The lure of violence

The lure of violence

The Right and the Edwardian crisis in Britain, 1901–1914

Alessandro Saluppo

MANCHESTER UNIVERSITY PRESS

Copyright © Alessandro Saluppo 2025

The right of Alessandro Saluppo to be identified as the author of this work has been asserted in accordance with the Copyright, Designs and Patents Act 1988.

An electronic version of this book has been made freely available under a Creative Commons (CC BY-NC) licence, thanks to the support of European Research Council (ERC), which permits non-commercial use, distribution and reproduction provided the author(s) and Manchester University Press are fully cited and it is indicated if any modifications or adaptations are made. Details of the licence can be viewed at https://creativecommons.org/licenses/by-nc/4.0/

Published by Manchester University Press
Oxford Road, Manchester, M13 9PL

www.manchesteruniversitypress.co.uk

British Library Cataloguing-in-Publication Data
A catalogue record for this book is available from the British Library

ISBN   978 1 5261 6487 2   hardback

First published 2025

The publisher has no responsibility for the persistence or accuracy of URLs for any external or third-party internet websites referred to in this book, and does not guarantee that any content on such websites is, or will remain, accurate or appropriate.

EU authorised representative for GPSR:
Easy Access System Europe, Mustamäe tee 50, 10621 Tallinn, Estonia
gpsr.requests@easproject.com

Typeset
by Deanta Global Publishing Services, Chennai, India

For Maria and Diego

Contents

List of figures	*page* viii
List of tables	x
Acknowledgements	xi
List of abbreviations	xiii
Introduction	1
1 How to shoot a rifle: the civilian rifle club movement and the problem of British military preparedness, 1899–1914	36
2 Custodians of the Empire: the Legion of Frontiersmen, 1904–1914	87
3 Race regeneration: nativist impulses and the drive for physical efficiency	117
4 'The revolt of the good citizens': Free Labour and practices of patriotic strikebreaking, 1901–1914	176
5 The arming of Ulster: the Home Rule crisis and the British League for the Support of Ulster and the Union	220
Conclusions	273
Select bibliography	283
Index	303

Figures

1.1	Lady Sybil Grey firing at the Miniature Bisley in *The Graphic*, 28 March 1903	page 50
1.2	The Society of Miniature Rifle Clubs: Competitions on the range of the Southfields Rifle Club in *The Bystander*, 13 September 1905	58
1.3	The Society of Miniature Rifle Clubs' Meeting at the Ham and Petersham Ranges in *The Illustrated Sporting and Dramatic News*, 4 August 1906	63
1.4	Lord Roberts firing the first shot in the new London and South Western Railway Rifle Range at Clapham Junction in *The Railway Times: A Journal of Finance, Construction, and Operation* 96, no. 18, 30 October 1909	65
1.5	Lord Roberts at the Miniature Rifle Club Meeting in the *Daily Mirror*, 4 July 1910	74
2.1	The Legion of Frontiersmen (London Command) in *The Sketch*, 12 July 1905	91
2.2	Frontiersmen in Coulsdon in *The Bystander*, 5 September 1906	99
2.3	Frontiersmen wrestling on horseback in *Penny Illustrated Paper*, 17 August 1907	104
3.1	Lieutenant General Sir Robert Baden-Powell, Lord Haldane, and a scout patrol leader at the Royal United Service Institution in *Daily Mirror*, 30 March 1911	164
4.1	William Collison in Chicago in *The Square Deal* 2, no. 6, January 1907	185
4.2	Composite image: (1) Badges, hats, truncheons, and armlets being served out to special constables at the Guildhall, London; (2) soldiers working as porters in Liverpool; (3) a butcher's shop unable to get supplies in Liverpool in *The Illustrated London News*, 26 August 1911	191

4.3	Members of the Civilian Force in uniform and armed with sticks in *The Illustrated London News*, 8 June 1912	206
4.4	The Civilian Police before deployment to the docks in the *Daily Herald*, 31 May 1912	207
5.1	Composite image: (1) Parade in honour of Carson in Portadown. Men with a dummy cannon, dummy rifles, and uniform caps; (2) Carson, Smith, Lord Londonderry, and J. B. Lonsdale at the saluting post in *The Sketch*, 2 October 1912	224
5.2	Sir Edward Carson and E. T. Smith inspecting Ulster volunteers in *The Illustrated London News*, 14 March 1914	228
5.3	Office of British League for the Support of Ulster and the Union in the *Evening Herald*, 11 June 1913	245
5.4	Form issued by the British League for the Support of Ulster and the Union in *The Sketch*, 3 December 1913	248
5.5	'New Fighting force for Ulster' in *The Daily Mirror*, 12 November 1913	253

Tables

1.1	Numbers of clubs affiliated with the Society of Miniature Rifle Clubs	*page* 72
5.1	Number of drill practices held by Unionist clubs and the number of people taking part in drills between November 1912 and December 1913	229
5.2	Quantity of arms believed to be in the possession of the Ulster Volunteer Force by December 1913 according to police reports	230
5.3	Estimates of the number of arms in possession of the UVF, the number of drilling practices, and the number of participants in drills according to police reports	232

Acknowledgements

Many people have helped and supported me in the process of writing this book. Matteo Millan gave me the invaluable opportunity to collaborate on the ERC project 'The Dark Side of the Belle Époque. Political violence and Armed Associations in Europe before the First World War – PREWArAs' (2017–2022). His unwavering encouragement, support and friendship have been a constant presence. His commitment to intellectual rigour, as demonstrated through his sharp observations and feedback, hopefully resonates throughout the following pages. I am grateful to a cohort of professors, colleagues and friends whose contributions have significantly influenced the construction of this project. Giulia Albanese and Marco Maria Aterrano provided significant scholarly assistance throughout the entire process of writing and constant motivation to finish this book. All the other members of the team PREWArAs – Andrea Azzarelli, Romain Bonnet, Amerigo Caruso, Nicola Camilleri, Assumpta Castillo Cañiz, Claire Morelon and Alexander Piahanau – have made significant contributions to this work by serving as meticulous readers of the numerous drafts submitted to them over the years. In Oxford, Martin Conway patiently listened and encouraged my research while I was a visitor at the Oxford Centre for European History (OCEH) in the Hilary Term 2018. He has since been a source of generosity and intellectual inspiration. Eugenio F. Biagini and the late Clive Emsley have also been kind enough to read, listen and offer advice to what were still embryonic and shapeless ideas. I am deeply indebted to Timothy Bowman, whose scholarly expertise and intellectual critique were pivotal in refining the academic foundations of this research. Thanks are also due to Andrew Stuart Thompson for allowing me consult his dissertation and George Gilbert, who helped to find materials at the British Library. Tessa Say, Edoardo M. Barsotti, Antonio Giuseppe Valletta, Travis Burgess and Brandon K. Gauthier were instrumental in the completion of this work. Gratitude is also extended to the anonymous peer reviewers who initially read the book proposal, providing favourable and constructive criticism.

The Bodleian Library, the National Archives, the Modern Record Centre (University of Warwick), the Biblioteca Storica (University of Padua), the New York Public Library and Columbia Libraries provided supportive environments for completing this project. I am particularly thankful to all their staff for handling my requests with remarkable competence and courtesy during a time of great difficulty caused by the COVID-19 pandemic. I would like to thank the History Department of Fordham University for its support and intellectual stimulation in the last two years. Of course, I would like to thank Manchester University Press for believing in this project before it was completed and for patiently awaiting its realisation.

Finally, I extend my sincere thanks to my family for their love, patience and the strength they provided, enabling me to bring this project to completion. I dedicate this work to them as a heartfelt token of appreciation for their enduring support and unwavering belief in my pursuits.

The book has received funding from the ERC under the European Union's Horizon 2020 Research and Innovation Programme (G.A. 677199 – ERC-StG2015 'The Dark Side of the Belle Époque. Political Violence and Armed Associations before the First World War').

Abbreviations

ASRS	Amalgamated Society of Railway Servants
ASU	Anti-Socialist Union
BBL	British Brothers' League
BCU	British Commonwealth Union
BF	British Fascisti
BLO	Bodleian Library, Oxford
BLSUU	British League for the Support of Ulster and the Union
BMJ	The British Medical Journal
BRL	British Rifle League
BRU	British Rifle Union
BSA	Birmingham Small Arms Company
BUF	British Union of Fascists
CIA	Citizens' Industrial Association
CIAA	Citizens' Industrial Association of America
CSL	Civic Service League
EES	Eugenics Education Society
FANY	First Aid Nursing Yeomanry
FLPA	Free Labour Protection Association
GOC	General Officer Commanding
GOC-in-C	General Officer Commanding-in-Chief
IML	Imperial Maritime League
INV	Irish National Volunteers
ITGWU	Irish Transport and General Workers' Union
NCU	National Citizens' Union
NF	National Fascisti
NFLA	National Free Labour Association
NL	Navy League
NLPEI	National League for Physical Education and Improvement
NP	National Party
NRA	National Rifle Association

NSL	National Service League
OMS	Organisation for the Maintenance of Supplies
PSARA	Preparatory School Air Rifle Association
PSRA	Preparatory Schools Rifle Association
RIC	Royal Irish Constabulary
SDF	Social Democratic Federation
SMRC	Society of Miniature Rifle Clubs
SWMR	Society of Working Men's Rifle Clubs
TNA	The National Archives at Kew
TRL	Tariff Reform League
UUC	Ulster Union Council
UVF	Ulster Volunteer Force
VADs	Voluntary Aid Detachments
VPF	Volunteer Police Force

Introduction

Whatever happens & whoever may
be the ultimate enemy, a people who can fight will
prevail in the long run over a people that can't. (Lord Milner)

Race improvement to-day is not a question of philosophy, but existence …
If the first law of life is self-preservation, England must choose
between State suicide and race-improvement. (Arnold White)

As the nineteenth century waned, Britain stood as the most advanced industrial society in the world, marked by dense urbanisation, social stratification and mobility and sophisticated institutional structures. The nation was on the threshold of popular democracy, a prospect that promised to irreversibly transform the very foundations of power and political leadership. Amid this epochal transition, all political factions were grappling with Britain's relative decline, the question of 'preparedness' in the face of mounting international tensions and rivalries, the growing assertiveness of the masses and the inexorable tide of moral and cultural change.[1] The Conservatives, long the standard-bearers of tradition and self-professed guardians of the nation, found themselves particularly besieged. Electoral defeats cast a pall over their future, while the pillars of their *Weltanschauung* – the Union, imperial and domestic security, social discipline and property rights – were groaning under the weight of modernity. As Britain's landscapes metamorphosed, British Conservatives faced a stark choice: adapt their 'social philosophy' or risk fading into irrelevance at a juncture where the future of the nation appeared to hang in the balance.[2] Between 1903 and 1914, persistent, acrimonious efforts within Conservative ranks to steer the party away from 'Salisburyan quietism' and counter a triumphant liberalism with a radical new strand of Conservative thought and action evolved into a broader 'crisis of Conservatism'.[3] This process of 'ideological redefinition' exposed the party to a potent strain of right-wing dissidence. Aside from pushing the party to internecine fragmentation over doctrinal principles and policies, this dissidence shifted it to something that more closely resembled a continental right-wing party than it had at any previous point in its history.[4] In the 1970s, Ian Gilmour, who insisted that 'British Conservatism' was not an -ism, went so far as to state that the Edwardian Conservative Party 'betrayed itself and came dangerously close to betraying the country'. The party had, to some extent, been hijacked by a tangle of 'radical Conservative' groups – particularly the tariff reformers – who had cast the teachings of Peel and Disraeli into oblivion and conducted the opposition in a manner that was 'fractious, inflamed, and, under Balfour's successor, Bonar Law, unconstitutional'.[5] More recently, in his analysis of the role of European conservative parties in democratisation processes, Harvard political scientist Daniel Ziblatt called the crisis of Edwardian conservatism 'a case of a democratic disaster averted'. From 1911 to 1914, under the spell of the 'radical right', the Conservative Party exhibited virtually all the maladies described in Juan Linz's taxonomy of semi-loyal and disloyal oppositions. Their defiance of constitutional norms became apparent from their ambiguous public statements on the use of force to gain power, their seeking of support from the armed forces, denying legitimacy to elected party leaders, labelling of opposition politicians as tools of foreign conspiracies and their support of actions that went beyond 'peaceful politics'.[6] While Ziblatt posited that the entire 'scenario' may have constituted 'high-stakes playacting' orchestrated by the Unionist leadership to extricate the party from an 'electoral precipice', the aggressive stance taken by Bonar Law and others during the Ulster Crisis may have arisen from excessive trust in their capacity to temper political tensions in an increasingly volatile environment or prevent these 'unpredictable' events from spiralling out of control. Undoubtedly, the many moderate observers already perturbed by the confluence of multiple crises – the controversy surrounding the House of Lords, the proliferation of industrial actions, the forcible nasal feeding of suffragettes and the arming of Ulster – saw the radicalism exhibited by the Conservative leadership and its 'Gothic auxiliaries' as yet another ominous sign of a more general loss of public composure and lucidity.[7]

Historians have conducted comprehensive analyses of the rightward shift of Edwardian conservatism, which have included: the origin and impact of Joseph Chamberlain's campaign for imperial preference; the purging of free traders by tariff reformers; the rise of patriotic and militarist pressure groups; the social and political realms of the 'diehards'; imperialist statesmen and ideologies; jingoism and xenophobia in electioneering tactics; manifestations of antisemitism; and the evolution of a new 'radical right' or 'radical Toryism' on the eve of war.[8] There is, however, a notable omission or at least inadequate exploration of the incubation and gestation of a 'culture of violence', or, more specifically, the development of propensities for, the advocacy of, or the descent into violent behaviours among conservatives or right-wing 'radicals'. This is, firstly, because there are generally few archival records concerning those who elevated violence to the status of a rational or ethical principle, and where they do exist, they are often difficult to identify. In particular, those obscure organisations that sprang from the middle ranks of society can only be traced through meticulous examination of newspapers, manuscripts, memoirs and other 'less authoritative' materials of the period. Secondly, this 'research gap' is a result of scholars accepting the assumption that the potential for political violence in Britain, at least until 1913, had been defused or even extinguished by the success of that long-term project of a peaceful society that had gradually materialised into a political culture of 'relative civility'.[9] As a result, the significance of right-wing incitement to and organisation of violence in pursuit of national efficiency, social discipline and law and order has not been given sufficient attention or has not been taken seriously enough.

This book endeavours to rectify this omission by focusing on the multi-faceted array of right-wing militaristic associations, xenophobic and antisocialist leagues and semi-military or paramilitary formations, whose central purpose was to arrest Britain's apparent ongoing decay and contribute to its rejuvenation. Rooted in crude social-Darwinist assumptions, the task of 'national revival' had a dual nature. Firstly, it involved preparing civil society for violence by instilling in the populace an unwavering faith in the effectiveness of physical force and 'racial virility' while eroding confidence in non-military methods for safeguarding Britain's world position. Many right-wingers fundamentally accepted Carlyle's inglorious argument that the ultimate question between two human beings was 'Can I kill thee, or canst thou kill me?' and used it to validate their assertion that war was inevitable and even beneficial. Hence, 'preparedness' was not only prudent, but deemed imperative for survival. The 'amateur military tradition' appeared woefully outdated during the Boer War years, prompting the Right to call for immediate adoption of universal military service or a thorough and widespread extension of the volunteer system. While tentative proposals for 'national service' were propagandised, the Right coordinated and provided the means for civilian marksmanship training to large numbers of 'patriotic citizens'. Every man, especially the young, had to master rifle handling, target acquisition, breath control, trigger discipline and efficient reloading – all essential skills in learning to kill. The Right aimed to mould men into strong, disciplined, self-sacrificing individuals prepared to serve their nation and uphold the social order. They aimed to restore those 'primal instincts' of self-preservation and propagation of the race that modern civilisation had been slowly atrophying. Sports were praised as they called upon a 'spirit of combat', 'energy and zeal' and 'masculine dominance'.

Through the stalking and killing of prey as practised in hunting, men were able to brutalise themselves. All of this would be in preparation for war, the 'highest form of vitality'.[10]

The mantra of 'military preparedness', which included calls for increased naval and military expenditure, was naturally accompanied by the cultivation of jingoistic suspicion of and intense hostility towards perceived external threats. These sentiments materialised in and were stoked by invasion literature, conspiracy theories, the cheap sensationalist press and the spread of 'Teutophobia' – a phenomenon that saw a spy in every German waiter, barber, shop assistant, clerk, porter or boot-blacker.[11] All this contributed to the radicalisation of large segments of the Conservative movement and fostered a climate of distrust in political institutions and politicians, which made it more difficult to hold reasoned and nuanced discussions about foreign policy and defence. It also led to the demonisation of those who held opposing views, effectively damning dissent as 'antinational' and fostering an atmosphere of intolerance.

Secondly, 'the politics of paranoia' escalated as far as advocating unconstitutional and violent means, supporting subversion and even courting the risk of civil war. The Khaki election had somewhat foreshadowed certain elements of this spirit of political intolerance, which had no place for pacifism, humanitarianism or cosmopolitanism. Liberals who had expressed milder or no support for the war were mobbed and had their meetings disrupted. Their very physical safety would have been at risk had they not been protected by the forces of law and order.[12] Five years later, the Right – the direct heir of that period of 'raving jingoism' – found it inconceivable that these 'Pro-Boers', 'Little Englanders' and 'Campbell-Bannermanites', who had exposed themselves to the charge of treasonous sympathy with the enemy, were installed in office at the head of the largest majority returned in seventy years. In their view, the men who had wanted and had fought the war had been silenced, and these much-despised, much-abused 'Kruger's supporters' had taken their places through a 'perfidious' alliance with the 'preachers of class war', American-backed Irish nationalists and 'alien plutocrats'. With the ministers of the Liberal government accused of not being Britons, but rather 'conspirators' and 'allies' of those whom the King's soldiers had fought, all those citizens who were driven by an unselfish devotion to the nation were called upon to continue the soldiers' fight. The Right was also called upon to oppose immigration and its perceived consequences: increased crime, cheap labour competition that lowered the standard of living in British industrial society, the formation of unassimilable 'cultural ghettos' and even 'racial degeneration', which they feared would relegate Britons to the ranks of 'mongrel races'. The Right had to combat 'pro-German internationalists', socialists, syndicalists, closed shop unions and the whole motley crew of 'traitors' who preached the 'gospel of class hatred' and incited workers to strike action and social disorder. Finally, the Right had to fight for imperial unity and the maintenance of the Union, for which it was primarily inspired by Ulster's grim determination.

The Right displayed unprecedented political aggressiveness and a certain susceptibility to populism. They attacked the 'political establishment', which they portrayed as rigged or apathetic to the 'real problems' of Britain and Britons, thus appealing directly to 'the people' and tapping into their fears and hatreds. To save the nation and the Constitution, the Right united reactionary 'patricians' who railed against 'the irresistible advance of democracy' and middle-class agitators. The former adopted the latter's incendiary rhetoric and intolerant impatience, while the latter adopted the former's bigotry. Thus it was that Tory aristocrats, such as Lord Abercorn, Lord Northcliffe, Lord Londonderry, Lord Willoughby de Broke, Lord Roberts and others, enthusiastically entered the realm of rebellion alongside adventurers, ringleaders, strikebreakers and ruffians. In certain instances, peers, baronets, admirals, generals and 'other great ones of the earth' filled the executive councils of leagues and associations whose origins could often be traced back to the poverty-stricken, densely populated alleys of London's East End, or the chaotic squalor of the ports and industrial areas.

In pursuing the 'national cause', the Right developed distinct agitational methods. However, these were not limited to the political and educational practices of special-interest nationalist groups, but also involved violent forms of 'grassroot mobilisation'. For example, the British Brothers' League (BBL) attacked Jewish refugees fleeing pogroms in Russia and Romania; the Volunteer Police Force (VPF) served as 'industrial shock troops' to break strikes, which were perceived as acts of treason against the nation and the future of the British people; while the British League for the Support of Ulster and the Union (BLSUU) was formed to recruit volunteers to join the Ulster Volunteer Force (UVF) and 'to stand in the trenches with those who are going to defend [the] common inheritance'.[13] Even the Legion of Frontiersmen, which espoused an ideology of physical exertion, risk-taking and the rejection of a perceived 'softness' in modern urban life, while at the same time incessantly stoking 'spy-mania', ultimately acted as bodyguards for Henry Page Croft and his Imperial Mission – much as the *Camelots du Roi* had done for the Action Française in the latter half of the 1890s. These groups operated beyond traditional party structures and parliamentary manoeuvring, and appealed instead to direct, impulsive and emotive notions of patriotism. They presented themselves as clear-eyed realists in a world enthralled by 'shortsighted self-seekers' and 'timorous men', and positioned their 'mobilisations' as the authentic voice of national interest. These groups considered it an esteemed duty to protect the nation, its honour and its homogeneity and guarantee its efficient organisation – even to the point of taking 'violent action' if deemed necessary.

Analysis of these cultures of violence demonstrates that the Edwardian Right was not far removed from the authoritarian and nationalist movements that were emerging across fin-de-siècle Europe.[14] At the risk of overgeneralisation, both British and continental 'rightist currents' attempted to transcend the limits of parliamentary democracy and neutralise the distinctive emancipative nature of liberal society by offering organic visions of national (or imperial) organisation and identity. By emphasising an organicist conception of the community, the British Right, especially after the Boer War, became oversensitive to the 'old formulas' of decadence and regeneration. This fuelled a pervasive feeling of 'us versus them', which manifested itself in demonising rhetoric, a conspiratorial mindset, 'anti-alienism' and the invocation of force.

The Edwardian Right, violence and the problem of definition

While the Conservative Party is no longer considered the 'Cinderella of Edwardian historiography', the nature and scale of right-wing mobilisations (e.g., pressure groups, militaristic bodies, etc.) in prewar Britain and their actual impact on political articulations are still open to speculation. At the same time, the porous border between the 'conservative right' and the 'radical right' – epitomised by the crossing of it by Conservative MPs, peers, regional and local officials, publicists and public intellectuals over specific issues or situations – had made the 'prewar British Right' particularly difficult to define. In 1965, historian J. R Jones wrote, 'In England … the term Right applies largely to groups within the Tory party'.[15] This narrow definition stemmed from English conservatism's strength and continuity, which led to the Right being simplistically equated with reaction. A Right existed and had considerable, sometimes even decisive, importance, especially in the turbulent prewar years. Jones added that the Right was radicalised in two stages. Before 1905, when the wounds of the Boer War were far from healed, it attacked the party leadership for being in a state of catatonic withdrawal and stupor in the face of the 'signs of decay' that appeared to undermine Britain's place in world affairs. After the Liberal landslide of 1906, Jones noted,

> [the Right] contended that power must be recovered, for the sake of the nation as well as the party, as, in their view, the Liberal government was following an antinational policy that would destroy the empire. Old leaders and traditionalists might be content to play the party game, observing its conventions and

treating the Liberal government as if it were respectable and responsible, but for the Right it must be destroyed before it destroyed the nation.[16]

While resistant to the irrationalist philosophies fuelling nationalist authoritarianism on the continent, the Right found early inspiration in the 'architect of the South African war', Alfred Lord Milner and the 'arch renegade of radicalism', Joseph Chamberlain. Their 'catastrophical theory of politics', as Lord Salisbury had called it, was a form of political behaviour characterised by an intense and pessimistic sense of urgency and by 'the radical nature of the changes proposed'.[17] Milner, who profoundly believed in the 'distinctive' mission of the English race, welded the task of imperial consolidation and organisation with social reformism with the aim of avoiding 'disintegration'. He regarded himself as a 'collectivist', but found the Marxist doctrine of class struggle repulsive. Instead he recognised a 'nobler socialism' that accepted the assertion of the nation as an organic unity. In Milner's view, the most pernicious danger to the empire came from 'liberal doctrinaires' and parliamentary politics. The former suffered from delusional egotism, bold hypocrisy and self-deception, while the latter was a 'system' where the ultimate power was exercised without regard for expertise and wherein party politics operated at its worst, reduced 'to mere husks of dead controversies'. The government was in the hands of 'a huge, unwieldy Cabinet ... and swamped by second-rate men', incapable of giving continuous thought and study to vital issues.[18] Milnerism, again in the words of Lord Salisbury, invoked 'a drastic change of method [of government] from the English system to the German system: from freedom to compulsion'.[19] Milner's crude judgement that politics was the last refuge of 'lazy minds' and 'corrupted souls' did not apply to Chamberlain. In 1903, the Colonial Secretary vigorously attacked the free trade doctrines of the Manchester School, whose 'high priests' were John Bright and Richard Cobden. He proposed a much closer integration of the empire, and warned that if his proposals were not implemented, 'England ... would sink from the comparative position which it has enjoyed throughout the centuries [and] it would be a fifth-rate nation, existing on the sufferance of its more powerful neighbours'.[20] Chamberlain failed to convince the party from within and left the Conservative cabinet in order to preach the new faith. His and his disciples' agitation for imperial preference and tariff reform created a rift in the Conservative Party that was as profound as that caused by Sir Robert Peel's conversion to free trade in 1846. When Chamberlain's health began to fail, his 'inspiring ideals' were continued and developed by the Right, and in particular by that youthful and radicalised sector of the party that was apprehensive about the rise of class politics and class consciousness, and frustrated with the 'intellectual fatigue' of the conservative Leadership. In 1906, following their electoral defeat, these self-professed champions of 'forward and constructive policies' launched a 'cannibalistic' witch hunt against free traders. Their unorthodox advocacy for an expanded state authority and 'social imperialism', and their pervasive belief in the idea of national sacrifice at the expense of individual rights and interests – all pursued with unusual aggressiveness and sectarian zeal – gave them the appearance, in Léon Gambetta's words, of '*Radicaux Autoritaires*'.[21]

Joseph Chamberlain's retirement and Lord Milner's reluctance to 'sully his hands' with politics left the Right deprived of a charismatic leader. Amid the controversy over the 1909 budget, the general elections of 1910 and the passage of the Parliament Act that 'limited the Veto' of the House of Lords, they turned to the ultra-reactionary Earl of Halsbury. The campaign for imperial preference merged with the battle to rescue the nation from the destructive policies of the Liberal government, catalysing the emergence of a new strain of 'radical conservatism'. Willoughby de Broke, described by George Dangerfield as 'not more than two hundred years behind his time', and no less ironically by historian R. C. K. Ensor as a fox-hunting nobleman, emerged as one of its foremost figures.[22] Under the label 'National Toryism', he cloaked the fundamental principles of the 'Tory tradition' in the contemporary rhetoric of efficiency, race regeneration and the 'metaphysical nation' – a nation with a higher 'ethical essence' that transcended and assimilated individuals. In doing so, he saw himself as defending the Constitution while addressing the 'whole vast problem of Heredity and Environment'. His vision gave prominence to preserving the national character through selective breeding, raising physically and mentally sound citizens in healthy, patriotic, religious surroundings, protecting domestic industries through tariffs, ensuring military preparedness, training a population to bear arms and raising awareness of the duties of British imperial citizenship.[23] To achieve these aims, he helped found the 'Reveille' group in October 1910 with Henry Page Croft and other tariff reformers. He was a member of the Halsbury Club, in charge of most of its organisation. When Asquith introduced the Third Home Rule Bill in the spring of 1912, Willoughby de Broke 'helped to raise the standard of revolt' by forming the BLSUU. The new body, which brought together one hundred peers and one hundred and twenty MPs, had close connections with the UVF and assisted them with recruitment and gun-running operations. According to one of his most perceptive historians, 'Willoughby de Broke's objectives were basically those of a traditional landed aristocracy', but 'his methods and emphases prefigured those of later rightist politicians, both British and continental'.[24]

Willoughby de Broke and his allies – 'Chamberlainites', Milnerites, Lord Carson, Leo Maxse and many others – cultivated that 'whole attitude toward politics' that Lord Hugh Cecil found 'intolerable'. Cecil was particularly troubled by their cult of a nationalism that kept personal liberties in general contempt.[25] In his classic analysis of the 'Right', Jones dissected the main elements of this 'attitude'. The Right saw the Liberal government as 'antinational' and they were alarmed by the growth of class politics. However, while more traditional conservatives viewed the political struggle primarily as a parliamentary contest, the Right instead interpreted the crisis of the prewar years as 'the logical and inevitable outcome of the pernicious, antinational principles of subversive radicalism, the principles of Cobdenism'.[26] *Manchesterismus*, with its free trade and other fundamental principles, was assigned the less than enviable status of 'a comprehensive doctrine of political destructiveness' due to its insensitivity to an organic conception of society and its propensity to sacrifice the national community to the clamour of sectional greed. The Liberal Party's appeasement of nonconformist grievances over Balfour's Education Act of 1902, the Land Bills, the disestablishment of the Welsh Church, Lloyd George's Budget of 1909 with 'its socialistic flavour', and, more dramatically, the Irish Home Rule Bill constituted incontrovertible proof of its antinational agenda. The Right, much like the *Boulangerists* in France, accused the Liberal government of corruption, and like the followers of the disgraced general, they could not conceal elements of their antisemitism. They believed that a *Plunderbund* composed of German-Jewish captains of industry and finance was behind the corrupt nature and 'internationalist' orientation of Liberal policies. For instance, while the reverberations of the Marconi Affair were still echoing, the National League for Clean Government was instituted to reform the party system and safeguard the integrity of British political institutions from the pernicious influence of 'alien votes and foreign gold'.[27] As expected, the Right abused the term 'traitor', and accused Churchill of being 'the Kaiser's *homme de confiance* in the Cabinet'.[28]

Aside from these vicious attacks *ad hominem* and *ad rem*, the Right sought to alert a 'complacent' public to the intensifying international threats, and in this they received the support of a sensationalist, manipulative, scaremongering press. While the empire remained their lodestar, crucial to Britain's standing in an increasingly competitive world, the issue of military preparedness became something of an obsession, with calls for conscription and an accelerated naval buildup. The Imperial Maritime League (IML) – an organ of the Right – broke away from the platitudes of the old Navy League (NL). However, it was the Ulster crisis that instilled in the 'Right revolt' intensity and bitterness. Most notably, as Jones observed, the UVF paramilitaries provided 'an example, model, or exemplar of what they hoped to achieve in the British Isles as a whole' – an energetic, disciplined, patriotic, Protestant community in which class divisions faded away and merged into one great, common purpose.[29]

Despite their reactionary militarist views, the Right proved amenable to institutional and social reform – albeit only when such restructurings were directed at bolstering national and imperial unity. This flexibility drew into their orbit a coterie of disaffected intellectuals: disillusioned liberals Hilaire Belloc and brothers Robert and Cecil Chesterton, and socialist heretics such as Robert Blatchford. In their quest for a 'Third Way', Belloc and the Chestertons conceived the doctrine of 'distributism' – an attempt to chart an economic course that would steer clear of both unbridled capitalism and Marxist socialism. While they did not elevate private property to the status of inviolable principle, they found common cause with the Right in their scathing critique of 'partitocracy' and what they decried as 'alien Liberal plutocracies'. Belloc, whose rhetoric resembled that of the French nationalist and anti-Dreyfusard Paul Déroulède, infused his political philosophy with a potent strain of antisemitism. Blatchford, instead, forged a curious alloy of 'jingo patriotism' and socialism – a synthesis so alien to English political culture at the time that it led to his political ostracism.[30]

In his analysis, J. R. Jones posited that the Right 'constituted an easily identifiable and formidable factor in English politics in the years before the war', but only when, as in the period 1910–1914, a series of crises converged. In more stable times, when ordinary political processes prevailed, the Right remained marginal and 'sealed' within the broader structures of the Conservative Party, unable to coalesce into a distinct political force.[31] In the late 1970s and early 1980s, historians attempted to refine their conceptualisation of the prewar British Right in order to delineate its defining characteristics. They questioned which social forces, political actors and intellectual programmes should be included under the label 'Right' and began to examine whether the Right was truly a coherent movement or merely a loose association of diverse groups with little common ground. They explored the role of the grassroots activism of right-wing movements – e.g., national pressure groups – in radicalising party politics. They questioned whether the Right could be studied in terms of 'proto-fascism'. Finally, they started to explore the possibility of identifying the transnational characteristics of right-wing movements with the aim of moving beyond country-specific analyses and uncovering broader patterns or commonalities across borders. In his introduction to *Nationalist and Racialist Movements in Britain and Germany before 1914*, Paul Kennedy conceded that if a consensus existed among the various contributors, it lay in the recognition that the years before the First World War had 'witnessed reverberations and changes – in the assumptions, practices, aims and political and social composition of many on the Right – which could not be contained within the operational area of an organised party'. Kennedy added:

New philosophies, new organisations and tactics, new social groupings surged into but also around and beyond the older Conservative party structures and programmes, often forcing changes in the latter yet never being fully assimilated into them. The concern about racial decay and eugenics, the agitations for conscription and protectionism in Edwardian Britain, the existence and influence of the Pan-German League, were phenomena which had no place in the traditional world of Bismarck and Salisbury.[32]

As early as 1975, R. J. Scally, who had argued that the formation of Lloyd George's wartime coalition government stemmed from the anti-democratic scepticism of social-imperialists, had lamented the lack of theoretical and ideological clarity in discussions of Edwardian political factions.[33] Some time later, Geoffrey Searle took up the challenge to provide an analysis of the 'radical right' during the Edwardian crisis. Despite the Right's complex stratification, Searle identified three distinct groups: traditional conservatives, the Chamberlainite and Milnerite factions who advocated social-imperialist policies and national efficiency, and the 'radical right'. The latter figured as 'a collection of super-patriots unable for one reason or another to identify with their natural party, or as a movement of rootless nationalists who felt alienated to a lesser or greater extent from all the major political organisations of the day'. It was formed by diehard Willoughby de Broke and the vitriolic editor of the *National Review*, Leo Maxse, and garnered support from other prominent critics of Edwardian society, including Arnold White, the Chesterton brothers and Hilaire Belloc. While subscribing to most of the ideals of imperial unity promoted by zealots Chamberlain and Milner, this radical right was populist, xenophobic, demagogic, militarist and jingoistic, and fomented war scares.[34] Aside from their eagerness to 'fight the Liberal enemy with the necessary ruthlessness and determination', the radical right developed a 'cult of violence':

> Whether calling for a preventive war against Germany or rushing forward to enlist in para-military bodies that could fight in Ireland, should civil war break out there, the Radical Right seemed to be positively eager for a bout of bloodletting that would put an end to sentimentality and humanitarian humbug and restore the British nation to its former manhood. Using the fashionable rhetoric of 'Social Darwinism', the Radical Right preached the necessity of struggle between nations, races and social types for the evolutionary progress of mankind. Moreover, these people lived in a state of perpetual tension, ever conscious of the fragility of the social order and the dangers that threatened it from within and without. Street fighting in London, bloody insurrection in India, the yellow peril, civil war in Ireland, a German army rampaging through the eastern countries looting and destroying: these were the fears that haunted the Radical Right and gave urgency to its writing and oratory.[35]

Searle refrained from linking Edwardian right-wing attitudes to later fascism and instead drew parallels with contemporaneous Wilhelmine German movements. He argued that radical nationalism found less fertile ground in Britain due to the absence of a *Mittelstand* and, more generally, the persistence of social trust and confidence in the reliability of political institutions.

In the 1970s, Alan Sykes critiqued the notion of a distinct 'radical right' within the Conservative Party, as well as the epistemological value of the various (and often obscure) labels used to characterise the Right's extremism. The radicalism of the diehards, particularly Willoughby de Broke, was aimed at returning the party to the basic principles of Toryism rather than a proposal for a new authoritarian theory of the role and function of the State. Sykes concluded that the defeats over Lloyd George's Budget and the Parliament Act, and the impending peril of Home Rule produced a 'major realignment of factions within the Right', with a broad spectrum of Unionists abandoning the conventional politics of restraint. By 1911, the 'radical right' was all 'but swamped in a sea of traditional Conservatives defending traditional causes'.[36]

Around the time Searle mapped the British Right's 'set of attitudes', Gregory D. Phillips offered a revisionist interpretation of the 'diehards' – the 112 peers who opposed the Parliament Bill of 1911. Phillips's analysis eschewed the conventional portrayal of this 'most maligned' group of aristocrats as politically disengaged 'backwoodsmen'. Rather, he posited them as forming a dynamic and 'constructive' section of the peerage preoccupied with agrarian economic decline, imperial defence, constitutional reforms and the political, social and moral direction of Britain generally. They advocated compulsory military service or, at least, a significant increase in military preparedness, a vast strengthening of the army and navy, protectionist economic policies, 'national efficiency', and physical and racial 'regeneration', with some adopting the theories and programmes of eugenics. Phillips believed that the diehards' militancy stemmed not only from reactionary or authoritarian reflexes, but also from that 'military ethic' to which a disproportionate number of peers had been exposed since the early years of their lives. Service in the armed forces, participation in reserve organisations and a firsthand experience of war (diehard families were always prepared to surrender their sons to the altar of war) instilled in them a sense of hierarchy, discipline and self-sacrifice. At the same time, it aggravated their 'restless anxieties' over Britain's present predicaments and uncertain future. It comes as no surprise that the diehards framed their political discourses in terms of battles between opposing forces, often employing militaristic terms such as 'fight', 'defend', 'attack' and 'surrender'.[37] As the Liberal government's tenure progressed, the diehards' political stance grew increasingly radical. They pursued a *politique du pire* and exhibited a willingness to contemplate extreme measures, including violence. This propensity was brought into stark relief by the Home Rule for Ireland issue, when prominent diehard peers actively encouraged and supported the formation of the UVF. For Phillips, those diehards, along with other enemies of Home Rule, 'were not bluffing, as the Liberals mistakenly believed ... [they] were prepared to spill blood to achieve their goals'. Only the outbreak of the First World War prevented the sedition they had preached and civil war from materialising.[38]

In a similar vein, David Cannadine in his monumental *Decline and Fall of the British Aristocracy*, remarked that the diehards' attitudes amounted to a 'quasi-revolutionary [...] rejection of the liberal, constitutionalist, patrician tradition in British politics':

> For the Tory die-hards, the next generation of aristocratic rebels, their sense of decline was more powerful, their hatred and resentment was more intense, and their defeat was correspondingly more bitter. By the 1900s, they saw the widespread decline of their own order and way of life; they contemplated with horror the twin evils of irresponsible plutocracy and proletarian democracy; they watched with scarcely concealed anger the feeble and vacillating leadership of the Conservative party; and they concluded that more drastic action was needed if the situation was to be retrieved. Accordingly, they espoused a violent, intransigent, seemingly anti-democratic credo, which skirted the very bounds of treason. They sought to arouse their lethargic and supine colleagues to the dangers of national and class decline. They attempted to defy the Liberal efforts to emasculate the House of Lords. And they were prepared to go to any lengths to prevent Home Rule and support the Ulster Loyalists.[39]

Though the diehards achieved little in a practical sense, their brand of militant extremism – which encompassed a willingness to defy laws and the legislature, to resort to extra-parliamentary and unconstitutional tactics and to preach violence and use it if necessary – pushed them ever closer to the 'aristocratic reaction' that historian Arno Mayer identified as spreading across the continent at the beginning of the century. In his essay on the domestic causes of the First World War, Mayer wrote that '[by 1914] even Britain, that paradigm of ordered change and constitutionalism, was approaching the threshold of civil war'.[40] While the Triple Alliance of miners', railwaymen's and transport workers' unions mobilised support within an increasingly restive Labour movement, Ulster became the rallying point for an influential and seditious 'conglomeration of conservatives and reactionaries'. This polarisation, characterised by a shift from parliamentary discourse to direct action, eroded the political centre. Mayer speculated that, had war not erupted in 1914, England might have spiralled into civil conflict, potentially inflicting irreparable harm to its parliamentary system.

Some years earlier, in his magisterial study on the development of industrial relations between 1906 and 1914, prominent economist Henry Phelps Brown remarked that

> To many observers, especially those to whom all [industrial] conflict was abhorrent, the last four years before the war seemed a time of remorselessly rising tension, of impending doom ... one quarrel broke out just when other quarrels were flaring up too. Something had come over people, they divided into irreconcilable camps, they declared their unswerving allegiance to antithetical principles, increasingly they preached violence and resorted to it.[41]

More recently, historians have noted that the industrial strife of the prewar years led some of the most 'reactionary sectors' of British capitalism to consider forming strikebreaking agencies and private police systems modelled on those in America. These sectors were convinced that the Liberal government was intentionally failing to protect their proprietorial rights and the country's productive forces.[42] Other scholars have described how the rise of trade unionism and the increasing frequency of strikes, especially in the essential industries, fuelled anxieties among conservative middle and upper classes about the growing power of the working class. Perceiving these industrial disputes as an outright attack on the stability and order of British society, these groups encouraged anti-labour mobilisations in response. These efforts garnered indiscreet support from some 'diehards' and sympathy from certain Tory 'whole-hoggers', who relished seeing the 'Cobden school' reaping the consequences of its 'cult of the self' at the expense of the 'national whole'. The recurring nature of volunteer strikebreaking, from the Great Unrest of 1911–1914 to the 1926 General Strike, was driven by consistent attitudes, values and ideological assumptions, and established this form of 'reactive' mobilisation as a prominent feature of the British Right.[43] Furthermore, other historians, in disagreement with the civilisational theory of Norbert Elias and his disciples, have pointed out that the Edwardian political elites displayed a perplexing tolerance for political violence. In this regard, Jon Lawrence wrote:

> If physical force and the threat of physical force, was an ever present feature of popular politics before the First World War, this was in part because professional politicians were frequently mythologised for their acts of bravery and strength in facing down disruption.[44]

Pre-1914 politics was still, in the words of Adrian Gregory, a 'bloody sport' and the Right was always ready to provide or recruit 'fists and muscle' to combat heckling.[45]

Arno Mayer's provocative thesis catalysed scholarly scrutiny of the 'domestic roots of diplomacy and decision making'.[46] Much inquiry has focused on Britain's societal militarisation – or, in Michael Geyer's terms, the policies, practices and appeals through which civil society configures itself for the production of violence.[47] Recent (and less recent) studies have provided a valuable opportunity to reconsider the pervasiveness of militarism in British society, even identifying its appeal within progressive circles. However, it is hard to dispute the fact that right-wing radicals and those many conservatives who had grown increasingly apprehensive about national defence issues exerted a virtual monopoly on the campaigns for military preparedness.[48] There is, instead, complete consensus among historians that the Boer War (1899–1902) 'marked a major watershed in British discourses on the concept of a nation in arms'.[49] The conflict exposed critical weaknesses in Britain's military structure, sparking renewed debates about the nation's capacity to wage future wars and safeguard its empire against increasingly powerful rivals. The ensuing 'conscription controversy' broadened into a wider examination of British modernity, particularly in comparison with Germany. This debate encompassed concerns about national efficiency, a perceived lack of masculinity, the effects of over-civilisation on 'the warrior qualities of the race', eugenics and 'physical fitness'. To combat the supposed signs of physical degeneration among the male population, the Right actively encouraged British youth to join militarised or semi-militarised youth movements, a prime example of these being the Boy Scouts. Girls and young women, too, were urged to enlist in auxiliary services with military purposes, such as the First Aid Nursing Yeomanry (FANY) and the Voluntary Aid Detachments (VADs).[50]

In politics, the Right spearheaded nationalist pressure groups, which, much like the *Wehrverein* and *Flottenverein* in Germany, the *Ligue Maritime* and *Ligue pour le service de trois ans* in France, and similar organisations across the European continent, operated with the aim of strengthening Britain's naval, land and air forces. The NL, the National Service League (NSL) and the Aerial League of the British Empire have received extensive historiographical attention.[51] In the 1990s, Frank Coetzee referred to the mobilisation of these (and other) pressure groups in terms of 'nationalist agitation'. He argued that 'the political practices and ideological precepts' pursued by these organisations were essentially directed towards determining 'what characteristics of behaviour entitled one to claim or to exercise membership within the national community'. The NL, the Tariff Reform League (TRL) and the Anti-Socialist Union (ASU), whose personnel were predominantly conservative, were faced with the dilemma of whether to function as aides-de-camp of the Conservative Party or to present themselves as distinct ideological formations, in which loyalty to the 'national cause' transcended conventional party orientations. The claim of being 'above-party' created tensions within these British *nationale Verbände*. For instance, after 1906 the NL split as a result of its refusal to back Conservative candidates, prompting the formation of a splinter group, IML. The right-wing IML insisted that true 'Navalists' should support the Conservatives, regardless of the Liberals' stance on naval issues. Eventually, the NL increasingly aligned with the Conservatives and prevailed over the IML, but these divisions may have prevented it from becoming as influential as the *Flottenverein*. From a grassroots perspective, the unconventional orientation of 'nationalist agitators' towards the party was the expression of a general scepticism among conservatives over the party's ability to meet new challenges. While recognising the potentially destabilising influence of these organisations, Coetzee posited that they ultimately served to bolster the Conservative Party's position. Their involvement extended beyond mere electoral support in by-elections. They were instrumental in identifying new constituencies and salient issues that facilitated the party's reconfiguration and its adaptation to the exigencies of the postwar milieu. In particular, Coetzee's analysis of the leagues' social constituencies shed light on the ways in which they expanded the Conservatives' appeal across the middle and lower-middle classes, effectively transforming the party from 'a loose conglomeration of agrarian interests to the predominant Party of government in urban, industrial Britain'. Coetzee's thesis provided a framework for understanding how what Seymour Lipset termed the 'radicalism of the centre' was contained and anaesthetised within the bastions of the Conservative Party – potentially explaining the failure of British fascism in the postwar years.[52]

In their search for a 'prefascist lineage', close observers and historians of British Fascism have also contributed to the investigation of radical nationalism's appeal in the Edwardian era.[53] Historian Thomas Linehan has written that during the Edwardian crisis 'a distinct vocabulary of protest began to take shape that would later find an echo in many of the anti-liberal arguments formulated by the fascists', and added that native fascism also inherited a 'tradition of extra-parliamentary activism' from the same period.[54] The long-standing debate on the 'affinities' between the *Weltanschauungen* and the practical politics of the Edwardian Right and the British fascists is not yet dead. In their quest for 'prefascist' ideas and thinkers some scholars have pointed out that the British Right was not entirely immune to the 'revolt against reason' which by the end of the nineteenth century had degenerated into a philosophy of will, instinctual action, elitism, racial hygiene and Splenglerian *Untergang des Abendlandes*. As historian Dan Stone wrote:

> Arnold White's militarism, the Edwardian popular leagues' demands for conscription and defence of empire, Lord Willoughby de Broke's 'National

Toryism', Oscar Levy's Nietzschean critique of an effete western ethic, Anthony Ludovici's call for a 'masculine renaissance', Karl Pearson's and W. C. D. Whetham's equation of eugenics with anti-alienism and anti-feminism, A. H. Lane's antisemitism, William Sanderson's vision of an organic society dedicated to 'service', Viscount Lymington's rural revivalism – all of these are, singly, elements of a reactionary, sometimes revolutionary-reactionary, ideology.[55]

He sums up these elements with the term 'extremes of Englishness', and it is only in combination that they could be considered as constituting something akin to proto-fascism.

By placing earlier thinkers in the philosophical tradition leading to fascism, historians have run the risk, as Edward R. Tannenbaum noted, of committing the *post hoc, ergo propter hoc* fallacy (after this, therefore because of this).[56] However, aside from the problem of causation, close observers and scholars of British fascism had the merit of unearthing and rescuing from oblivion a number of right-wing organisations and groups, including the anti-alien and antisemitic organisation the BBL. In addition, they have paid particular attention to the 'paramilitary aspect' prevalent in many Edwardian right-wing formations. This militaristic inclination manifested itself in those organisations formed to counter the perceived 'revolutionary threat' posed by socialists and militant trade unionists, and reached its zenith during the 'Ulster Crisis'. During this time, the radical right not only sponsored the UVF but also orchestrated the BLSUU.

Scholarly interest in Edwardian conservatism has remained unabated in recent years. E. H. H. Green's inexhaustible intellectual curiosity has led to a general re-examination of the 'crisis of conservatism' and the role of 'radical conservatives' in transforming the Party's identity. The term 'radical conservative' was preferred over 'radical right' to differentiate developments in the British Right from those in the continental Right.[57] In analysing the ideas and programmes of the major parties on the extreme right in Britain from the early twentieth century to the present day, Sykes wrote that the radical right 'was neither a political party, nor a single, unified political movement nor a completely coherent ideology [...] its salient attitudes were sometimes virtually indistinguishable from mainstream Conservatism'. However, he recognised that it was possible to identify some 'ideological genericizations' in the elements that constituted the phenomenon, from Social Imperialism to the BNP. The radical right was 'intensely nationalist or hypernationalist'. It held the traditional view of society as an 'organic whole', a 'harmonious' aggregate cemented by a common past, a common spirit and a common will. In the best reactionary tradition, it was inclined to see any approaching dark cloud as portending disaster. The radical right strove for the 'regeneration of existing society and the regeneration of the individual physically, mentally and morally', and while it imagined a 'a new man' it yearned for a past more mythical than real. It opposed liberalism, democracy, socialism, internationalism and 'vulgar modernity'. From this perspective, the pristine 'radical right' – the Edwardian Right – was a form of conservative dissidence that had emerged from a profound 'sense of crisis' and that relied on economic protectionism, imperial unity, national efficiency, social discipline and racial regeneration to support the national awakening.[58] More recently, N. C. Fleming has examined the 'morphological transformations' of 'Right-Conservatism' between 1900 and 1939. The Edwardian era, Fleming argues, rather than heralding modern reactionary politics, marked a pivotal moment in the evolution of British conservatism. This transformation was manifested in three vectors of dissent: empire-first Unionists, 'the legion of leagues', and the diehards. United in demanding more aggressive opposition, yet divided on specifics, these factions catalysed the restructuring of the party and changes in leadership style, which were bequeathed to the Conservative Party in the interwar period.[59] Other historians have devoted specific attention to the semi-secret Confederacy and its commitment to purging the party of all who adhered to the free trade orthodoxy. Some have identified Leo Maxse and his *National Review* as the epitome of the radical right. Others have traced the history of the IMF and examined the circulation of ultranationalist arguments within the British media.[60] All studies agree that the Right injected into the Conservative Party a spirit of impatience, demands for immediate and decisive action, a strong proclivity for conspiratorial thinking and a rhetoric marked by aggressive threats and martial metaphors.

In this work, the term 'Right' is employed as a sort of heuristic device encompassing the diverse ideological tendencies, styles of action, modes of communication, worldviews and attitudes that are inherent to and often transcend the 'conservative position'. Drawing on existing literature, this book defines the 'Edwardian Right' as a phenomenon of 'radical nationalism'. Stemming from a compulsive preoccupation with the perceived decline of the national community, this movement generated forms of mobilisation that radicalised to the point of deformation the 'conservative core' – namely, respect for tradition, an organic society, authority and order, a sense of duty and self-sacrifice, imperial unity and patriotism, and the defence of private property and enterprise. By elevating war to the status of an 'index' of national health, the Right fought perceived 'internal enemies' and were in favour of extensive programmes of military preparation and regeneration in every sphere of national life, whether political, economic, social, cultural or moral. These efforts were aimed at guaranteeing the 'survival' of the national organism and subsequently enhancing its potential warlike capacity.

The British Right and the lure of violence

This volume analyses right-wing responses to the Edwardian crisis in Britain (1901–1914), highlighting how the surge in right-wing extremism, both internal and external to the Conservative Party, coincided with the solidification of a culture predisposed to the 'production of violence'. This culture was manifested in diverse ultra-nationalist organisations, civilian policing entities, private military associations and paramilitary formations. The study reconstructs the system of beliefs and the practices of those right-wing actors who fostered the cult of armed and martial force, and promoted national virility, 'law and order', imperial unity and, where necessary, violent resistance to the disintegrative forces of liberalism, socialism, materialistic hedonism and cosmopolitan pacifism. This 'lure of violence' was well stated by Willoughby de Broke in his article 'The Coming Campaign':

> The sacrifice of the sanctity and dignity of the Sovereign for the purpose of handing over the Empire to the despotism of the reigning caucus, and making it a sign and proverb among all the nations, is never likely to be accomplished pacifically. Even if a claim could be plausibly established that the scheme had been ratified by some kind of majority, the attempt to carry it out, would bring us dangerously near to the exercise of physical force, which still remains the ultimate sanction of Parliamentary Government.

Accordingly, every loyal citizen was duty-bound to bear their share of the sacrifices necessary to defend society and its members from those who were consumed by 'jealousy of imperial power' and who sought to undermine national defence and stoke hatred between classes to a fever pitch.[61]

Based on this premise, the book is divided into five chapters, each presenting one or more of the movements or organisations that mobilised to deal with one or more of the predicaments that Britain appeared to be facing: military unpreparedness, want of manhood, physical degeneration, strikes and industrial strife, the Irish question and the imperial crisis. In contrast to preceding scholarly works, this study allocates significantly less attention to those pressure groups (e.g., the NL, the ASU, the NSL, etc.) whose strategies were partly educational and partly political, and instead focusses more on those organisations that provided a 'performative' outlet for the cultivation of an ultra-nationalist, masculine, efficient, 'vigilantist', soldierly citizenry.

The first chapter presents how the Right raised the issue of proficiency with weapons as the first duty of a citizen. The setbacks endured during the Boer War and the conspicuous deficiencies in military training and equipment forced the Conservative government to initiate a comprehensive programme of military restructuring in 1904. However, long before this, right-wing factions had responded by either championing universal compulsory military training or, as an alternative to conscription, remobilising 'patriotic volunteering'. The Navy's pivotal role in securing Britain's coastlines was never really put under discussion. Nonetheless, a current of feeling was emerging that the nation's internal security should not be entrusted solely to the Regular Army, but rather to its own citizenry. Accordingly, adequately trained, organised, armed and equipped citizens should shoulder the responsibility of safeguarding their homes, while the role of professional soldiers remained indispensable in defending the Empire. This concept was by no means new. In the past, every citizen's right – and responsibility – to defend their country had not only been acknowledged, but had also found expression in a variety of 'voluntary official' bodies (e.g., the Yeomanry and Volunteer corps) and voluntary civil bodies, including sundry uniformed youth organisations.[62] Nonetheless, especially after the Norfolk Commission concluded that the auxiliary forces were unfit to defend the country, the concept of 'civilian preparedness' took on renewed urgency. As the Boers excelled in shooting, the Right launched a popular campaign for improving marksmanship. Britons had to learn (or relearn) to kill at a distance with the utmost accuracy, certain of hitting their targeted enemies at up to two hundred yards. The genesis of this 'rifle movement' can be traced back to comments made by Lord Salisbury at a gathering of the Primrose League in 1901, where he drew attention to the deficiencies in British marksmanship and introduced the principle of 'One Man, One Rifle'. Later, Lord Roberts assumed the leadership of the Society of Miniature Rifle Clubs (SMRC) and became a fervent advocate of improving the nation's skills in arms. Drawing inspiration from the 'shooting traditions' of the Netherlands and Switzerland, Lord Roberts proposed establishing rifle clubs in every village, and encouraging people of all ages, boys in particular, to participate in shooting during their free time. By the summer of 1914, the civilian rifle movement had attracted over half a million citizens. In addition, the Right consistently pressed school authorities to add rifle shooting to the school curriculum. Firearms training was necessary to instil in pupils a perception of violence as an inherent, unchanging facet of the natural order. War was among the 'sternest' and most ineluctable realities of existence and going to war meant preparation in peacetime.[63]

Another important instructive observation taken from the Boer War was that the Boers were trained from childhood to ride horses, study the terrain, take cover and endure lengthy marches and harsh environmental conditions. Despite having no strict conventional military structures, they had acquired habits of obedience and self-sacrifice. British soldiers, unaccustomed to 'life in the wilderness', initially found themselves at an immense disadvantage against this elusive and mobile foe. It was after a year or so of fighting that they learned the primitive yet essential lessons of 'how to find the way, how to scout, to travel, and to save horseflesh'.[64] Only then were they able to effectively cope with the hardships imposed on them by man and nature. For the Right, the blame for this 'painful adaptation' lay primarily in modern civilisation, which had contributed to the erosion of self-reliance and self-sufficiency. Abundance had not only created leisure, it had bred idleness, effeminacy and the gratification of individual desire. It had blunted natural impulses, 'surplus vitality' and the 'exuberant manners of life', while spreading a rancid odour of decay. In other words, modernity was making men smaller and more vulnerable. To revive the virility of those deep-chested, broad-shouldered forefathers, who had 'carved an empire out of the wilderness', it was necessary to recreate as closely as possible the conditions under which it had flourished – and nothing was better adapted to this task than popularising frontier skills and instilling them in the imagination of the youth. For instance, as historian John M. MacKenzie noted, hunting as the principal survival skill of pioneers played a dual role in the preservation of the 'imperial race': it served as a formative experience for the imperial elites and at the same time as practical training for war. It thus perpetuated the inherent predatory instinct present in all human beings.[65]

Against this backdrop, the second chapter outlines how the creation of the Legion of Frontiersmen in 1904 garnered predictable support from right-wing conservatives, who saw it as bringing together British men for the cause of national and imperial defence and guiding them in the fulfilment of their duty to God, King and country. Founded by Roger Pocock – frontiersman, cosmopolitan, bohemian and writer – the Legion's aim was to provide military training for men who would act as local guides, advisors or intelligence operatives across the empire during times of crisis. They promoted schemes of internal and coastal defence against the 'German peril' and organised themselves to meet the threat of foreign espionage. Despite the Army Council's continual refusal to officially acknowledge the Legion, the Frontiersmen undertook the responsibility of publicly advocating for games that would provide training for warfare. This included instruction in horsemanship, marksmanship and martial arts, expertise in drill, marching proficiency and the essential qualities defining a 'soldierly bearing'. Not infrequently, they took on roles as scoutmasters for the newly established Boy Scouts, where they endeavoured to develop endurance, grit, self-assurance and the courage perceived as vital for imperial defence, all in the interests of maintaining the race at a high pitch of physical and moral efficiency and to nurture future generations capable of fulfilling the responsibilities handed to them by fate and Providence.[66]

The Frontiersmen sympathised with the policies of 'Imperial Preference and Protection' believing these would cement the empire. Those who obstructed this imperial development were perceived as 'enemies', or at best 'mentally torpid'. When the Imperial Mission led by Henry Page Croft intensified its campaign by sending Imperial 'Pioneers' throughout Britain, the Frontiersmen offered to steward its rowdy meetings and prevent Radicals from infiltrating and disrupting them. At the Lambeth Baths, as Croft recounted, the Legionnaires went 'into battle with real purpose. Men and women were screaming, blood was flowing, teeth were disappearing, and the ringleaders were roughly deposited down the steps'.[67]

The Boer War dramatically brought to the surface the 'stigmata of degeneration' when an appalling number of recruits were rejected because of physical deficiencies. The Right lay the blame at the twin curses of immigration and urbanisation. The first 'curse' derived from an imperfect syllogism: 'racial dissolution' due to interbreeding and a 'defective blood stream' that had come to Britain through Eastern European immigrations, introduced signs of degeneration; degeneration predisposed individuals to a general decline in physical vigour, mental acuity and moral fibre, and *pari passu* affected the 'efficiency' of the country, including its military preparedness; hence racial degradation might be said to be the cause of most of the problems of British life. The only way to escape this was a total ban on the immigration of 'undesirables', paupers, criminals, the 'diseased' and 'mental defectives'. For this purpose, as presented in the third chapter, the Right directly participated or assisted in the formation of several anti-alien and antisemitic associations, the most vociferous and most conspicuous of which was the BBL. Established in 1901 by Captain William Stanley Shaw, this body originated from the contention that the arrival of poor immigrants from Romania and Russia was flooding the labour market with cheap labour and further congesting the already teeming East End of London. The League, with forty-five thousand members throughout Stepney, Hackney, Bethnal Green, Shoreditch and Saint George's, pressed Parliament to enact stringent immigration restrictions under the slogan 'England for the English'. Organised along military lines, the BBL preached violence, propagated antisemitic hate and incited mob rioting. They taunted the Liberals for being pro-alien and unconcerned with the daily needs of British citizens. The passing of the Aliens Act of 1905 subdued the movement at a moment when words were transforming into deeds. The spectre of the BBL was evoked in the wake of the Houndsditch outrage, the 'Siege of Sidney Street' and whenever the Liberal government's application of the expulsion powers granted by the Act seemed insufficiently stringent.⁶⁸

According to the Right, urban life and, more generally, the 'haste of modernity' was another influential factor contributing to racial degeneration. Cities were often synonymous with overcrowding, inadequate sanitation, malnutrition, overwork and mental strain, as well as hooliganism, 'the exaggeration of sex', inebriety and other 'indulgent' behaviours. Eugenics seemed desirable to the Right, but controlled change in the inherited biological nature of men was something complex, even when limited to reducing dysgenic traits and 'artificial selection' through the differential birth-rate between the social classes. Certainly, for the Right, the remedy for progressive degeneration did not lie in 'socialistic illusions', or in the ethical notion of welfarism, but rather in strengthening the race with rigid prescriptions of discipline, hierarchy and order. Exasperated by the sense of 'internal dissolution', which was being manifested in the 'behaviour' of Home Rulers, socialists, trade unionists and suffragettes, the NSL expanded its mission beyond national defence, elevating universal military service as a catalyst for physical, moral and industrial efficiency. Specifically, it was argued, a period of compulsory military training would greatly improve the health, posture, mental acuity, stamina and 'personal hygiene' of all men, particularly those from the nation's humbler social strata. This improvement in individual well-being would in turn contribute to an improvement in the overall 'vigour of the nation'. In addition, military training would instil in the men a heightened sense of patriotic responsibility, self-sacrifice, obedience and respect for authority. The army was the medium through which the 'finest breed of men that the race had generated' could be nurtured. In essence, it embodied the exaltation of a productive, robust, assertive and virile ideal, held to be essential for halting or retarding the process of 'degeneration' and for preserving Britain's position in the world.⁶⁹

The Right was certainly not united on the merits of universal military-style training. Many argued that the pretext of military necessity put at risk the fundamental principles of freedom, held so sacred by the British people. A compromise was found in strengthening and expanding the 'old volunteering spirit' and at the same time attempting to secure for every child in the country a complete course of physical and pre-military training. Historians have examined the prewar militarisation of British youth in its minutest details, including its advocacy by the Left.⁷⁰ However, it was on the Right that a 'philosophy of force' with its directive to preserve and 'foster the savage in the male youth' became a practical moral code and an antidote to decay. The strength of a nation ultimately depended upon the strength of the individuals that comprised it. However, achieving military and physical efficiency required more than the government enacting sanitary laws or providing cities with good water, proper drainage and safe food. It was incumbent upon citizens to ensure the 'protection and continuity of the race'. While fears of physical degeneration had taken hold in the minds of British subjects, the Right introduced a series of schemes and initiatives to improve the physical fitness and morale of the younger men of the country. For inspiration, they turned to models of military training for school age youths both within and outside the empire. For instance, the Australian preparatory military training programme was vigorously advocated by the NSL and may have inspired Henry Page Croft's Citizen Army, which recommended starting physical exercises and military training for boys on their first day of school at the age of six and continuing with them up to the age of twenty.[71] The Right also supported the formation of many patriotic, civic, health and philanthropic organisations focused on improving the physical fitness of boys in their 'age of immaturity', primarily by imitating Adolf Spiess's gymnastics system, which had been adopted in Swiss schools.[72] The ultimate objective was to guarantee the maximum physical efficiency of the largest possible cohort of young men in anticipation of future military training. Preparation was to include drill, comprising exercises with and without arms and rifle shooting, and the cultivation of robust health habits.[73]

Physical education was directed to the formation not only of good soldiers, but also of good citizens. The Right thereby effortlessly interlocked the pursuit of health and vigour with martial respect for the virtues of honour, loyalty and morality. Military drills, for instance, taught boys the proper wearing of uniforms, the meticulous upkeep of shoes, marching in precise 30-inch steps at a pace of 120 steps per minute and the rigid manoeuvres of a regular army. More significantly, these drills had to instil in schoolboys the habit of precise, unwavering obedience to authority, particularly when a crisis situation called for the Fifth Commandment to be disobeyed. The old Latin adage *mens sana in corpore sano* was gradually transformed into the more 'reactionary' ideal of 'social efficiency', which basically meant the subordination of the individual to the superior interests of the national collective.[74] Moreover, regular and robust physical exercise was envisioned as a deterrent to the dissipation of 'vitality', which was attributed to the vice of onanism and other 'bad habits'. Thus, juvenile energy, instead of being wasted in masturbation, should be directed or 'sublimated' into violent muscular effort. Right-wingers insistently invited Britons to train in martial arts and combative sports, particularly boxing, wrestling, ju-jitsu, bartitsu, savate and stick fighting, to rouse the virility of a 'disappearing manhood'. This 'unleashing of manhood' latched with the powerful rhetoric of masculine citizenship and efforts to preserve rigid gender boundaries at a time when the Suffragettes were sending shock waves through the general public by agitating for extension of the franchise to women.[75]

The concept of social equality never found expressive (or emotional) resonance within the Conservative imagination and the most reactionary factions harboured concerns that its realisation would hasten the erosion of civilisation. Certainly, as the fourth chapter shows, the Right revered social harmony, stability and security, implying that its policy was to strike effectively at all sources of disorder and to reconcile all classes in the unity of a living faith – Britain. Above all else, socialism stood indicted for propagating unpatriotic sentiments among the working classes, resulting from its efforts to supplant patriotism with the ideals of humanitarian internationalism and the 'world brotherhood of all those who toil'. The socialist doctrine of 'class war' and the manner in which it was habitually preached by 'evolutionary' and revolutionary socialists alike was conjectured to have not only wreaked havoc on the peace of the community, but to have also been detrimental to the imperative of national and industrial efficiency. In 1908, the Earl of Malmesbury wrote that

> Organisms are subject to malignant growths, to the evil effects of bacilli, and to the influences of germs. From this rule the political organism is not exempt. We have in our midst a growth which has sprung into a poisonous weed of huge proportions. The trouble in our house to-day is the dry-rot of Socialism.[76]

Collectivist influences were seen to be materialising across all domains of national life, posing a threat to the constitution and exerting pernicious pressure on legislation concerning capital and land. Meanwhile, the 'seductive teachings' of socialism were, like a potent narcotic, subtly sabotaging national defences and allowing the people's healthy spirit of discipline and unity to dissipate.

The Right considered it unfair to accuse the Liberal government of being solely responsible for the sad state of affairs. By permitting the Trade Disputes Act to pass through the House of Lords *nemine contradicente*, Balfour had connived in establishing a privilege for trade unions at the expense of the country. It was said that only deluded minds could fail to see that this piece of 'legislative hypocrisy', which jeopardised the sanctity of contract, gave the unions immunity from civil damages and legalised the 'terrorism' of peaceful picketing, was a harbinger of calamities. From this vantage point, the Right needed no great effort of the imagination to portray the 'Great labour unrest', which exploded in the years immediately before the war, as a crime against the nation. In the 'terrible summer' of 1911, seamen went on strike just after the Kaiser had sent a warship to Agadir and – outrageously – a week before George V's coronation. In Southampton at the end of July, the hitherto intractable shipping magnates conceded to the workers' demands for higher wages and overtime rates. The effect on dockers, lightermen, coal porters and other classes of waterfront labourers in London and other major English ports was, as one historian wrote, 'electric' and thousands upon thousands of men downed tools.[77] In mid-August, while the maritime strikes dragged on, a railwaymen's strike, instigated by rank-and-file pressure on the union leadership, thrust England for the first time into a general strike. The 'quadrilateral of English industrialism' was virtually paralysed. Troops were called in and disputes were settled, although amid much violence and 'savage rioting'. The 'most eventful summer of the British proletariat' inevitably exacerbated right-wing instincts for vigilante action.[78] While charges of treason, disloyalty and conspiracy were levelled at trade union leaders and organisers, and the Liberal government was accused of sacrificing the country on the altar of political expediency, the Right actively promoted and facilitated the formation of middle-class unions, citizens' patrol groups and voluntary special police forces to protect strikebreakers. 'Patriotic citizens' were encouraged to rise up and 'take the law into their own hands', with the aim of preventing organised labour from holding the state and society to ransom. On the eve of the war, brigades of volunteers had sprung up around the country, a tangible expression of their 'social instinct of self-preservation'.[79]

While anti-labour schemes of civilian mobilisation unfolded, the revival of Home Rule raised among the conservative Right the fundamental question, as J. A. Hobson bluntly put it, of whether it was desirable to 'abandon the constitutional methods, in which they have hitherto put their trust', or 'fall back upon [the methods] of physical force'.[80] The 1911 Act of Parliament had delivered a single decisive blow to the last effective bulwark of privilege, property and 'traditional authority', giving the House of Commons complete liberty to carry out forthwith the people's wishes. According to its indefatigable critics, it had left the Constitution at the mercy of sectional party interests and 'electioneering vanity'. Preservation of the Union and the Ulsterites' resistance gave Conservatives an opportunity to bring the government to its knees. However, toying with treason for the sake of Ulster was not merely shallow political opportunism, instead it served the much deeper purpose of 'recapturing' the Constitution and protecting it from future attacks by a 'degenerate Liberalism' that since 1884 had betrayed imperial interests and from the growing menace of socialism. Historians have very carefully examined the history of the Home Rule crisis and have conducted exegetical readings of the speeches and pronouncements of Unionist front benchers and peers, and all those who carried weight and influence in the party. They have charted how Bonar Law's heedless 'rodomontade at Blenheim' and the bellicose posturing of Sir Edward Carson developed into a festival of seditious talk and fraternisation with rebellion. Much attention has been directed at Conservative support for the arming of the Ulster

Volunteer Force, their adventurous gun-running operations, their tampering with the Army and their ignominious attempts to involve the King. Despite the excesses they have charged British Unionists with, historians have given the impression that their threat to use any means, even the worst and most reprehensible, to defeat the 'conspiracy' of the 'revolutionary committee' was simply a ploy to force a fresh election.[81] While this interpretation has merit, it is also true that the dynamics of escalation, as many contemporaries recognised, were impossible to predict and control. The preparation for and willingness to use violence, together with an emotional rhetoric that suppressed any rational or effective calculation, could have had unpredictable results. The Right, mindful of the risks, were playing with fire and gradually losing their sense of restraint.

It was, of course, no secret that men were being armed and trained in England and Scotland to support the UVF. After outlining the relationship between UVF and Conservative leaders, the fifth chapter specifically reconstructs the story of the BLSUU. Founded by Willoughby de Broke, it recruited men to go over to join, train and fight along the Ulster Volunteers. Among them was Frank Percy Crozier, to whom the British government would later assign the command of the 'Black and Tans' in Ireland. With hundreds of agents scattered throughout Britain, the BLSUU played an important role in procuring weapons and providing financial assistance and training to Captain James Craig and his Ulstermen.[82] It also became a conduit of intelligence, particularly regarding 'unusual army manoeuvrings'. The gravity of the BLSUU's treasonable military preparations certainly diminishes the credibility of the 'bluff theory', while vividly illustrating the lengths the Right was prepared to go to. The organisation, whose activities, insults and threats had had a marked effect on Tory public opinion and had greatly contributed to the unsettling prospect of an impending civil war, could claim over ten thousand members by the time of the 'Curragh incident'.[83] It gave, in the words of its leader, 'flesh' to Bonar Law's speech at Blenheim.[84] It also provided the organisational framework on which the British Covenanters would build their movement. In the summer of 1914, the increase in semi-military companies or outright 'private military forces' connected with the BLSUU and their blatant preparations for the use of force against Irish nationalists was at its height. The sense of dread and foreboding at impending war became disturbingly palpable. Nevertheless, with the onset of the Great War, 'friends' and 'foes' declared a truce and the acrimony stemming from the 'Irish complications' suddenly faded into insignificance in the face of the awful carnage.

The rumblings of the Edwardian era sanctioned the 'strange death of Liberal England'. But the crisis of the old order and the advent, or at least the promise, of the new order also convulsed British conservatism.

Nonetheless, the Right was either too loyal or too weak to break away from the Conservative Party, although it did produce forms of mobilisation and a 'culture of violence' that gradually solidified into a 'tradition'. In a curious paradox, the myriad postwar anti-Bolshevik organisations that reassembled around the defence of order and property and became an important rallying point for disgruntled middles classes emulated the abusiveness of their Edwardian predecessors. At the same time, this 'tradition' contributed to either the development of an idiosyncratic-nativist interpretation of fascism – 'a glorified Boy-Scoutism for adults' – or the neutralisation of those political spaces in which potential imitators of Mussolini could flourish.

Notes

1 On the Edwardian period, see Sir Robert C. K. Ensor, *England 1870–1914* (Oxford: Oxford University Press, 1936); Élie Halévy, *History of the English People in the Nineteenth Century*, translated as *Imperialism and the Rise of Labour* (London: Ernest Benn, 1951) and *The Rule of Democracy* (London: Ernest Benn, 1952); George Dangerfield, *The Strange Death of Liberal England* (London: MacGibbon & Kee, 1935; reprinted 1983). See also Donald Read, *Edwardian England, 1901–15* (London: Harrap, 1972); Paul Thompson, *The Edwardians* (London: Weidenfeld & Nicolson, 1975); David Powell, *The Edwardian Crisis: Britain 1901–1914* (London: Palgrave Macmillan, 1996); Roy Hattersley, *The Edwardians* (London: Little, Brown, 2004); Simon Heffer, *The Age of Decadence: Britain 1880 to 1914* (New York: Random House, 2017).

2 On the Edwardian Conservative Party, see, among others, Robert Blake, *The Conservative Party from Peel to Churchill* (London: Eyre & Spottiswoode, 1970); Lord Butler (ed.), *The Conservatives: A History from Their Origins to 1965* (London: Allen & Unwin, 1977); John Ramsden, *The Age of Balfour and Baldwin, 1902–1940* (London: Longman, 1978); David Dutton, *'His Majesty's Loyal Opposition': The Unionist Party in Opposition, 1905–1915* (Liverpool: Liverpool University Press, 1992); Anthony Seldon and Stuart Ball (eds), *Conservative Century: The Conservative Party since 1900* (Oxford: Oxford University Press, 1994); Stuart R. Ball, *The Conservative Party and British Politics, 1902–1951* (London: Longman, 1995). More recently, David Thackeray, *Conservatism for the Democratic Age: Conservative Cultures and the Challenge of Mass Politics in Early Twentieth Century England* (Manchester: Manchester University Press, 2013). For an extensive bibliographical essay on the Conservative party, see Stuart Ball, 'The Conservative Party since 1900: A Bibliography', in Seldon and Ball (eds), *Conservative Century*, pp. 727–772.

3 E. H. H. Green, *The Crisis of Conservatism: The Politics, Economics, and Ideology of the British Conservative Party, 1880–1914* (London: Routledge, 1995), pp. 1–23.

4 On party factionalism, Neal Blewett, 'Free-Fooders, Balfourites, and Whole-Hoggers: Factionalism within the Unionist Party 1906–1910', *Historical Journal* 11 (1968), pp. 95–124; Alan Sykes, 'The Confederacy and the Purge of the Unionist Free Traders 1906–1910', *Historical Journal* 18 (1975), pp. 349–366; David Dutton, 'The Unionist Party and Social Policy 1906–14', *Historical Journal* 24 (1981), pp. 871–884; Corinne C. Weston and Patricia Kelvin, 'The Judas Group and the Parliament Bill of 1911', *English Historical Review* 99 (July 1984), pp. 551–563. Jane Ridley, 'The Unionist Social Reform Committee 1911–14: Wets before the Deluge', *Historical Journal* 30 (1987), pp. 391–413.

5 Ian Gilmour, *Inside Right: A Study of Conservatism* (London: Hutchinson, 1978), pp. 32–33.

6 Daniel Ziblatt, *Conservative Political Parties and the Birth of Modern Democracy in Europe* (Cambridge: Cambridge University Press, 2017), pp. 139–171. Ziblatt refers to the classic work by Juan J. Linz and Alfred Stepan (ed.), *The Breakdown of Democratic Regimes* (Baltimore, MD: Johns Hopkins University Press, 1979), pp. 27–34.

7 E. H. Phelps Brown, *The Growth of British Industrial Relations* (London: Macmillan, 1959), p. 332. The prominent British economist wrote: 'Events which stir the emotions, in the same way boost one another's signals when they are in a circuit with one another, and their aggregate effect is greater than the sum of the effects they would take separately'. On this 'factor of reverberation' which accounted for the anxieties that the prewar crisis inspired, see also Standish Meacham, 'The Sense of an Impending Clash', *American Historical Review* 77 (December 1972), pp. 1343–1364.

8 On the Right in Edwardian Britain, see, in particular, J. R. Jones, 'England', in Hans Rogger and Eugen Weber (eds), *The European Right: A Historical Profile* (Berkeley, CA: University of California Press, 1966), pp. 29–70; Geoffrey R. Searle, 'Critics of Edwardian Society: The Case of the Radical Right', in Alan O'Day (ed.), *The Edwardian Age: Conflict and Stability, 1900–1914* (London: Macmillan, 1979), pp. 79–96; Geoffrey R. Searle, 'The Revolt from the Right in Edwardian Britain', in Paul Kennedy and Anthony Nicholls (eds), *Nationalist and Racialist Movements in Britain and Germany Before the First World War* (London: Palgrave Macmillan, 1981), pp. 21–39; Alan Sykes, *The Radical Right in Britain* (Basingstoke: Palgrave Macmillan, 2005); Alan Sykes, 'The Radical Right and the Crisis of Conservatism before the First World War', *Historical Journal* 26 (1983), pp. 661–676; Barbara Storm Farr, *The Development and Impact of Right-Wing Politics in Britain, 1903–1932* (New York: Garland, 1987); Neil C. Fleming, *Britannia's Zealots, Volume I: Tradition, Empire and the Forging of the Conservative Right* (London: Bloomsbury Publishing, 2020); David Thackeray, 'Rethinking the Edwardian Crisis of Conservatism', *The Historical Journal* 54, no. 1 (March 2011), pp. 191–213. On the diehards, Gregory D. Phillips, *The Diehards: Aristocratic Society and Politics in Edwardian England* (Cambridge, MA: Harvard University Press, 1979); Ronan Fanning, '"Rats" versus "Ditchers": The Diehard Revolt and the

Parliament Bill of 1911', in Art Cosgrove and J. I. McGuire (eds), *Parliament and Community* (Belfast: Appletree Press, 1983), pp. 191–210. On the origins and impact of Joseph Chamberlain's policy of tariff reform, Alan Sykes, *Tariff Reform in British Politics* (Oxford: Oxford University Press, 1979).

9 See, for example, Paul Langford, *Englishness Identified: Manners and Character 1650–1850* (Oxford: Oxford University Press, 2000); Robert Colls, *Identity of England* (Oxford: Oxford University Press, 2002); Peter Mandler, *The English National Character: The History of an Idea from Edmund Burke to Tony Blair* (New Haven, CT: Yale University Press, 2006). For a 'revisionist approach', Donald C. Richter, *Riotous Victorians* (Athens, OH: Ohio University Press, 1981). For a survey of the changing pattern of violence in modern and contemporary England, Clive Emsley, *The English and Violence since 1750* (London: A&C Black, 2005).

10 John M. MacKenzie, 'The Imperial Pioneer and Hunter and the British Masculine Stereotype in Late Victorian and Edwardian Times', in J. A. Mangan and James Walvin (eds), *Manliness and Morality: Middle-Class Masculinity in Britain and America, 1800–1940* (New York: St. Martin Press, 1987), pp. 188–189.

11 For the concept of Teutophobia, see A. J. A. Morris, *The Scaremongers: The Advocacy of War and Rearmament 1896–1914* (London: Routledge & Kegan Paul, 1984).

12 See, for example, Michael D. Blanch, 'British Society and the War', and Bernard Porter, 'The Pro-Boers in Britain', in Peter Warwick (ed.), *The South African War: An Anglo-Boer War, 1899–1902* (Harlow: Longman, 1980), pp. 210–238 and 239–257.

13 Willoughby de Broke's emphatic appeal for armed resistance appeared widely in the British press between 12 June and 14 June 1913. See, for instance, the *London Evening Standard* and the *Belfast News-Letter*.

14 For an overview of radical and authoritarian nationalism in late nineteenth-century Europe, see Stanley Payne, *A History of Fascism* (Madison, WI: University of Wisconsin Press, 1995), pp. 35–69.

15 Jones, 'England', p. 29.

16 Ibid., p. 32.

17 BLO Salisbury to Selborne, 10 August 1904, Selborne Papers, 5/89.

18 Citations in Robert J. Scally, *The Origins of the Lloyd George Coalition: The Politics of Social Imperialism 1900–1918* (Princeton, NJ: Princeton University Press, 1975), p. 159.

19 Bodleian Library, Salisbury to Selborne, 20 May 1908, Selborne Papers, 5/207–212.

20 *Mr. Chamberlain's Speeches*, edited by Charles W. Boyd, with an introduction by Austen Chamberlain, Volume 2 (Boston, MA: Houghton Mifflin Company, 1914), p. 368.

21 Austen Chamberlain, *Politics from Inside* (London: Cassell, 1936), p. 81.

22 Dangerfield, *The Strange Death of Liberal England*, p. 48; Ensor, *England 1870–1914*, p. 428.

23 Willoughby de Broke, 'National Torysm', *National Review* 58 (1912), pp. 413–427.
24 Gregory D. Phillips, 'Lord Willoughby de Broke and the Politics of Radical Toryism, 1909–1914', *Journal of British Studies* 20 (1980), pp. 205–224.
25 William S. Rodner, 'Conservatism, Resistance and Lord Hugh Cecil', *History of Political Thought* 9, no. 3 (Winter 1988), pp. 529–551.
26 Jones, 'England', p. 48.
27 See, for example, Kenneth Lunn, 'Political Anti-Semitism before 1914: Fascism's Heritage', in Richard Thurlow (ed.), *British Fascism* (London: Routledge, 2015), pp. 20–40.
28 Jones, 'England', p. 50.
29 Ibid., p. 53.
30 Ibid., pp. 54–57.
31 Ibid., pp. 57–58.
32 Paul Kennedy, 'The Prewar Right in Britain and Germany', in Kennedy and Nicholls (eds), *Nationalist and Racialist Movements in Britain and Germany*, p. 2.
33 Scally, *The Origins of the Lloyd George Coalition*, p. 19.
34 Searle, 'Critics of Edwardian Society', p. 85.
35 Ibid., p. 94.
36 Sykes, 'The Radical Right and the Crisis of Conservatism', pp. 675–676.
37 Phillips, *The Diehards*, pp. 82–110.
38 Ibid., p. 155.
39 David Cannadine, *The Decline and Fall of the British Aristocracy* (New Haven, CT: Yale University Press, 1990), pp. 501–502.
40 Arno Mayer, 'The Domestic Causes of the First World War', in Leonard Kreiger and Fritz Stern (eds), *The Responsibility of Power* (London: Macmillan, 1968), pp. 292–293.
41 Phelps Brown, *The Growth of British Industrial Relations*, p. 332.
42 See, for example, Ralph Darlington, 'Strikers versus Scabs: Violence in the 1910–1914 British Labour Revolt', *Labor History* 63, no. 3 (2022), pp. 332–352; Alessandro Saluppo, 'Strikebreaking and Anti-Unionism on the Waterfront: The Shipping Federation, 1890–1914', *European History Quarterly* 49, no. 4 (2019), pp. 570–596.
43 On prewar anti-labour vigilantes and middle-class unions, Saluppo, 'Vigilant Citizens: The Case of the Volunteer Police Force, 1911–14', in Matteo Millan and Alessandro Saluppo (eds), *Corporate Policing, Yellow Unionism, and Strikebreaking, 1890–1930* (Abingdon: Routledge, 2020), pp. 222–241. On the continuity of forms of civilian anti-labour mobilization, Liam Ryan, 'Citizen Strike Breakers: Volunteers, Strikes, and the State in Britain, 1911–1926', *Labour History Review* 87, no. 2 (2022), pp. 109–140.
44 Jon Lawrence, *Speaking for the People: Party Language and Popular Politics 1867–1914* (Cambridge: Cambridge University Press, 1998), pp. 178–193. Quote on p. 188.

45 Adrian Gregory, 'Peculiarities of the English? War, Violence and Politics 1900–1939', *Journal of Modern European History* 1 (2003), pp. 44–59.
46 See, for instance, Zara Steiner, *Britain and the Origins of the First World War* (London: Macmillan, 1977).
47 Michael Geyer, 'The Militarization of Europe, 1914–1945', in John R. Gillis (ed.), *The Militarization of the Western World* (New Brunswick, NJ: Rutgers University Press, 1989), pp. 65–102, at p. 79.
48 See, in general, Anne Summers, 'Militarism in Britain before the Great War', *History Workshop* 2 (Autumn 1976), pp. 104–123.
49 Jörn Leonhard, 'Nations in Arms and Imperial Defence: Continental Models, the British Empire and Its Military before 1914', *Journal of Modern European History* 5 (2007), pp. 287–308.
50 On youth organizations, John Springhall, *Youth, Empire and Society: British Youth Movements, 1883–1930* (London: Croom Helm, 1977); John Springhall, 'The Boy Scouts, Class and Militarism in Relation to British Youth Movements 1908–1930', *International Review of Social History* 16, no. 2 (1971), pp. 125–158; Paul Wilkinson, 'English Youth mMvements, 1908–30', *Journal of Contemporary History* 4, no. 2 (1969), pp. 3–23; M. Blanch, 'Imperialism, Nationalism and Organized Youth', in Richard Johnson, John Clarke and Chas Critcher (eds), *Working-Class Culture: Studies in History and Theory* (London: Hutchinson, 1979), pp. 103–120.
51 W. Mark Hamilton, 'The "New Navalism" and the British Navy League, 1895–1914', *The Mariner's Mirror* 64, no. 1 (1978), pp. 37–44; Matthew Johnson, 'The Liberal Party and the Navy League in Britain before the Great War', *Twentieth Century British History* 22, no. 2 (2011), pp. 137–163; R. J. Q. Adams, 'The National Service League and Mandatory Service in Edwardian Britain', *Armed Forces & Society* 12, no. 1 (1985), pp. 53–74; Roger T. Stearn, 'The Last Glorious Campaign: Lord Roberts, The National Service League and Compulsory Military Training, 1902–1914', *Journal of the Society for Army Historical Research* 87, no. 352 (2009), pp. 312–330; Michael John Allison, *The National Service Issue, 1899–1914* (PhD diss., University of London, 1975); Rowan G. E. Thompson, *The Peculiarities of British Militarism: The Air and Navy Leagues in Interwar Britain* (PhD diss., University of Northumbria at Newcastle, 2019).
52 Frans Coetzee, *For Party or Country: Nationalism and the Dilemmas of Popular Conservatism in Edwardian England* (Oxford: Oxford University Press, 1990).
53 The literature on the origins and development of British fascism is extensive. See, generally, Colin Cross, *The Fascists in Britain* (London: Barrie and Rockcliff, 1961); Robert Benewick, *The Fascist Movement in Britain* (London: Allen Lane, 1972); Kenneth Lunn and Richard C. Thurlow (eds), *British Fascism: Essays on the Radical Right in Interwar Britain* (London: Croom Helm, 1980); Richard Thurlow, *Fascism in Britain: A History 1918–1985* (Oxford: Basil Blackwell, 1987); Thomas Linehan, *British Fascism, 1918–1939: Parties, Ideology and Culture* (Manchester: Manchester University Press,

2000); Martin Pugh, *Hurrah for the Blackshirts! Fascists and Fascism in Britain Between the Wars* (London: Pimlico, 2006).
54 Linehan, *British Fascism*, p. 17.
55 Dan Stone, *Breeding Superman: Nietzsche, Race and Eugenics in Edwardian and Interwar Britain* (Liverpool: Liverpool University Press 2002), p. 3.
56 Edward R. Tannenbaum's review of Zeev Sternhell, *Maurice Barrès et le nationalisme francais* (1972) and of Robert Soucy, *Fascism in France: The Case of Maurice Barrès* (1972), *AHR* 78 (1973), pp. 1478–1480.
57 Green, *The Crisis of Conservatism*.
58 Sykes, *The Radical Right in Britain*, pp. 2–3 and 11–33.
59 Fleming, *Britannia's Zealots*, *Vol. I*, pp. 35–76.
60 John A. Hutcheson Jr., *Leopold Maxse and the National Review* (New York: Garland, 1989); Larry L. Witherell, *Rebel on the Right: Henry Page Croft and the Crisis of British Conservatism, 1903–1914* (Newark, NJ: Associated University Press, 1997); Andrew Dougall, *Mediatizing the Nation, Ordering the World: Struggles for Redemption in Britain and the United States* (Oxford: Oxford University Press, 2024), pp. 82–124.
61 Willoughby de Broke, 'The Coming Campaign', *The National and English Review* 56 (1910), pp. 59–70.
62 See, among others, Ian F. W. Beckett, *The Amateur Military Tradition, 1558–1945* (Manchester: Manchester University Press, 1991); Ian F. W. Beckett (ed.), *Citizens Soldiers and the British Empire, 1837–1902* (London: Routledge, 2012); Stephen M. Miller, *Volunteers on the Veld: Britain's Citizen-Soldiers and the South African War, 1899–1902* (Norman, OK: University of Oklahoma Press, 2007).
63 The prewar civilian rifle movement has been conspicuously ignored by the historiography.
64 Roger S. Pocock, *The Frontiersman's Pocket-book* (London: John Murray, 1909), p. 2.
65 MacKenzie, 'The Imperial Pioneer and Hunter and the British Masculine Stereotype', pp. 176–198; J. A. Mangan, *'Manufactured' Masculinity: Making Imperial Manliness, Morality and Militarism* (London: Routledge, 2014).
66 On the Legion of Frontiersmen, see Michael Humphries, '"The Eyes of an Empire"': The Legion of Frontiersmen, 1904–14', *Historical Research* 85, no. 227 (2012), pp. 133–158.
67 Henry Page Croft, *My Life of Strife* (London: Hutchinson, 1948), p. 59.
68 On the BBL, see, generally, Sam Johnson, '"Trouble is Yet Coming!": The British Brothers League, Immigration and Anti-Jewish Sentiment in London's East End, 1901–1903', in Robert Nemes and Daniel Unowsky (eds), *Sites of European Antisemitism in the Age of Mass Politics, 1880–1918* (Waltham: Brandeis University Press, 2014), pp. 137–156.
69 Matthew Hendley, '"Help Us to Secure a Strong, Healthy, Prosperous and Peaceful Britain": The Social Arguments of the Campaign for Compulsory Military Service in Britain, 1899–1914', *Canadian Journal of History* 30, no. 2 (1995), pp. 261–288.

70 Matthew Johnson, *Militarism and the British Left, 1902–1914* (Basingstoke: Palgrave Macmillan, 2013).
71 In Australia, the Defence Acts – enacted in succession between 1903 and 1914 – provided that military instruction given in schools was part of the system of national defence. Training for Australian male citizens was divided into three cycles: junior cadets (ages twelve to fourteen), senior cadets (ages fourteen to eighteen) and adult service (ages eighteen to twenty). The programme primarily comprised daily physical training sessions lasting a minimum of fifteen minutes and elementary marching drills. Alongside these, a variety of subjects were taught, including miniature rifle shooting, swimming, organised running exercises, first aid and, in naval training areas, instruction in mariners' skills, navigation and basic signalling techniques. These cadets, functioning as military bodies without uniforms, were guided by a specialised team of physical training instructors, and supervised by school inspectors for the defence department. Senior cadet training, spanning four years and commencing at fourteen years old, required registration after completing necessary qualifications at thirteen and fourteen years of age. The senior cadet training consisted of forty drills each year, with four whole-day sessions lasting not less than four hours, twelve half-day sessions of not less than two hours, and the remainder as night drills lasting not less than one hour. The minimum service requirement for senior cadets was consistently set at sixty-four hours per annum. The comprehensive four-year course covered essential foundational aspects for military service, including marching, arms handling, marksmanship, physical drills, first aid, guard duties, tactical company training in field manoeuvres and basic battalion exercises, emphasising a strong inculcation of discipline. The training was supervised by Army officers and non-commissioned and warrant office, and each senior cadet had to pass four annual tests of 'efficiency'. Upon reaching eighteen, cadets transitioned into adult service, being assigned to a specific branch based on personal preference or specialised qualifications. The programme, it was said, had led to moral, attitudinal and physical improvements in the youth.
72 Under the Act for the military organisation of the Swiss Republic, the cantons were entrusted with arranging calisthenics courses for young men, overseen by specialised trainers. 'Preparatory gymnastics' would provide neuromuscular training and correct posture, and would enhance coordination, strength and endurance in school-age boys. Concurrently, the federal government had the responsibility to foster initiatives and associations focusing on the physical development of young men from when they left school to when they began military service.
73 For an overview of the history of military drill for pupils in elementary schools, Alan Penn, *Targeting Schools: Drill, Militarism and Imperialism* (Portland, OR: Woburn Press, 1999).
74 Samuel Hynes, *The Edwardian Turn of Mind* (Princeton, NJ: Princeton University Press, 1968), pp. 254–306.

75 See, for example, Ina Zweiniger-Bargielowska, 'Building a British Superman: Physical Culture in Interwar Britain', *Journal of Contemporary History* 41, no. 4 (2006), pp. 595–610; Emelyne Godfrey, 'Urban Heroes versus Folk Devils: Civilian Self-Defence in London (1880–1914)', *Crime, Histoire & Sociétés/ Crime, History & Societies* 14, no. 2 (2010), pp. 5–30.
76 Lord Malmesbury (ed.), *The New Order: Studies in Unionist Policy* (London: Francis Griffiths, 1908), p. 7.
77 Ensor, *England 1870–1914*, p. 440.
78 On the Great Unrest, see the recent work of Ralph Darlington, *Labour Revolt in Britain 1910–14* (London: Pluto Press, 2023).
79 J. E. Williams, 'The Leeds Corporation Strike in 1913', in Asa Briggs and John Saville (eds), *Essays in Labour History 1886–1923* (London: Palgrave Macmillan), pp. 70–95.
80 John A. Hobson, *Traffic in Treason: A Study of Political Parties* (London: T. F. Unwin, 1914), p. 7.
81 On the Home Rule Crisis, see Anthony Terence Quincey Stewart, *The Ulster Crisis* (London: Faber and Faber, 1967); Patrick Buckland, *Irish Unionism I: The Anglo-Irish and the New Ireland 1882–1922* (Dublin: Gill and Macmillan, 1972), and *Irish Unionism II: Ulster Unionism and the Origins of Northern Ireland 1886–1922* (Dublin: Gill and Macmillan, 1973); David George Boyce and Alan O'Day, *The Ulster Crisis: 1885–1921* (London: Macmillan, 2006); Gabriel Doherty (ed.), *The Home Rule Crisis 1912–14* (Cork: Mercier Press, 2014); Alvin Jackson, *Home Rule: An Irish History, 1800–2000* (Oxford: Oxford University Press, 2003); Charles Townshend, *Political Violence in Ireland: Government and Resistance since 1848* (Oxford: Clarendon Press, 1984). The crisis can also be examined through the biographies of the key participants: Edward Marjoribanks and Ian Colvin, *The Life of Lord Carson* (3 vols., London: Victor Gollancz, 1932–1936); Alvin Jackson, *Sir Edward Carson* (Dublin: Dundalgan Press, 1993); Robert Blake, *The Unknown Prime Minister: The Life and Times of Bonar Law* (London: Eyre & Spottiswoode, 1955); F. H. Crawford, *Guns for Ulster* (Belfast: Graham and Heslip, 1947) and Richard Greville Verney Willoughby de Broke, *The Passing Years* (London: Constable, 1924).
82 On the UVF, see Timothy Bowman, *Carson's Army: The Ulster Volunteer Force, 1910–22* (Manchester: Manchester University Press, 2017).
83 Daniel Jackson, *Popular Opposition to Irish Home Rule in Edwardian Britain* (Liverpool: Liverpool University Press, 2009).
84 Jeremy Smith, *The Tories and Ireland, 1910–1914: Conservative Party Politics and the Home Rule Crisis* (Dublin: Irish Academic Press, 2000), p. 273.

1

How to shoot a rifle: the civilian rifle club movement and the problem of British military preparedness, 1899–1914

> High courage, sound health, power of endurance, discipline, organisation, and leading –
> under the existing conditions of war all become more or less subservient to marksmanship at the supreme moment. (Lord Roberts)
>
> No doubt but ye are the People, absolute, strong and wise
> Whatever your heart has desired, ye have not withheld from your eyes.
> On your own head, in your own hands, the sin and the saving lies. (Rudyard Kipling's *The Islanders*)[1]

'Had our men been trained to shoot better', Lord Roberts wrote in a letter to *The Times* dated 12 June 1905, 'most of the unfortunate incidents which had to be deplored during the Boer War would never have occurred'.[2] The Boer War had stridently proved to Britain and the world that good marksmanship overshadowed all other skills in battle. Accordingly, 'Bobs', as Lord Roberts was reverently named by Rudyard Kipling in his 1893 poem, urged that the ordinary citizen should have known, and should, if necessary, have been compelled to know how to aim and fire a rifle. The Right, which took pleasure in repeatedly pointing out that the triumphs of Crécy, Agincourt and Poitiers were attained because English archers shot 'further and straighter' than their enemies, concurred that training in rifle marksmanship should have been strongly encouraged among the public, if not made outright compulsory. Since the 'gloomy days' of the Black Week of December 1899, when British forces suffered a series of ignominious defeats at the hands of the Boers, the guardians of imperial greatness and honour (as right-wingers professed themselves) had stirred the rise of a civilian rifle club movement.[3] Encouraged by Lord Salisbury's announcement that the government intended to provide shooting facilities for civilian instruction, a grassroot mobilisation ensued, aiming to supplement and expand upon the initiatives undertaken since the 1860s by the Volunteers. In 1903, the SMRC was formed, and under the leadership of Lord Roberts, began forming clubs for twenty- to fifty-yard shooting. Air guns also sprang up with mushroom-like rapidity, while spontaneous 'Homeland Defence Leagues' announced their intention to teach young men to 'shoot straight'. The roll of 'shooting clubs' first mounted in southeast England – the heartland of 'gentleman Torysm' – then expanded throughout the country. Gradually, newspapers began reporting that shooting ranges were emerging in the most unconventional locations, such as church crypts, house rooftops, barns, cellars and quarries. The Right and those Conservatives who more intensely felt a sense of dread for the conditions of military unpreparedness promoted marksmanship by bestowing shooting prizes and cups. The diehard Lord Denbigh urged the necessity for 'Sunday rifle practice' in the face of the increasing 'German peril'.[4] Others such as Sir Herbert Bulkley Mackworth-Praed offered a challenge trophy to be competed for by the members of the Association of Conservative Clubs.[5] Contrary to expectations, members of the NSL – both before and especially after Lord Roberts became the champion of compulsory service – showed genuine and practical support for the civilian rifle movement. Though sceptical that national defence could rely solely on amateur marksmen, British proponents of conscription viewed rifle clubs as complementary to their goal of improving military efficiency. They also considered them a sort of 'preparatory stage' toward the future introduction of mandatory military service, especially since 'the principle of compulsion' was still opposed by the majority of British citizens in 1914 and would remain 'out of the field of practical politics' until 1916.

The chapter reconstructs the history of this mobilisation for civilian marksmanship, examining its symbiotic or mutualistic relationship with the NSL and those other prewar militaristic initiatives which attempted to rearticulate the military obligations of citizenship. It explores how this movement helped prepare British society for the production of violence and preservation of the 'primitive instinct for fighting and killing' – an instinct that would eventually be unleashed in wartime.[6] It stresses how the effort to provide citizens, in particular young men, with the opportunity to become proficient marksmen was motivated not only by the aim of developing lethal skills, but was also informed by a broader ideal of armed citizenry on which the security of the nation depended. A man who refused to learn how to shoot to defend his own people was not a real man, but a traitor to his God, to his country and to his family.

The civilian rifle club movement, 1900–1914

The idea of organising civilian rifle shooting for the purposes of national defence was by no means a new one. In the midst of the French invasion scare of 1859–1860, some of the most influential leaders of the Volunteer movement founded the National Rifle Association (NRA). Its mission was to 'give permanence to Volunteer corps, naval and military, and to encourage rifle shooting throughout the Queen's dominion'.[7] Another goal of the NRA, during a period of rapid technological change – from muzzleloader to breechloader, from percussion caps to metallic cartridges, from single-shot to repeating and magazine systems, from self-cocking hammer guns to hammerless designs and from black to smokeless powder – was to promote 'the art of gun-making and science of gunnery'.[8] The NRA expected to fund its operations through voluntary subscriptions, match entrance fees, prize donations and charges for range services. The War Office's donation was limited to camp equipment and half a million rounds of ammunition for use at the NRA's annual prize meeting. It also provided regular soldiers to preside over the matches as range officers, record keepers and markers in the trenches. While receiving no direct government funding, the NRA enjoyed the personal patronage of the royal family and prominent courtiers. As well as instituting The Queen's Prize for Volunteers, Queen Victoria fired the inaugural shot at the NRA's first annual meeting on Wimbledon Common in June 1860, with a Whitworth rifle which had been fixed on a machine rest and carefully aimed to strike the bull's-eye.

The first step taken by the NRA was to establish county associations, 'wishing to see the taste for rifle shooting widely diffused and thoroughly nationalised'.[9] By 1889, eighty county associations had formed across Britain, each adopting the national organisation's regulations. In 1890, the NRA received a Royal Charter, conferring it authority over all matters connected with rifle practice outside the regular army and moved its annual prize meeting to the Bisley ranges. However, the NRA had already strayed from its original vision of making rifle shooting 'the pastime of the people'. 'Little by little', as gunmaker W. W. Greener observed, 'the truly military element obtained ascendency, and ultimately the NRA meeting became little more than a gathering of Volunteer delegates and competitions with the service rifle'.[10] Match rifles typically featured .303 magazine rifles of the Lee-Metford or Lee-Enfield patterns or Mannlichers, with specifications restricting weight to 10 lb, length to 52 inches, and calibre to .315, and mandating non-telescopic sights. By the summer of 1899, popular interest in rifle shooting had declined to a regrettably low point and some critical commentators noted that it was entirely plausible that forty-nine out of every fifty citizens had never fired a rifle in their lives.[11]

The neglect of marksmanship would bring upon the country 'many unfortunate days'. On 11 October 1899, the Boer republics of the Orange Free State and Transvaal declared war on Great Britain. Immediately, fast-moving commandos swarmed across the western frontier into the territory secured to Britain by the Bechuanaland or Warren Expedition and overran half the colony of Natal. The British army was forced into a precipitous retreat from its advanced positions and was surrounded by the Boers at Ladysmith early in November.[12] The humiliating reverses at Stormberg and Magersfontein in the 'Black Week' of December appeared to confirm the prophetic visions of Jean de Bloch, whose *The War of the Future in Its Technical, Economic and Political Relations* had just been translated into English from the Russian original.[13] The events in South Africa were in fact proving that the huge improvements in the range, rapidity of fire and accuracy of modern weapons had favoured defence over offence and made it impossible for attackers to seize entrenched positions without the risk of enormous losses. In these new realities of warfare, close-quarter marksmanship under stressful conditions and quick-fire methods had become of vital importance. Unfortunately, since the early stages of the war, the rifle skills of British troops had lagged lamentably behind those of the Boers. The notable difference in shooting skills raised serious public concerns over the lack of British military preparedness. In the monthly literary magazine *The Nineteenth Century*, the renowned adventurer and hunter William Adolphe Baillie-Grohman lamented the unacceptably low level of British marksmanship, which was due largely to the inadequate promotion of rifle shooting as a popular pastime on a par with football, rugby and cricket. Rifle practice as a sport was limited to a 'few hundred members of long-range rifle clubs' and a 'fad of the well-to-do leisured classes'. To amend this state of affairs, Baillie-Grohman proposed:

> easily available butts for the citizen to practice at (Sundays included); enforced rifle practice at all schools for youths of fifteen upwards; for the poorer classes of the population free use of arms and ammunition under proper superintendence at ranges which can be reached without expense or loss of time; and finally, a law that shall compel every youth of eighteen years of age who has received benefits at the hands of the State – such as Board School education or free bringing up – to acquit himself of his debt to the taxpayer by serving for one or two years in the Army.[14]

The 1899 report on musketry training by the Regular Forces stationed in the United Kingdom, which included the School of Musketry, the Militia, the Yeomanry and the Volunteers, revealed that the soldiers received three days of individual rifle practice every year, while nine days were dedicated to field exercises.[15] Marksmanship training did not include any form of *Gefechtmäßiges Schießen* (warfare shooting) as practised by the German Army, but rather involved firing at bull's-eye targets at fixed distances. Predictably enough, when confronted with the mobility of the Boers and their snap shooting skills, the British troops were found to be woefully lacking. Their shortcomings required immediate and careful correction.[16]

The proficiency of the Boer marksmen had been largely considered a natural, quasi-inborn trait. Almost all Afrikaners had learned their rifle shooting skills from childhood and maintained them through hunting game and fowl. 'They became unerring riflemen through the same education that made the American pioneers among the finest shots in the world', John C. Ridpath and Edward Sylvester Ellis wrote in their extensive account of the vicissitudes of the Boer War.[17] When urbanisation began to threaten this 'natural marksmanship', the governments of the Transvaal and Orange Free State, particularly after the Jameson Raid of 1895, made 'every effort […] to preserve the old skill and interest in rifle-shooting, which it was feared would vanish with the vanishing elands and gemsbok'.[18] In an article in the *National Review*, naturalist and author C. J. Cornish contrasted the encouragement that shooting received in the two republics with the situation in Britain and recommended that 'the rudiments of rifle shooting should be applied universally as part of the school system'.[19] Proposals to teach military drill and exercise in British schools were not unusual. Conscious of the inadequacy of Britain's military forces, the Earl of Meath had established the Lads' Drill Association in 1899 aimed at providing the 'Systematic physical and military training of all British lads, and their instruction in the art of the rifle'.[20] At the outbreak of the war, the Reverend G. Sale Reaney recommended that all boys be committed to compulsory military drill after leaving school.[21] Similarly, famous physician and pharmacologist Sir Lauder Brunton wrote that 'every able-bodied man should, in case of need, be qualified to take part in the defence of the country' and schools had to play a decisive role in instilling in the youth 'a warrior-like spirit'. Education curricula should include the methodical and developmental teaching of rifle shooting:

> a course of instruction with […] toy guns, elementary drills and skirmishing, and games calculated to teach scouting, use of cover, etc. gradually progressing to firing caps, miniature cartridge practice, and more advanced skirmishing exercises, and culminating in cadet corps armed with rifle or carbine and trained to regular military exercises.[22]

The introduction of military training and rifle practice into schools was left largely to the discretion of the local education authorities. At the beginning of the war, various school boards applied to the Army Ordnance Department for carbines and dummy rifles. In Sheffield, the School Management Committee deemed 'that seventh standard boys in the schools be provided with dummy rifles such as are used by the Boys' Brigades for drill, as requested by the instructor'.[23] The proposal to arm schoolboys was opposed by nonconformist circles and was later withdrawn. The arming of children and the transformation of playgrounds into rifle ranges in order to mould the youth into a bulwark of defence remained a contentious issue right up until the war.

Meanwhile, faced with the urgent need of making rifle practice more accessible to the general public, Lord Roberts made the NRA the official body through which the War Office could promote the ideal of the citizen-soldier. Guidelines were issued to those citizens wishing to establish rifle or miniature rifle clubs in affiliation with the NRA.[24] This appeal for rifle clubs was also taken up by Rudyard Kipling and other celebrities, who recommended private rifle practice on the grounds of national defence. The poet of imperialism and empire, for instance, reacted to the defeats of 1899 by opening a rifle club in his Sussex village of Rottingdean.[25] Sir Arthur Conan Doyle, who had served as a volunteer doctor in South Africa, likewise championed the notion of a vast corps of civilian riflemen effectively protecting the British Isles. Doyle wrote that 'With modern weapons every brave man with a rifle is a formidable soldier, and there is no longer the need for a hard training and a rigid discipline which existed when men fought in platoons and performed complicated evolutions upon the field of battle'. By pointing to the 'enormous' advantage of defence over attack, and of a stationary force against a mobile one, Doyle stated it was legitimate to claim that 'a country of hedgerows would, with modern weapons, be the most terrible entanglement into which an army could wander', downgrading 'the bugbear of an invasion of Great Britain to an absurdity'.[26] Doyle's proposal, advocating for arming a million civilians with rifles, had a significant impact on public opinion and appealed to those who had faith in the importance of superior numbers in war, though it was also criticised for its crude, radical, impractical and 'dangerous' nature.[27]

Reality quickly tempered illusions of 'gigantic armed crowds'. Given that rifle clubs or associations were private bodies, the costs of weapons, ammunition, train fares to ranges and markers could not be met by public funds, yet they were unaffordable by many citizens. To resolve this pressing problem, influential military and public figures suggested that rifle practice could be conducted with inexpensive .22 calibre rifles and ammunitions. Furthermore, since the maximum effective range of the .22 calibre was 1,325 yards, far less than the approximately four thousand yards of the service cartridge, small-bore or miniature rifles could more easily meet the safety requirements of the ranges. At the end of February 1900, the Earl of Leven and Melville asked the government to 'consider the establishment in towns and villages of short-range shooting galleries of 100 yards, to be open at night as well as by day, where Militiamen and Volunteers might, under a qualified instructor, practice the use of the regulation or some similar rifle adapted for a short range'.[28] The use of miniature calibres on much smaller ranges would, as Major W. T. Dupree of the Second Hants. Artillery Volunteers claimed, afford 'the opportunity for all classes to practice with the rifle and carbine at all times'.[29] A Bill was later introduced to the House of Commons to facilitate the acquisition by borough and county councils of suitable lands for rifle ranges.[30] Around this time, unable to find long ranges, Birmingham marksmen began using air guns for target shooting. They formed a club, which attracted thousands of members, and which later became the National Air Rifle Association (with Lord Roberts at its head as patron). The Preparatory Schools Air Rifle Association (PSARA) also came into being in 1905.[31]

In April, the former commanding officer of the Royal Engineers in Natal, Major General C. E. Luard, put a motion to the Technical Education Committee requesting that 'an application be made to the Board of Education to authorize 'rifle shooting as a subject for instruction under the Technical Education Act'. If the reply to the application were favourable, the Technical Education Committee would be expected to take steps towards effecting the proposal according to the provisions contained in a document entitled 'The draft of a Bill for making further provision for instruction in the Science and Art of Rifle Shooting in England and Wales'. The motion was carried, but the Bill did not get any further.[32] Nonetheless, the following month at the annual meeting of the Conservative Primrose League, the prime minister, Lord Salisbury, delivered his famous 'One Man One Rifle' speech. After painting a most alarming picture of the British international situation, Salisbury stressed the urgent need to set up civilian rifle clubs and advance 'the means of learning the handling of rifles placed in the hands of every man within reach of his own cottage':

> if once the feeling can be propagated abroad that it is the duty of every able Englishman to make himself competent to meet an invading enemy, if ever, God forfend, an invading enemy should appear – if you once impress upon them that the defence of the country is not the business of the War Office but of people themselves, learning in their own parishes the accomplishments which are necessary to make them formidable in the field, you will then have a defensive force which will not only repel the assailant if he comes but will make the chances of that assailant so bad that no assailant will ever appear.[33]

The appeal for establishing civilian rifle clubs was evidently connected to Salisbury's opposition to conscription, serving as a response to the torrent of articles, pamphlets and speeches that had begun advocating compulsory military service in the wake of the 'South African lesson'.[34] In 1900, historian

George Gordon Coulton stood as an early advocate of compulsory military training with his book *A Strong Army in a Free State*, drawing inspiration from the Swiss militia system.[35] More consequentially, in 1901, George F. Shee published *The Briton's First Duty: The Case for Conscription*, in which he proposed the establishment of a 'pan-Britannic Militia', a mass reserve force that encompassed 'all able-bodied white men throughout the Empire'. Its role was to assist in 'home defence' and 'to fill up the casualties in the ranks of the foreign-service Army in time of war'. In Shee's scheme, every 'militiaman' would undergo one year of military service between the ages of eighteen and twenty-three, while those from maritime communities would instead contribute to the Naval Militia. Subsequently, 'militiamen' would transition to the Militia Reserve, which would comprise three segments analogous to the German Reserve, *Landwehr* and *Landsturm*. The First Reserve would comprise men aged eighteen to twenty-five years, the Second Reserve men aged twenty-five to thirty, and the Third Reserve – never to be assigned to foreign service – men up to the age of forty. The training plan for each reserve category was as follows: First Reserve men were to complete two eight-week training sessions during their term; Second Reserve men would engage in two two-week training sessions; the Third Reserve would be asked to attend two week-long training sessions. Shee believed that the benefits of such a scheme would not be limited to strengthening national security in case of invasion or to providing a solution to the question of imperial federation by 'uniting the whole of our race in the strong bonds of a brotherhood-in-arms', but would also include the cultivation of a profound patriotism, unaffected by the 'gross inequality' of the ballot system, and the bringing together of 'all classes of the community'.[36]

In January 1902, Shee presented a paper on compulsory military service at a session of the Royal United Service Institution presided over by Lord Newton. The presentation attracted significant attention and was discussed further in three subsequent meetings. Notable contributors to the debates included Admiral Sir Nathaniel Bowden Smith, Admiral Sir Edmund Fremantle, Colonel Brookfield MP, Colonel Pilkington MP, Colonel Howard Vincent MP, the Duke of Wellington, General Seely (who was a Conservative at the time), Lord Hardinge, Robert A. Yerburgh MP, Sir John Colomb and Robert Giffen. Finally, on 26 February 1902, a meeting was held at Apsley House on the invitation of the Duke of Wellington and attended by Leo Amery and Leopold Maxse, among others. During this meeting, a decision was made to establish the NSL.[37]

The Duke of Wellington served as its first president, and was succeeded by Lord Raglan, who, in turn, relinquished the position to Field Marshal Lord Roberts in 1905. During this time, the executive committee was composed of Admirals Sir Gerald Noel and Sir Nathaniel Bowden Smith, Earl

Curzon, John Wolfe Barry, Edward Tennant, Lord Hardinge, Lord Meath, Lord Milner and several other prominent political and military figures. The ranks were bolstered by 'radical right' activists, imperialists and those who had 'Germany on the brain'.[38] Recognising the unpopularity of conscription on the continental model or any form of compulsory service, the NSL proposed a very timid program: individuals aged between eighteen and twenty-two years who were not enlisted in the Regular Army or the Navy, nor serving in the Mercantile Marine, nor joining any of the auxiliary forces, would be required to undergo two months of training, under canvas, followed by an additional fourteen days of training in each of the subsequent three years.[39] Due to tensions between hard-line conscriptionists and proponents of the 'Swiss system' of military training, the initial proposal was later revised 'in the interest of vagueness', leaving the duration of service deliberately unspecified.[40]

Meanwhile, Salisbury's advocacy of rifle practice for national defence led to the establishment of the British Rifle League (BRL) with its headquarters in London. The League was in no way connected to the Volunteer Corps or its regulations. Since January 1900, schemes for a national association that called 'into life all over Great Britain rifle clubs with ample facilities for civilians to acquire the ABC of rifle shooting' had been drafted in imitation of the popular rifle shooting associations in Switzerland, Bavaria and Tyrol.[41] The BRL, founded by the proprietors of the weekly military journal, *The Regiment*, aimed to combine into one association all civilians 'who desire[d] to be able to defend their country in case of invasion'.[42] From the summer of 1900, the League began encouraging the formation of rifle clubs. All citizens, except those who were serving in the armed forces, were invited to enrol on payment of a small annual subscription of six pence. Once thirty or more members from one town or village had signed up, steps were taken to establish a rifle club. To encourage the formation of clubs, the BRL donated a rifle to any member who managed to recruit thirty or more new members in their own county or district of residence. In Manchester, the secretary of a local rifle club received a miniature rifle – a Martini-Henry pattern – for his successful recruitment of thirty aspiring marksmen.[43] Appeals were made to landowners to provide facilities for rifle practice. In Pontarddulais, a town in the county of Swansea, the Duke of Beaufort offered land on the Cefn Drum Mountain for a range.[44]

In spite of the difficulties in procuring ranges, rifle clubs or associations affiliated to the BRL sprung up throughout Britain. At the launch of a BRL club in Pontypridd, the *Western Mail* commented that: 'Independent, intelligent sharpshooters … who are able to use the rifle effectively have proved so valuable to the Boers for defensive purposes that it is not surprising to find enthusiastic men turning … their attention to the establishment of rifle clubs independent of government control, with the object of fostering the art of rifle shooting'.⁴⁵ By February 1902, the BRL had gained 5,252 members. 'Every day adds from fifty to sixty fresh members to our roll-call, say, at the rate of 900 per month', the secretary of the BRL, Captain H. Brook-Ascough stated in a letter to editor of the *Pall Mall Gazette*.⁴⁶ Three months later, the membership of the league had risen to eight thousand. Twenty-four rifle clubs were affiliated to the BRL, 'with branches being formed in East London and Johannesburg in South Africa'.⁴⁷ By the end of the 1902, the BRL's membership had reached ten thousand one hundred. Both miniature ammunition and service rifles with Morris tubes were used at indoor (twenty-five yards) and outdoor ranges (up to six hundred yards).⁴⁸

In the summer of 1900, a meeting of the civilian rifle clubs of England was convened at the Council House in Birmingham. In the presence of the Lord Mayor, the delegates drew attention to the difficulty 'all classes of people' faced in meeting the conditions for membership of the NRA. They also pointed out that it was extremely difficult for many ordinary citizens to comply with the 'red tape and restrictions of the Volunteers and attend so many drills a week'. In view of these grievances, a resolution was passed to request the government to waive gun licences for rifle clubs and charge them the same rates for cartridges as the Volunteers. It was also decided that a provisional committee should be elected for the purposes of drafting a scheme for the establishment of a British Rifle Union (BRU).⁴⁹ At the end of the year, a resolution was passed at a meeting of various rifle clubs held at the London Polytechnic Institute bringing the BRU into formal existence. The aim of the new organisation was 'the encouragement of the art of rifle shooting, and the protection and development of civilian clubs'.⁵⁰ In seeking to promote the usefulness of rifle clubs 'as a means of materialising the vast stores of otherwise merely latent strength in the country', the BRU intended to put pressure on the government to support marksmanship among citizens by providing:

> 1) Rifle ranges at convenient centres, whereupon regulars, volunteers, and rifle clubs shall alike practice rifle shooting; 2) Service rifles and ammunition for individual members or clubs, and Morris tubes and ammunition for clubs – all at government cost price; 3) Exemption from gun licence duty in respect of all service rifles.⁵¹

Efforts would be made to press railway companies into offering members the same benefits they accorded to Volunteers. All rifle clubs, whether affiliated to the NRA or not, were invited to join the BRU. However, mainly because of lack of support from public figures, the Union never progressed beyond its initiatory stage.

Around the same time, Major General Luard set about forming an organisation to promote and encourage rifle shooting among the country's labourers. In the field of rifle shooting, as described by a historian, Luard played a role akin to Lord Elcho in the context of the Militia ballot and Lord Meath in imperial youth movements.[52] On 23 March, a meeting was held at Mansion House in London presided over by the Lord Mayor for the purpose of inaugurating the Society of Working Men's Rifle Clubs (SWMR). Lord Roberts, who had succeeded in reversing the military situation in South Africa and had repeatedly stressed the national importance of rifle shooting, consented to act as its provisional president, though he would not formally assume the office until his retirement from active service. Members of the aristocracy, such as the Earl of Dudley and diehards like the Duke of Westminster and the Duke of Norfolk, pledged financial support. In the presence of numerous dignitaries, Major General Luard stated that the SWMR was 'in the nature of an experiment' and might be called a 'new departure'. Its essential purpose was 'to reach the sources which had not yet been touched either by the Volunteer movement or otherwise'. These untapped pools of potential marksmanship were the 'vast body of working men's clubs and institutes throughout the country'. Luard was careful to explain that the new society did not intend to intrude on either volunteering or Army recruitment. Rather, it would 'devote itself entirely to the training in halls and galleries where miniature ammunition could be used, and so inculcate some of the principles of the [rifle shooting] art'. There was no intention to ask the government for financial assistance, as 'the gentlemen of the country will contribute to the funds'.[53]

The first resolution submitted to the meeting was couched in the following terms: 'That the foundation of the Society of Working Men's Rifle Clubs, for facilitating rifle shooting, more especially in the evening, with small-bore rifles and inexpensive ammunition, as an ordinary branch or recreation by working men's and working boys' clubs and institutes be now proceeded'. Harold Boulton, vice-chairman of the Federation of Working Men's Social Clubs, who had proposed the resolution, argued that 'the working class had made great sacrifices in common with other classes during the present crisis [and] were prepared go further'. The whole-hearted cooperation of all classes of the community was of paramount importance to home defence, and the responsibility of learning how to shoot a rifle was a 'new form of patriotism'. The resolution was seconded by Mr. Douglas Eyre of the Federation of the London Working Boys' Club and Institute Union. It was also supported by Major William Evans Gordon, military diplomat and anti-immigration Conservative MP for Stepney, and by Colonel W. J. Alt, who represented the Association of Conservative Working Men's Clubs. The resolution was adopted with only two dissenters. The Lord Mayor of London then moved a second resolution which was an appeal to the Chancellor of the Exchequer to exempt members of the SWMR from payment of gun licence duty. He pointed out that the success of the organisation depended on inter-club rifle matches, and these would be adversely affected unless the need for a licence was removed or the law was amended. The motion was seconded and carried unanimously.[54]

By the end of the summer, the patriotic appeal of the SWMR drew interest and applications from cities such as London, Liverpool, Birmingham and Belfast, numerous other towns, the London Diocesan Church Lads' Brigade, the Jewish Lads' Brigade, Oxford House, several schools, the Second V. B. Royal Fusiliers and other Volunteer Corps, the Admiral Superintendent at Chatham and the officer commanding the cavalry depot at Canterbury.[55] In an attempt to further the society's progress, a booklet entitled 'Miniature rifle clubs and how to form and conduct them' was issued. To establish a rifle club, fully equipped with target apparatus, rifles and ammunition, the booklet recommended securing a hall or a room of forty feet or more in length and a sum of £15 to cover initial costs. Many letters were sent to the SWMR headquarters seeking information regarding Major General Luard's recent invention of a portable apparatus on which stationary, disappearing and moving targets could be mounted.[56]

At the beginning of October, the SWMR donated Winchester repeating rifles, Winchester model 190 .22 calibre rifles and moving carton-targets protected by Siemens plate steel safety screens to the West Newington Conservative Club for the inauguration of their new shooting range. In addressing the members of the club, Major General Luard stated that different ideological orientations within the association were coming together under the banner of military preparedness, and that 'on the whole the Society of Working Men's Rifle Clubs had a grand prospect of success in town and country'.[57] A few months later, in a letter to the *St. James Gazette*, Luard reiterated that 'the time should be not far distant when the public opinion of all classes of both sexes of the community will hold it shameful in any able-bodied man or lad to be entirely ignorant of the use of some weapon of defence, of which the rifle is the most potent'.[58] Yet despite this show of optimism, the response of working people to the SWMR's appeals was little more than lukewarm. In Oxford, a club was formed to offer those men who could not have spared 'the time for the full training of a Volunteer, the means of learning the use of the rifle at fixed and movable targets'.[59] A match manufacturing company in Bromley-by-Bow, Messrs, R. Bell & Co., instituted a rifle club at the works for their employees.[60] The management of Messrs. Jaeger & Co., a well-known clothing company, established a miniature rifle range on their premises, 'wishing to make everything easy for their staff to learn the use of the rifle'.[61] Not all employers, of course, welcomed the SWMR's aim of providing the working class with shooting facilities. An unnamed business owner told a reporter from *The Star* that he 'feared bullets during strikes':

> At present with a clear sky and calm public mind, the idea of these clubs is very attractive to many as strengthening our natural defences, but I am surprised, I confess, at the manner in which its promoters have absolutely ignored the future. Look at the American coal strike of this year, and the Chicago railway strike of a few years ago, and the riots and bloodshed that accompanied them. The real reason for that is that in America the habit of going armed is such more prevalent than it is here, and that the workman on strike does not hesitate to shoot at non-unionists, or the policeman, or the sheriff's deputies. [...] in times of great strikes, of tremendous public excitement, and bitter controversy, it may be a dangerous thing that angry hungry men have learned to use the army.[62]

For the proponents of civilian rifle shooting, these concerns were curiously insignificant. The advantages of arming wage earners seemed to outweigh the risks of replicating American industrial violence.

By the end of 1902, 125 clubs with a membership of seventeen thousand had affiliated to the SWMR.[63] Arrangements were then being made in collaboration with the BRL to hold what was called a 'Miniature Bisley' at the Crystal Palace on 23 March 1903. The two associations, which were negotiating an amalgamation, agreed that the competitions should be open to all civilians and Volunteers, whether members of a rifle club or not. The use of any rifle fitted with a Morris tube or using other miniature ammunition would be permitted and ranges were to be twenty-five yards in length. Stationary, moving and disappearing targets were to be used 'and various novel conditions introduced, bearing as much as possible on minor but important lessons derived from the late war'.[64] Colonel Longstaff of Ridgelands presented a cup for the competition: made of silver, at intervals around the body were twelve lions' heads bearing twelve escutcheons on which the names of the winners could be engraved.[65]

At the opening ceremony of the 'Miniature Bisley', General Sir Ian Hamilton, one of the society's vice-presidents, declared that 'the men who joined those clubs were not content with being taxed to pay for others who would risk their lives on their behalf, but they wanted to do something themselves for the defence of the country'.[66] Earl Grey, another vice-president, added that 'every man ought to be taught how to shoot, in order, if necessary, to be able to take part in the defence of his country. Boys and girls at school should be given the benefit of a systematic physical training. The objects of the Society would not be realised until there was a miniature range in every school yard'. Lady Sybil Grey then opened the programme by firing the first shot on the range, which had been temporarily erected in the central transept of the Crystal Palace.[67] A total of 1,967 entries for the twenty-three competitions were submitted. The press reported that the novelty of the 'Miniature Bisley' attracted a large crowd.[68]

From February 1903, the SWMR informally absorbed the BRL with its fifty-four rifle clubs and eight thousand five hundred subscribing members. The society also took over the league's trophies, including the Gamage Challenge Shield and the Sandow Challenge Bowl, together with a subscription roll of between £300 and £500. Liabilities for an estimated £200 were also assumed. After the incorporation was formalised on 15 May, the society's name was changed to the SMRC. Major General Luard remained Chairman of the Executive Committee, while the Duke of Norfolk became the first Chairman of the Board. By now, 173 rifle clubs were affiliated to the new organisation, whose motto was 'Look Forward'.[69]

In the meantime, the NRA, which had regarded its principal goal as being the promotion of effective marksmanship with service rifles, began to permit the miniature .22 calibre rifle at Bisley.

New competitions at one hundred yards to be shot with miniature rifles, the Morris tube and service rifles fitted with breech adapters were announced in the spring of 1900.[70] At the general winter meeting of 1901, the board of the NRA claimed that its efforts to foster a 'taste for rifle shooting' among the people were meeting with 'signal success'. The association had acquired 108 affiliated rifle clubs, amassing more than ten thousand members 'most of whom could never have been able to join the Volunteers'.[71] Another result of this drive to train marksmanship was the construction of over fifty miniature ranges and twelve long ranges, while 'over sixty of the volunteers' ranges, twenty private ranges – including Bisley and Runnymede – and twelve military ranges [were] used by clubs for their practice'.[72] The following year – King Edward VII's coronation year – the number of affiliated rifle clubs increased to 224 with an overall membership of eighteen thousand. Moreover, the American tycoon, William Waldorf Astor, who had relocated to Britain in 1890, donated £10,000 to the NRA to help promote rifle clubs in towns and villages, 'the clubs consisting of civilians and volunteers or civilians only'.[73] In a letter to the association, the scion of the 'Landlords of New York' remarked that

> The war in South Africa has taught us the importance of training every able-bodied Englishman in the use of the rifle. Beyond this, a remarkable feature in the life of an English country laborer is the absence of organized recreation [...] There seems no better method of giving these men a national form of amusement than by extending their facilities for rifle practice.[74]

Figure 1.1 Lady Sybil Grey firing the first shot at the Miniature Bisley. *The Graphic*, 28 March 1903. Image © Mary Evans Picture Library

One of the trustees of the Astor fund, Sir Arthur Conan Doyle, had long argued that the rifle club movement should be supported because the alternative was conscription, and that the acquisition of basic rifle marksmanship constituted a citizen's duty.[75]

At the end of 1903, the SMRC and the NRA had taken on the task of preventing a repetition of the South African embarrassment. Some months earlier, Major General Luard delivered a lecture entitled 'Rifle shooting as a winter evening pursuit' at the Royal United Service Institution.[76] Luard argued that, in spite of the lack of government encouragement and assistance, there had been constant private initiatives for the establishment of rifle clubs since the Boer War. However, what had been done thus far was not nearly enough to convince the working people 'to learn the most efficacious way in which they may, to some extent, guard against the chances of national disaster and disgrace'. To amend this situation, elementary rifle shooting should be brought by any means 'into the category of national games'. With regard to the means of popularising rifle shooting, Luard suggested that preliminary marksmanship training could be given in rooms, halls or galleries of forty to sixty feet in length and artificially illuminated. These short, indoor ranges opened up possibilities for shooters whose jobs or schooling prevented daytime practice, especially during the winter months. Also, a great advantage offered by small bore rifle ranges was that they could be conveniently located in urban areas. As the essence of this pastime was competition, Luard stressed the importance of standardising the rules, regulations and equipment for small bore rifle shooting. To this end, the .22 calibre rifle loaded with a .22 short cartridge was considered the most satisfactory low-powered gun. The Morris tube or any adaptor that could be fitted into the breech of a service rifle was also acceptable. Given that the costs of ranges and ammunitions were relatively affordable, miniature rifle shooting allowed people who would not otherwise have been able to do so to participate. In the discussion that followed the lecture, the Assistant Inspector-General of Fortifications, Lieutenant Colonel C. B. Mayne R. E., asserted that miniature rifle shooting was of particular value in training individuals to use service weapons. However, referring to the classic book *Stonewall Jackson and the American Civil War* by the British military historian Colonel George F. R. Henderson, Mayne argued that Confederate soldiers were 'born shots, riders and scouts', but they lacked that 'collective discipline which is so necessary for the winning of battles, as well as for offensive operations'.[77] Therefore, while a high standard of marksmanship was of extreme, if not vital, importance, discipline could not be neglected. Lieutenant General E. Gunter of the East Lancashire Regiment argued that the SMRC had to put itself in communication with 'the great employers of labour':

There is a feeling in some parts of the country against putting the rifle in the hands of people at all, because it is said to lead to militarism. But after all, militarism or not, the country must be defended, and the best way to defend the country is to accustom the lads and boys of the country to the use of the rifle.[78]

Lieutenant Colonel O. T. Duke of the Fifth Battalion Rifle Brigade recommended the amalgamation of the SMRC, the NSL and the Lads' Drill Association 'for the great object of making the youths of the country fit to defend our shores'. Miniature rifle shooting should be to service rifle shooting what elementary or secondary schools were to higher education.[79]

At the beginning of 1904, an estimated sixty to sixty-five thousand civilians were regularly practicing rifle shooting in the country. In the London metropolitan area alone there were 104 clubs, some of which were affiliated to neither the NRA nor the SMRC. There were three ways in which civilian rifle shooting was practised: on registered ranges with service rifles, on short or protected open-air ranges with commercial medium-power rifles and cartridges with reduced charges, and in indoor short ranges with miniature rifles or service rifles fitted with tubes or adapters enabling the firing of miniature ammunitions. The majority of rifle clubs with a regularly established range were owned by the County Associations, which organised prize meetings for Volunteers and Yeomanry and were generally affiliated to the NRA. The situation regarding the miniature rifle was quite different. It appeared that the SMRC was still unable to do for shooters what the Marylebone Cricket Club had done for cricketers or the Amateur Athletic Association for athletes.[80] For instance, attention was frequently drawn to the failure of numerous clubs to comply with the regulations prescribed by the SMRC regarding the standardisation of target dimensions, ammunition and other items. In addition, the SMRC, unlike the NRA, received no funds from wealthy benefactors like Astor, and had to make repeated appeals through the press or privately to any wealthy citizen disposed to make a donation to the society. Nevertheless, on 18 February, Lord Roberts retired from the War Office and formally took on the presidency of the SMRC, dedicating himself to placing the civilian rifle movement on a larger and firmer basis.

The Norfolk Commission, the Elgin Report, and the Esher Committee, along with Leo Amery's series of articles in *The Times* (later republished as 'The Problem of the Army'), laid bare the blunders of the Boer War and revealed structural weaknesses in British military organisation. The Army clearly required extensive reform, but the plans proposed by St John Brodrick and Hugh Arnold-Forster proved costly, inadequate, and politically contentious. Faced with this impasse, Lord Roberts – then still a member of the Committee of Imperial Defence – directed his efforts 'to see a rifle club in every village, and the men and boys of the nation practising shooting in their leisure time as do the citizens of Holland and Switzerland'.[81]

Lord Roberts's tireless campaign to make every English boy a marksman, advanced through endless public speeches and articles in the press, led to an immediate increase in miniature rifle clubs and indoor ranges across the country. As a result, the NRA and the SMRC decided to jointly hold a Miniature Prize Meeting at Olympia from 25 to 30 April 1904. The ranges of twenty and fifty yards were set up in the arena where a few months earlier William F. Cody, alias Buffalo Bill, had presided over the Congress of the World's Horsemen. There were 564 entries for the nine competitions and shooters were mostly equipped with Stevens, Winchesters and the Francotte cadet model. A prize for riflewomen was introduced, 'the first of a long series of ladies' competitions which have been a feature of the SMRC for years past'.[82] The Olympia event, the *Westminster Gazette* wrote, afforded

> proof of the already great and still increasing popularity in this country of low-power, or 'miniature' practices. The days have been left far behind when small rifles were regarded as mere toys, or the practice of shooting them fitting only as a concomitant of the frolic of the countryside yokel at the annual 'mop', or hiring fair.[83]

In a letter to *The Times*, Earl Grey, recently appointed Governor of Canada, stressed the effectiveness of miniature rifle practice and urged a response to Luard's appeals to public duty.[84] The Secretary of State for War, Arnold-Forster, who had previously not shown particular enthusiasm for the possibility of marksmanship training with miniature rifles, attended the closing day of the meeting, showing 'much interest in the fire'.[85]

Although the miniature rifle prize meeting incurred financial losses, 'it showed in other respects such evidence of success, that it was thought advisable to repeat the experiment', A. P. Humphry and T. F. Freemantle wrote in their history of the NRA. Furthermore, the distinct features of miniature rifle shooting made it feasible to hold meetings in different parts of the country.[86] Birmingham was initially selected to host the second annual meeting, but following disagreements over the rules and regulations for the conduct of matches, the event was moved to Exeter.

Since its foundation, the SMRC had affiliated over two hundred local rifle clubs. In a letter on the subject of rifle shooting published in December 1904, the Duke of Norfolk urged that miniature rifle shooting 'should be made the greatest of national games' with the purpose of educating the masses 'to guard their territories which their forefathers and contemporaries have placed in their charge'.[87] He appealed for any unused music or dance halls, saloons, schoolhouses or any other suitable place to be converted into indoor ranges. Despite the progress made, the Duke of Norfolk lamented the insufficient financial resources that were preventing the 'patriotic movement' from offering opportunities and incentives for rifle practice. He therefore appealed to the public 'to offer more assistance in carrying out the work of national defence'.[88] Commenting on Norfolk's letter, the *Pall Mall Gazette* wrote 'Politicians and strategists may differ upon theories of army organization, but if a population is steadily developed with a practical acquaintance with the use of firearms, the disputes and errors of its rulers must lose half their power for mischief'.[89] A short time later, the Metropolitan Rifle Club, an organisation affiliated to the SMRC, formed the London League 'for the promotion of a grand competition on the lines of the cricket and football leagues'.[90]

Though the country had recognised, or rather was recognising the importance of rifle shooting, the measures being taken to provide indoor and outdoor ranges were still unsatisfactory. The SMRC's first annual report noted the 'non-existence of sites suitable for service rifle ranges near populous centres', which represented an effective barrier 'to any considerable use of service rifles by civilian rifle clubs'. It was also noted that the 'education of our countrymen in the art of marksmanship can only be effected by means of low power and miniature rifles'.[91] The only miniature rifle range in southeast London was located in a hotel cellar.[92] It was obviously more difficult to establish ranges in large cities than in small towns or villages. In villages, in particular, vacant spaces with backstops could almost always be found. Residents of a village in Kent installed a forty-yard range in the village hall, and on one evening a week they fired their Winchester repeaters at stationary, moving and disappearing targets, timing the shooting by metronome. All the equipment was donated by the SMRC.[93] In Tavistock, Devon, the town council placed the market hall at the disposal of the local SMRC-affiliated club to hold competitions, which were open to rifle and air clubs, school and cadet corps, and lads' brigades.[94]

In early 1905, Lord Roberts officially intervened in the political controversy over military preparedness. Contrary to the Committee of Imperial Defence's assessment, he maintained that an invasion of Britain remained entirely possible and argued that citizens must prepare for home defence before 'the enemy was at the gates'. In this regard, in an article entitled 'The Army as it was and as it is', Roberts argued that the discipline fostered by self-denial and self-reliance was superior to that of the barracks. However, while he preferred volunteers to conscripts, he insisted that 'Men of all classes […] must be prepared to undergo such a modicum of training as will make them useful as soldiers when called upon by their country for personal service in time of need'. Britain's security, Roberts maintained, rested upon establishing a 'prepared citizenry' through a programme of universal training. An essential component of this scheme was the military preparation of youth through drill exercises and rifle shooting until they reached service age.[95]

In a letter to *The Times* in June, Lord Roberts again stressed that it was 'a matter of the highest importance, not only to the Regular Army and the Auxiliary Forces of this country, but to the Empire at large, that rifle shooting should be made a national pursuit'.[96] He pointed out that there was a widespread quest for efficiency in the use of rifles in the English-speaking world. In the United States, the National Board for the Promotion of Rifle Practice, having received the approval of the Secretary of War, had drawn up plans for educating young men over fifteen years of age in the handling of rifles and in proficient marksmanship. The National Rifle Association of America had then been entrusted with carrying out these recommendations. Among the British colonies, Natal had introduced compulsory military training in its school curricula, while the desire for rifle practice had grown considerably in Australia and Canada. The situation was much more complicated in Britain. The NRA, Lord Roberts wrote, had done excellent work towards 'the attainment of high standards of efficiency in musketry', without, however, reaching 'the nation as whole'. The paucity of ranges in a densely populated country and, in part, the costs of service rifles and ammunition were reputed to be responsible for the meagre popularity of rifle shooting. To overcome these obstacles, miniature ammunition to be fired with either small-bore rifles or service rifles fitted with adapters had been introduced. The SMRC was precisely formed with the aim of organising and conducting these shooting methods. Since then, Lord Roberts continued, interest and participation in the various aspects of rifle shooting had certainly increased, but it was still deemed insufficient for national defence purposes and unless some system of obligatory instruction in the fundamentals of rifle shooting were enforced in all schools, it was impossible to completely dispel the impending shadow of conscription. For 'Bobs', who was set to become the president of the NSL, rifle shooting represented a delicate compromise between the safeguarding of individual liberty and the demands of military preparedness. Therefore, in order to systematically and practically advance civilian marksmanship, he held that:

> it is essential that rifle clubs should be formed under the patronage and supervision of the Lord Lieutenant of counties and of mayors of all important towns, while branches should be established in the smaller towns and villages, until every man in the country shall have within his reach the means for practicing rifle shooting as a pastime after his day's work is over and thus fit himself to take up arms for his country should the need arise.[97]

To put this scheme into effect, Lord Roberts launched a 'patriotic appeal' to raise £100,000 for civilian rifle training. His battle cry was widely discussed and proposals for encouraging shooting activities were put forward.[98] *The*

Field magazine reported that someone had gone so far as to suggest that 'no man should have a vote unless he could produce a certificate of efficiency in shooting'.[99]

Lord Roberts's plea for financial assistance evoked very little response. Presiding over a meeting of the SMRC, he stated that 'The effect of the replies received was that the matter was one for the government and not for individuals'.[100] Despite this failure, Lord Roberts asserted his intention not to let matters rest and regardless of what the government might do – and he hoped that they would do more concerning the problem of ranges and grants of rifles to cadet corps – there was still much work for the association to do, namely, promote rifle shooting and undertake the task of standardising and formalising shooting practices.[101] At the meeting, the board of the SMRC reported that since 1 January of that year fifty-nine new clubs with a combined membership of 4,873 had been formed and associated to the society. This raised the number of affiliated clubs to 221 with an overall membership of nearly fifteen thousand riflemen. The number of individual subscribers to the SMRC had also increased to 974. Over approximately one year, 195 silver medals were awarded in competition. Furthermore, as a result of the society's encouragement of rifle shooting among public and preparatory schools, fourteen rifle clubs were established and 'enrolled as units' of the SMRC. During the meeting, it was also mentioned that a number of clubs had been authorised to use 'orthoptic sights', which was criticised by military experts whose opinion was that these devices did nothing to help develop the skills that were necessary for marksmanship with service rifles, but instead only appeared to satisfy the interests of pothunters and 'adepts in fancy shooting'.[102]

Lord Roberts's 'patriotic appeal' failed to raise the necessary funds to give rifle shooting a satisfactory foundation. However, it vigorously reignited the never wholly subdued debate on military training in schools and colleges. In the Commons, Conservative Sir Elliot Lees asked the First Lord of the Treasury 'whether, in view of the opinion expressed by Field Marshall Roberts that training in rifle-shooting can be effectively given by the use of miniature ranges [and] whether such training can be provided through the medium of the Education Department'. The prime minister, Arthur J. Balfour, answered that the educational system was not designed nor intended for military training.[103] A few weeks later, in a speech to the House of Lords, the Earl of Meath quoted a passage from an article Lord Roberts had published in the literary magazine *The Nineteenth Century and After*, in which the former Commander-in-Chief wrote that 'it is the bounden duty of the State to see that every able-bodied man in this country ... undergoes some kind of military training in his youth'.[104] To strengthen his argument, Meath went on to refer to Admiral Charles Beresford, Major

General Edmund Barrow, General Ian Hamilton, Lord Rosebery and others, who had recently put forward arguments in favour of the introduction of compulsory military training for boys of school age.[105] Shortly afterwards, Meath donated a Winchester rifle, cartridges and cardboard targets to the headmaster of a village school in Surrey.[106]

By the end of 1905, thirty-five new clubs had become affiliated to the SMRC, including the Jewish Lads' Brigade and its more than one thousand members. A further eighteen clubs set up new ranges. Even the Bishop of Salisbury took similar steps, while Reverend T. G. Wilson took on two hundred schoolboys in Plaistow to train them in camp life and miniature rifle shooting. In Newcastle, the Northern Counties Industrial Rifle League was being formed with the aim of providing training in rifle shooting to 'those engaged in shipyards, factories, and engineering works'.[107] Prize rifle competitions were run in Cheshire, Devon, Lancashire, Northumberland, Tyne and Wear and Scotland.

The rising popularity of the civilian rifle movement and the mounting criticism of British gunmakers for not manufacturing miniature rifles, unlike their continental and North American rivals, convinced the War Office to take steps to design a miniature or cadet rifle.[108] The technical design of this rifle, which would serve for both drill and target exercise, and a plan for standardising civilian practice with small-bore weapons were discussed by a committee that included members of the NRA and the SMRC. After extensive comparative tests, the outcome was a .22 calibre bolt action, single shot rifle with the same sight as on the short Lee-Enfield. The rifle was designed to be effective at a range of no more than one hundred yards. The W.O. miniature rifle did not live up to expectations, its defects including frequent burst cases.[109]

In November 1905, Lord Roberts submitted a six-page memorandum to the Committee of Imperial Defence recommending, among other provisions, a legislation requiring all able-bodied youths, upon reaching age eighteen or nineteen, to undergo mandatory military training until achieving basic proficiency as 'citizen-soldiers'. These men would then be required to complete annual musketry training until age thirty. Lord Roberts also advocated that all able-bodied men should be liable for service anywhere in the Empire during national emergencies.[110] Anticipating the government's cold, if not openly hostile, opposition to his plans, Roberts resigned from the Defence Committee and accepted the presidency of the NSL, which had long courted him. From this position, he launched a two-pronged offensive – advocating both national service and civilian marksmanship – two initiatives that converged on the single point of 'military preparedness'.

Lord Roberts's apprehension that Britain was not exempt from the laws that had governed the decline and fall of empires was further fuelled by the

58 *The lure of violence*

Figure 1.2 The SMRC: Competitions on the range of the Southfields Rifle Club. *The Bystander*, 13 September 1905.
Image © Mary Evans Picture Library

general election of 1906, which brought the Liberals, led by the 'Pro-Boer' Henry Campbell-Bannerman, into power. The 'empire's greatest soldier' then put all his prestige and missionary fervour at the disposal of the NSL, transforming it from a 'small extremist association' into a sizeable and influential national pressure group. By 1910, under a barrage of public meetings, lantern lectures, conferences, publications, posters, and other means, the NSL reached sixty-two thousand members, and by the eve of the war, it boasted two hundred and seventy thousand.[111] Lord Roberts also helped establish the National Defence Association, whose members included the *Morning Post* editor Howell Arthur Gwynne and the *Daily Express* publisher Sir Arthur Pearson.[112]

Throughout this period, the seventy-three-year-old Lord Roberts maintained his unwavering regimen of rifle club inaugurations, visits, and inspections. At the end of January 1906, the Colonial Consignment & Distributing Co. Ltd. established a miniature range at Nelson's Wharf, Lambeth, 'for the benefit of the company's officials, clerks and workmen'. In opening the range, Lord Roberts said he was delighted to see rifle clubs springing up everywhere, from 'the top of a warehouse to a crypt of a church'.[113] As evidence of the progress of the civilian rifle movement, the SMRC began publishing its official organ, *The Rifleman*. Edited by the secretary of the society, Hyam Marks, the red-covered magazine would report on the activities of local clubs (news, matches, etc.), air their grievances, and provide a range of information on rifle practice. 'I hope that the society's new paper', Lord Roberts wrote, 'will aid in placing before the men and youths of Great Britain the desirability of knowledge of rifle shooting, in order that they may fit themselves to take their share in the defence of the country should occasion for their service ever arise'.[114] The first issue, dated April 1906, reported that over one hundred clubs had been added to the society since the previous summer. Henceforth, air gun and air rifle clubs were allowed to affiliate to the SMRC. Matches for air gunners were arranged at the third annual meeting of the society, which was held at the Birmingham headquarters of the First V. B. Royal Warwickshire Regiment.[115]

In an interview in the *Daily Mirror* at the end of May, Marks stated that since Lord Salisbury's speech to the Primrose League, 'the condition of this country from the point of view of marksmanship has been completely revolutionised', and that Britain was pretty determined to carry out Lord Roberts's ideas. He then listed the achievements of the SMRC:

> Three hundred and fifty rifle clubs are affiliated to our society. We have enrolled eighteen new clubs within a fortnight [...] The Metropolitan Gas Company's miniature rifle club now numbers no fewer than 500 members.

> The District Messengers Association have converted a basement into a very smart-looking miniature gallery [...] The Army and Navy Stores are constructing a range on their roof, and the Merchant Taylors' School are endeavouring to adapt one of their schoolrooms for a similar purpose. The Boys' Home Industrial School have fitted up their mess-room as a miniature gallery. Chalk pits, passages, sheds, and barns are also being utilised all over the country in the endeavour to convert the rising generation into a nation of marksmen. Ladies are taking very kindly to shooting as a pastime, and young boys and girls of thirteen years of age have made some extraordinary scores.[116]

In July, after months of pressure, the Army Council officially recognised the SMRC and granted it equal powers and similar privileges to those enjoyed by the NRA, including exemption from gun licence duty for its clubs and members.[117] At ten shillings per annum, the cost of the licence was not trivial. The concessions granted by the Secretary of State for War, Richard B. Haldane, resulted in a marked increase in the number of affiliated clubs.[118] At the annual meeting of the SMRC, held as usual at the Royal United Services Institution, Lord Roberts said that he was delighted to see that women were also 'taking an interest in rifle shooting'.[119] Around that time, Gertrude Silver appealed to her fellow countrywomen to unite in steering the 'boyhood of Britain' towards military efficiency. Writing in *The Times* and again later in the *Fortnightly Review* she called on mothers 'to encourage and induce the boys of every family and of every class to learn to drill and to shoot'. Understanding their military duties and improving their physical condition would better prepare boys to fight in the impending wars.[120]

In addition to or in collaboration with the SMRC, other societies attempted to extend rifle practice in schools. In 1905, The Preparatory Schools Rifle Association (PSRA) was founded with Lord Roberts as president with the objective of encouraging rifle shooting in preparatory schools through practice with both miniature and air rifles. In 1906, the PSRA sent round a questionnaire to all preparatory schools listed in the Public School Yearbook for 1905 to obtain information on whether they taught boys shooting and physical drill, what facilities they had for rifle shooting, and whether they had a cadet corp. Out of the 248 replies, seventy-five headmasters stated that they provided teaching in rifle shooting.[121] In twenty of these schools, shooting practice was compulsory, while in the rest it was a 'privilege' or optional. Only twelve schools were categorically opposed to shooting. Among the 'shooting schools', fifty used miniature rifles, mostly the Winchester .22 single shot bolt action and the Martini-Henry. There was unanimous agreement that large rifles fitted with Morris tubes were too dangerous for boys. Air guns were generally regarded as useful complements to small-bore rifles rather than substitutes for them. Forty-two schools had outdoor ranges of lengths ranging from fifteen to over thirty yards. Other schools had accommodated indoor ranges in what were normally ordinary classrooms for air-gunning. Eleven schools were affiliated to either the NRA (seven) or the SMRC (four), while fifteen belonged to the PSARA.

While the costs of fitting out ranges and understandable concerns about safety might have deterred preparatory schools from offering rifle practice, the teaching of physical and military drill was something different. Physical drill was taught in 88 per cent of the schools, and military drill was compulsory in 122 schools. In addition, several schools expressed the desire to form a cadet corps, but they all cited major obstacles: 'The government gives more trouble than help', one headmaster said, 'With infinite difficulty, we now get an allowance of 60 rounds of .303 ammunition per head, and the regulations for its use are absurd'.[122]

However, in 1906 the Board of Education approved the teaching of rifle shooting on an experimental basis as part of the curriculum of a small number of public elementary schools. At the village of Shoreham in Kent, the administrators of the local school planned to instruct boys who had reached the age of twelve in: '1) The construction of the different parts of the rifle; 2) Sight and Sighting; 3) Position of the body; 4) Holding the rifle; 5) Aim and Pull off without cartridge and 6) Target practice with cartridge'. A suitable range was set up at the back of the gymnasium and the headmaster was appointed instructor.[123]

The approval given by the President of the Board, Augustine Birrell, to these educational experiments met with severe criticism from those who opposed the military training of the youth. The International Arbitration League, whose secretary was the Liberal MP Sir William Randal Cremer, who was awarded the Nobel Peace Prize in 1903, condemned the sanctioning of rifle teaching in schools. A resolution passed by the League's board stated that 'To teach boys the art of killing, under the pretext that it is necessary for the purposes of defence, is calculated to brutalise our youths by developing a fighting instinct and strengthening their combative natures'.[124] The socialist paper, *The Worker*, also deplored the institution of rifle training in schools claiming it encouraged 'brutality'.[125] At the end of the school year, the Board of Education resolved that military instruction with arms was inappropriate for children.[126]

While the controversy was raging, the NRA opened a Boys' Camp at Bisley. Under the direction of Major General Cheylesmore, boys from those elementary and public secondary schools without a uniformed cadet corps were given 'a week's training in drill and shooting'. A jubilant *Evening Standard* commented that while 'Mr. Haldane is cogitating over the formation of the National Army, that army is quietly coming into being'. The

Boys' Camp at Bisley was proving 'that most boys have a natural turn for soldiering'. The newspaper *Crown*, under the title 'The Nucleus of a new Army', voiced similar praise. It also added that in 'the last year nearly 110,000 young men and boys received some form of drilling and training in the use of the miniature rifle, and that 55,000 others received military training but no instruction in shooting'. There was no doubt that the army of the future lay in schools.[127]

At the end of 1906, the civilian rifle movement was growing apace. The SMRC had affiliated more than four hundred clubs and since Lord Roberts's appeal the press had been focussing increasing attention on civilian marksmanship. The high number of entries and large public attendance at the Miniature Bisley Meeting in November 'demonstrated unmistakable progress in the cult of rifle shooting'.[128] The proprietors of *Smith's Weekly* donated a million rounds of ammunition to the clubs affiliated to the SMRC, a gift that would have enabled 'some thousands of the rural members of the clubs to develop their shooting powers by increased opportunities for practice'.[129] Railway companies also took on the task of encouraging shooting skills among the civilian community by offering lower fares to SMRC members travelling to rifle practice or to shooting matches.[130] The railway manager Sir Charles John Owens, who later joined Henry Page Croft's Imperial Mission, set up an indoor miniature rifle range of the London and South Western Railway Rifle Club at Claphan Junction Station. The FIAT Motor-Car Company even decided to award a silver trophy at the 1907 Birmingham Miniature Rifle Meeting.[131]

With such remarkable progress, the SMRC decided to proceed with grouping the clubs into county associations. This plan received further impetus when Her Majesty the Queen Consort presented the society with 'The Queen's Cup', an annual challenge cup with a value of one hundred guineas. As a gesture of her personal interest in the advancement of marksmanship among 'the great mass of the nation', the medals were to be presented to the successful competitors at Buckingham Palace.[132] Teams of ten men selected by each county committee would compete in 'The Queen's Cup'. Establishing representative bodies of the SMRC in each county was complicated by rumours that Haldane's new army scheme would have required each county to form a body which would be responsible not only for all the auxiliary forces in the county, but also for promoting rifle shooting. The SMRC also had to deal with competition from The Patriotic Society. Founded by Major General Luard, who had previously severed his links with the SMRC, and presided over by the Marquess of Camden, the new organisation aimed to speed up the advancement of rifle shooting throughout the United Kingdom. The newly formed society presented competition prizes at the Bisley Boys' Camp in the form of oak shields with

How to shoot a rifle 63

Figure 1.3 The SMRC's Meeting at the Ham and Petersham Ranges. Illustrated Sporting and Dramatic News, 4 August 1906.
Image © Mary Evans Picture Library

silver mountings: 'on the head of each shield a figure of Britain [lay] on eight-pointed ground, supported by cross-rifles, and on the scroll below the inscription [were] the words: "England must wake up"'.[133] In the early summer of 1908, The Patriotic Society held an exhibition meeting at the Hall of the Royal Horticultural Society, where they held rapid fire competitions with magazine and automatic rifles.[134] A few months later, a distraught Luard, whose wife had been murdered in mysterious circumstances, died by suicide. Reflecting on his efforts to advance rifle practice in the country from the SWMR onwards, Luard had written 'My main object throughout has been to give better security to the lives of Englishmen in the land battles of the future, perhaps a near future'.[135] Following his death, The Patriotic Society was absorbed by the SMRC.

In 1907, ballistic engineer and marksman Edward J. D. Newitt was given authorisation by the board of the SMRC to publish '*The Citizen Rifleman*', a small volume dealing with subjects such as the construction of indoor and outdoor ranges, the value of marksmanship and all matters connected with miniature rifles and match and target shooting.[136] Newitt, an early promoter of the civilian rifle movement and member of the famous Southfields Rifle Club, delivered a lecture to the London Chamber of Commerce in which he stated that only 7 per cent of the male population had 'military aspirations', while the remaining 93 per cent were 'an unrealised asset from the point of view of national defence'. He went on to highlight 'the failure of British gunmakers to supply the initial demand for rifles by miniature clubs', allowing cheaper, foreign-made rifles to be imported into England, and concluded that the fact that '150,000 of our nation had already been induced to take some interest in rifle-shooting was not to be ignored, though the limits of development of the Movement were a long way from being reached'.[137] Not long before, Lieutenant General Lance, speaking as the SMRC's representative, had reminded the Church Lads' Brigades and the Boys' Brigade that good and loyal citizenship demanded practice in rifle shooting.[138]

By the end of summer 1907, miniature rifles were 'fast becoming a feature of town and country life',[139] and the number of clubs affiliated to the SMRC had risen to 793.[140] However, the society's growth was somewhat hindered by its apparently weak financial situation. Since Lord Roberts's appeal, only £5,148 had been received in donations and the society was operating at a financial loss each year. Nonetheless, with grants from Lord Roberts's fund and the generous patronage of its board, the society was able to continue its work'.[141] It published literature, held meetings and continued to give awards and prizes to rifle clubs at an estimated value of £10 a week. The consequent need to make rifle contests as popular as the inter-Imperial cricket matches had been or at least on a level with the meetings held by the *Deutscher Flottenverein* (Navy League) in Germany, put pressure on the

Figure 1.4 *The Railway Times: A Journal of Finance, Construction, and Operation* 96, no. 18 (30 October 1909), p. 446

SMRC to mobilise local patriotism to the fullest possible extent. According to the *Daily Telegraph*, the civilian rifle movement had to follow the example of the Football Association, which had 'captured industrial democracy as no passion in sport had appealed to it before'.[142] There was no better incentive for rifle practice than arousing civic rivalries. Under the auspices of the SMRC, numerous matches were organised between neighbouring clubs under Miniature Bisley rules. International matches against teams of marksmen from Canada, Australia and the United States were also arranged. When reports came in that English riflemen had been outmatched by their opponents, Lord Roberts laid the blame on the inadequate military training of the youth at home compared to foreign countries. 'In America, the boys were taught to shoot from an early age', he argued, 'Even in China they have their boy cadets between nine and sixteen years of age, and if a population of four hundred million could be taught to shoot accurately and a proper proportion of them some day became soldiers they would be a great power in the world'. Lord Roberts also stressed the urgency of improving British rifles, ammunition and sights.[143]

While numerous initiatives surfaced with the aim of reinvigorating British manhood and marksmanship, Henry Page Croft proposed a National Citizen Army, which amounted to universal military training. The scheme consisted in a comprehensive training schedule that included daily half-hour drills for schoolboys comprising physical exercises and military activities, including firearm handling. During their final two years of school, students would engage in rifle practice at miniature ranges and would earn certificates upon completing the musketry course. To maintain interest in military matters beyond school, Rifle Clubs and Boys' Brigades were supported and membership encouraged. The proposal also envisaged a tiered defence structure with expanded forms of Militia, Yeomanry, and the Territorial Army for national and imperial defence. Croft concluded that 'if it be loss to learn the art of serving one's King and Country, even the extreme faddists will have to admit that the character of the British race will gain, in that its manhood will learn discipline and acquire steadiness, whilst the physique of the nation will be greatly improved'.[144]

With the polarisation of the international system and the country's Germanophobic mood, the command of the Legion of Frontiersmen – a force established in 1904 with the purpose of recruiting former servicemen or individuals with a knowledge of bush craft for service around the British Empire – lamented the use of foreign ammunition, in particular German cartridges, by the large majority of miniature rifle clubs.[145] Predictably, the issue triggered a heated public debate. To clarify why the rifle clubs were unable to use English cartridges, the Legion's secretary, Hyam Marks, explained to the *Globe*:

> As to the general use of foreign ammunition at miniature rifle ranges, I can say at once that its proportion to that of English ammunition used must be quite 100 to 1. It is difficult to estimate what amount that involves, but there are about 2,000 miniature rifle clubs in existence, with a membership approximately of 200,000. Roughly speaking, I should say that 100 million rounds of ammunition are fired each year for practicing purposes, so it is obvious that a fairly large sum is represented [...] The cause of this extensive use of foreign ammunition, regrettable as the fact may be, is simply that riflemen find it better and more reliable than that manufactured here, though the prices of the home article compare very favourably with those of the German.

Marks further explained that some of the provisions of the Explosives Act were responsible for higher production costs at home than abroad. For instance, if British manufacturers filled their cartridges with a charge of six grains, of which not more than 25 per cent was fulminate of mercury, they would have been classified as 'detonators'.[146] He therefore asked the government to step in and either modify the law or guarantee costs above a certain price, otherwise, nine-tenths of the SMRC's annual budget for cartridges (£7,000 to £10,000 for fifteen to twenty million rounds) would go to Germany.[147]

Marks' argument was unconvincing, or at least insufficiently convincing to many. For instance, some members of the rifle clubs felt that it was unpatriotic to buy ammunition from the Rhenish Westphalian Explosives Company rather than from the King's Norton Metal Company,[148] which at that time was Britain's largest manufacturer of ammunition for miniature rifles. The Miniature Ammunition Company had procured the sole right to sell the King's Norton .22 cartridges at cheaper rates (11s 6d per thousand), but only to clubs affiliated to the NRA. In response to an enquiry by the *Morning Post*, the director of the King's Norton Metal Company, H. Melville Smith, dismissed public rumours that there was no good .22 calibre ammunition on the British market. Such was the quality of their .22 cupro-nickel cartridge, known as the 'Carton', that in using it riflemen were sacrificing neither efficiency nor patriotism. 'Possibly one explanation', he argued, 'why German ammunition was so much favoured by the Society of Miniature Rifle Clubs is that it is the cheapest', and most of the clubs depended on profits from the sale of accessories and ammunition for their maintenance. Melville Smith also declared that the SMRC 'had been very anxious to make a contract with us, but as we have made certain arrangements with the National Rifle Association, we were unable to fall in with their arrangements unless they asked the permission of the National Rifle Association, which they refused to do'. As a result, numerous SMRC affiliated clubs had also joined the NRA in order to obtain King's

Norton ammunition at low cost. In conclusion, Melville Smith accused the Home Office's restrictions and free imports of severely hindering the ability of English cartridge makers to meet market demands.[149] German tariffs on British ammunition were onerous, while German ammunition, in line with free trade principles, was not subject to duties or regulations. To the further disadvantage of British manufacturers, France had forbidden the importation of .22 cartridges.[150]

In the meantime, the SMRC and the NRA had sought permission from the Gun and Ammunition Trade Section of the London Chamber of Commerce to purchase stockpiles of old Martini-Henry rifles from the War Office for subsequent resale at a lower cost.[151] The request followed British gunmaker W. W. Greener's achievement in converting the Martini-Henry to fire .22 bullets. The introduction of the 'converted Martini-Henry' sparked 'the real boom in the civilian rifle movement'.[152] British gunmakers had only recently begun taking a serious interest in miniature rifles. The Birmingham Small Arms Company (BSA) and the London Small Arms Company had obtained government permits to manufacture the W.O. 1906 miniature rifle.[153] Its design made the rifle more expensive than other models of the same calibre already on the market. It came as no surprise that the Birmingham manufacturers contested the government's decision to sell thousands of Martini-Henrys to the SMRC and the NRA, pointing to the fact that selling converted rifles would 'put competition out of the question'. Furthermore, Taylor Peddie of the BSA denounced the SMRC's action as outright illegitimate.[154] The society replied that 'if the civilian rifle movement was to be furthered, it was essential that shooting appurtenances should be placed within the reach of those whose position did not admit of their paying fancy prices for such articles'.[155]

The extraordinary increase in the number of clubs was proof that the rifle club movement had become popular and 'that rifle shooting was becoming a national sport'.[156] By the spring of 1908, over one thousand three hundred clubs with about one hundred thousand members had affiliated to the SMRC. It was around this time that the BSA, which used American techniques of mass production, decided to enter the contest. Various patterns of high velocity sporting rifles, sporting carbines, air rifles and miniature bolt rifles were sent out from their factory in Small Heath. The BSA miniature rifle went 'into the home of the many' and 'found its way all over the British Empire, into France, Norway, Sweden, Denmark, and, before the war started, even Germany'.[157]

At the end of 1908, Lord Roberts made a fresh appeal to working men's clubs, inviting them to convert their premises into indoor miniature ranges of fifteen to twenty-five yards. A solid wall reinforced by iron plates behind the targets, a couple of acetylene lamps, one on either side of the target, and an oil lamp directly above the firing point were all that was needed to set up a good range. Martini-Henry rifles converted to .22 bore were offered to SMRC members at a cost of twenty-four shillings each, and ammunition at five shots a penny. If there was not sufficient space for a miniature range, air rifle ranges of eight and ten yards were recommended. 'Rifle shooting has also its patriotic side', Lord Roberts wrote. By becoming an expert shooter 'a man is at least doing something towards rendering himself able to defend his country, and it is constantly found that miniature rifle shooting is an incentive to enlistment in the Territorial Army'. The rifle clubs were therefore to function as feeders to the reorganised force, established in 1907 by the amalgamation of the Militia, Volunteers and Yeomanry with the aim of providing support to the regular Army.[158] Major Clive Morrison Bell, who was about to resign from his position as the SMRC's organising secretary to pursue a political career as Unionist MP for Honiton, likewise declared that 'England could not be saved by Rifle Clubs, but those Clubs [have been] excellent feeders for the defensive forces in preparing for any contest that might suddenly come upon the country'.[159]

Efforts to forge closer ties between rifle clubs and Lord Haldane's citizen army dovetailed with the NSL's broader campaign to introduce compulsion into the Territorial Army Scheme. The League advocated for training all able-bodied men aged eighteen to twenty-one within the ranks of the Territorial Army. Infantry recruits would complete four months in camp, while recruits for other army branches would serve up to six months. This initial training would be followed by three years of annual musketry courses and two-week camps. These trained men would remain liable for home defence service in the Territorial Army until age thirty, but only called upon in a time of grave emergency declared by Parliament. Additionally, compulsory military and physical training would be introduced for youths aged fourteen to eighteen, conducted through secondary and public school curricula, affiliated cadet corps or authorised youth training organisations. The League estimated that, within four years of implementation, the Territorial Army would include four hundred thousand active members and a hundred and fifty thousand recruits undergoing training, while a reserve force of trained men would grow to approximately six hundred thousand by the conclusion of their service liability period. On 19 May 1909, the 'National Service (Training and Home Defence) Bill' was put before the House of Lords by Lord Newton, and seconded by the Duke of Norfolk, Lord Milner and other prominent peers. Despite Lord Roberts reiterating his belief that British military policy 'involve[d] a wilful gambling with the safety of the country and of the Empire', the Bill was defeated on its Second Reading by a vote of 123 to 103.[160] That ninety-eight Unionist peers sided with Lord Roberts, against seventy-five who opposed him, revealed how the movement for conscription had gained significant traction within the Conservative establishment. Following the two elections of 1910, the League stated that 155 MPs supported the conscription cause, with eighty of them being regular members of the League. In 1903 there were only three MPs in the House of Commons who were known to support 'national service'.[161]

Lord Roberts's 'last glorious campaigns' were pervaded by the 'German threat'. In 1906, he composed an appreciative introduction to the novel *Invasion of 1910: with a full account of the siege of London* by the popular author and journalist William T. Le Queux. In the preface to the book, which seems to have sold over a million copies, Le Queux significantly wrote that 'ever since Lord Roberts formulated his plans for the establishment of rifle clubs [...] the idea occurred to me to write a forecast [...] which would bring home to the British public vividly and forcibly what would really occur were an enemy suddenly to appear in our midst'.[162] In 1907, the NSL urged the Committee of Imperial Defence to revisit 'the question of invasion', convinced of the potential for a German assault on British shores. The NSL then rejected the inquiry's conclusions, which asserted that Britain would remain secure as long as it upheld naval supremacy.[163] 'Invasion propaganda' resumed, if it had ever stopped, with equal fervour and reached paroxysmal levels during the 1908–1909 Dreadnought scare and the 1911 Agadir crisis, the penultimate in the series of crises that preceded the First World War. Even prior to the dispatch of the German cruiser Panther to South Morocco, Lord Roberts succeeded in passing a motion with ninety-nine votes in favour and forty against, declaring that given the changed strategic situation in Europe, the House of Lords observed with growing concern 'the inadequate military arrangements of His Majesty's Government for the defence of this country and His Majesty's Overseas Dominions'.[164] Months later, speaking in Manchester, Lord Roberts notoriously declared 'now in the year 1912, just as in 1866 and just as in 1870, war will take place the instant the German forces by land and sea are, by their superiority at every point, as certain of victory as anything in human calculation can be made certain. Germany strikes when Germany's hour has struck'.[165] The German menace, as conjured in the public imagination by Lord Roberts, found ready champions in Admiral Lord Charles Beresford – a stalwart advocate of national service who was pressing upon the country the need for a substantial increase in cruisers and destroyers – and, more unexpectedly, in the 'rogue socialist' Robert Blatchford, whose *Daily Mail* articles warned of Germany's supposed ambition to dismantle the British Empire.[166] All this contributed to a climate of increasingly neurotic moods, misdirected passion, and 'bellicism' – a form of social fatalism that rested on the belief that war was inevitable and a necessary part of the struggle for survival among nations.[167]

Spy-mania and invasion scares, coupled with the vast 'literature of the next war', stimulated the expansion of the miniature rifle movement. It was speculated that 'In a few years, if the same rate of progress is maintained, every village throughout England will have its club and every man will have an opportunity of becoming proficient in the use of the rifle'.[168] In February 1909, the NRA announced that the number of members registered in its rifle clubs had reached 102,752. Since the founding of the rifle club movement, 1,350 clubs had become affiliated to it – many of them also belonged to the SMRC. Since their introduction in 1901, 'Skilled Shot' certificates had been awarded to nine thousand eight hundred shooters, while over eleven thousand had received 'Rifleman' certificates, first granted in 1903. The hundred thousand riflemen asked for by Lord Roberts in his 1905 appeal had finally been reached.[169] The SMRC also reported a record increase in new rifle clubs of 260 in the first six months of 1909. 'We can estimate that thus twenty-five thousand members have come to us since January 1st', secretary Marks told the *Leeds Mercury*. The time had come, he added, for the War Office to recognise the society beyond its exemption from gun licences and to incorporate it 'in a national reserve, with military status in war'.[170] A month later, at the annual meeting of the SMRC, it was announced with jubilation that rifle shooting was finally taking its place as 'a national sport', as most of its practitioners were drawn from the middle and working classes. The society had grown across the entire country, especially in Oxford, Norfolk, Lincolnshire, Somerset, Cambridgeshire and Staffordshire. Furthermore, despite the stubborn opposition of those who considered that 'the teaching of a boy to shoot [was] tantamount to teaching him to murder', miniature rifle shooting had been eagerly taken up in boarding schools, including Eton and Malvern.[171] The SMRC also provided free training to the junior branch of the IML, which had recently seceded from the NL and was to channel radical-right sentiments and visions into the cause of navalism.[172]

Around this time, the SMRC, eager to dispel the 'German ammunition controversy', had placed orders with Messrs. Eley Brothers and Messrs. Kynoch for a total of eleven million rounds of ammunition.[173] They also purchased a large quantity of old Martini-Henry rifles from the government to convert into miniature rifles. Curiously, these rifles, a quarter of a million altogether, were packed and stored in a subbasement of Lloyds Bank in central London and for a time they were even suspected of being a secret German arsenal.[174] In July, the SMRC faced fresh accusations of

Table 1.1 Numbers of clubs affiliated with the Society of Miniature Rifle Clubs

Numbers of clubs affiliated with the SMRC			Increase
30 June	1902	28	38
–	1903	63	55
–	1904	178	85
–	1905	221	43
–	1906	360	139
–	1907	823	463
–	1908	1315	492
31 December	1908	1539	224
30 April	1909	1768	229

Source: 'Rifle Shots', *Chard and Ilminster News*, 5 June 1909

unpatriotic behaviour when the *John Bull* magazine reported that the converted Martini-Henrys supplied to clubs were fitted with Belgian barrels. The society denied using foreign barrel components, explaining that it had initially contracted C. G. Bonehill of the Belmont Fire Arms and Gun Barrel Works to convert a few thousand Martini-Henry rifles, but later, when it was brought to their attention that foreign materials were being used, they demanded the Birmingham gunmaker use only British materials. As to the statements that the SMRC was a 'shabby trading concern … hucksters of every possible appurtenance', they gave assurances that the profit deriving from the sale of shooting accessories was entirely 'devoted to furthering the formation of additional clubs, the holding of rifle meetings throughout the country at which members of the clubs compete, and to awarding prizes for shooting'.[175]

The year 1909 had been successful for the SMRC with 546 new rifle clubs joining the society bringing the total number of affiliated clubs to two thousand.[176] This positive trend continued into the new year, with 'new clubs coming in at the rate of 40 per month'.[177] Nevertheless, this growth was still not considered sufficiently satisfactory and in the first monthly issue of *The Rifleman*, Lord Roberts reiterated his conviction that by undergoing training in the use of a rifle, citizens were not only indulging in a pleasurable pursuit, but also 'performing one of the most important duties of patriotism'. In addition to Lord Roberts's foreword, the official organ of the SMRC published Rudyard Kipling's *The Parable of Boy Jones* and a satirical poem by the editor of *Punch*, Owen Seaman, which exhorted women to show their public spirit by 'giving the 'cold shoulder' to members of the opposite sex who decline[d] to fit themselves for the purposes of the national defence'.[178]

By the summer of 1910, Lord Roberts and many NSL supporters had lost confidence in the Territorial Army's ability to defend Britain in the event of an attack. This mistrust was likely exacerbated by the limited training provided to the 'Terriers' – only thirty drills per year, typically held in the evenings for around two hours, along with a two-week annual camp. In response to the League's critiques, Haldane commissioned Sir Ian Hamilton to publish *Compulsory Service*, which made a compelling case for 'voluntary service'. Lord Roberts countered with *Fallacies and Facts* (1911), written with the assistance from Leo Amery and historian John Adam Cramb. As the controversy intensified, Lord Roberts further emphasised the importance of good marksmanship. He persuaded the *Daily Mail* to establish an annual competition open to all miniature rifle clubs across the British Empire.[179] 'I am most anxious that every man and youth belonging to the empire shall obtain a thorough knowledge of rifle-shooting', he wrote.[180] Soon after, the former Commander-in-Chief attended the SMRC's meeting at the Petersham Range, where he was received by a guard of honour formed by Boy Scouts and Australian cadets.

In the introduction to the SMRC handbook for 1912, Lord Roberts wrote that 450 new miniature rifle clubs had affiliated to the society in the previous year:

> Great business firms, railway companies, schools, units of the Regular and Territorial Forces, boys' organisations, cities, boroughs, and villages all appear to be anxious to fit themselves as far as may be possible by voluntary effort to take their share in the defence of their country if and when called upon to do so.[181]

Meanwhile, the large increase in rifle shooting devotees in Northern Ireland, particularly among Unionist circles, resulted in the establishment of clubs and ranges throughout the region, a number of them affiliated to the NRA and the SMRC. The Committee of the Dublin Civil Service Rifle Club organised an All-Ireland Miniature Rifle meeting at Ballsbridge in the early spring of 1910.[182] For the occasion, *The Irish Times* offered a silver cup for a competition for schoolboys and Boy Scouts. In August 1912, at the opening ceremony of the Kingsbridge Miniature Rifle Club, which had been formed by residents of the Ballynafeigh and Newtownbreda districts of Belfast, the new secretary of the SMRC, Colonel Winter, announced that three thousand five hundred clubs throughout Britain were affiliated to the society and that in the last two years the number of Irish clubs had more than doubled. He went on to say that 'several hundred thousands of men and women had through their instrumentality been taught the use of the rifle and, in addition to that [...] a loftier sense of patriotism'.[183] With the escalation of the Home Rule crisis and the Unionists ready to abandon constitutional means,

74 The lure of violence

Figure 1.5 Lord Roberts at a Miniature Rifle Club Meeting, *Daily Mirror*, 4 July 1910. With thanks to the Trinity Mirror. Digitised by Findmypast Newspaper Archive Limited

the government was forced to tighten procedures for the formation and membership of rifle clubs. As it was, affiliation to the SMRC entitled members to carry rifles to and from the ranges and provided a legal framework for firearms training. The authorities therefore established that the SMRC could not grant affiliation to any club without prior inspection and approval of the ranges by the War Office. Rifle clubs were obliged to submit a list of their members every year to the Irish Executive at Dublin Castle, who then decided whether or not to grant authorisation.[184] Not surprisingly, the following summer, many rifle clubs in Ulster had their affiliate licences cancelled. A sign of the government's state of alarm over the situation in Ulster, was their call for the Boy Scouts to return their .22 calibre carbines. Protest was made to the Lord Lieutenant, who was asked to reconsider the matter, as no similar requirements were placed on English rifle clubs, to which Lord Aberdeen bluntly replied: 'It is regretted that in the existing circumstances the Irish Government are unable to approve of the application for a renewal of the affiliation'.[185] The Belfast correspondent of the *Pall Mall Gazette* reported that 'The government evidently presume that these clubs, which now number 140, will immediately be disbanded; but in the majority of cases such will not be the case'.[186] This defiance on the part of the clubs was legally justified as the orders of the government were made *ultra vires* and had no statutory warrant. The sole power to revoke a range licence was contained in Army Form K. 1314 ('Certificate as to safety on a miniature club'); other than this the authorities had no power to order the SMRC to withdraw a certificate of affiliation and exemption granted to any club.[187] Furthermore, constabularies could only take the name and address of a club member carrying a rifle, but could not confiscate his weapon. This legal impasse allowed the clubs to continue shooting.[188]

In his introduction to the 1914 Handbook of the SMRC, Lord Roberts wrote that, although the movement had made good progress, his ideal of 'every man a rifleman' was far from fulfilled. A tribute was paid to the women members of the society for honing their skills in the art of rifle shooting. In his conclusion, he stressed once again the connection between the responsibilities of good citizenship, patriotism and marksmanship training:

> No man should have a voice in the legislation of his country who is not prepared and equipped to take part in its defence. The man who cannot shoot is absolutely useless in the fighting line. A man who cannot shoot should be ashamed to possess the Parliamentary vote.[189]

By the outbreak of war, about four thousand five hundred clubs had joined the civilian rifle movement. Brigadier General Percy Lake, the newly appointed honorary secretary of the SMRC, invited those who were unable to go to the front to go to their nearest range and learn how to shoot. Many clubs began offering all male citizens the free use of their rifles, ammunition and targets.[190] All rifle competitions were discontinued in order to preserve ammunition. To those members who asked whether miniature rifle clubs could be turned into 'some sort of irregular unit for home defence', the SMRC replied with a circular in which it was suggested that miniature rifle clubs should become 'local centres of a semi-military character, where men can train themselves and make themselves fit to take up arms if and when called upon to do so'. With this in view, it was suggested teaching prospective recruits the rudiments of the 'use and handling of the rifle, squad-drill, taking cover, extending, advancing, retiring, and fire control'.[191] At the end of August, Lord Kitchener asked the NRA and the SMRC to form corps of musketry instructors for the purpose of training the thousands of recruits that were volunteering for service in the 'New Army'. A month later, Lord Roberts delivered his last appeal:

> I am proud of my rifle clubs. I am proud of the society that binds them together. I am proud of the unanimity with which all the clubs at this time of national emergency are placing their ranges, the personal services of their members, and in many cases their arms and ammunition, at the service of the Territorial Force, the National Reserve, and of all others who either for practice or instruction desire to shoot. Now is the time to put to the test your years of preparation, your skill with the rifle, your patriotism.[192]

Since the Boer War, civilian rifle clubs had done an enormous amount of groundwork in training a not insignificant segment of the male population in the use of the rifle. Before being killed near Ypres in 1914, Harcourt Ommundsen wrote that a surprisingly high number of those who enlisted in Kitchener's Army 'had their first introduction to a Service Rifle through the medium of these .22 service weapons'.[193] At the same time, while the NSL's agitation for national service failed to make its proposal into law, the civilian rifle movement created a robust culture that raised rifle shooting from a leisure pursuit to an essential asset of good citizenship and patriotism. It provided British men with the training needed to fulfil their common-law obligation to participate in the defence of the homeland. This aspect was exemplified by the words of an anonymous writer, 'A Marksman', who at the turn of the century declared: 'the man who can hit the target is a more useful citizen than he who can not'.[194] The tremendous development of rifle clubs also contributed to stirring up of Germanophobia and instilling a psychological state of readiness for war among the British people. Finally, the act of aiming, sighting and firing a rifle appears to have provided a cathartic release from the pervasive culture of muscular, militarised masculinity that saturated and agitated the imaginaries of the Right and, more broadly, nearly all aspects of Edwardian society. 'Few things have more attraction for the average man and boy', wrote the *Navy & Army Illustrated* 'than a firearm. Anything that will propel a missile is dear to the masculine heart [...] the gun or rifle becomes the object of fierce, overmastering desire'.[195]

Notes

1. Quotation with which the SMRC prefaced its pamphlet *Miniature Rifle Clubs, and How to Form and Conduct Them* (London: Society of Working Men's Rifle Clubs, 1902).
2. Lord Roberts, 'Rifle Shooting as A National Pursuit', *The Times*, 12 June 1905. This article is reprinted in Elliott Eraus Mills and Frederick Sleigh Roberts, *Speeches and Letters of Field Marshal Earl Roberts, K.G. on Imperial Defence* (London: Simpkin, Marshall, Hamilton, Kent & Company, Limited, 1906), pp. 93–108.
3. No scholarly work has been devoted yet to the analysis of the civilian rifle club movement and, more specifically, to the efforts of private citizens to promote rifle marksmanship in the aftermath of the Boer War.
4. Phillips, *The Diehards*, pp. 87–88.
5. 'Games and Pastimes', *The Bystander*, 7 October 1907.
6. For a definition of militarisation, see Geyer, 'The Militarization of Europe, 1914–1945', pp. 65–102, at p. 79. See also, in the same volume, Geoffrey Best, 'The Militarization of European Society, 1870–1914', pp. 13–29.
7. On the NRA, Susie Cornfield, *The Queen's Prize: The Story of the National Rifle Association* (London: Pelham Books, 1987); Alfred Paget Humphry and Thomas Francis Freemantle, *History of the National Rifle Association During Its First Fifty Years, 1859 to 1909* (Cambridge: Bowes and Bowes, 1914); John Randal MacDonnell, *The National Rifle Association: A Sketch of Its History and Progress, 1859–1876* (London: W. J. Johnson, 1877). On the Volunteer Movement, Ian F. W. Beckett, *Riflemen Form: A Study of the Rifle Volunteer Movement 1859–1908* (Havertown: Pen and Sword, 2007); Hugh Cunningham, *The Volunteer Force: A Social and Political History 1859–1908* (London: Croom Helm, 1975); Cecil Sebag Montefiore, *A History of the Volunteer Forces from the Earliest Times to the Year 1860: Being a Recital of the Citizen Duty* (London: [publisher not identified], 1908); Robert Potter Berry, *A History of the Formation and Development of Volunteer Infantry* (London: Simpkin Marshall & Co., 1903).
8. W. W. Greener, *Sharpshooting for Sport and War* (London: R. A. Everett, 1900), p. 156.
9. Letter sent by the Council of the NRA to Lords Lieutenants, 16 August 1860. Reprinted in Humphry and Freemantle, *History of the National Rifle Association*, p. 34.

10 Greener, *Sharpshooting for Sport and War*, p. 156. See also from the same author, *The Gun and Its Development*, eighth edition (London: Cassell, 1907), pp. 727–763.
11 William A. Baillie-Grohman, 'Rifle Shooting as a National Pursuit', *The Nineteenth Century: A Monthly Review* (September 1899), pp. 367–382.
12 On the Second Boer War, Michael Barthorp, *The Anglo-Boer Wars* (Poole: Blandford Press, 1987); Eversley Belfield, *The Boer War* (London: Leo Cooper, 1975); Owen Coetzer, *The Anglo-Boer War: The Road to Infamy* (Rivonia: William Waterman, 1996); Donal Lowry (ed.), *The South African War Reappraised* (Manchester: Manchester University Press, 2000); Bill Nassom, *The South African War, 1899–1902* (Oxford: Oxford University Press, 1999); Pretorius Fransjohan, *The Anglo Boer War, 1899–1902* (Cape Town: Don Nelson, 1985); Thomas Pakenham, *The Boer War* (New York: Random House, 1979).
13 Jan Bloch, *Modern Weapons and Modern War: Being an Abridgment of 'The War of the Future in Its Technical, Economic and Political Relations'*, with a prefatory conversation with the author by W. T. Stead (London: G. Richards, 1900). On the impact of Jean Bloch's analysis of war on British military thought in the years before the First World War, T. H. E. Travers, 'Technology, Tactics, and Morale: Jean De Bloch, the Boer War, and British Military Theory, 1900–1914', *The Journal of Modern History* 51, no. 2 (1979), pp. 264–286.
14 William Adolphe Baillie-Grohman, 'Marksmanship Old and New', *The Nineteenth Century: A Monthly Review* 47, no. 279 (March 1877–December 1900), pp. 753–766.
15 Report on the musketry training of the regular forces serving at home: including the School of Musketry, and also on the musketry training of the militia, yeomanry cavalry and volunteers during the year 1898 (London: Her Majesty's Stationery Office, 1899).
16 Spencer Jones, '"Shooting Power": A Study of the Effectiveness of Boer and British Rifle Fire, 1899–1914', *British Journal for Military History* 1, no. 1 (2014), pp. 29–44; Spencer Jones, '"The Shooting of the Boers Was Extraordinary": British Views of Marksmanship in the Second Anglo-Boer War, 1899–1902', in Karen Jones, Giacomo Macola and David Welch (eds), *A Cultural History of Firearms in the Age of Empire* (Farnham: Ashgate, 2013), pp. 251–266.
17 John C. Ridpath and Edward S. Ellis, *The Story of South Africa: An Account of the Historical Transformation of the Dark Continent by the European Powers and the Culminating Contest Between Great Britain and the South African Republic in the Transvaal War* (Chicago, IL: J. M. Moore & Company, 1899), p. 436.
18 Maurice Harold Grant and John Frederick Maurice, *History of the War in South Africa, 1899–1902* (London: Hurst and Blackett Limited, 1906), p. 80.
19 C. J. Cornish, 'A Chance for the Public Schools', *The National Review* 35, no. 205 (1900), p. 83.
20 On the Lads Drill Association and the development of military and physical drill in elementary schools, Penn, *Targeting Schools*.

21 Reverend G. Sale Reaney, 'The Civic and Moral Benefits of Drill', *The Nineteenth Century* (1900), pp. 396–399.
22 Sir Lauder Bruton, *Collected Papers on Physical and Military Training* (published privately, 1915), 3 (2 July 1901).
23 'Sheffield School Board. The Children and Dummy Rifles', *Sheffield Evening Telegraph*, 15 February 1900.
24 Conditions for Affiliation of Rifle Clubs and Miniature Rifle Clubs to the National Rifle Association in Thomas Francis Freemantle, *The Book of the Rifle* (London: Longmans, Green and Co., 1901), pp. 536–538.
25 Letter to James M. Conland, 2 December 1900, in *The Letters of Rudyard Kipling: Volume 3: 1900–10*, edited by Thomas Pinney (New York: Palgrave Macmillan, 1995), p. 39.
26 Arthur Conan Doyle, *The Great Boer War* (London: Smith, Elder & Co., 1900), pp. 515–516.
27 See, in particular, Lonsdale Hale, 'Sham versus Real Home Defence', *Nineteenth Century and After* 49, no. 288 (February 1901), pp. 248–267.
28 'Rifle Ranges', *Volunteer Service Gazette and Military Dispatch*, 9 March 1900.
29 [No title], *London Evening Standard*, 1 March 1900.
30 House of Commons, Rifle ranges acquisition. A bill to facilitate the acquisition of rifle ranges, Bills and Acts, 42 (paper number), Vol. 4, 1902.
31 W. W. Greener, *The Gun and Its Development*, 8th ed. (London: Cassell and Company, 1907) pp. 756–757.
32 'Technical Education Report', *Maidstone Journal and Kentish Advertiser*, 17 May 1900.
33 'The Government and the Empire', *The Times*, 10 May 1900; 'Lord Salisbury's Address to the Primrose League', *The Manchester Guardian*, 10 May 1900.
34 See, generally, the monthly *Reviews* in 1900 and 1901; the *Journal of the Royal United Service Institution* and the *United Services Magazine* for some years past; pamphlets such as Lieutenant Colonel W. C. Underwood (1901). See also Doyle, *The Great Boer War*, and Samuel Smith, *My Life-Work* (London: Hoddern and Stoughton, 1902).
35 George Gordon Coulton, *A Strong Army in a Free State: A Study of the Old English and Modern Swiss Militias* (London: Simpkin, Marshall, Hamilton, Kent, 1900).
36 George F. Shee, *The Briton's First Duty: The Case for Conscription* (London: Grant Richards, 1901), pp. 174–208.
37 Allison, *The National Service Issue*, pp. 1–41; Stearn, 'The Last Glorious Campaign', pp. 313–314.
38 Frank McDonough, *The Conservative Party and Anglo-German Relations, 1905–1914* (Basingstoke: Palgrave Macmillan, 2007), pp. 109–110.
39 Stearn, 'The Last Glorious Campaign', pp. 312–330.
40 Allison, *The National Service Issue*, p. 25. R. J. Q. Adams and Philip P. Poirier, *The Conscription Controversy in Great Britain, 1900–1918* (London: Macmillan, 1987), p. 11.

41 William Adolphe Baillie-Grohman, 'A British Rifle League', *The Scotsman*, 29 January 1900.
42 'Sunderland Rifle Club', *Sunderland Daily Echo and Shipping Gazette*, 17 August 1900. This was the first press mention of the League.
43 'District Volunteer Notes', *Manchester Evening News*, 22 January 1901.
44 'British Rifle League', *South Wales Daily News*, 5 May 1902.
45 'British Rifle Club: Formation of a Club at Pontypridd', *Western Mail*, 26 February 1902.
46 'The British Rifle League', *Pall Mall Gazette*, 12 February 1902.
47 Ibid., 5 May 1902.
48 Ibid., 20 October 1902.
49 'Conference of Civilian Rifle Clubs:. Proposed National Rifle Union', *Sheffield Independent*, 28 June 1900.
50 'British Rifle Union', *London Evening Standard*, 29 November 1900.
51 'Bradfield', *The Berkshire Chronicle*, 23 February 1901.
52 Allison, *The National Service Issue*, p. 69.
53 'Working Men's Rifle Clubs: An Extraordinary Movement. New Form of 'Patriotism', *The Daily News*, 25 March 1901; 'Rifle Clubs for Working Men: Meeting at the Mansion House', *Volunteer Service Gazette and Military Dispatch*, 29 March 1901.
54 Ibid. On the formation of the SWMR, see also Richard Price, *An Imperial War and the British Working Class: Working-Class Attitudes and Reactions to the Boer War, 1899–1902* (London: Routledge & Kegan Paul, 1972), pp. 221–223.
55 'Major General Luard on Rifle Shooting Clubs', *Kent and Sussex Courier*, 11 October 1901; 'Rifle Shooting', *The Army and Navy Gazette, & c.*, 4 January 1902, p. 19.
56 Harold Marks, *Miniature Rifle Clubs, and How to Form and Conduct Them* (London: Society of Working Men's Rifle Clubs, 1902).
57 'Working Men's Rifle', *The Morning Post*, 5 October 1901.
58 'Rook Rifles and Others', *St. James Gazette*, 7 January 1902.
59 'The Rifle Club', *The Oxford Times*, 6 December 1902.
60 [No title], *Volunteer Service Gazette*, 12 December 1902.
61 'The Inauguration of the Jaeger Company's New Miniature Rifle Range', *Volunteer Service Gazette and Military Dispatch*, 20 October 1905.
62 'Rifles for Workers: An Employer Fears Bullets during Strikes', *The Mid-Sussex Times*, 21 October 1902.
63 'Rifle Clubs Popular', *Stroud News and Gloucester County Advertiser*, 29 February 1903.
64 'London Miniature Bisley', *Pall Mall Gazette*, 7 November 1902.
65 'Society of Working Men's Rifle Clubs', *The Graphic*, 3 January 1903.
66 In 1885, General Sir Ian Hamilton published *The Fighting of the Future* in which he advocated the importance of learning the basic skills and techniques of accurate shooting. See R. Bryan Nichols, *Ian Hamilton: A Study in Military Biography and the Literature of War, 1870–1914* (PhD diss., Naylor University, 1969).

67 'The Miniature Bisley', *London Evening Standard*, 24 March 1903.
68 'The Miniature Bisley: Opening of a Novel Competition for Rifle Clubs', *Manchester Courier*, 28 March 1903.
69 [No title], *Volunteer Service Gazette and Military Dispatch*, 6 November 1903.
70 'Official Notices: National Rifle Association', *Volunteer Record & Shooting News*, 28 April 1900.
71 'National Rifle Association', *Sheffield Daily Telegraph*, 28 February 1901.
72 [No title], *Shooting and Fishing: A Journal of the Rifle, Gun and Rod* 30, no. 5 (16 May 1901).
73 'National Rifle Association: Mr. Astor's Munificent Gift: The Rifle Club Movement', *Sheffield Daily Telegraph*, 6 February 1902.
74 [No title], *Shooting and Fishing: A Journal of the Rifle, Gun and Rod* 31, no. 21 (6 March 1902).
75 'National Rifle Association', *Volunteer Service Gazette and Military Dispatch*, 7 February 1902.
76 C. E. Luard, 'Rifle Shooting as a Winter Evening Pursuit', *Journal of the Royal United Service Institution* 47, no. 2, (1903), pp. 1044–1050.
77 Ibid., pp. 1051–1052.
78 Ibid., p. 1053.
79 Ibid., pp. 1054–1055.
80 'Civilian Rifle Shooting', *Exeter and Plymouth Gazette*, 26 January 1904. The article was originally published in *The Daily Telegraph*.
81 Harcourt Ommundsen and Ernest Herbert Robinson, *Rifles and Ammunition and Rifle Shooting* (London: Cassell, 1915), p. 187.
82 Ibid., p. 192.
83 'Cult of the Miniature Rifle: Popularity of Low-Power Practices', *Westminster Gazette*, 28 April 1904.
84 Lord Grey, 'Miniature Rifle Clubs', *The Times*, 29 April 1904.
85 'The Miniature Bisley', *London Evening Standard*, 2 May 1904.
86 Humphry and Freemantle, *History of the National Rifle Association*, p. 433.
87 'Miniature Rifle Shooting', *Westminster Gazette*, 3 November 1904.
88 Lord Norfolk, 'Rifle Shooting as a Winter Evening Pursuit', *The Times*, 4 November 1904.
89 'Occasional Notes', *Pall Mall Gazette*, 4 November 1904.
90 'Rifle Range Gossip', *Pall Mall Gazette*, 26 November 1904.
91 'Miniature Rifle Clubs', *London Evening Standard*, 23 March 1905.
92 'Rifle Range in Hotel Cellar', *Daily Mirror*, 17 January 1906.
93 'Miniature Rifle Shooting', *Volunteer Service Gazette and Military Dispatch*, 3 February 1905.
94 'Municipal Assistance for Air Gunners', *Birmingham Mail*, 19 August 1905.
95 Lord Roberts, 'The Army – As It Was and As It Is', *The Nineteenth Century and After* 57 (January 1905), pp. 1–26.
96 Lord Roberts, 'Rifle Shooting as a National Pursuit', *The Times*, 12 June 1905.
97 Ibid.

98 Arthur Conan Doyle, Lord Meath and Second Baron Ebury, 'Rifle Shooting as a National Pursuit', *The Times*, 14 June 1905; John Seely et al., 'Rifle Shooting as a National Pursuit', *The Times*, 15 June 1905; J. St. Loe Strachey and Robert Yerburgh, 'Rifle Shooting as a National Pursuit', *The Times*, 21 June 1905.
99 'Lord Roberts on Rifle Shooting', *Field*, 17 June 1905.
100 'Rifle Shooting Appeal', *Evening Star*, 27 July 1905.
101 'Society of Miniature Rifle Clubs', *Volunteer Service Gazette and Military Dispatch*, 28 July 1905.
102 'Military Matters', *Globe*, 29 July 1905.
103 Hansard, House of Commons (HC) Debates (Deb), Fourth Series, Vol. 148, Col. 232 (27 June 1905).
104 Lord Meath referenced Lord Roberts's article in *The Nineteenth Century and After*.
105 Hansard, House of the Lords (HL) Debates (Deb), Fourth Series, Vol. 141, Cols. 543–563 (20 February 1905). See also Reginald Brabazon, 12th Earl of Meath and Mary Jane (Maitland) Brabazon Meath, *Thoughts on Imperial and Social Subjects* (London: T. Cardner, Darton & co. ltd, 1906). More generally, on the 1905 debate on universal military training in elementary schools, Alan Penn, *Targeting Schools*, pp. 118–128.
106 'Military Training for Schoolboys: Letter to the Editor of The Times', *The Times*, 1 December 1905.
107 'Lord Roberts Open a Rifle Range', *Lloyd's Weekly Newspaper*, 12 November 1905.
108 'New Miniature Rifle: Warning to the Home Gun Trade', *Birmingham Mail*, 7 September 1905.
109 'The W.O. Miniature Rifle', *Arms & Explosives* 15, no. 178 (July 1907), p. 90.
110 'Memorandum for the Consideration of the Committee of Imperial Defence', quoted in Allison, *The National Service Issue*, pp. 82–83.
111 On the NSL's propaganda methods, see Stearn, 'The Last Glorious Campaign', pp. 316–318.
112 Linehan, *British Fascism*, pp. 22–23.
113 'Lord Roberts and Rifle Clubs', *Volunteer Service Gazette and Military Dispatch*, 26 January 1906.
114 'Magazine for Riflemen', *Western Daily Press*, 11 April 1906.
115 'Society of Miniature Rifle Clubs', *Volunteer Service Gazette and Military Dispatch*, 4 May 1906.
116 'Nation of Riflemen: Societies and Companies All Over the Country Follow Lord Salisbury's Famous Advice', *Daily Mirror*, 30 May 1906.
117 'Promotion of Rifle Shooting. Haldane's Concession', *London Evening Standard*, 7 July 1906.
118 [No title], *Globe*, 21 July 1906.
119 Quoted in Penn, *Targeting Schools*, p. 140.
120 Gertrude Silver, 'An Appeal to the Women of England', *The Times*, 28 July 1906; Gertrude Silver, 'Women and War', *Fortnightly Review* 80 (July–December 1906) (Vol. 86 Old Series), pp. 714–723.

121 'Military Efficiency in Preparatory Rifle Shooting and Drill in Preparatory Schools', *The Public Schools Year Book* (London: Swan Sonneschein & co. Ltd, 1906), pp. 415–424.
122 Ibid., p. 420.
123 *School Government Chronicle* 76 (22 September 1906), p. 239.
124 *The Arbitrator: Organ of the International Arbitration League* 343 (October 1906), p. 48.
125 *The Worker*, Huddersfield Socialist Party, 20 July 1906.
126 Penn, *Targeting Schools*, pp. 134–136.
127 Quotes from both the *Evening Standard* and *The Crown* in 'The Boys' Bisley, *The Herald of Peace and International Arbitration*'. Published under the auspices of the Peace Society, 1 September 1906, pp. 265–266.
128 'Notes of the Week', *Volunteer Service Gazette and Military Dispatch*, 30 October 1907.
129 'Aid for Rifle Clubs: Promise of Million Rounds of Ammunition', *Birmingham Daily Gazette*, 17 January 1907.
130 'Concession to Riflemen', *Nottingham Evening Post*, 11 November 1907.
131 'Open to All Who Shoot', *Daily Mirror*, 26 June 1907.
132 'The Queen and Her Cup', *The Graphic*, 27 July 1907.
133 '"Boys'" Bisley: Prize Shooting', *Westminster Gazette*, 2 August 1907.
134 'The Rifle Shooting Exhibition', *Woolwich Gazette*, 8 May 1908.
135 'National Safety: Up-to-Date Rifle Shooting', *Daily Telegraph & Courier* (London), 15 November 1907.
136 Edward James D. Newitt, *The Citizen Rifleman* (London: George Newnes, 1906).
137 'Civilian Rifle Clubs', *Globe*, 30 May 1907.
138 'Youthful Marksmen', *Hastings and St Leonards Observer*, 25 May 1907.
139 'Miniature Rifle Clubs', *The Westminster Review* 167, no. 1 (1907), pp. 35–40, at p. 35.
140 'Last Night's News Items', *Daily Mirror*, 4 July 1907.
141 'Rifle Shooting Encouragement Fund: Balance Sheet', *Evening Mail*, 14 February 1908.
142 'To-Day', *Daily Telegraph & Courier* (London), 25 February 1908.
143 'Short Range Shooting', *Morning Post*, 3 June 1908.
144 Henry Page Croft, 'A Citizen Army', in Lord Malmesbury (ed.), *The New Order: Studies in Unionist Policy* (London Francis Griffiths, 1908), pp. 255–268.
145 'Frontiersmen Using German Cartridges', *Birmingham Daily Gazette*, 20 March 1908. On the Legion of Frontiersmen, Humphries, 'The Eyes of an Empire'.
146 German producers generally used between seven and eight grains, 80 per cent of which was fulminate.
147 'German Ammunition: Foreign Cartridges Used by Rifle Clubs: A Hint to the War Office', *Globe*, 23 March 1908.

148 'Ammunition for Rifle Clubs', *Morning Post*, 13 October 1908; 'Rifle Clubs and German Ammunition', *The Scotsman*, 14 January 1909; 'German Cartridges for British Rifle Clubs', *Globe*, 20 January 1909; 'The World, the Flesh and the Devil', *John Bull*, 5 June 1909.
149 'German Ammunition for British Rifle Clubs', *Morning Post*, 1 October 1908; 'A Manufacturers' Letter', *Globe*, 22 January 1909.
150 'The Advantage to the Foreigner', *Globe*, 18 January 1909.
151 'Miniature Rifle', *Morning Post*, 3 April 1903.
152 Ommundsen and Robinson, *Rifles and Ammunition*, p. 193.
153 The National Archives (TNA): WO 32/9087, General and Warlike Stores: Small Arms (Code 45(J)): Proceedings of Miniature Rifle Committee Permission to manufacture.
154 'Grievance of the Gun Trade: Complaints against Rifle Club's Society', *Birmingham Daily Gazette*, 3 April 1908.
155 'Gun Trade Grievance: Reply from the Miniature Rifle Clubs Society', *Birmingham Daily Gazette*, 4 April 1908.
156 'Society for Miniature Rifle Club', *Sporting Life*, 3 June 1908.
157 Ommundsen and Robinson, *Rifles and Ammunition*, p. 197. In 1912, at the annual general meeting of shareholders in the Birmingham Small Arms Company, it was stated that 'Business in our sporting and miniature rifles still shows steady growth, and the demand for the B.S.A air rifle, especially abroad, has exceeded our expectations; new market has been opened up, and we now regard this as a steady, permanent trade'. See also 'Birmingham Small Arms Company, Limited', *Economist*, 5 October 1912, p. 636.
158 'Miniature Rifle Clubs', *Globe*, 2 October 1908. On the Territorial Army, see Peter Dennis, *Territorial Army, 1906–1940* (Woodbridge: Royal Historical Society, 1987).
159 'Major Morrison Opens Sidmouth M.R.C. Range', *Exeter and Plymouth Gazette*, 6 November 1908.
160 See, generally, Adams and Poirier, *The Conscription Controversy*, pp. 39–41.
161 Stearn, 'The Last Glorious Campaign', pp. 322–323.
162 William Le Queux and Herbert Wrigley Wilson, *The Invasion of 1910: With a Full Account of the Siege of London*, Introductory Letter by Field-Marshal Earl Roberts (London: E. Nash, 1906). On fictional depictions of war and invasions in late Victorian and Edwardian Britain, see Christian K. Melby, 'Empire and Nation in British Future War and Invasion-Scare Fiction, 1871–1914', *The Historical Journal* 63, no. 2 (2020), pp. 389–410; Michael Hughes and Harry Wood, 'Crimson Nightmares: Tales of Invasion and Fears of Revolution in Early Twentieth-Century Britain', *Contemporary British History* 28 (2014), pp. 294–317.
163 Allison, *The National Service Issue*, p. 114.
164 Denis Hayes, *Conscription Conflict: The Conflict of Ideas in the Struggle for and Against Military Conscription in Britain between 1901 and 1939* (New York: Garland, 1973), p. 109.
165 Ibid., pp. 111–122.

166 Robert Blatchford, *Germany and England: The War That Was Foretold* (New York: Edward J. Clode, 1914).
167 On the concept of bellicism, see Michael Howard, *The Causes of War and Other Essays* (London: Unwin, 1984). On the 'literature of the next war', see Ignatius F. Clarke, *Voices Prophesying War: Future War 1763–1984* (Oxford: Oxford University Press, 1966).
168 'Rifle Shots', *Chard and Ilminster News*, 12 December 1908.
169 '100,000 Riflemen: Bob's Appeal Answered', *Hull Daily Mail*, 3 February 1909.
170 'Rifle Club's Record: Members Ask for Military Status in Wartime', *Leeds Mercury*, 28 May 1909.
171 'Rifle Shots', *Chard and Ilminster News*, Saturday 5 June 1909.
172 N. F. Fleming, 'The *Imperial Maritime League: British Navalism, Conflict, and the Radical Right, c.1907–1920*', *War in History* 23, no. 3 (2016), pp. 296–322. See also N. F. Fleming, 'Navalism and Masculinity Before the First World War', in Karen Downing et al. (eds), *Negotiating Masculinities and Modernity in the Maritime World, 1815–1940* (New York: Palgrave Macmillan, 2021), pp. 245–265.
173 'British Preferred', *Manchester Evening News*, 20 May 1909.
174 'The Supposed German Arsenal: Mystery Solved', *Globe*, 26 May 1909.
175 'Society of Miniature Rifle Clubs', *John Bull*, 17 July 1909.
176 'Miniature Rifle Shooting', *Chard and Ilminster News*, 22 January 1910.
177 'What the Society of Miniature Rifles Really Is', *The Rifleman*, February 1910.
178 Ibid., July 1910.
179 'Empire Rifle Contest', *Daily Mirror*, 4 July 1910.
180 'A New Shooting Contest', *Northern Whig*, 4 July 1910.
181 'The Handbook and Calendar for 1912 of the Society of Miniature Rifle Clubs', published by the Society at Arundel House, Arundel Street, London, 1912.
182 'All-Ireland Miniature Rifle Meeting at Ballsbridge', *Dublin Daily Express*, 15 February 1910.
183 'Kingsbridge Miniature Rifle Club', *Northern Whig*, 5 August 1912.
184 'Rifle Club Movement', *Belfast News-Letter*, 16 August 1912.
185 'Rifle Clubs Prohibited', *Globe*, 27 August 1913.
186 'Ulster's Preparations: The Government and the Rifle Club', *Pall Mall Gazette*, 29 August 1913.
187 'Ulster Rifle Clubs: Defiance of Irish Executive', *Dublin Daily Express*, 24 September 1913.
188 On Unionist clubs affiliated to the NRA and SMRC, see Bowman, *Carson's Army*, pp. 21–22.
189 'The Handbook and Calendar for 1914 of the Society of Miniature Rifle Clubs', published by the Society at Arundel House, Arundel Street, London, 1914.
190 'Every Man Must Learn to Shoot', *Dundee Evening Telegraph*, 12 August 1914.
191 'Miniature Rifle Clubs and Service', *The Scotsman*, 21 August 1914.

192 'Lord Roberts and Rifle Clubs', *Berwickshire News and General Advertiser*, 22 September 1914.
193 Ommundsen and Robinson, *Rifles and Ammunition*, p. 190.
194 Greener, *Sharpshooting for Sport and War*, p. 153.
195 'The Rifle Club Mania', *Navy & Army Illustrated* 12, no. 219 (18 April 1901), p. 74.

2

Custodians of the Empire: the Legion of Frontiersmen, 1904–1914

We preach in advance of the Army,
We skirmish ahead of the Church,
With never a gunboat to help us
When we're scuppered and left in the lurch.
But we know as the cartridges finish,
And we're filed on our last little shelves,
That the Legion that never was 'listed
Will send us as good as ourselves. (Rudyard Kipling, *The Lost Legion*, 1895)

The old spirit [of the tribal ancestors of the English] moves us to migrate,
we burn still with untamable, inextinguishable savagery, abhorring walls,
and roof – the entire house of civilized restraint. We ask, we adventurers, the
earth for our bed, the stars for our clock, the morning chill for our reveille,
the ends of the earth for our portion,
and in the path of our world-grabbing savagery the shuttles of Fate are
weaving the fabric of Empire. (Roger Pocock, 1906)

The Boer War brought into dramatic relief the problem of imperial overstretch. The search for new schemes and strategies for protecting the Empire from external aggression and securing its uncertain frontiers became increasingly urgent. As a result, Conservative ranks found themselves caught between a party increasingly exposed to the pressures of committed conscriptionists and influential Navy advocates, and an electorate traditionally hostile to experiments in military compulsion and large military spending. For most of the conservative public, the obvious deficiencies of the British voluntary system could be remedied by reigniting the duty of every citizen to take his full share of responsibility in the work of imperial defence. The logical corollary of this sense of 'patriotic obligation' was the formation of military or quasi-military organisations, which, both in peacetime and in situations of armed conflict, had the avowed purpose of assisting the regular forces of the Crown. A typical and perhaps one of the most extravagant examples of this popular or grassroots militarism was the Legion of

Frontiersmen.¹ Founded in 1905 by writer and adventurer Roger Pocock, this paramilitary force was originally aimed at recruiting men with previous military training and experience in hunting in the wild or just a keen taste for adventure to carry out intelligence and reconnaissance (scouting) operations in the service of the Army in the event of an emergency. 'A special force for seeing and hearing, a Field Intelligence Corps', as Pocock put it.² This chapter reconstructs the organisational features of this private body, which claimed the right to organise, equip and train citizens for home and imperial defence. It traces the Legion's attempt to popularise essential military knowledge through the 'public staging' of field exercises and through manoeuvres, often conducted under simulated combat conditions, and by promoting practice in the use of weapons. It also examines the persistent efforts of the Legion to provide all male Britons with access to instruction in the skills, tactics and techniques necessary for survival in the most remote and inhospitable regions of the Empire. Instruction in frontier skills was provided to the male public not only for the purposes of imperial defence, but also as an antidote to the 'impotency' of bourgeois masculinity. The press regularly reiterated that the Legion of Frontiersmen was for those men who, in the 'waste places of the earth' and in war, had found their manhood. Finally, although historians have emphasised that the Legion cultivated an apolitical image and included members with diverse political views – such as the radical and pacifist Sir Francis Vane – this chapter demonstrates that, at least after 1909, the Legion experienced a noticeable rightward shift in its ranks.³ Some frontiersmen formed ties with right-wing political organisations, providing uniformed stewards for their meetings and rallies. Others engaged in murky mercenary or 'filibustering' activities. Nearly all opposed the Irish Home Rule, and some even offered to assist and fight alongside the Ulsterites in their resistance. Against this background, by 1914, the Legion had acquired a global membership of ten thousand, making it Britain's largest irregular, self-governed military organisation.

The dream-come-true army

In 1904, Pocock conceived the idea of establishing a Legion of Frontiersmen to defend the Empire.⁴ Poor military intelligence and the serious logistical problems encountered by British troops during the Boer War had provided him with inspiration. Pocock also reflected on how the particular skills of the 'frontiersmen' (men who had lived and fought in the furthest outposts of the Empire) in collecting, processing and evaluating information on foreign territories had been entirely misapplied in the Veldt:

We tumbled over each other to get to the last campaign, not as Frontiersmen of some small usefulness in guerrilla service, but as soldiers, the professionals of war. Outnumbering the Boers, we Frontiersmen of the Empire, instead of beating them at their own game, frittered away our strength playing at soldiers, imitating Tommy. It is with no grudge, but with loving admiration, that we own up now how well he knew his business. We could have helped him more had we come not as amateurs, but as intelligence agents, as guides, as scouts, as pioneers, as horsemen for flying raids, with our own leaders and organisation, our own methods, tools and weapons, a corps of Frontiersmen, to help the Army in bringing the war to a swifter, more decisive, and more merciful ending.[5]

The first shots of these 'Rough Riders of the British Empire' were not fired, as Pocock might have wished, under a sky lit by the blaze of battle, but in the conservative protectionist press. At the beginning of April 1905, while fanning the flames of tariff agitation, the *Daily Express*, the *Daily Mail* and other London daily papers announced that a meeting had been convened at Lord Lonsdale's private residence for the purpose of organising a civilian intelligence service.[6] Letters apparently approving the project were received from a distinguished body of soldiers, including Admiral Sir William Robert Kennedy, General Sir Redvers Buller, General John French, General Reginald Pole-Carew, Lord Methuen and Lord Tweedmouth. On 10 April, in the presence of several peers, Conservative Members of Parliament, military officers, war correspondents and explorers, the Legion of Frontiersmen was officially inaugurated. The organisation, which was named in prosaic reference to Rudyard Kipling's poem *The Lost Legion*, aimed to promote imperial interests in times of peace and mobilise for imperial defence when the God of war called for sacrifice. To these ends, the Legion intended to recruit 'men trained and qualified by previous military service, or by working in wild countries, or at sea, who, for various reasons, do not or cannot serve in the existing Military Forces of the Empire'.[7] The organisers and others who expressed support for the Legion were convinced that there was a substantial and still largely untapped reservoir of men whose experience and training made them particularly fitted for military pursuits. This 'splendid fighting material' was expected to act as an auxiliary force and help the Army to avert calamities such as those that had occurred in the Boer War. More specifically, the frontiersmen, when fully organised, could be deployed as guides, pioneers, scouts, mounted infantry, saboteurs and spies. The Legion's peacetime activities would revolve around sports and games that afforded training for war, including the martial arts, horse riding and shooting.[8] Driving this preparedness was the widespread apprehension, if not outright alarm, among the frontiersmen (and their backers) that

Britain might become entangled in a major European war. 'We frontiersmen', Pocock emphatically stated in the summer of 1905, 'have subdued the wilderness, and there is little wilderness left us to conquer, so that our usefulness is coming to an end, except in the defence of that Empire which we have helped to found'.[9]

Five days after the inaugural meeting, in a letter to Frederick White, Comptroller of the Royal North-West Mounted Police, Pocock declared that the idea of a 'civilian, self-supporting and self-reliant' legion was influenced by his experience as a trooper in the North-West police. 'I confess', Pocock said, 'that the whole project of the Legion is a device for catching and holding in the service of the Empire, ex-policemen of all Police outfits like myself. We are all intolerant of British tactics of surrender, and strategy of flight, as we saw them when we fought in South Africa'. Opposed to stiff posturing and drill books, the frontiersmen were to be completely independent of the War Office or any government subsidy. 'If we fight again for the Empire, we must have our own organisation, our own methods, not those of any civilized army', Pocock concluded, in tribute to the traditional philosophy of citizen soldiering. White replied with courteous scepticism that the raising of an armed force outside the regular military chain of command, no matter how patriotic and willing to serve the Empire it might be, would encounter 'insurmountable difficulties, particularly during an extended period of peace'. The obstacles to official recognition and a fear of deadlock gave the Legion cause for concern.[10]

To draw the public's attention, Lord Lonsdale, explorer, hunter, master of foxhounds and colonel of the Westmorland and Cumberland Yeomanry, was placed at the head of the Legion. Having gained as much fame for his intrepid expedition from Prince Patrick Island to the Pacific as notoriety for his philandering, Lonsdale was entrusted with nominating a committee for the purpose of advancing and administering the organisation of the new force. He appointed Conservative MP Henry Seton-Karr – a member of the NL, protectionist, big-game trophy collector and organiser of yeomanry regiments – as chairman of the executive council. Future British fascist Major Lord Brudenell-Bruce was placed at the helm of the finance committee, while Colonel William Charles Eldon Serjeant – a barrister and veteran of the Boer War – was nominated general adviser to the council. Many renowned names appeared to have embraced the Legion in some sort of official capacity, including the Earl of Meath, the Earl of Onslow, Viscount Esher, Lord William Seymour, General Michael Rimington and Prince Louis of Battenberg, the latter having previously received from Pocock intelligence regarding the Russian naval base of Libau.[11]

At the end of June 1905, a Legion Club was inaugurated at the Red Lion tavern in Fleet Street, London. 'The gathering', a correspondent of *Lloyd's*

Figure 2.1 *The Sketch*, 12 July 1905. Image © Mary Evans Picture Library

Weekly wrote, was a very 'picturesque one'. Some of the participants, including Pocock, wore the Legion's uniform of grey shirt and trousers, yellow neckerchief, boots with spurs and a Baden-Powell hat with a wide leopard-skin band; a revolver in a holster and a bandolier around waist completed the attire. There was also a display of badges, insignia and medals earned by frontiersmen in various conflicts and battles.[12] Meanwhile, Pocock's patriotic plan to gather all those men who were 'hunting for trouble' instead of indulging themselves in the comforts of civilised life, was attracting new supporters. Commands of the Legion were announced during organisational tours around the country.

Despite a steady stream of illustrious endorsements and martial enthusiasm, the growth of the Legion was nonetheless hampered by financial insecurity. Furthermore, Pocock and other organisers, who came mostly from Conservative ranks, feared that the new Liberal government would be less friendly or even hostile to their organisation.[13] In December 1905, following legal advice, the Legion began seeking formal sanction from the authorities. Certain provisions of the Foreign Enlistment Act (1870) made it *de facto* unlawful to enrol members and charge them subscription fees without the approval of the Crown. After several attempts, a delegation of frontiersmen was finally allowed to plead their case before the newly formed Army Council. At the hearing, Sir Neville Lyttelton, the Chief of the General Staff, enquired as to what the Legion would do in case of war with Germany, to which a spirited Pocock replied 'Blow up the Kiel Canal, Sir!'[14] On 15 February 1906, the War Office replied to the Legion's request for recognition as follows:

> The Secretary of State for War desires me to inform you that he is in sympathy with the aims and objects of the above Legion and the formation of an organization on the lines suggested appears to him to be free of difficulty. Mr. Haldane also requests me to state that he thinks the Legion well advised as regards its principles of organization, set forth in paragraph 4 of the private and confidential circular which you have submitted, providing that 'the Association shall be self-governing and self-supporting, in time of peace'. He, therefore, recognises the Legion as a purely private organization, in no way connected with any department of State, but one which, should a suitable occasion arise, [...] he might be able to utilise.[15]

Predictably enough, this clumsily worded response was susceptible to misinterpretation. The frontiersmen opportunistically announced through the press that the Legion had been approved by the Secretary of State for War, obliging War Office representatives to point out that the Legion, being a private body, had not received official sanction nor recognition from the government. Common law allowed a man to arm himself and assemble his friends in defence of his house, but no more. Raising an organisation for the purpose of military training, including the use of firearms, was therefore patently illegal. However, wearing a uniform in public places, unless it entailed serious disturbance, was permissible. The War Office drew attention to the fact that Haldane had only 'taken cognizance' of the Legion's aims and objects, although the clarification fell on deaf ears.[16]

After Haldane's cordial but indefinite expression of sympathy, the Legion markedly increased its organisational efforts and established its central headquarters in London at 6 Adam Street. In the April 1906 issue of *The Fortnightly Review*, Pocock gave a wildly optimistic view of the workings of the Legion and its potential recruiting field, estimating that the organisation could reach a pool of six hundred and twenty thousand men in the Empire. Of these, only a twentieth would be entitled to wear the frontiersman's badge, which displayed the Union Jack charged on the cross of St George and the text 'God guard thee', these being the words on General Gordon's signet ring. Pocock added that 'the citizen unwilling to fight for home defence is not a man, but only a social error'. In this respect, the Legion offered nothing but 'what the State had the right to demand, the fitness of every citizen for war'. This service was, of course, to be paid for without dipping into the taxpayer's purse. With the aim of making the Legion financially self-sufficient, three classes of membership were offered, each with an annual fee: Class A was formed of members who 'pledged military service'; Class B, 'members qualified but not pledged'; and Class C, 'Honorary – not qualified for military service'. To supplement the individual subscriptions, local councils and commands were invited to raise funds by 'donations, grants from municipalities or employers, profits from indoor entertainment or outdoor sports, or any means short of larceny'. As had been previously announced, military sports and exhibitions in frontier skills would form the bulk of the Legion's activities in times of peace. Packing, riding and shooting competitions and other military exercises served not only for the amusement of members, but also as a means of selecting the fittest guides, scouts, troopers and pioneers. While the ordinary method of training soldiers was drill and discipline, the frontiersmen would be trained in close association with entertainment. In the matter of equipment, the Legion would, as far as funds permitted, provide horses, ranges, rifles and all materials. In case of war, as Pocock put it in a flight of poetic imagination, Legion squadrons would gather topographical intelligence and carry out attacks on the enemy's rear installations.[17]

At around the same time, the ubiquitous Sir Arthur Conan Doyle, who was a member of the general council, suggested that the Legion would appeal to Britain's motorists. Motor cars, which had been noticeably present in his latest detective stories, represented a potential asset for swift coastal defence. Should fears of invasion morph into a concrete threat, he wrote in *The Times*, thousands of motorists 'could instantly fill up their cars with picked riflemen drawn from their own immediate neighbourhood, and convey them with a week's food, their rifles, and their ammunition to the danger point'. The government was expected to provide two thousand rounds of ammunition to each motorist. In his recommendations, Conan Doyle may have been impressed by the continental armies' use of motor cars in manoeuvres, training and other exercises.[18] In France, Automobiles Charron, Girardot & Voigt (CGV), for instance, had manufactured a car fitted with a rapid firing Hotchkiss gun mounted in a revolving turret. In Germany, a four-cylinder Opel-Darracq car covered with 6 mm Krupp steel armour and fitted with two Mauser guns was tested in 1903.

The magazine *The Car: A Journal of Travel by Land, Sea & Air*, edited by Lord Montagu of Beaulieu, expressed interest in Conan Doyle's idea and arranged to interview Pocock. The Legion's founder explained that the organisation was talking with the foremost motorist associations of the kingdom to determine the feasibility of the coastal defence scheme. He stressed that the frontiersmen would not transport troops to avoid interfering with the government, but would engage essentially in reconnaissance work. In this connection, the Legion might use cars for the purpose of 'carrying explosives by which to blow up bridges in the enemy's rear, and so cut off his supplies'. Pocock also said that motor vehicles could easily convey Rexer automatic machine guns given their portability and lightness. This recoil-operated weapon weighed only 17.5 lb (about 60 lb less than other machine guns) and had a firing rate of three hundred rounds per minute. When not in use, the two legs forming its support could be easily folded back against the barrel. According to Pocock, the Rexer could be used 'from behind a hedgerow, whilst the car retired behind the hill'.[19]

While speculations on the military side of the Legion abounded, M. H. De Hora was appointed as London's commandant of the Legion of Frontiersmen and was assisted in this role by J. C. Best, a veteran of the Indian Mutiny of 1857. Like Pocock, De Hora had been many things in his life: cowboy, scout, explorer, seaman, pearl diver, mining engineer and guerrilla fighter in various South American campaigns. If it was indeed true that the War Office had recognised the Legion, someone suspiciously observed, De Hora was the only American citizen in charge of a fighting unit of the British army.[20] Nonetheless, the appointment of men like De Hora prompted the conservative press to call the Legion 'the most romantic body of men in the world'.[21] Certainly, the biographies of some of the most famous frontiersmen abounded with daring and dazzling feats. Harry de Windt had explored almost every corner of the world, and the 'hunger and filth' he had endured in his voyages was described in highly popular books published at the beginning of the century. Captain de Crespigny was a famous steeplechase rider and hunter, whose life was replete with brushes with death, and it was said of him that no other living man had more broken bones. C. J. Cutcliffe Hyne was another intrepid frontiersman, whose splendid imagination gave birth to the mythical continent of Atlantis. Another novelist bitten by the bug of imperial defence was Morley Roberts, who had been a sailor before the mast and had tramped the world from the Sandwich Islands to Manitoba. Conan Doyle, Sir Henry Rider Haggard and other frontiersmen had similarly explored the most remote corners of the world and had engaged in all kinds of adventurous employment.

At the beginning of summer 1906, the Legion offered to place a contingent of five hundred frontiersmen at the disposal of the Natal government in the event the Bambatha Rebellion should spread. However, this 'jingoist proposition' met with many obstacles. Reservations were held concerning whether members would be allowed to carry arms and ammunition without a licence, although frontiersmen did carry guns in public. Inquiries were made to Whitehall and officials answered that the only possible way in which an organisation like the Legion could legally train in the use of firearms or other weapons was as a rifle club, which could, as we have seen, be legitimately organised by private effort. Predictably, requests by the Legion to purchase ammunition for target practice at reduced rates were refused by the authorities on the grounds that the organisation was not affiliated to the NRA.[22] These legal complications drove many frontiersmen to the join the most accessible ranks of the SMRC.

Official attitudes poured a certain amount of cold water on Pocock's enthusiasm. Nevertheless, in a provocative interview given to the *Pall Mall Gazette*, he again stated that if the Legion had been formed before the Boer War, 'we would have saved two years' fighting'. It was the lack of an intelligence branch of the army in the field that had prolonged the hostilities. Adding to this display of narcissism, Pocock informed the interviewer of his intention to form 'maritime and motorcar branches' of the Legion. The latter would see car owners proceeding to the 'seat of war' with the aim of assisting in rear operations, while the former would be formed of yachtsmen for service as 'raiders and pioneers afloat'.[23] At the end of the year, steps were finally taken to form a 'maritime branch' of seafarers, who were expected to serve, either ashore or afloat, in case of war.[24] This scheme of a 'coastal reserve' was later endorsed and enthusiastically supported by the former Conservative MP for Woodbridge (and future member for Chelmsford), Captain Ernest George Pretyman.[25]

Given that the Legion was hampered by want of funds, these plans appeared more like exercises in imagination. To deal with its financial difficulties, the Legion arranged a fundraising event at the Royal Botanic Society's Gardens, which included the performance of a one-act play (*The Open Door*) by dramatist Alfred Sutro, an exhibition of the School of Ju-jitsu and a pastoral performance of Act V of *A Midsummer Night's Dream*. Participants sang a song composed for the Legion by actor Edward Sass titled 'Frontiersmen', which went like this:

> Out from the woods of the great North-east,
> Under the Austral Sky,
> From the South and the North, they'll all come forth
> At the sound of the Mother's cry!
> And each at his post, where the danger is most,
> Will stand as a sentry then:
> Britishers all, to stand or to fall,
> The Empire's Frontiersmen.

After the theatrical and variety entertainments, the frontiersmen reproduced a bivouac. At the end of this *mise-en-scène*, Lord Lonsdale declared 'I feel, like Mr. Haldane, that if the Army must be reduced, the British nation can be trusted. There are others ready to defend the Empire'.[26]

Meanwhile, an assortment of variously uniformed commands sprang up across the country. A local command of the Legion was formed in Newcastle on the initiative of military figures. The inaugural committee recommended a uniform that was to be generally adopted, which consisted of a pair of riding breeches, a light blue shirt, a black scarf and the classic Baden-Powell hat. In addition, each member was armed with a revolver and had to wear a distinctive badge bearing the inscription *Mitis et Fortis* (Meek and Strong). Land for drilling and training was found at Whitley Bay, a seaside town near the mouth of the Tyne, while representatives of a local shipping firm even guaranteed free passage to all members who volunteered to go to Natal.[27] A command was also inaugurated in Manchester in the presence of military historian and Conservative politician, Sir Lees Knowles. About twenty persons enrolled. Members were expected to wear khaki breeches, a khaki shirt with sewn-on red neckband, shoulder straps and wristbands and puttees. It was distinctly understood that hierarchies in the command were not a question of social standing.[28] In Birmingham, about fifty 'patriots' attended the inauguration of the local command, asserting the citizens' right to form in their own way and under their own authority a military unit for the defence of the Empire. The chosen uniform was a green flannel shirt, green cord breeches and a green slouch hat.[29] At the first gathering of the Leeds Command, Pocock, who was attired in complete frontiersman rig, boasted: 'Eighteen or twenty months ago, it was thought a wild-cat scheme. It is not a wild-cat scheme now: it is an army on which the sun never sets'.[30] Addressing the recently formed Bradford Command, Cutcliffe Hyne said that the Legion had been formed because Great Britain was vulnerable to foreign attacks, and one of the causes of this 'frailty' was the lack of love that many, perhaps too many, Englishmen had for their own country. The frontiersmen's self-understanding as 'citizen soldiers from the outposts', who had banded together to protect the Empire as much from external enemies as from individualistic and unpatriotic tendencies within society, became an explicit leitmotif. The *Daily Express*, which was wholeheartedly sympathetic to the Legion's cause, wrote that '[the game of the frontier] is loathed and feared by the Little Englander, the ultra-humanitarian, the advocate of Indian sedition and Irish riot, of Socialist disloyalty and of general discontent, for it keeps alive the spirit that has made England what she is, and fosters the determination to maintain her as such at all costs'.[31]

Since its inception, the Legion's lack of formal recognition effectively prevented it from organising regular, systematic training for its members. Instead, it arranged periodical rides and certain forms of military exercises. From time to time, these 'militaristic stunts' turned into melodramatic fiascos. For instance, the widely advertised competition between two teams of frontiersmen to pack-ride from Charing Cross to Brighton and back finished in embarrassment when both teams failed to return to London in the allotted time, drawing widespread mockery in the press. It was said that the immoderately extravagant apparel of the 'cavalcade' – Mexican saddles, slouch hats, boots and spurs, glittering burnishers and snazzy yellow handkerchiefs – had caused some inattentive bystanders to ask if the circus had come to town. 'Evidently regarding the parade as a picnic', the *Daily Mirror* sardonically wrote, 'the horses demanded oatmeal and water at every likely inn'. In response to these defamatory insinuations of insobriety, an offended Pocock wrote that the legion 'has got to be taken seriously [...] it is not a joke'.[32] Evidently, there was no room for drunkards in the ranks of the Legion, and this despite Pocock's scandalous praise of 'hopeless drunkards' in battle.[33]

Right after the Brighton ride, another similar challenge was planned – this time from Birmingham to Leicester – to prove that it was possible for horses to be ridden one hundred miles in a day. Colonel James Magnus, from the Seventh (Manchester Artillery) Volunteer Artillery, acerbically commented that frontiersmen were 'heroes who wanted to be patriots with no trouble, no expense, no discipline. They would not be the slightest use in time of war ... and might consider themselves jolly lucky if they were shot by the enemy instead of by themselves'. Magnus, who deplored the lack of military spirit in the middle classes, suggested that the ablest and fittest frontiersmen should think about enlisting in the reserve forces, while the others could continue playing 'Buffalo Bill upon the highways and byways'.[34]

In order to acquire a new, more respectable and more respected status, the Legion regularly participated in patriotic demonstrations and celebrations such as Empire Day and Trafalgar Day. They were also present at the annual commemorations of soldiers fallen in the Boer War. In Birmingham, for instance, the Legion of Frontiersmen gathered with the Birmingham Association of South African Service Men, veterans of the Crimean War and men of the Naval Brigade for a memorial ceremony at Cannon Hill Park.[35] Mounted frontiersmen frequently supplied military escorts for burials of deceased veterans. Invariably suspicious of any manifestation of military patriotism, the socialist *Labour Leader* teasingly commented that a 'troop of warriors, with the fire of patriotism burning fiercely within their Imperialistic bosoms [...] have determined to save the British Empire from the machinations of its foe, and to protect it from each and from every invader [...]. With Lord Lonsdale as Field Marshal of the[se] Buffalo Bills we are safe at last'.[36]

Commentators on military affairs sometimes expressed concern that the Legion's popularity, like that of the rifle clubs, could draw recruits away from the Militia and Volunteers. In response, Pocock, in a conversation with a *Manchester Evening News* reporter, underscored the value and limitations of the Legion, stressing that it would not interfere with any of the existing forces as it enrolled mostly veterans, explorers, hunters and sailors:

> We must not take ourselves too seriously. The functions of guides, scouts, pioneers, and swift horsemen do not replace those of an army, and they have not been thought important enough to be paid for as valued service apart from the main work of a field force. To produce these services as the work of an arm of the forces would cost some millions of pounds a year, money better spent on the main purpose of war which is fighting. Our only value is that we can organize such services at no cost of the State in time of peace.[37]

By late 1907, the Legion appeared to have gathered momentum, with several commands already in place or in the process of being set up in the United Kingdom and the colonies. An Irish Command was formed in Dublin with the Southern Unionist MP James Campbell presiding over the inaugural meeting.[38] In Glasgow, after a reading of General Aleksey Kuropatkin's book on the Russo-Japanese war, Lieutenant Colonel Verner concluded that military victory could not be achieved by the army alone – it must have the nation behind it. He had therefore decided to form a command of frontiersmen.[39] Public meetings were held for the purpose of promoting branches of

Figure 2.2 Frontiersmen passing Coulsdon on their ride to Brighton. *The Bystander*, 5 September 1906.
Image © Mary Evans Picture Library

the Legion in Cambridge, Cardiff, Gloucester, Grimsby, Malvern, Stafford, Wigan and York.

At this stage, the Legion's total membership was a little under two thousand men, of whom over one thousand were pledged to active service. Its 1907 annual report, which was presented at the first general meeting, offers valuable insights into the Legion's recruitment and membership. The records of two hundred members – ostensibly selected at random – showed that their average age was thirty-three, 146 had served in the army, while others had volunteered or rendered voluntary service under a foreign flag. Many had been awarded commissions and decorations for their conduct. Regarding their professional and personal qualifications, the records showed that:

> Twenty-Four of them have had the valuable emergency training of frontier mounted police; there are 46 cowboys and stock-riders, including 20 horsebreakers and rough-riders, 44 men have been hunters, 12 trappers, eight voyagers, 22 freighters and mail-riders, 26 explorers, 40 prospectors and miners, 38 had sea-training, and 40 are qualified in various branches of engineering. Fourteen have been guides, 14 foresters, 16 lumbermen, 12 packers, eight special correspondents, six doctors.

Many frontiersmen spoke foreign languages, from Hindustani, Chinese and Swahili to French, German and Russian. However, while military experience and skills abounded, the Legion's operational perspectives appear to have been unsatisfactory. The report lamented the fact that many of the commands raised around Britain 'were still weak in numbers and cannot, at the present, all be taken seriously as effective units'. Many needed horses, arms and ammunition. Scarcely any groundwork had been laid for a well-organised transport system, although Colonel Mark Meyhew of the Army Motor Reserve (Volunteer Motor Corps) was forming a 'motor-car branch'. All this meant that the organisation was still unable to raise 'a complete field intelligence corp'. The situation was further complicated by financial concerns. The published balance sheet showed receipts of £1,033 10s and a balance in hand of £36 16s 8d.[40]

The lack of facilities and equipment might have driven some frontiersmen to procure them in some other manner. The appointment of the organiser and commanding officer of Driscoll's scouts in the Boer War, Colonel Daniel P. Driscoll, as the head of the London Command certainly helped win the confidence of some high-ranking military officers. And so the first 'Legion camp' was held in the spring of 1907 at the invitation of General Sir Henry Rundle, general officer commanding the North-Eastern District, in York. On that occasion, a Legion scout delivered a lecture on reconnaissance and scouting to the general staff.[41] In the county borough of Hanley,

Staffordshire, the frontiersmen joined the Volunteers and Yeomanry in a military tournament that included 'tent pegging, pushball, lemon cutting, obstacle races, artillery competitions, physical drill and gymnastics display, and a tug of war'. The event concluded with the simulation of a battle engagement.[42] In Newcastle, Colonel H. A. Erskine, Third Volunteer Battalion Northumberland Fusiliers, authorised the Legion to train in St George's Drill Hall.[43] At Cheltenham, a revolver range was placed at the disposal of the members of the local command by the Captain of the Second Volunteer Battalion, Gloucestershire Regiment.[44] Occasionally, frontiersmen, in particular the London, Northern and Yorkshire commands, were permitted to join Territorial battalions in local manoeuvres, field exercises and target practice.[45] In the summer of 1909, some fifty representatives of the Northern Command of the Legion of Frontiersmen attended the second Northumberland Territorial Infantry Brigade camp.[46] Not surprisingly, this collaboration between active members of the regular and auxiliary land forces of the Crown and an unlawful paramilitary formation irritated the War Office. A new paragraph was specifically added to The King's regulations and orders for the army (449a), which stated:

> In order that the privileges granted to recognized units shall not lose their value by being granted to unrecognized bodies, no one on the active list of the army as defined in para. 1 is permitted, without the express sanction of the Army Council, to take official cognizance of or to assist officially any private association which is not recognized by the Army Council as forming part of the army or of the educational and training establishments supplementary thereto.[47]

In September 1910, the War Office warned the Legion that these amendments to the King's regulations 'operate as a bar to the grant by local military authorities of facilities to the members of the Legion of Frontiersmen for association with any of the forces comprised in the Army in military drill, parades, or tactical exercises'.[48]

Naturally, questions and doubts as to the nature of the Legion were not confined to Whitehall. The *Globe* correspondent on military matters commented that it could easily become 'a thorn in the side of authorities and the cause of awkward complications if permitted too free a hand'.[49] Similarly, the Labour MP (later Minister of Labour) George H. Roberts said before the House of Commons that he found it 'somewhat anomalous that it should be in the power of private individuals to organise what is practically a military force in our own country'.[50] Accusations of 'amateurish soldiering' were also constantly levelled against the frontiersmen. With reference to the rifle clubs and the Legion, an anonymous contributor to the *Birmingham Daily* wrote: 'why are all these attempts at soldiering allowed to flourish, or even exist? From the point of view of national defence, they are merely the tares among the wheat'.[51] On the eve of the war, the *Daily Citizen*, with much less tact, defined the Legion as a 'stick-at-nothing body of janissaries',[52] while H. G. Wells noted that it was a force 'equipped to war, oh! in Arizona in 1890'.[53]

With constant reiteration that Providence helped those who helped themselves, the Legion improvised their activities or adapted them to the resources at hand. An annual march through Kent was arranged, covering about 150 miles and providing plenty of opportunities for 'exercises, instruction and revolver practice'. At a training camp in Whitley Bay, the frontiersmen were allowed to carry on with their ordinary professions during the day, but were ordered to attend the camp at night, where they were 'engaged in mimic warfare, scouting movements, military evolutions and night attacks'. The camp was expected to last a month.[54] In the Medway Valley, near Maidstone, a camp was arranged where small units of frontiersmen were trained in infiltration tactics. Much attention was devoted to night training and the Legion put forward ideas for the advancement of civilian marksmanship.[55] For instance, while miniature rifle shooting was gaining greater popularity, frontiersman R. B. Townsend published *The Complete Air-Gunner*, which explained how to gain proficiency in the handling of air guns. Townsend was convinced that ordinary porches and gardens could be readily fitted out as rifle ranges.[56] In Manchester, Grand Duke Mikhail Aleksandrovič Romanov inaugurated the first rifle range opened by frontiersmen.[57] The promotion of rifle practice was combined with public lectures on explosives, gunnery, topography and the principles of hippology.[58]

Running in parallel with practical and theoretical military training was an extensive programme in 'burlesque militarism', including displays of horsemanship, swordsmanship, stick fighting and martial arts. In Manchester, for instance, the Legion ran an 'assault-at-arms' programme, which included 'sword, bayonet, foil and singlestick combats, tugs of war, boxing contests, and exhibitions illustrative of camp and frontier life'. Another feature of the programme was two relay bike rides – one from Newcastle, the other from Portsmouth – with the goal of demonstrating the usefulness of bicycles for dispatch.[59] In Norwich, frontiersmen offered a 'marvellous display of lasso throwing, stock whipping, etc.'[60] In Newcastle, the Legion, in collaboration with the Tyneside branch of the Physical Culture Society, held a four-day festival of gymnastics exercises.[61] In Birmingham, the frontiersmen held a military 'gymkhana' at the Handsworth Flower Show.[62] There was no doubt that these exhibitions appealed to the editors of illustrated magazines and popularised 'warlike arts'.

In addition to martial spectacles, frontiersmen also began to put in regular appearances at local festivals, fairs, pageants, masquerades, tournaments and other special occasions, most of the time as security stewards. Green-uniformed members of the Legion escorted 'Lady Godiva' and her maids through the streets of Coventry.[63] The Legion attended the annual Saturday Lifeboat Processions that were held in numerous northern cities before the outbreak of the war to raise funds for the Royal National Lifeboat Institution. On the occasion of the 1909 Manchester Lifeboat Saturday, a correspondent of the *Manchester Courier and Lancashire General Advertiser* wrote that 'the Legion of Frontiersmen – who seemed born and bred to ride in procession – looked veritable dare-devil fellows'.[64] The participation of the Legion in these popular events was conceivably aimed to solicit support and to 'entice the unwilling shillings into its coffers'.

From 1908 onwards, Pocock and other frontiersmen consistently sought to convince the authorities of the Legion's value and desirable characteristics, aiming to secure official financial assistance for its military activities. De Hora, before being expelled for misconduct, requested 'arms, ammunition, and saddlery' from the War Office. An unnamed MP made a 'personal request' to Haldane, asking for a loan of rifles for the frontiersmen among his constituents. The Legion applied to the General Officer Commanding-in-Chief (GOC-in-C), Ireland, to hold a camp of instruction for one hundred and fifty members at the Curragh. However, the GOC-in-C refused, reminding them that since 1905, the Army Council had consistently refused to give official recognition to the Legion 'in any shape or form', and, as a civilian organisation, it was only 'allowed to carry arms and train on sufferance'.[65]

Around the time frontiersmen claimed to have uncovered machine guns, five thousand rifles and ammunition on City Road in London, along with an arms cache beneath a hotel in Bournemouth, Pocock repeatedly wrote to Lord Errington, private secretary to Charles Hardinge, the Permanent Under-Secretary of State for Foreign Affairs, offering intelligence assistance.[66] In October 1908, Colonel Serjeant wrote to the Foreign Office, offering the services of the Legion to assist in the 'prevention of gun-running in Morocco or elsewhere'. He added that he regularly provided information obtained from Legion members 'to the India Office, and various other departments concerned'. A 'Far Eastern Command' – a group of British expatriates based in China's major coastal cities – requested priority access to the arms stored in British consulates in the event of disturbances.[67] The Foreign Office's polite lack of interest turned to outright distrust when two senior special branch officers concluded that certain information about gun-running, which involved accusations of corruption against the police, was unsubstantiated or downright false.[68] This embarrassing *faux pas* inevitably harmed the Legion's credibility and may have dealt a fatal blow to any

Figure 2.3 Frontiersmen wrestling on horseback in Kent. *Penny Illustrated Paper*, 17 August 1907. Image © The British Library Board. All Rights Reserved

hope of recognition as an intelligence gathering agency. Some years later, in a preposterous exhibition of megalomania, Pocock wrote that the Legion was responsible 'for the ten-year lull before the World-storm broke ... the years in which the Legion engaged all the lawless adventurers as videttes, watching the frontiers ... We had set the whole of the wolf-pack to guard the sheep'.[69]

Besides counter-espionage, some of the better informed and, more often, imaginative frontiersmen continued to warn the public and the authorities of the inevitable prospect of war and the possibility of an imminent German invasion.[70] 'The alarmist authors guided by Lord Roberts were nearly all members of the Legion', Pocock candidly acknowledged.[71] In 1903, frontiersman Erskine Childers published *The Riddle of the Sands*, a best-selling work of fiction which vividly laid out the plans for an invasion of Britain from the East Frisian Islands. The book ran to many editions and fuelled an exasperating spy paranoia. Another frontiersman, William Le Queux, had been frantically waving the flag and banging the drum of British vulnerability since 1894. The things he foreshadowed in the 560 closely printed pages of *The Invasion of 1910* (published in 1906) made the British people's flesh creep with disquiet and appears to have been taken very seriously by the intelligence community. Astonishingly, as one historian has noted, the evidence presented by the future Brigadier General James Edmonds to a subcommittee of the Committee of Imperial Defence regarding German espionage was apparently based on Le Queux's *Spies of the Kaiser*.[72]

The belief – which the Legion encouraged – that a vast network of German spies existed in Britain was bolstered by the feeling that the British authorities were not doing enough to deal with a possible (or imminent) German invasion. In Colchester, while outlining the Legion's *raison d'être* and speculating on what might happen in the case of war with Germany, Pocock said that forty or fifty thousand German reservists were scattered around the country and were ready in the case of war to sabotage the railroads and telegraphs, burn stores and strategically sink steamers loaded with Portland cement across the fairways and anchorages of ports.[73] The editor of the *Daily Express*, Ralph D. Blumenfeld, also a frontiersman, was persuaded that the *Deutsches Heer* was 'well represented in East Anglia', but every time he attempted to call attention to this infiltration [of German agents] he was pilloried 'by the radicals'.[74] Conjectures on the number of German reservists in Britain ready to mobilise upon an order from Berlin reached grotesque proportions.[75] Colonel Driscoll calculated that three hundred and fifty thousand German soldiers were living on British soil. Considering that the peacetime strength of the German army was six hundred and fourteen thousand servicemen of all ranks, the calculation was downright absurd.[76]

Predictably, when the Reichstag passed the Fourth Naval Bill in March 1908, many wondered if an invasion of England by sea really was feasible after all. This disquieting prospect drove the formation of an organisation closely linked to the Legion of Frontiersmen to be known as the Coastal Reserve. 'The idea', the assistant editor of the *Pall Mall Gazette*, Gerard Fiennes, wrote in 1913, 'was to get all the longshore fishermen, tug masters and men, bargemasters, yachtsmen, and suchlike, to bind themselves to perform certain services in the event of war, not combatant in their nature (unless otherwise required), but likely to be of considerable assistance to fleets and flotillas'.[77] The Coastal Reserve was expected to provide training in pilotage and navigation, operating a motorboat, signalling, identification of warships and firing discipline to the seafaring and shoreside workforce. Branches were rapidly established (or attempts were made to establish them) at Yarmouth, Lowestoft, Harwich and other port towns on the east coast, as the eastern seaboard from Duncasby Head to South Foreland was believed to be completely bare of defence. The head of the Coastal Reserve was Pretyman, who had served as Civil Lord of the Admiralty between 1901 and 1903, and among its backers was Erskin Childers. The naval authorities, which had been authorised by the 1903 Naval Reserve Act to raise and maintain a force of volunteers, appeared at first to be interested in the project, but then the Admiralty, acting on a report by a naval officer, decided not to recognise the Coastal Reserve.[78]

The schemes of coastal defence, which appeared to be little more than attempts at reviving the defunct Royal Naval Artillery Volunteers under a different name, went hand in hand with the organisation of war games (map manoeuvres). As the *Norfolk Chronicle* reported,

> Last week, Lowestoft Marine section of the legion tested their ability to enter Yarmouth unseen, between 8.30 and midnight. Yarmouth was supposed to have been captured and in the hands of the enemy. All bridges and railways were barred, and the Yarmouth section of the Legion was allotted the task of guarding the town frontiers. With the aid of their spy, the Lowestoft men very cleverly succeeded in delivering [...] two despatches.[79]

In conducting these exercises, a great deal of attention was devoted to military cycling. Ten battalions of Territorial cyclists were raised, and the North Staffordshire command of the Legion established a corps of Cyclist Guides, whose topographical knowledge of the county would be very helpful in the case of invasion.[80] Cyclist Guides were then formed in Norfolk, Surrey and Kent. The qualifications for enrolment were in good physical condition and 'knowledge of the county within a radius of fifteen miles'.[81]

On several occasions, Pocock had disconsolately stated that English boys were 'losing their manliness and grit'. According to the founder of the Legion, this 'general decline in manliness' was embarrassingly visible the moment youngsters left for the colonies.[82] To toughen up boys approaching manhood, two members of the Legion organised an Imperial School of Colonial Training at Shepperton.[83] More importantly, in this quest to turn the boys into robust and vigorous youths, many frontiersmen became scoutmasters of the newly formed Boy Scouts. At the first annual scout rally, held at the Crystal Palace in 1909, frontiersmen carried out a simulated attack on a farm where the scouts where encamped, while members of the Territorial Forces performed the role of defenders. This war game was intended to display the scouts' skills as non-combatants during a battle. The *London Evening Standard* correspondent described the scene as follows:

> Up come the Legion of Frontiersmen on prancing steeds; in rush more enemy; along fly more supports; the Englishman's Home is afire … The boy audience by this time is delirious and howls strange war-cries. But the scouts at work on the field of carnage do not seem to lose their heads. Quietly, as though they were on parade, they go about their work. Gatling guns crash, maxims pour forth a hail of lead and nickel, enemy retires, defenders advance, shells burst in the air, but scout ambulance men, scout signallers, and scout cycle messengers are cool and collected … it was all very exciting.[84]

According to one of his biographers, Baden-Powell, who watched the 'Battle of Sydenham' from the stands, was dismayed by this stentorian exhibition of truculent militarism.[85]

The want of 'practical fighting men' was apparent in *The Frontiersman's Pocket Book*, a 463-page volume compiled and edited by Pocock with sixty-nine contributions from professional soldiers, trappers and pioneers, forming a veritable 'encyclopaedia of soldiering in miniature'.[86] Arranged in five thematic sections, the *Pocket Book* dealt with the ordinary training of a frontiersman, means of transportation, whether by horse or motor vehicle, scouting, shooting, signalling, explosives, medical and surgical care, personal hygiene and morale. In his opening article, the hunter and naturalist Henry Anderson Bryden argued that modern society had caused the values of self-help and self-reliance to atrophy: 'Even the training of European armies has for centuries tended to eliminate these characteristics, which in warfare are, in truth, such essential factors in the strength and effectiveness of a regiment, a battalion, and an army corps'.[87] Nothing had made this deterioration more apparent than the Boer War, where British soldiers had seemed disoriented and helpless. In the chapters on morale, A. J. Dawson, editor of the *Standard of Empire*, maintained that Britons were 'in need of the advantages to be gained from discipline, self-denial, and a clear sense of grave responsibility than anything else'. In view of this, the most important lesson they were learning from the Legion of Frontiersmen was that 'the able-bodied man who declines to undergo any form of military training is not quite a complete man'. The motherland expected everybody to fulfil the responsibilities of citizenship.[88] With the scout movement spreading throughout the Empire, miniature rifles on the rise and the Territorial force in search of new recruits, *The Frontiersman's Pocket Book* was a great success and new editions were printed in 1911 and 1914.

At the Legion's annual general meeting, held at the end of August 1909, Pocock was ousted as overall commandant. His eccentric behaviour, including the unfounded declaration that *The Times* had opened a 'patriotic fund' to finance the Legion and his infelicitous challenging of the editor of *The Modern Man* to a duel,[89] had blemished the organisation's already poor image in the corridors of power.[90] In place of Pocock, the council appointed Colonel Serjeant. The reorganisation of the leadership, including the headquarters staff, was apparently aimed at curbing some of the most folkloric tendencies of the organisation in favour of a more routinary military discipline. To this end, the Legion took steps to enrol all veterans (officers, WOs, NCOs and ex-soldiers of the regular forces) in the county of London in the Volunteer Reserve scheme.[91] Serjeant also informed the press that the Legion of Frontiersmen was prepared to assist the authorities in maintaining an adequate supply of horses for the Army, for which he drew up a plan which pledged to raise between three and five hundred thousand horses from all parts of the Empire at £27 10s per head.[92] The Legion's tireless zeal in uncovering imagined spy networks and saboteurs led to the formation of groups like the Loyal British Waiters' Society. Influential voices, such as J. L. Garvin, editor of *The Observer* and confidant of Tory leadership, argued that thousands of German waiters, barbers and other personal service trades were gathering intelligence on military and naval installations. In this fight against an 'enemy' supposedly lurking in hotels, restaurants and clubs, Serjeant played a prominent role.[93]

By the end of 1909, the Legion's membership was a little over three thousand men. It should be noted that the bulk of its membership was no longer in the United Kingdom, but largely in the colonies. Despite its modest organisational growth, Serjeant brazenly boasted that 'directly and indirectly the Legion had under its control no less than 100,000 Boy Scouts'.[94] The boastful, lofty speeches, however, could not disguise the fact that the Legion was still facing funding challenges. The average gross revenue for the three preceding years had been about £700 per annum and there was no hope of receiving any direct financial help. 'Our whole difficulty is one of money', Seton-Karr wrote to Sir Edward Grey in March 1909.[95]

While the Legion managed to survive on small financial resources, the links between some of the frontiersmen and political organisations of the radical right became apparent. District organisers of the TRL had not infrequently taken an active part in the management of the Legion.[96] More alarmingly, frontiersmen in uniform were seen acting as stewards at the inaugural meeting of the Imperial Pioneers in Walworth. When a heckler shouted 'Who paid for the Boy Scouts?' disorderly scenes broke out.[97] Other frontiersmen had been seen in a similar gathering and with the same responsibilities at Battersea. Years later, Henry Page Croft recalled having received 'a sporting offer from the Legion of Frontiersmen to steward our next mass meeting at the Lambeth Baths'.[98] The question of uniformed frontiersmen in the service of a political organisation caused a great deal of public consternation. Serjeant initially played down the issue as a gross misunderstanding, then issued an order prohibiting members from attending political meetings in uniform.[99] Despite these pronouncements of apoliticism, members of the Legion were reported to have joined the anti-union Civilian Force in 1912. In the case of a national strike, they would operate as 'flying squadrons' to transport essential goods.[100] Others enrolled in the national reserve of special constables, primarily to assist the police in coping with disorders arising out of strikes, while others demonstrated their sympathy for William M. Power's Volunteer Civil Force.[101]

Naturally, the anti-sectarianism the Legion prided itself on was further damaged by the Home Rule Crisis, which saw frontiersmen in strong support of Ulster. The antisocialist gun-runner, Sir William Bull MP, was honorary colonel of the Legion's Hammersmith squadron.[102] In Birmingham, rumours persisted that the Legion of Frontiersmen had offered its services to fight for Ulster,[103] and other stories suggest that frontiersmen had volunteered to train the UVF.[104] Driscoll, who was left in command of the Legion after Serjeant's withdrawal, denied these allegations but was unable to entirely dispel suspicion.[105] Behind the scenes, Driscoll and various local contingents continued to press their offers for 'intelligence operations' at home and abroad.

Alongside a certain vulnerability to political contamination, the Legion was constantly under suspicion of mercenary-related activities. In 1908, Pocock reported to the Foreign Office that he had received a request for 'four or five good all round men from J. D. Tighe from Butte (Byutt) Montana'. This singular petition specified that 'no Jews or Swedes' would be accepted.[106] Three years later, Portuguese royalists made a futile request for Colonel Driscoll's assistance in preparing their attack on Chaves. 'Some time ago', Driscoll admitted, 'a gentleman called upon me and inquired whether I was willing to take up the matter of recruiting forces for Portugal'. He later resolved that the Legion should have nothing to do with it.[107] During the first days of China's Republican Revolution, frontiersman Arthur Sowerby led a British delegation in rescuing foreigners in Sianfu (Xi'an).[108]

At the outbreak of war, Colonel Driscoll approached the War Office offering to deploy his men along the French coast to 'clear the country of all detached bodies of the enemy'. The War Office adamantly refused. However, on 8 September 1914, General Bethune inspected 683 Legion members and delivered a positive assessment, describing them as 'toughs' well suited for irregular warfare and noting Driscoll's effective leadership. After pestering the War Office to allow its members to serve as infantry wherever needed, the Legion was authorised to raise and send a battalion to Major-General Wapshare in British East Africa. Three months later, the 1,166 men forming the Twenty-Fifth (Service) Battalion, Royal Fusiliers (Frontiersmen), under the command of the 'swashbuckler' Colonel Driscoll, arrived in the colony. The battalion faced fierce combat and suffered heavy casualties, including the renowned big-game hunter F. C. Selous among the fallen. For its efforts, the battalion was awarded the battle honours of East Africa, 1915–1917, Beho-Beho, Kilimanjaro and Nyangao.[109]

Back in Britain, however, the Legion's activities continued to draw criticism. The Surrey branch faced objections from the Eastern Command's General Officer after issuing notices under 'O.H.M.S.' (On His Majesty's Service), while organisations like the Territorial Force Association continued to withhold recognition. In Leeds, a voluntary organisation criticised the frontiersmen, accusing them of using questionable recruitment methods and attempting to pressure tribunals into forcing exempted individuals to join the Legion.[110]

After the war, the Legion faded from visibility until 1923, when its new president, Lord Loch, sought to revive it. Loch informed the War Office of his intention to reorganise the Legion, claiming that '9,000 members' had been killed during the war and that the organisation was now weakened. He requested renewed recognition based on the Legion's wartime record, though the War Office remained cautious. Despite Loch emphasising 'the anti-Bolshy side of the Legion's activities' at a time when Stanley Baldwin's government was reactivating the Supply and Transport organisation and presenting parliament with a Special Constable Bill to make permanent the provisions of the 1914 Act, the Army Council merely extended the same level of 'cognisance' as in 1906. The word 'recognition' for the Legion was to be avoided.[111]

All things considered, the story of the Legion of Frontiersmen in the prewar years lies at the intersection of militarism and right-wing politics, as its members embraced sympathies for tariff reform, imperial unity and a renewed 'ultra-patriotism'. While the Legion revered Lord Roberts and shared his concerns about war preparedness, it opposed conscription.

Instead, it radicalised the principle that every citizen should voluntarily take on as much responsibility as possible in the work of imperial defence – without legal compulsion. The Legion believed this could be achieved by mobilising 'unutilised' volunteer resources. Through training in marksmanship, terrain exercises, war games and manoeuvres, the Legion aimed to prepare the public for the use of force in Britain's defence. It also contributed significantly to invasion scares and anxiety about future wars. At the same time, spreading rudimentary elements of military training and cultivating a 'psychological predisposition for war' responded to a prevailing fear – especially acute among right-wing circles – that Britain, if relieved of its 'military burden' and softened by the refinements of an 'effete modernity', would face decay. The Legion, thus, promoted a rejection of 'civilised restraint' in favour of toughness, strength, tenacity and resilience. Committed to combatting national degeneration, Driscoll declared, 'There is no race on God's earth like the British, but there is a canker eating at the heart, and it must be cut out'.[112]

Notes

1 On the Legion of Frontiersmen, see Geoffrey A. Pocock, *Outrider of Empire: The Life and Adventures of Roger Pocock (1865–1941)* (Edmonton: University of Alberta Press, 2007); Geoffrey A. Pocock, *For Adventure and for Patriotism: 100 Years of the Legion of Frontiersmen* (Chichester: Phillimore, 2004); Humphries, 'The Eyes of an Empire', pp. 133–158; Robert H. MacDonald, *The Language of Empire: Myths and Metaphors of Popular Imperialism, 1880–1918* (Manchester: Manchester University Press, 1994), pp. 162–170.
2 Roger Pocock, 'For Men Who Found Their Manhood', *The Nautical Magazine: A Technical and Critical Journal for the Officers of the Mercantile Marine.* Enlarged Series 78 (July–December 1907), pp. 208–211.
3 On the apolitical stance of the Legion of Frontiersmen, see Humphries, 'The Eyes of an Empire', p. 138. Citing Andrew Thompson, Humphries wrote: 'In a number of ways, the Legion of Frontiersmen closely fitted the paradigm for imperial pressure groups [...] It organized itself with a general council, filled with peers, ex-generals, and various other well-known names (including the Earl of Onslow, Lord Esher, and Sir Arthur Conan Doyle), the majority of whom had little involvement in the legion's activities; it had its own periodicals; and there is no evidence of executive members having any significant involvement in other patriotic leagues'.
4 On Boxing Day, 1904, Pocock had advanced for the first time the idea of the establishing the 'Legion of Frontiersmen'. In a letter to the *Morning Post*, titled 'The Legion that never was listed', he wrote: 'Permit me in your columns to suggest the formation of an organization of frontiersmen resident in the Kingdom. An applicant for membership would offer evidence that he has

done real frontier work in such employments as the following: Explorer, scout, hunter or trapper, prospector or alluvial miner, cowboy or stock rider, cargador, or trader among savages, pearler, sealer, whaler, seaman or sea apprentice, trooper in the Irregular Cavalry or Mounted Police, or War Correspondent [...] Its objects would be good fellowship, mutual help, and possibly service to the State in time of war [...] It is time that the Legion was listed'.

5 Roger Pocock, 'A Forecast of the Legion of Frontiersmen', *The Fortnightly Review* 79, new series (Vol. 85, old series) (January–June 1906), p. 722.
6 'The Legion of Frontiersmen: New Corps of Keen Men Is to Be Organised at Once', *Daily Express*, 10 April 1905, and many others.
7 See, among other sources, 'The Legion of Frontiersmen', *The Cavalry Journal* 1, no. 4 (January–October 1906), pp. 367–368.
8 Accounts of the inaugural meeting appeared in numerous newspapers. See, as an example, 'The Defence of the Empire', *London Evening Standard*, 11 April 1905.
9 Quoted in Humphries, 'The Eyes of an Empire', p. 146.
10 Quotations in this paragraph are from Pocock, *Outrider of Empire*, pp. 190–191.
11 'The Legion of Frontiersmen', *London Evening Standard*, 27 March 1906. See also Mark Kerr, *Prince Louis of Battenberg: Admiral of the Fleet* (London: Longmans, Green and Company, 1934), p. 175.
12 'The Legion of Frontiersmen', *Lloyd's Weekly News*, 25 June 1905.
13 Pocock, *Outrider of Empire*, p. 194.
14 Roger Pocock, *Chorus to Adventurers: Being the Later Life of Roger Pocock ('a Frontiersman')* (London: John Lane, 1931), p. 38.
15 Secretary of the War Office (Permanent Under-Secretary of State) Colonel E. W. D. Ward, KCB to Secretary of The Legion of Frontiersmen, 15 February 1906 (20/General Number/2605 [6.1] in TNA: WO 32/10426.
16 TNA: WO 32/10426. See also Hansard, HC Deb Vol. 3, Col. 703 (5 April 1909).
17 Pocock, 'A Forecast of the Legion of Frontiersmen', pp. 720–732.
18 Sir Arthur Conan Doyle, 'Motor-Cars and Coast Defence', *The Times*, 12 April 1906.
19 'Motor-Cars and Coast Defence: The Legion of Frontiersmen and Its Work', *The Car: A Journal of Travel by Land, Sea, and Air* 205 (25 April 1906), 297.
20 'Not an Englishman: Legion of Frontiersmen Has an American for Its Colonel', *Daily Mirror*, 13 October 1906.
21 'A New Legion of Frontiersmen: The Most Romantic Body of Men in the World', *Tyrone Constitution*, 27 April 1906.
22 TNA: WO 32/10426, 'History of the Legion: as Obtainable from War Office Files', 'Appendix 'A' – Applications and Offers (1906–1913)'.
23 'The New Legion of Frontiersmen: Its Value in War', *Pall Mall Gazette*, 15 June 1906.
24 'Maritime Frontiersmen', *Portsmouth Evening News*, 31 December 1906, and many others.

25 Pocock, *Chorus to Adventurers*, p. 36.
26 'A Camp Fire in Regent's Park', *Pall Mall Gazette*, 11 July 1906.
27 'Legion of Frontiersmen: Proposed Force of Natal', *Newcastle Daily Chronicle*, 10 July 1906.
28 Manchester Archives and Local Studies, M540/3, Legion of Frontiersmen, newspaper cuttings.
29 'Legion of Frontiersmen. Birmingham Command Formed', *Birmingham Mail*, 27 July 1906.
30 'Frontiersmen: Commando Formed in Leeds', *Leeds Mercury*, 23 October 1906.
31 'The Bushman's Bible – Text-Book on How to Live in the Open – Rules of the Game', *Daily Express*, 13 April 1909. Quoted in Humphries, 'The Eyes of an Empire', p. 148.
32 'Cowboys' Brighton Ride', *Daily Mirror*, 3 September 1906; 'Cowboys' Long Ride – Frontiersmen Arrive Back Safe in London after the Perils of the Brighton Road', 4 September 1906.
33 'Legion of Frontiersmen', *Western Daily Press*, 30 January 1907.
34 'Colonel's Racy Speech: Volunteering Instead of Footballing', *Manchester Evening News*, 1 November 1906.
35 'Empire Day', *Birmingham Daily Gazette*, 16 May 1907.
36 'British Buffalo Bill', *Labour Leader*, 25 January 1907.
37 'Legion of Frontiersmen: An Unarmed Force', *Manchester Evening News*, 18 January 1907.
38 'Legion of Frontiersmen: Inauguration of Irish Command', *Dublin Daily Express*, 22 January 1907.
39 'Garrison Gossip', *Berwickshire News and General Advertiser*, 2 April 1907.
40 'The Legion of Frontiersmen', *Volunteer Service Gazette and Military Dispatch*, 26 June 1907.
41 'Notes of the Week', *Volunteer Service Gazette and Military Dispatch*, 10 April 1907.
42 'Military Tournament', *Staffordshire Sentinel*, 28 June 1907.
43 'The Legion of Frontiersmen in the North', *St. Georges's Gazette*, 30 March 1907.
44 'Legion of Frontiersmen', *Gloucestershire Echo*, 19 June 1907.
45 Letter from Sir Henry Seton-Karr to Sir Edward Grey, 22 March 1909, in TNA: FO 800/111. The letter includes a memorandum explaining the situation of the Legion.
46 'Territorials in Camp: Three Thousand Men under Canvas at Berwick', *The Berwick Advertiser*, 18 June 1909.
47 The King's Regulations and Orders for the Army 1912; Reprinted with amendments published in Army Orders up to 1st August 1914, Directorate and Commission Agencies, paragraph 449a (London: H. M. Stationery Office, Harrison and Sons, printers, 1916). See also TNA: WO 32/10426.
48 Letter was published in *The Frontiersman* 9 (September 1910). See Humphries, 'The Eyes of an Empire', p. 151.

49 'Military Matters', *Globe*, 20 July 1907.
50 Hansard, HC Deb Vol. 14, Col. 1404 (8 March 1910).
51 'Territorial Notes: Rifle Clubs and Amateurish Soldiering', *Birmingham Mail*, 7 April 1910.
52 'London Chat', *Daily Citizen*, 25 May 1914.
53 Herbert George Wells, *An Englishman Looks at the World: Being a Series of Unrestrained Remarks upon Contemporary Matters* (London: Cassell Limited, 1914), p. 30.
54 'In Camp at Hartley', *Newcastle Evening Chronicle*, 17 June 1907.
55 [No title], *London Evening Standard*, 10 February 1908.
56 Richard Baxter Townshend, *The Complete Air-Gunner* (London: L. Upcott Gill Publisher, 1907).
57 'Frontiersmen's Rifle Range', *Manchester Courier and Lancashire General Advertiser*, 23 December 1907.
58 'Legion of Frontiersmen', *Chelmsford Chronicle*, 24 January 1908, and many others.
59 'Legion of Frontiersmen', *The Times*, 21 January 1907, and many others.
60 'The Norwich Military Tournament', *Norfolk News*, 21 November 1908.
61 'Four Days Fête Opened in Newcastle', *Newcastle Daily Chronicle*, 14 November 1907.
62 'Handsworth Flower Show', *Birmingham Daily Gazette*, 27 July 1908.
63 'The Godiva Procession', *Coventry Evening Telegraph*, 2, 8 and 9 August 1907.
64 'Lifeboat Saturday', *Manchester Courier and Lancashire General Advertiser*, 17 September 1909. On the 'Lifeboat movement', see James C. Dibdin and John Ayling, *The Book of the Lifeboat: With a Complete History of the Lifeboat Saturday Movement* (London: O. Anderson & Ferrier, 1894).
65 TNA: WO 32/10426, 'History of the Legion: as Obtainable from War Office Files', 'Appendix 'A' – Applications and Offers (1906–1913)'.
66 Morris, *The Scaremongers*, p. 414, f. 65.
67 TNA: WO 32/10426, 'History of the Legion: as Obtainable from War Office Files', 'Appendix 'A' – applications and offers (1906–1913). See also Humphries, 'The Eyes of an Empire', p. 140.
68 Report from New Scotland Yard, reference 6088/42/a, 26 Feb. 1909, in TNA: HD 3/139.
69 Pocock, *Chorus to Adventurers*, p. 54.
70 On the Edwardian spy literature, see David French, 'Spy Fever in Britain, 1900–1914', *The Historical Journal* 21, no. 2 (June 1978), pp. 355–370; Morris, *The Scaremongers*; Thomas Hitchner, 'Edwardian Spy Literature and the Ethos of Sportsmanship: The Sport of Spying', *English Literature in Transition, 1880–1920* 53, no. 4 (2010), pp. 413–430; Danny Laurie-Fletcher, *British Invasion and Spy Literature, 1871–1918* (London: Palgrave Macmillan, 2019).
71 Pocock, *Chorus to Adventurers*, p. 56.
72 Humphries, 'The Eyes of an Empire', p. 142. In 'The Invasion of 1910', the Legion of Frontiersmen fought alongside the fictional 'League of Defenders of the British Empire'.

73 'Frontiersmen', *Evening Star*, 13 May 1907.
74 R. D. Blumenfeld, *R. D. B.'s Diary, 1887–1914* (London: William Heinemann, 1930), p. 223.
75 Charles Lowe, 'About German Spies', *The Contemporary Review* 97 (January 1909), pp. 42–56.
76 'The German Army in England – Is the Government Aware That We Have Three Hundred Thousand Foreign Soldiers in Our Midst?', *Penny Illustrated Paper & Illustrated Times*, 22 May 1909.
77 'Ships and Sailors: The Proposed Coastal Reserve', *Pall Mall Gazette*, 27 January 1913.
78 On maritime frontiersmen, Suffolk Record Office, Lowestoft Branch, Covehithe, Legion of Frontiersmen, ref. 1300/31/12–14. See also *The Lowestoft Journal and Suffolk County Record*, in particular 1908–1914.
79 'Legion of Frontiersmen', *Norfolk Chronicle*, 8 August 1908.
80 'Legion of Frontiersmen', *Staffordshire Sentinel*, 21 March 1908.
81 'The Legion of Frontiersmen', *Yarmouth Independent*, 2 January 1909, and many others.
82 'Roger Pocock', *Pearson's Weekly*, 20 August 1908.
83 'A Novel School', *Norfolk News*, 9 May 1908, and many others.
84 'Boy Scouts' Rally', *London Evening Standard*, 6 September 1909.
85 Tim Jeal, *Baden-Powell* (London: Hutchinson, 1989), p. 410.
86 'If You Had to Play Robinson Crusoe', *The Sphere*, 22 May 1909.
87 *The Frontiersman's Pocket-Book* (London: John Murray, 1909), p. 2.
88 Ibid., p. 380.
89 On the 'duel affair', see *The Modern Man: A Weekly Journal of Masculine Interests*, 20 and 27 February, 6, 20 and 27 March, 17 April. The challenge was issued in response to an article titled 'The Legion of Humbugs', 16 January 1909.
90 TNA: WO 32/10426. The adjutant-general General Ian Hamilton, for instance, assessed the Legion as an 'essentially unmilitary organization'.
91 'Veteran Reserve for the County of London', *Kentish Mercury*, 29 July 1910, and many others.
92 'The Shortage Horses', *Army and Navy Gazette*, 19 February 1910.
93 *The Frontiersman* 3 (March 1910), p. 35.
94 'Legion of Frontiersmen', *London Evening Standard*, 23 May 1910.
95 TNA: FO 800/111, Miscellaneous S.
96 See, for instance, 'New Conservative Agent', *Manchester Courier*, 21 January 1909. The article describes the case of frontiersman Harry Heydeman, who served for some time as organising and general secretary of the Manchester and District Division of the TRL and then Agent to the Otley Conservative and Unionist Association.
97 'Imperial Preference Mission', *The Times*, 13 April 1910.
98 Croft, *My Life of Strife*, p. 59.
99 'Those Pioneers! How They Hoodwinked the Legion of Frontiersmen', *The Daily News*, 16 April 1910.

100 'London Letter: Civilians for Public Protection', *Aberdeen Press and Journal*, 19 January 1912.
101 'Wild Women: Volunteer Civil Force Dealing with the Problem', *London Evening Standard*, 10 June 1914.
102 [No title], *Daily Telegraph & Courier*, 23 October 1907.
103 'Political Crisis: Ulster Arming: Rifles and Ammunitions Ordered in the Midlands', *The Birmingham Daily Mail*, 30 November 1910; 'Birmingham Volunteers Ready for Duty', *Birmingham Mail*, 17 July 1914.
104 'A Radical Discovery', *Belfast Weekly News*, 8 January 1914.
105 *The Frontiersman* 51 (March 1914), pp. 61–63.
106 TNA: HD 3/139, secret service funds; gun-running; purchase of presents; payments to agents: 1909.
107 *The Frontiersman* 22 (October 1911), p. 158.
108 Keith G. Stevens, 'The Shensi Relief Column and the Legion of Frontiersmen, China Command, 1911–12', *Journal of the Royal Asiatic Society Hong Kong Branch* 51 (2011), pp. 171–206.
109 TNA: WO 32/10426, 'History of the Legion: as Obtainable from War Office Files', 'Appendix 'A' – Applications and Offers (1906–13)'. See also Edward Paice, *Tip & Run: The Untold Tragedy of the Great War in Africa* (London: Orion Publishing Group, 1991); Humphries, 'The Eyes of an Empire', p. 135.
110 Ibid.
111 Ibid.
112 The *Frontiersman* 24 (December 1911), 184.

3

Race regeneration: nativist impulses and the drive for physical efficiency

When I have borne in memory what has tamed
Great Nations, how ennobling thoughts depart
When men change swords for ledgers. (William Wordsworth, *When I Have Borne in Memory*, 1802)

In his Sidgwick lecture at Cambridge University on 25 January 1908, former Prime Minister, A. J. Balfour, asked how it came about that 'civilization wears out and great communities decay' and whether or not there was any satisfactory evidence of such a process of degradation. Although Balfour could not give any conclusive answers to these questions, they were not merely intellectual rhetoric. Rather, they revealed how Balfour, who was well read in evolutionary biology and a member of the Eugenics Education Society (EES), was ready to accept the axiom that all human societies went through childhood, maturity and old age, and were consequently inherently mortal, exactly as all individuals are. It followed that national decadence was analogous to man's senescence. This was certainly a permissible biological analogy in a time when application of the crude principles of natural selection to human affairs was standard and was elevated to the dignity of a scientific principle. Balfour, who appeared to attribute little or no importance to the possible effects of germinal change upon the course of civilisations, argued that 'The flexible elements in any society, that which is susceptible to progress or decadence, must be looked for rather in the physical and psychical conditions affecting the life of its component units, than in their inherited constitution'. Going on to describe these conditions, he spoke of 'a mood of deep discouragement, when the reaction against recurring ills grows feebler, and the ship rises less buoyantly to each succeeding wave, when learning languishes, enterprise slackens, and vigour ebbs away'. In this view, the fate of the Roman Empire, which Balfour sketched impressionistically and allusively, provided an all too effortless case study of decline and fall and was likely to raise fears in the most apprehensive minds about the future of Britain.[1]

In conservative circles, theoretical speculations on 'retrogressive degeneration' in political and social matters had become increasingly prominent as the electoral franchise was extended. In 1883, the Marquis of Salisbury, while uneasily pondering whether democracy and empire were compatible, wrote that history had 'not yet furnished us with material wide enough or minute enough for constructing anything like a science of diseases and decay of States'. The most important (and perhaps less obvious) inference to be drawn from his remarks was that society would undergo various stages of degeneration, atrophy and necrosis. These processes might be caused by anything that at once interfered with, weakened or threatened to destroy the cohesion, functional harmony and vitality of the imperial body. In this regard, Lord Salisbury saw party and class politics as two potent factors of 'disintegration'.[2] Predictably, with the steady advance of democracy, the physical, mental and moral efficiency of the people became a serious preoccupation for conservatives and their rivals alike – the former being notably less inclined to believe in the progressive postulates of human perfectibility.

At the dawn of the twentieth century, concerns that racial decline might over time bring about the collapse of the empire had taken hold of the British Right. As expected, immigration, urbanisation, materialism, 'anarchy' and moral decay were identified as significant contributing factors in the emergence or exacerbation of these tendencies to degeneracy. The shocking experience of finding many of the recruits who had volunteered for the Boer War to be physically unfit underscored the need for a 'healthy stock'. This fuelled nativist impulses and led to the emergence of a patriotic movement centred on physical regeneration. Against this background, the first part of this chapter investigates the history of the xenophobic and fiercely antisemitic BBL. This organisation was formed with the aim of curbing the immigration of destitute aliens, thus preventing them having a potentially negative impact on the national body.[3] The second part of the chapter explores the initiatives of organisations that advocated for the highest levels of 'physical efficiency'. Their shared goal was to combat the perceived racial degeneration of the population while promoting values such as virile manhood, athleticism, hygiene, social discipline and readiness for national defence.

'Britain for the British': the British Brothers' League, 1901–1914

'When I founded the BBL and organised the Alien Agitation in East London in 1901', William Stanley Shaw recalled in the *Daily Mail* on 26 April 1928, 'destitute Aliens were pouring into this country at the rate of over a hundred thousand a year. Many were undesirable and unclean in their manners and habits, many were diseased, many were criminal'. After indulging in timeworn racial prejudices and suspicions, he concluded that 'Alien immigration has been a curse to this country and has injured a national life beyond repair'. For this, he accused politicians of allowing 'the scum of Eastern Europe' – Jews and other immigrants alike – to enter and 'infect' the country. Naturally, Shaw's article, which was reprinted in a book authored by Lieutenant Colonel A. H. Lane, Chairman of the National Citizens' Union (NCU), and all too predictably entitled *The Alien Menace*, revived in many readers' minds memories of the fierce controversy which had raged across East London a quarter of a century earlier.[4]

Since the late nineteenth century, the boroughs of Stepney, Poplar, Bethnal Green, Shoreditch and Hackney had become the first port of call for immigrants and a fertile ground for xenophobia and 'populist nativism'. As early as 1886, ardent eugenicist and antisemite Arnold White together with Lord Dunraven financed the Society for the Suppression of the Immigration of Destitute Aliens, the first organisation in Britain to advocate for the control of immigration. It was followed five years later by the Association for Preventing the Immigration of Destitute Aliens.[5] By nourishing fears of an 'alien invasion', these short-lived bodies helped put pressure on the two houses to discuss the question of immigration. In 1888, a select committee was appointed to examine the immigration laws of other countries and to report on whether it was desirable to impose restrictions on the admission of aliens. Beyond recommending that the Board of Trade collect immigration statistics, no legislative steps were taken as a result of the inquiry. However, the 'restrictionists', or anti-aliens, did not give up and they appeared to intensify their pressure as time passed. In particular, some conservatives began to question the principle that 'freedom of immigration' was an incontrovertible and beneficial feature of free trade. In 1894, at a meeting held in Bradford under the auspices of the Primrose League, Joseph Chamberlain declared that 'the time has come when we ought to make some regulations to restrict and limit the immigration of alien paupers into the country'. The labour market was oversaturated and there was no need to 'increase competition for the benefit of persons who [were] not altogether a very desirable style of resident'.[6] A few weeks later, the Marquis of Salisbury, then leader of the opposition, introduced a Bill in the House of Lords to make provision for amending the law relating to immigration. The first part contained measures to allow the government to prohibit the entry of destitute foreigners who were likely to become dependent on public funds. The second part lent support to the actions of police authorities in deporting foreign anarchists and other individuals considered 'dangerous'. Britain could no longer afford to serve as a 'sanctuary for political refugees and the oppressed'. Salisbury's Bill was not passed into law. In 1898, with the Conservatives in control of parliament, the Earl of Hardwicke introduced a new Bill, which provided for the inspection of passengers at certain ports and prohibiting the entry of any alien who was found by immigration inspectors to be 'unfit'. The Bill passed all its stages in the upper house, but was not introduced in the House of Commons. The timidity of the Conservative cabinet on the 'immigration problem' precipitated right-wing, extra-parliamentary action.[7]

In the years 1899–1900, a few thousand Romanian Jews escaping persecution found refuge in England.[8] This wave of migration provided a prime opportunity for the most fervent anti-alienists to remobilise. Among them was Major William Evans-Gordon, the Conservative MP for Stepney, a constituency known for its large immigrant population. Disappointed by the absence of an Aliens Bill on the government's agenda, he decided to pledge cooperation with the BBL, whose rallying cry was 'Britain for the British', and to give outspoken support for it.[9] Aided by the *Daily Express* and the *Daily Mail*, the League aimed to secure the passage and vigorous enforcement of restrictive immigration laws, arguing that the employment of cheap foreign labour was 'taking out the bread from English mouths'. The new anti-alien body was expected to be structured on military lines with 'bands', brigades, companies, battalions and so on. Each 'band' was to be formed of ten men, who would appoint a leader.[10] In an interview to the press, Shaw, the commander-in-chief of this 'army', declared that aliens were 'eating out the heart of the East End and some of the provincial cities, notably Leeds'. He expected to raise fifty thousand men to prevent the East End from becoming 'the dustbin of Europe'.[11] With this aim, posters were affixed to walls and handbills were distributed throughout the East End inviting residents to enrol in the League.[12] From the very outset, Shaw was at pains to explain that the term 'alien' did not apply exclusively or primarily to Jews.

In May 1901, a public meeting was held at Stepney Meeting House under the chairmanship of long-standing Conservative MP for Mile End and brewer, Spencer Charrington. Major Evans-Gordon was also present on the platform alongside Conservative MPs Walter Murray Guthrie and Thomas Dewar. With the intention of demonstrating that the BBL was neither anti-semitic nor politically biased, Evans-Gordon read letters of support from the Conservative MP for Limehouse, Harry Samuel, the Conservative MP for South-East Bethnal Green, Samuel Forde Ridley, and the Liberal MP for Poplar, Sidney Buxton. He also stated that the Jewish Board of Guardians, which had been repatriating immigrants to Eastern Europe for years to avoid overburdening its charitable operations, sympathised with the aims of the League. Evans-Gordon went on to argue that the League was essentially a protest against 'the dumping down of foreign paupers' on British shores and should be seen as an exercise in prevention rather than intolerance, being undertaken before the situation got out of control. Amidst cries of approval, Evans-Gordon listed all the detrimental effects of the 'invasion' upon the native population – overcrowding, high rents and 'abominable' unsanitary conditions – and asserted that 'we must think of our own people first. We cannot afford to be charitable at the expense of our own flesh and blood'. At that point, someone reminded the speaker that he was elected thanks to the 'Jewish vote' and now he was 'running them down'. Pandemonium ensued. When order was restored, Evans-Gordon moved the first resolution:

> That this meeting of inhabitants of the Borough of Stepney, having heard the objects of the British Brothers' League, expresses its hearty approval of such objects and pledges itself to use every effort (irrespective of Party) to further the work of the League in its endeavour to put an end to the influx of destitute aliens – a matter which has become an intolerable grievance to our own people and a cause of misery to the immigrants themselves.

The resolution having been seconded by Shaw, Spencer Charrington invited amendments. Isaac Salomon, secretary of the Boot and Shoe Workers' Union, tried to take the floor, but was immediately overwhelmed with derision and booing. The noise was so loud that Solomon had to write his proposed amendment on a piece of paper and hand it to the chairman to be read at a suitable time. Solomon's amendment insolently suggested the insertion of the words: 'that this meeting believes that nothing short of the complete organization of industry by the people themselves, and the total abolition of private ownership of the means of life, will solve the question of pauperism'. Predictably, a torrent of protests and insults swept the room. To further inflame the situation, a working man rushed to the stage and invited the meeting to vote on the issue of whether 'no more Jews should be brought in this country'. Almost all hands went up, leaving a puzzled Solomon – apparently the only hand not raised – to wonder if the new organisation was a veritable 'British brotherhood'. The amendment was put to the meeting (and apparently lost), while some socialists, probably foreigners, began to chant the *Marseillaise.* Fights broke out, hastening the conclusion of the gathering.[13] Right after this tumultuous birth, one of the League's most influential backers, Colonel Sir Howard Vincent, Conservative MP for the Central Division of Sheffield, made a vain attempt to move a resolution in the House of Commons on the immigration of destitute aliens – the same Colonel Vincent who had previously presented a Bill to legislate for the restriction of immigration in 1897 and again in 1898.[14]

The sympathetic, if not enthusiastic, response of many Tory MPs to the establishment of the League pressured Shaw to say that the new body was not 'an appendage of the Conservative Party'.[15] While vague claims of political neutrality were uttered, the League's ranks rapidly filled with antisemites and racists of all stripes. A very short time passed before hostile letters began pouring into the *East London Observer*. An anonymous 'British Brother' wrote: 'Let Major Gordon, Mr. Dewar, Mr. Charrington, Mr. Steedman, and Mr. Crooks join together and force the powers-that-be to intervene, for if something is not done the time will come when there will be a flame kindled before which the anti-Semitism of the continent will pale'.[16] Such threats caused a great deal of public worry and consternation. Someone pointed out that the BBL served only to incite racial hatred against the Jewish people.[17] What made the situation appear even more alarming (and perplexing) was the strong endorsement given by Conservative politicians to the more demagogic and choleric rhetoric of the anti-alien movement. Furthermore, as a general appeal for contributions had fallen on deaf ears and the only two persons acknowledged as financial backers were Evans-Gordon and a moderate councillor for Stepney, William Spencer Beaumont, suspicions were raised over the League's sources of funding. Shaw promptly replied to this scepticism warning 'certain Jews' that there 'was a limit to the patience of the working men of East London'.[18] Meanwhile, some organisational steps were taken. One hundred men were to form a section, while ten sections would form a ward. The sections were lettered, respectively, A, B, C, D, E and so on, while the wards were numbered first, second, third, fourth, etc. Each section was expected to nominate a delegate to represent it on the Executive Committee, the body that decided the general policy to be pursued. The League was also expected to cooperate with the recently formed Parliamentary Alien Immigration Committee, which was pressing the government to pass immigration laws.[19]

From its inception, the League's members and sympathisers consistently berated anyone who reminded them that Christian and humanitarian motives should prevail over self-interest. 'Radicals and Liberals' were accused of being insensitive to the plight of British workers. Unsurprisingly, amid the jingoism fuelled by the Boer War, they were swiftly labelled as traitors.[20] Others were accused of raising the 'bogey' of antisemitism for political purposes.[21] In response, Shaw frequently pointed out that regardless of whether the alien pauper worshipped Jesus Christ, the God of Abraham or Allah, he had to leave the country. The reasons consistently cited were as follows: immigration resulted in an excess of unskilled labour, leading to wage depression, a decline in the standard of living and increased unemployment among British workers. It contributed to overcrowding and unsanitary housing conditions. The impoverished living conditions of immigrants fostered disease, weakness and 'feeble-mindedness'. Physical deterioration was accompanied by moral degeneration, sexual immoderation and a rise in criminal activity. Alien pauper immigration, as Shaw asserted, 'corrupts our children, owing to the vile things that they have to see and hear'.²²

In the early summer of 1901, the Londoners' League briefly joined the BBL in the fight to restrict immigration. Once again Conservative MPs appeared to have played a decisive role in establishing a new movement whose aim was to solve the issue of overcrowding in South and East London. As a start, the new organisation sent a deputation to the Home Secretary, Charles Ritchie, the President of the Local Government Board, Unionist Walter Long and the President of the Board of Trade, Gerald Balfour. All of them promised legislative remedies for the housing problem. Despite the fanfare, the Londoners' League suddenly fell into oblivion and was only brought to light again by its connection with the BBL.²³

With the publication of alarmist reports of the arrival of 'swarms of aliens', the BBL held a second public meeting in mid-August at the Fountain Meeting Hall in Stepney. Before a large audience, Shaw declared that the fight for legislation to protect British standards of living was largely dependent on the people, rather than in the hands of rapacious politicians. In similar populist tones, Alderman J. L. Silver of the Borough of Stepney complained that the East End was becoming the 'muck-hole of the world'. As proof of their bipartisanship, John Williams Benn, London County Councillor and popular Progressive Party whip, was invited to speak. He urged the League to moderate their anti-alien zeal, an appeal to reasonableness that did little to placate the more turbulent spirits. The following resolution was carried by acclamation:

> This meeting of East London British residents views with indignation and alarm the ever-increasing hordes of foreigners settling in these parts ... and while urging the Government to deal with the unrestricted immigration of destitute aliens, hereby records its determination to make every legitimate effort in its endeavour to remedy this growing evil and pledges itself not to relax its efforts until this unhappy state of things is satisfactorily altered.²⁴

By the end of the summer, the BBL appeared to be gaining momentum and word of its objectives began to circulate, sparking growing interest across the country. The Provisional Executive Committee issued a circular in which they requested 'an Act of Parliament imposing heavy penalties on owners and captains of ships, landing, or attempting to land, any person in this country liable to become a public or private charge'. They believed that in order to bring about legislative change a 'body of resolute and determined Britishers' united for action was necessary. The circular concluded by posing a rhetorical question: 'If a great country like the United States of America, with its immense territory, its boundless natural resources, has found it absolutely necessary to restrict the immigration of alien paupers, how much more must a small country like England stand in need of similar restriction?'[25]

Certainly, the League's extremism scared many East Enders, who were generally left with the impression that Shaw and the League's devotees were nothing more than antisemitic hatemongers. Ominous corroboration of this perception came from the numerous League activists (and sympathisers) who admired the work of the French antisemite Max Régis, or complained that Stepney Borough Council had begun to publish notices in Yiddish alongside English. In a long letter published in the *East London Observer*, Arthur Stockton, a member of the League's executive committee, tried to offer a more moderate portrayal of the organisation. However, his letter had a more detrimental than beneficial impact. After quoting reports by the medical officer for Stepney and the work of Edward Bowmaker on working class dwellings, Stockton wrote:

> A peaceful invasion of the kind to which Great Britain is now being subjected is far more disastrous to the labouring world than an armed invasion is to the nation. It is impossible to recoil and recover from the sword's effects, but alien invasion is slowly and surely undermining the constitution of our country – our birthright. Our ancestors fought for the ground we stand on, inch by inch, and paid for it with their lives. Have we no call therefore, to guard the legacy of our forefathers for this and future generations? [...] We cannot afford to sleep while Europe laughs and England goes the way of Rome; and we must not allow the heart of our Empire to canker and corrupt while we consolidate the outer portions.[26]

The spectre of a dying Rome loomed large: the shiploads of 'undesirable aliens' brought daily into London docks and then carted into the East End appeared to Stockton (and those likeminded) as something akin to the Goths, Huns and Vandals amidst the ruins of the Roman Forum.

While the League was attracting significant press attention, it faced protests and continued to struggle to secure the necessary financial support, despite receiving endorsements from prominent conservative figures. Sir Arthur Conan Doyle, among others, praised the anti-alien movement and contributed half a guinea to it.[27] Interestingly, certain Tory critics were less troubled by the League's racism and propensity for violence and more concerned with the possibility that the animosity towards landlords who rented their houses to immigrants or manufacturers who employed them might become the foundation for a broader assault against property.[28]

In September 1901, with the League facing financial difficulties and the frustratingly slow progress of its efforts, Shaw resigned as its president.[29]

However, the timely surge in membership in Bethnal Green spared him from disillusionment. The recruitment of over one hundred affiliates representing 'all shades of opinion' placated Shaw to the extent that he temporarily withdrew his resignation.[30] Efforts to mobilise the substantial reservoir of anti-alien sentiment among native East Enders were finally being met with some success. During this period, numerous letters expressing sympathy and mainly praising Shaw's 'crusade' poured in. One of these, from Colonel Vincent, offered encouragement to the League's chairman: 'The more public attention is aroused to the evils of alien immigration, without restriction, the better. If the Britons … will not help themselves, no one will help them. If they do not prioritize this, and only this, in their politics, they and their children must expect to suffer'.[31]

On 19 October, a third public meeting of the League was held at Pott Street school in Bethnal Green. The seating capacity of several hundred was not enough for the crowd and many were turned away. Opening the meeting, secretary Stockton announced that the League now had five thousand members, about six hundred of whom, he claimed, had paid the membership fee. After that, Shaw took the floor. As usual he blamed immigrants for converting the workshop of the world into 'the casual ward of Europe'. The English working man had 'to make room for the scourings of Russia, Roumania and elsewhere', and as a consequence of this 'inrush of filthy humanity' the 'best blood' was leaving the country. Most parts of the East End, he added, had been inundated by destitute foreigners and 'their houses were more rabbit hutches than human habitations'. Given this dire situation, the League's task was to safeguard the homes and jobs of natives. His speech was received with loud cheers and some cries of 'Shame!' Shaw believed that the government needed unequivocally to be pressured into passing legislation.[32]

As a result of the meeting, the League began to grow and spread. Membership increased and committees were formed in Poplar, Bromley and Bow. Recruitment was extended beyond the East End, but met with negligible success.[33] Besides organisational matters, everyone there felt that anti-alien violence was not very far off. At the end of October, an anonymous witness told the press that in St. George-in-the-East 'a number of foreigners were about to take possession of certain houses when they were attacked by a number of Englishmen. The furniture was broken, and windows were smashed, and a crowd of many hundreds witnessed the scene'.[34] A month later, a certain H. J. Kelsey put up a BBL poster in the window of his stationer's and newsagent's shop. Kelsey, who had helped to establish the Hackney Branch of the League, had been boycotted or subjected to other reprisals by Jewish customers. The matter was brought before the Central Executive Committee as it was considered intolerable that someone could dictate to an Englishman what he should or should not exhibit on his property.[35]

While the situation in the streets was becoming tense, the League approached the Home Secretary with the suggestion that the naturalisation fee be increased. It was also proposed that foreigners provide evidence of financial means to support themselves and demonstrate skilled work experience in order to gain entry.[36] In the meantime, the 'Brothers' attacked local authorities for neglecting the problem of housing, which, it was said, had been exacerbated in certain areas by the continuous arrival of aliens from Eastern Europe. When someone like H. H. Gordon, civil engineer at the Metropolitan Borough of Stepney, used official information from the Board of Trade to try to demonstrate that the relationship between overcrowding and immigration might have been exaggerated or misconstrued, he was met with the response that statistics were merely 'fairy tales'.[37] Not infrequently, prominent 'Labour men', such as William C. Steadman and Will Crooks, who criticised the League, were accused of caring more for foreigners than Britain and Britons.[38]

While the organisational and political battles were heating up, the BBL received the endorsement of Alec P. Matheson, senator of the Australian Commonwealth. In a conversation with Shaw, Matheson, who was at the time fighting to exclude the Aboriginal people from voting and to maintain a 'White Australia', said that immigration of 'coloured' aliens was 'a burning question as they tended to reduce the rate of wages and generally lower the standard of living'. However, he added that immigration was not only a labour question, but a national one as well, which demanded immediate action. In this light, the BBL was a movement of self-defence.[39]

As 1901 drew to a close, racial tensions in the East End were high. In a meeting held at Limehouse Town Hall in mid-November, which was attended by Matheson, 'a large body of working men' acted as stewards to prevent disruption by protesters. A resolution was passed by Alderman Silver accusing the government of apathy and collusion with 'sweaters and slum landlords'. He added that the Borough Council was packed with members of Toynbee Hall and therefore opposed to the restrictions on immigration. Following this 'preamble', Councillor A. T. Williams announced that the League had faced two 'political defeats'. The first was when the London City Council 'contemptuously rejected' a resolution to establish a committee to determine the number of foreigners arriving at various ports. The second was when, in relation to the housing problem, a resolution put before Stepney Borough Council asserting that unrestricted immigration was the primary cause of overcrowding was rejected by ten councillors, most of them 'members of the Jewish persuasion'. Williams added that 'The most astonishing argument' put forward by these 'anti-restrictionists' was that alien immigration was necessary to improve the race. Amidst laughter and cries of derision, Williams turned to the prospect of legislation, arguing that the 'people' had to exert significant pressure on Parliament to achieve anything. Amendments to the King's Speech were promised. Senator Matheson concluded the proceedings by articulating the classic repertoire of racial prejudices and unfounded assumptions about British racial superiority.[40]

Sometime later, in an article published in the *Pall Mall Gazette*, Alderman Silver clarified the League's position and compared it with that of the Anglo-Jewish community. He wrote that Jewish and Christian communities in the East End were 'common sufferers' in the face of the 'alien invasion':

> Their trades, like ours, are being ruined; their rents, like ours, are being increased to an unparalleled extent; their rates and taxes, like ours, are being increased as a direct result of this invasion; and their health, like ours, is being endangered, and their sense of decency shocked, by the terrible amount of overcrowding which exists in the districts of St George's East, Stepney, and Whitechapel.

Naturally, he repeated the mantra that the League was not antisemitic and those who thought otherwise were 'wanton mischief-makers' or people who were benefitting from immigration. However, Silver specified that while the League supported legislation to exclude indigent aliens, the Anglo-Jewish community championed the broader distribution and anglicisation of these people. The League considered this programme of assimilation to be at the least impracticable and 'very much like the process of emptying a bath by unstopping the waste pipe and yet allowing the supply line to remain full on'. Silver went on to say that the League gave voice to the grievances of thousands of citizens who were invoking the government to act on their behalf. The League had a 'popular mandate' to achieve and bring to fruition their aspirations. Silver added that 63 MPs had already 'pledged up to the tilt to support a restrictive measure'. Evidence of the deleterious effects of the 'unrestricted invasion of foreigners' – undercutting of wages, and increases in house rents and taxes levied for welfare purposes – convinced even the most sceptical of these MPs that it was necessary to enact legislation.[41]

Desperate for funds, the various League sections organised concerts and musical recitals to attract the support of wealthy patrons. Barrister and Conservative MP for South Hackney, Thomas H. Robertson presided over one of these events.[42] At the inaugural meeting of the Conservative Working Men's Club in Bethnal Green, which was attended by Albert Yorke, Sixth Earl of Hardwicke and Under-Secretary of State for India, and other party dignitaries, Forde Ridley MP congratulated the 'workmen of that part of London' for organising themselves in the BBL.[43]

With the new year, the Liverpool, Manchester and provincial newspapers began to devote space to demands for legislation coming from the East End.[44] Even the novelist Marie Corelli expressed sympathy for the League: 'Our first duty is to ourselves', she wrote to Shaw, 'and the maintaining of our position with honour. British work, British wages and British homes should be among the considerations of the British government'.[45] The fight for immigration legislation was a matter of 'patriotism and necessity'. It is interesting to note that in the eyes of some 'restrictionists', the alien problem was bristling with not only economic and social, but also military side issues. Lieutenant Colonel George A. Leach wrote significantly that 'in the event of any European war in which this insular country – notably, nowadays, unproductive of food – may be engaged we should have to subsist, as far as can be judged, an enormous comparatively pauper alien proletariat in addition to our own. Unless, therefore, the nation is on the alert and prudent measures by State legislation are predetermined, we shall have the wolf at our very doors and the heart of the Empire will be in jeopardy'. In Colonel Leach's reflections, fears of military unpreparedness were intertwined with a string of myths about the communion between labour and disloyalty.[46] Other, more sober observers saw the dangers that Britain would face if other countries, particularly the United States, imposed restrictions on immigration, which could lead to an uncontrolled surge in migration into Britain.[47]

By this time, as historian John A. Garrard documented, a 'growing savagery' began to shape the anti-alien agitation campaign.[48] For instance, in response to a smallpox outbreak, an anonymous contributor to the *Pall Mall Gazette* proposed the formation of a Pink Ribbon League, an anti-immigration organisation that would be composed of individuals determined to seek protection from the perceived evil of alien immigration by appealing to the 'High Court of Parliament'. To symbolise their commitment, each member would wear a pink ribbon in their buttonhole. Furthermore, it was incumbent upon every member to raise awareness of the alien question and encourage public discourse on it in all possible settings – 'at the dinner table, in the railway train, in the tramcar, in the tube, on the earth and under the earth'. The anonymous writer believed that in this way public opinion would be alerted to the dangers brought about by 'the loathsome wretches who come grunting and itching on our shores'. The smallpox then spreading through London was 'caused by the scum washed to [British] shores in the dirty waters flowing from drainpipes', while the ordinary well-to-do Englishman was forced to 'suffer the agonies of vaccination'. Besides these sanitary concerns, the anonymous writer asked the public to consider the 'moral effect produced by constant contact and companionship with the dregs of Europe and Asia':

The cockney, the London working-man, is by nature a clean beast ... but to live in the midst of people who never wash ... who are utterly ignorant of the most rudimentary sanitary arrangements, a people who can see no reason for bathing the body, for ventilating the room, or for cleansing household utensils; a people, in short, who live as the beasts live – this is to rob the working man of his glimmering idea that cleanliness is something useful. With such neighbours he grows careless, 'slummocky' indifferent; and when once an Englishman gets dirty his religion topples like a house of cards.

The alien question was primarily a 'Jewish question'. 'These careful, dirty hoarders of money are buying up property every day, and when the houses are bought out go the English occupiers and in come the Poles, the Russians and the Italians'. The East End of London, the writer concluded, did not belong to England 'but to the Jews'.[49] Aggressive, anti-alien schemes and language were not isolated occurrences. The first biographer of Oscar Wilde, Robert H. Sherard, described immigrants in Britain as 'filthy, rickety, jetsam of humanity, bearing on their evil faces the stigmata of every physical and moral degradation'.[50]

At the beginning of 1902, the League's resolutions and press releases couched in intimidatory language were becoming a source of much worry to Jews and political opponents alike. In a lecture delivered at St. George's and Wapping under the title 'Rocks ahead for Socialism', socialist Ernest E. Hunter argued that one of the 'rocks' that was looming ahead was the rampant antisemitism that the BBL was stirring up among the working class. It would be the task of socialists to turn workers away from the pernicious lures of hatred and bigotry.[51] These warnings did not in the least deter the League (and its sister organisation, the Londoners' League) from organising further and more frequent public demonstrations. Some of the most fervent supporters of these events were Conservative agents – in certain cases, as in Bromley, they were themselves the initiators of the League's branches.[52]

On 15 January, prior to the opening of parliament, the League held a large demonstration at the People's Palace, which drew over four thousand people. In light of rumours that 'socialists and foreigners' would be attempting to break up the meeting, the League recruited two hundred and sixty stewards from its own ranks. According to the *East London Observer*'s correspondent, these men were 'big, brawny, stalwarts, dock labourers, chemical workers from Bromley, and operatives from Shoreditch, Bow, Poplar, Stepney, Bethnal Green, & Mile End'. Arrangements were also made to protect the chairman, Major Evans-Gordon, and other speakers from possible attacks. Before the event started, 'the Stepney contingent [of the League] followed by the Hackney, Shoreditch, and Bethnal Green battalions, carrying banners and singing national songs to the accompaniment of drums and divers[e] kinds of musical instrument' appeared at the entrance of the Queen's Hall. Such were the 'patriotic instincts' generated by this military-like procession that the audience broke out in jubilation and a zealous organist played the strains of 'The Soldiers of the Queen', 'God Bless the Prince of Wales', 'There Is No Place Like Home' and 'Britons Never Shall Be Slaves'. When a semblance of quiet had been established, Major Evans-Gordon said that he was impressed by the 'remarkable unanimity' of opinion around the problem of immigration. This was a matter of loyalty to 'our own country', which went beyond party lines or any dictate of religious prejudice. 'When the choice is forced upon us', he argued, 'we must choose our own flesh and blood and see that we are provided for before we accept the rejected burdens [...] of other nations'. Amid much cheering, letters of support from a number of prominent and less prominent 'restrictionists', including several Conservative MPs, were read out. The Reverend Arthur Edison Dalton, Rector of Stepney Parish and Rural Dean, gave his blessing to the meeting. Then came Shaw, who first warned the audience 'not to allow the red herring of religion to be drawn across the trail'. Following this, he said that if the country were invaded, 'the man behind the gun' should be an Englishman. In the midst of loud cheers and vehement applause, Arnold White moved the first resolution, which declared that the housing problem was insoluble until the immigration of destitute foreigners was completely restricted. The government, he remarked, had to redeem its promises and throw off the shackles which 'the great European financiers' had endeavoured to impose upon it (and thus upon the people's will) by lobbying for mass immigration. His inflammatory rhetoric, which drew on classic antisemitic themes (i.e., Jewish political conspiracies; charges of disloyalty, etc.) was accompanied by ferocious cries of 'Down with the foreigners', 'Wipe 'em out', 'Give it them', etc. White's resolution was seconded by Alderman Silver and applauded with notable enthusiasm. Liberal 'restrictionist' Henry Norman, MP for South Wolverhampton, proposed the second resolution, which affirmed that unrestricted immigration lowered the standard of living. He said that 'This is England. It is not the backyard of Europe; it is not the dustbin of Austria and Russia', and given the opportunity he would have a billboard erected at the mouth of the Thames bearing the following words: 'No rubbish to be shot here'. Councillor Williams seconded the resolution before launching into a bitter invective against immigrants as reservoirs of cheap labour and contributors to insanitary employment conditions. Then William's voice took on a solemn cadence as he intoned a prayer:

> Let us work for those who love us,
> For those who hate us, too;
> For the goal that lies before us,

Ever nearer to our view.
For the wrong that need assistance;
For the haven in the distance,
And the good that we may do.

New resolutions were passed and recommendations made, including an appeal to the government 'to fulfil forthwith the pledges [on immigration] given by Lord Salisbury, Mr. Ritchie, Mr. Chamberlain and other Ministers of the Crown'. Afterwards, 'some foreigners' angrily rose in protest. The stewards intervened and 'unceremoniously bundled [them] outside into the cold'. The meeting closed with the audience singing 'God Save the King' with great 'patriotic fervour'.[53] Soon after, according to a press report citing an anonymous source, some Jews were chased down the Mile End Road.[54]

The People's Palace rally gave rise to a wave of antagonism and criticism. Intemperate speeches and threats of violence made by the organisers, as well as the hiring of stewards to repress dissenting voices, were highly deprecated.[55] John Brown, who had been chairman of the Board of Guardians for over a decade, regarded 'the agitation carried on by the British Brothers' League as calculated to have very evil results in the way of fomenting racial hatred'.[56] An anonymous 'municipalist' warned the League not to overstep the 'bounds of prudence, and allow the more fiery contingent of their adherents to drag them into the arena of racial antagonism, with all its attendant horrors and miseries to both sides'.[57] Other critics went so far as to compare the League's aims with the determination of the Boer government to proscribe the admission of Uitlanders to full citizenship.[58] 'Tattler' wrote in *Justice*, the weekly newspaper of the Social Democratic Federation (SDF), that he had 'no objection to a foreign workman simply because he is a foreigner. The English workman who blacklegs me is more my enemy than the German workman who is prepared to stand by me in maintaining a standard rate of wages, or in striving for better conditions'. Therefore he entirely disagreed with the League's nativist tones and purposes.[59] Some months later, the same newspaper commented that the League 'was nothing but an organisation against the pauper alien, and a subterfuge of the East End employers to shift the responsibility of sweating from the sweater to the sweated'.[60] At a meeting of the Jewish Federated Tailors' Union', trade unionist Lewis Lyons commented that ironically the League 'had their offices in the same building as the Free Labour Association'.[61] In addition to expressing their concerns over the excessive demagoguery and aggressive boastfulness exhibited by the League's leaders, some Jews decided to form an 'Aliens' Defence League'.[62]

While the BBL appeared satisfied with the progress they had made, the government was still resisting being pressurised into passing legislation. Gerald

Balfour MP, President of the Board of Trade, refused to meet a delegation of the Central Executive Committee of the League, explaining that he had been in private communication with Major Gordon-Evans and that was enough.[63] There was no doubt in the minds of the more thoughtful Conservative politicians that the racist activities of the East End rabble-rousers could become a source of embarrassment in the future. Unsurprisingly, the League did nothing to dispel this impression and its members continued to deliberately spread false news and grossly exaggerate the 'invasion'. For instance, the public were told that a notice reading 'No English need apply' had been put up in the East End. Shaw was so outraged by this likely fictitious occurrence that he composed a modest poem, which went as follows:

> Sons of the world's first freemen! Sons of a martial race!
> Sons of a thousand heroes for ever Fame's roll to grace!
> Must ye to the strangers' children, at the bid of the strangers' gold,
> Give place in the land of your fathers, abandon your rightful hold.
> Of the England your fathers bled for, of the land that they fought to free.
> And left for their children's children?
> Surely, this should not be!
> O spirits of bygone heroes! O souls of England's best!
> Can ye in the grave find slumber, can ye in the grave find rest,
> Whilst your sons with their wives and children, go forth in the winter cold,
> At the bid of the strangers' children, by the power of the strangers' gold?
> Not by the blood and sinews, not by the strong right arm,
> Not by the right of conquest, not by war's bold alarm,
> Drive they your children's children out from their father's home,
> Seeking a rest by the wayside, forced by the stranger to roam!
> But by the golden image, at whose feet the stranger bows,
> By the crime that the world holds righteous, by the crime that law allows,
> By the right of the man with plenty, his poorer brother to grind,
> That he for his surplus lucre, an increased return may find.
> List now! ye old-time spirits, list to the bastard cry!
> In England, O mother of nations, 'No English need apply!'
> Stand now, ye sons of England, cry 'Halt!' to the foreign hordes!
> That would filch the rightful heritage, won by your father's swords.
> Cry 'Back' to the silent foemen, who land in the early dawn,
> Seeking to drive the home-birds out from their birthright nest,
> Playing the part of the cuckoo, with a cunning insidious zest.
> Cry 'Back' to the silent invader, back to our rampant sea!
> Back to the lands that sent ye, defiling the home of the free!
> Get ye beyond the billows, let the ocean's cleansing wind,
> Play between your corrupted legions and our wholesome English kind.
> List now! ye old-time spirits, list to the bastard cry!
> In England, O mother of nations, 'No English need apply!'[64]

On 28 January, Major Evans-Gordon tabled an amendment to the King's Speech setting out the urgent need to introduce legislation to cure the 'evils' of unrestricted immigration. Gerald Balfour, who remained obstinately unconvinced of the effectiveness of restrictive laws, said that there were sufficient grounds for an inquiry before legislation. While it was unclear whether this inquiry into alien immigration would take the form of a Select Committee or a Royal Commission, there was no doubt that the Tory government was trying to evade the issue, which might have created trouble for the party.

Despite (or perhaps because of) these developments, some of the most zealous members of the League persisted in publishing letters threatening the Jewish community. One stated: 'The British Brothers' League will make it so hot for the Jews, that the aliens will be glad to ask mercy of Russia or Roumania, as that mercy will be mild compared with the mercy of England'.[65] Shaw attacked the novelist Thomas H. H. Caine for having stated at a Zionist meeting in Shoreditch that he, as an Englishman, deeply regretted the anti-alien agitation. Caine, who had supported Hovevei Zion in response to the 1881 anti-Jewish pogroms in Russia, was vilified as an example of 'that thoughtless but numerous class who believe in being generous at other people's expense'.[66] Shaw recommended that Caine and other 'comfortable Englishmen' take a walk through the East End on a Sunday morning, predicting that when they had finished they would likely feel their blood 'tingling with indignation'. Responding to this hail of threats and verbal abuse, the Liberal MP for Whitechapel, Stuart Samuel, admonished Shaw and told him he would be held responsible and accountable if the situation escalated. As an afterthought, Samuel provocatively asked for the League's balance sheet.[67]

With the 'alien debate' raging in the columns of the local press, members of the League expressed their antisemitic sentiments with greater force and defiance. Shaw, who persistently repeated that the League had nothing whatever to do with religious prejudice, wrote: 'If a crusade against the Jews was started in East London, a hundred thousand Britons would flock to the standard of the leader in the twinkling of an eye'.[68] A League sympathiser contended that 'England ... must protect her own, and conserve the rights of her children from the cupidity and the grasping and pitiless instincts of the Jew'.[69] Another urged the workers to 'wield their arms, like some octopus, and seize them [the Jews] in a relentless grasp'.[70] Adding further fuel to the fire, the League circulated a pamphlet which declared: 'alien Jews are in possession of large shops and factories, who but a few years ago landed in England almost penniless'.[71] All of this was taking place when the English antisemite Joseph Banister published *England under the Jews*. In the eyes of this self-proclaimed champion of 'English race feeling',

Britain had been transformed into 'a dumping ground for the human refuse of other lands'. He vehemently argued that indiscriminate and unrestricted immigration led to racial and moral degeneration. Banister reserved his praise solely for Colonel Vincent, who 'seems to have been fairly successful in arousing the public to the gravity of the evil'. It is hardly surprising that Banister's book, which had several reprints, was much admired by League members.[72]

In consequence of this outspoken antisemitism, the hitherto (at least reputedly) impartial *East London Observer* felt morally bound to denounce the League's methods:

> In the last quarter of a century there have been many popular agitations in East London, having varied objects and conducted by singular methods. We do not, however, remember any agitation fostered by greater impropriety or one having had a quicker descent to the gutter, than the anti-alien movement, which, as promoted by the British Brothers' League, is more than half based on ignorance, bolstered up by prejudice, and is justified only by selfishness [...] As the agitation against the aliens proceeds, the more violent become the agitators, the grosser their exaggerations, the fouler the abuse of those who happen to differ from them. The British Brothers' League does not command general confidence; its disposition to pothouse methods and use of beery support must increase suspicion.[73]

The *East London Observer*'s accusations came as the League was forming new branches around the East End. Another large public meeting was held in St. George's, which again avowed the absolute necessity of restrictive legislation. However, the League's organisers were reluctantly coming to terms with the fact that, despite their relentless campaigning, their message was not gaining ground in the country, even in industrial and port cities which had in recent years seen an increase in their foreign populations.[74]

In late March 1902, a Royal Commission was established to investigate alien immigration. Presided over by Lord James of Hereford, its members included Lord Rothschild, the Hon. Alfred Lyttelton, Sir Kenelm Digby (Under-Secretary for the Home Office), Major Evans-Gordon, Henry Norman MP, and William Wallace (Clerk to the Guardians of Whitechapel). A short time later, Shaw resigned from his position as President and Chairman of the League, citing personal reasons. However, he remained watchful and critical of his successors. Despite his departure, the anti-alien agitation continued. A leaflet was issued, apparently without the authorisation of the Executive Committee, stating that 'If you or any of your friends have suffered by the alien Jews coming here, now is the time to say so'.[75]

In early May, the Hackney Branch of the League organised a parade which passed through the Jewish quarters of the East End:

> Their progress was witnessed by thousands of aliens who offered some slight opposition in Brick Lane, but a strong posse of police kept order. In Old Montagu Street the British Brothers, waving large banners and accompanied by a band, which played patriotic airs, such as 'Britons never shall be slaves', gave vent to their feelings shouting, 'Go back to Jerusalem'.[76]

Following this provocative gathering, the League convened its inaugural annual meeting at St. George-in-the-East Town Hall. Reports indicated a purportedly satisfactory growth in membership, now at forty-five thousand, and boasted of 'scores of branches'. However, these numbers appeared to have been greatly exaggerated, considering that at the time of Shaw's resignation the membership was in fact between ten and twelve thousand, and only one thousand five hundred of them had paid the sixpence subscription fee.[77] The League's major donors included Colonel Vincent, Forde Ridley, A. T. Williams, Conan Doyle and the Coppersmiths Company. In the internal election, Silver secured victory over Arnold White and ascended to the position of President.[78]

Meanwhile, the 'Brothers' started appearing before the Royal Commission, presenting evidence in support of their 'restrictionist' claims. The chairman of the executive committee, James William Johnson, stressed that 'there is a feeling growing stronger and stronger in our breasts against this treatment (i.e., displacement of natives), an undercurrent [...] working quietly and silently, unseen'. And although he did not mean it as a threat, he argued 'that unless something is done this feeling is bound to grow, and no one can fairly expect us to go on tamely submitting to the present state of things for ever'.[79] By the end of summer 1902, public attention was focused not only on the sessions of the Royal Commission but also on the election for a councillor for the St. George-in-the-East ward of the Borough of Stepney. This political contest pitted the Unionist candidate J. Gibbs, a City Imperial Rough Rider in South Africa and a League member, against the Liberal Dan Haggarty. Playing on anti-immigrant sentiments, Gibbs won by a narrow margin.[80]

At the beginning of autumn, racial tensions in the East End were once more nearing breaking point. Viscount Mountmorres wrote in the *Daily Mail* 'No one acquainted with London east of Aldgate Pump can conceive the bitterness of feeling which prevails. Anti-Semitic crusades are openly preached with all the vigour and all the wrath which characterized the Jewish persecutions in Eastern Europe half a century ago'.[81] This hatred frequently turned into minor cases of violence and the columns of the local press were filled with stories of fights between natives and foreigners.[82]

The premature death of President Silver in October 1902 was a severe blow to the organisation and intensified internal dissension. A few months later, the East End press prophesied the League's imminent dissolution and its reconstitution into an association with the primary task of pressing (and giving aid to) local authorities to enforce housing and sanitary regulations.[83] The secretary of the League, H. G. Barnett, denied the rumours; he wrote that 'The struggle against our foe during the past years' war is not yet finished' and considered it the duty of all Englishmen to defend themselves against the 'invasion'. Barnett also expected that the League's ranks would be swelled with veterans returning from South Africa, and as he declared on the East End press: 'the Reservists who have fought most nobly for their King and country, to land once more on old England's shores to find the Home in which they were born is now occupied by these aliens, this is the recompense they get for their services'.[84] To demonstrate the League's vitality, open-air meetings were held around London before Christmas. At the same time, a petition signed by forty-five thousand East Enders protesting against alien immigration was formally presented to parliament.[85] Even Shaw reappeared on the scene, begging that the empire not be sacrificed for cheap labour and shoddy work.

In the spring of 1903, the League's campaign was proceeding vigorously. The Conservative MP for Hoxton, Claude Hay, unfurled a new banner for the Shoreditch branch of the League before one thousand people.[86] When Prime Minister Balfour announced that no legislation on alien immigration would be adopted that year, the executive committee issued a hurried call for an emergency meeting. The constantly active and extremely outspoken Shaw viewed the Royal Commission as nothing more than a political stratagem, which an alien-controlled government was using to 'keep things quiet'. This lack of legislative initiative would, according to the founder of the League, by 1913 turn London 'into an important Jewish city on the Thames'. Shaw pointed out that unrestricted immigration was not only the most perfidious threat to the British race (and to the empire), but also an inexhaustible reservoir of social unrest and discontent among the masses of British working people. On the political plane, of course, this implied socialism.[87]

In those days, the League was also becoming aware of the advisability of entering into communication with the Immigration Reform Association. Founded in February 1903 and presided over by the Earl of Donoughmore, the aim of this organisation was to strengthen public opinion in favour of the expulsion of 'undesirable' aliens and to convince parliament of the need for restrictive legislation. Its widely circulated pamphlets laid stress on the presumed 'social evils' arising from immigration. The Duke of Sutherland, the Earl of Wolseley, Lord Ardilaun and Lord Colville of Culross accepted positions as vice-presidents, while the committee included Henry Seton-Karr and another fifty MPs.[88] Amidst the proliferation of new 'restrictionist' bodies, the controversial Protestant preacher Job Williams addressed a crowd of several hundred in Victoria Park and urged them to stand firm against the 'the papal element' brought into the country by swarms of immigrants.[89]

With the approach of summer, there were increasing signs of further intensification of anti-alien agitation. The League issued twenty thousand handbills blaming the 'pauper destitute' for lowering the English standard of living and decency. At the same time, a meeting of the Shoreditch Branch of the League unanimously resolved 'That all candidates for local and Parliamentary honours be asked to state their views upon Alien Immigration. That no candidate will receive any support unless he supports the object of this [British Brothers] League; and that only a plain and decisive answer be accepted'.[90]

In August, after forty-nine public sittings and examination of 175 witnesses and officials, the Royal Commission submitted its final report before the House. Summing up, the commissioners concluded that:

> A larger number of aliens have during the last twenty years entered the country. This number is much in excess of those who had in previous years reached us. The excess is mainly composed of Russian and Poles, who belong for most part to the Jewish faith. There seems to be no reason to anticipate that under present conditions the number of alien immigrants arriving here in future years will be diminishing [...] No case has been established for the total exclusion of such aliens [...] but in the interests of the State generally, and of certain localities in particular, the entrance of such immigrants into this country and their right of residence here should be placed under conditions and regulations [...] The greatest evils produced by the presence of the alien immigrants here are overcrowding caused by them in certain districts of London and the consequent displacement of the native population [...] special regulations should be made for the purpose of preventing aliens at their own will choosing their residence within districts already overcrowded [...] Efforts should be made to rid the country of criminals (and other objectionable characters) [...] The causes that have so largely tended to produce the conditions above referred to will probably continue, and if this be so, the evil will unless checked by legislative or administrative measures, year by year increase and intensify.[91]

These disquieting conclusions were followed by recommendations of a distinctly drastic nature. Briefly put, these concerned the establishment of a Department of Immigration with 'the power of making and enforcing orders and regulations which may be made applicable to immigration generally, or to vessels arriving at or from certain ports, or to certain classes of immigrants'. Authority to enforce the regulations would be assigned to officers, whose duty would be to determine whether the alien seeking admission fell within the category of 'undesirable' – criminals, paupers and the physically and mentally disabled. Any such 'undesirable' alien might be ordered by a Court of Summary Jurisdiction to leave the country, and the subsequent expulsion of the 'undesirable' and his or her reconveyance to the port of departure would be at the expense of the shipping companies. To keep out 'undesirables', the commissioners recommended that all immigrants undergo a medical examination and any who were found to have a contagious disease or a physical or mental deficiency were to be detained and deported. It was further proposed that 'prohibited areas' be created for aliens in order to alleviate or prevent overcrowding. Far less controversial were the proposals regarding the expulsion of convicted aliens. The Royal Commission concluded by asking the government to move quickly to adopt their recommendations 'as they can be introduced without recourse to parliament'.[92] Dissenting memoranda were signed by Sir Kenelm Digby and Lord Rothchild, who, while acknowledging the critical nature of the situation, believed that 'immigration problems' could be combated by more rigorous application of existing laws on housing and sanitation.

The BBL wholeheartedly approved of the report presented by the Royal Commission and expressed their gratitude to those 'restrictionist' MPs and anti-alien agitators who had directed (and were carrying through) the 'patriotic campaign'. In a fervour of enthusiasm, the new president, A. C. Rodgers, travelled to Scotland with the aim of establishing branches of the League there. In Edinburgh, he met representatives of the Scottish Tailors' and Tailoresses' Association, whose members had recently gone on strike after employers had imported foreign labour. The object of the meeting was 'to discuss ways and means of dealing with what is fittingly termed the Jewish complaint'.[93] In a letter, 'smacking with patriotism' and citing the opening line of Robert Burns's poem *Scots Wha Hae*, Rodgers called upon the Edinburgh Trades Council to support the battle against immigration.[94] In the meantime, in collaboration with the Immigration Reform Association, 'demonstrations' in Sheffield and other cities of the Kingdom were announced.[95] In the Midland Counties, Trade Councils and Trade Unions expressed some sympathy with the League's aims.[96]

At the end of 1903, the League held regular public meetings and issued countless resolutions to pressurise the government into carrying out the Royal Commission's recommendations. Major Evans-Gordon published *The Alien Immigrant*, in part a report of his investigation into the conditions of the Jews in Eastern Europe, in part a justification of his 'restrictionist' views. In mid-November, a meeting was held in the Queen's Hall of the People's Palace under the auspices of the Immigration Reform Association and with the participation of 'a large number of members of the British

Brothers League'. The chairman, David John Morgan, then Conservative MP for Walthamstow, restated that London was not the dumping ground of 'people of no use' and certainly not the stage for 'vendettas'. Supporting the resolution moved by Thomas H. Robertson, Conservative MP for Hackney South, who had urged the government to act immediately and boldly, Independent Liberal MP Cathcart Wason proposed sending a few thousand Jews to Palestine. Claude Hay added that the time had come to acknowledge the 'alien problem' as a national one and blamed foreign governments for letting criminals go free and move to British shores.[97] Besides meetings and talks, the League mobilised for the London Metropolitan Borough Council elections, which were held in November 1903. Twenty-thousand leaflets were printed and distributed, carrying the message to vote only for 'restrictionist' candidates. To the disappointment of the Conservatives, the elections resulted in considerable gains for the Progressive Party.[98]

For the BBL, the new year (1904) started as the last one had ended, with a continuous stream of meetings. At Shoreditch Town Hall, Claude Hay called on the government to fulfil its promise to return Britain to the British. He added that London was infested with foreign criminals and that the 'alien influx', like a 'hideous, loathsome bacillus was floating and soaking into all industrial centres of [the] nations'. The Dean of Norwich, William Lefroy, in crude, populist language expressed his belief that the people should take the matter into their own hands.[99] While Evans-Gordon repeatedly warned of the future dangers of unrestricted immigration, the secretary of the League, Alfred Walmer, began a friendly correspondence with the violently antisemitic Irish Redemptorist priest John Creagh, who was at the time inciting a boycott of Jews in Limerick. In addition to this unequivocal proof of antisemitism, members of the League warmly praised the Australian Immigration Restriction Act (1901), which was designed to keep Australia 'White', and agreed to have copies of the legislation printed for circulation.[100]

As expected, when parliament reassembled in February, the government included in the King's Speech a measure 'for the purpose of dealing with the evils consequent on the Immigration of Criminals and Destitute Aliens into the United Kingdom'. The BBL felt that its insistent voice was finally being heard. On 29 March, Aretas Akers-Douglas, the Home Secretary, introduced the Aliens Bill, which sought to put into force all the recommendations of the Royal Commission. Its second reading was scheduled for 25 April and after a lively debate was carried by a majority of 124. Nonetheless, it soon became clear that the Bill was badly conceived and required substantial alteration. It essentially imposed upon the Home Secretary the highly improbable task of determining the position and the fate of every alien passenger disembarking in British ports. In a letter to *The Times*, Sir Kenelm

E. Digby, formerly Permanent Secretary of the Home Office, pointed out that 'no more serious injury could be done to a public department than to impose upon it duties which it cannot possibly perform'.¹⁰¹ The government appeared to be taken aback by these significant reservations. To the consternation of the Liberals, in June Akers-Douglas moved that the Bill be referred to the Standing Committee on Law instead of allowing it to be dealt with by a committee of the whole House. After six sittings, in which the committee had only considered three lines in one clause, the government withdrew the Bill and placed responsibility for this failure to obstruction by 'radicals led by some conservative renegades'.¹⁰²

With the withdrawal of the Bill, the League promised to continue fighting against the 'influx' of destitute aliens and resolved to take vigorous action during the ensuing autumn. Balfour's assurance that that the government would certainly attempt to deal with the 'alien problem' early in the following session was met with much scepticism and a certain ironic humour. The 'restrictionists' reserved some of their sharpest attacks for Winston Churchill, who had recently crossed the floor of the House to become a Liberal and who had privately boasted to have personally 'wrecked the Bill', and for Ivor Guest, Walter Runciman and Sir Charles Philips Trevelyan, all of whom had been nominated to the Standing Committee on Law by the Committee of Selection.¹⁰³ In a lengthy letter to the members of the League, Colonel Vincent wrote that 'these defenders of the alien within the United Kingdom are the protectors of Chinese labour in the Transvaal' and that every vote for them (and their party) was a vote for the aliens.¹⁰⁴

As the summer of 1904 faded, anti-alien agitation resumed. Delegates of the Parliamentary Alien Immigration Committee met government ministers, while Robert Sherard, who was known for his controversial book *The White Slaves of England*, began to draft *The Child Slaves of Britain*, in effect a vicious attack on the 'filthy alien'. In December, the League criticised the Bishop of Stepney for having dared laud the industriousness and thriftiness of the immigrant population.¹⁰⁵ With the Mile End by-election in sight (January 1905), the 'Brothers' organised several meetings, including one attended by one thousand five hundred people at the Mile End Waste. A manifesto was issued appealing to electors to vote for the candidate who supported drastic immigration restrictions and the 'expulsion of the most unnatural class of human being, who are mostly Russian, Polish and Rumanian Jews'. The event closed with a call for continuous agitation and revolt against the 'terrible alien evil' and the 'false friends' of the British working classes.¹⁰⁶

On 18 March 1905, a new Bill was introduced in the House of Commons. It differed from the previous year's abortive measure by omitting the Royal Commission's recommendations concerning registration and the issue of 'immigrant congestion' in urban areas. Instead, it proposed to restrict the entry of 'alien steerage passengers' and 'immigrant ships' to eight designated ports, where immigrants would be required to undergo assessment by an immigration officer and examination by a medical inspector. Following this assessment, they could be either granted admission into the United Kingdom or rejected as 'undesirables'. Exclusion was based on four main criteria: a lack of means of subsistence, physical or mental 'infirmities' that might burden public funds, a criminal conviction abroad for a non-political extraditable crime, or a previous expulsion order under the Aliens Act. A person denied entry could appeal to an Immigration Board composed of individuals with magisterial, business or administrative experience. The Bill also ensured the right of asylum for 'destitute aliens' who could demonstrate that they were seeking refuge from political or religious persecution. If passed into law, it would grant the Home Secretary the authority to expel 'undesirable' aliens in cases where a court, including a court of summary jurisdiction, certified that the individual had been convicted of a crime and recommended expulsion instead of, or in addition to, a fine or imprisonment. A foreigner could also be expelled if such a court determined that he or she had received relief from Poor Law authorities within twelve months of their last entry into the country, was a vagrant, lived in unsanitary conditions due to overcrowding or had been convicted elsewhere of a crime as defined by the Extradition Act of 1870.

There was no question that the Bill was much more modest in scope than had been expected. 'The advocates of extreme measures', the journalist Myer Jack Landa wrote, 'made no attempt to disguise their disgust'.[107] As far as its members were concerned, the League had surrendered itself to a clique of political wirepullers and bowed to the demands of factions. All attempts to persuade the government to reintroduce the clauses that had been removed from the previous measure, or at least some of them, were fruitless. The new legislative act passed through the Commons and was then approved without amendment in the Lords. It received the Royal assent on 11 August. 'By a strange irony', wrote the *Jewish Chronicle* commenting on the 1906 general election, 'the Liberal Party which displayed so unsympathetic a demeanour towards the Aliens Bill, [was] now called upon to inaugurate the operation of the Aliens Act'.[108]

The story of the BBL could have ended here, but it did not. With the introduction of 'humanitarian' amendments to the Act by the new Liberal Home Secretary, Herbert Gladstone, 'restrictionists' called for renewed anti-alien agitation and more stringent measures. In particular, after Gladstone had instructed immigration officers to grant the 'benefit of doubt' to those immigrants who maintained that they were refugees from political or religious persecution, Conservatives distributed a malicious handbill entitled

The Aliens Act Made Useless: Our Ports Reopened to Criminal, Pauper and Diseased Aliens. The Liberals faced accusations of 'unduly lax' administration of the Aliens Act and, of course, that their alleged 'rampant pro-alienism' demonstrated 'the falsity of their pretended sympathy with the working classes'.[109] Addressing Mid-Hertfordshire Conservatives, diehard anti-immigrationist Henry Page Croft deplored the fact that 'there were welcomed into this country Anarchists, aliens of the criminal type, the diseased, scum of the earth. They came here and undermined the British constitution, and caused vast discontent among the working classes'.[110] From late 1908 onwards, the *East London Observer* reported attempts to revive the BBL, which greatly increased in the aftermath of the Houndsditch murders. 'The time has arrived to form a new British Brothers' League [...] to pass a drastic law to stop the influx of a horde of bloodthirsty assassins and the expulsion of all undesirables', wrote an anonymous contributor to an East End local paper. While this vigilante spirit soon dissipated and nothing was in fact done, it was a sinister reminder that the germ of intolerance was still there.[111] Thereafter, and notwithstanding the antisemitic sentiments stirred by the Marconi Scandal, the BBL gradually receded into obscurity.[112]

The outbreak of hostilities helped to some extent to clear the League's reputation, mainly as a result of the activities of Sir Edward Carson's Unionist War Committee and its demands for drastic revision of the naturalisation laws. In September 1918, about ten months after the Balfour Declaration was made public, Shaw proposed reorganising the BBL in a new form. The aim would be to provide demographic relief to East and North-East London, as well as parts of Manchester and Leeds, by transferring 'the Jews to Palestine, Syria and the Euphrates Valley under the auspices of the British government'.[113] Shaw, who had recently retired from the Territorials on account of ill-health, reasoned that the League supported the restoration of Israel to the ancient homeland as soldiers would not tolerate finding 'alien Jews' getting richer and richer while they were fighting in the Flanders.[114] Once again, as so often before, the Jews were cast as parasitic and disloyal, an inner enemy. The new League seems to have died at birth (and in spite of Lloyd George's electoral offer of 'Britain for the British, socially and industrially').

The BBL emerged as the first 'private' endeavour in Great Britain during the twentieth century to organise along paramilitary lines. Operating in a territory highly susceptible to racial tensions, it skilfully employed the weapons of racial demagoguery and the fervour fuelled by the Boer War to stoke native resentment against immigrants, particularly Eastern European Jews. It cast doubt on the patriotism and loyalty of their political adversaries, questioning their commitment to the British cause. The League advocated a policy of 'restriction and selection' aimed at curtailing the influx of undesirable immigrants and preserving racial purity. At the same time, it incited its members and followers to engage in acts of violence and create disturbances if the government failed to fulfil its promises. In light of these exhortations, it is not surprising that historians see the BBL as an incipient precursor to fascism.[115]

The want of stamina: the Right and the question of national physique

At the onset of the new century, immigration was just one of the social predicaments that concerned 'Britannia's zealots'. Aside from immigration, indications were emerging that the social conditions of urban centres were playing a critical role in the decline of the British people's physical and mental vitality. The squalid, overcrowded tenements, unsanitary factories and inadequate nourishment afflicting the labouring classes, rampant crime, idleness, and any form of moral waywardness were viewed as insidiously devouring the very essence of society like a malignant cancer. In the view of the conservative Right, 'physical inefficiency', whether due to environmental conditions or hereditary factors, was a paramount threat to military strength and potential. There was no doubt that the defence of the empire required robust, healthy, fecund bodies, and in their pursuit of this objective the prevailing sentiment among conservatives, as articulated by one historian, was moral condemnation of the weak and destitute rather than Christian compassion and social reform.[116]

In 1901, initial alarms were raised regarding the widespread lack of physical fitness for military service among the British youth. In his book *Efficiency and Empire*, Arnold White deplored the fact that a staggering 60 per cent of the men who had volunteered for army service at the Manchester recruiting depot in 1899 'were found to be physically unfit to carry a rifle and stand the fatigues of discipline'. In addition, only 40 per cent of those fit met the undemanding standards of muscular power and chest measurement laid down by the military authorities. For the staunchly antisemitic, anti-immigration journalist, there was little reason to believe that the situation was any different in other major British towns, and it might have been even worse. To make matters worse, 'while Britain's population [was] replenished not wholly but increasingly from its least desirable specimens', its world competitors were not showing signs of deterioration in physical stamina.[117] Several months later, Benjamin Seebohm Rowntree corroborated White's findings. In his seminal *Poverty, A Study of Town Life*, Rowntree presented compelling data on the suboptimal physical efficiency among the working classes, a deficiency that was evident in the numbers of recruits seeking enlistment in the army who were deemed physically unfit.

Between 1897 and 1901, the combined data from York, Leeds and Sheffield (three thousand six hundred applicants) revealed a cumulative rejection rate of 26.5 per cent. The reasons for rejection were wide-ranging and included defective vision, hearing impairment, underdeveloped physical attributes (such as chest size, weight or height), diminished intellectual capacity, dental decay, deformed limbs and various diseases. Rowntree noted, furthermore, that among those accepted 29 per cent were classified as 'specials', denoting individuals slightly below the established standard, but who were granted a trial period in the army to enhance their physical fitness. Taking both rejected applicants and 'specials' into account, a staggering 47 per cent of potential recruits fell short of the army's health and physical standards. This was substantiated at the national level by the Annual Report from the Inspector-General of Recruiting for 1900, referenced by Rowntree, which found that the average rate of rejection due to a range of ailments and 'want of physical development' between 1896 and 1899 was roughly 37 per cent. In 1900, this figure dropped to 28 per cent due to revised guidelines that instructed recruiting officers to proceed with medical examinations of recruits only when there was a reasonable probability of them passing.[118] Military recruitment figures, as the leading Liberal imperialist, Earl Grey wrote in *The Times*, 'cast a lurid light on the future which awaits the nation'. The future Governor General of Canada added that the 'population reared in the sunless slums of our smoke-enveloped cities' would, unless intermixed with the more robust classes, probably either be impotent or produce an 'infirm and rickety posterity'. In reference to the principle of efficiency, an ideal that was steadily gaining devotees within conservative circles as well, Earl Grey proposed carrying out an anthropometric study of school children throughout the country, collecting 'weights and measurements' being crucial to protect that human reservoir destined to bear the burden of the empire.[119]

In January 1902, the debate over the 'deterioration of the national physique' intensified significantly as Major General Sir John Frederick Maurice provocatively posed the question, 'where to get men?'. Analysing the figures, he came to the conclusion that 'a state of things in which no more than two out of five of the population below a certain standard of life are fit to bear arms, is a national danger which cannot be met by any mere schemes of enlistment, and that true patriotism requires the danger be recognized'. Mindful of his father's 'Christian-socialist' teachings, Sir Maurice attributed the causes of 'physical decadence' to purely environmental rather than hereditary factors. He therefore recommended that a substantial nationwide effort be made to counteract physical decline, involving both general and local initiatives and primarily focused on education. This endeavour would include training mothers on the fundamentals of infant care and ensuring that every child had the opportunity for robust physical development through gymnastic exercises.[120]

By this time, it became increasingly difficult to determine the exact boundary between the quest for physical efficiency and the quest for military preparedness. Arguments for and against the militarisation of school children reached new heights. *The Times* featured a series of articles entitled *National Training and National Defence*, underlying which was the principle that the nation's military efficiency ultimately rested on physical vigour, martial spirit and discipline.[121] The first article stressed that physical education and the development of young individuals, 'upon which their fitness to bear arms depends', was fundamental for the survival of the Empire. Another, no less important matter, it said, was the need to broaden the narrow foundation on which the military system rested, which would ensure that 'every able-bodied youth [would be] gradually trained to take his share, if called upon, in his country's defence'. *The Times* cited a letter from Lord Balfour directed to School Boards and managers in Scotland, in which the Conservative leader emphasised the educational importance of military drill, stating that 'not only does it tend to improve manual dexterity and to render more alert the faculties of observation, but it is also pre-eminently useful in developing those habits of comradeship, of responsibility, and of individual resource, which are of supreme importance, not only to the nation as a whole, but to the individual pupil'. The newspaper went on to suggest that in the last twelve years the Board of Education had rescued physical training from almost absolute neglect. The new Code of 1890 had mandated all elementary school headteachers to ensure proper arrangements were made for instruction in 'Swedish or other drill or other suitable physical exercises'. The 1901 Day School Code had established that 'The course in Physical Training should be carried on continuously throughout the school years for not less than one hour in each week for each class, and for not more than one half-hour for each class on any one day'. In 1902, the Board of Education in collaboration with the War Office issued the *Model Course of Physical Training, for Use in the Upper Departments of Public Elementary Schools*. This curriculum, which *The Times* described as 'quite excellent', was designed on the basis of Army training methods and consisted in military drill accompanied by exercises with dumbbells and barbells. Schools were encouraged to hire instructors 'preferably with training in the Army Gymnastic Course', and, generally, to refer to the War Office publication *Infantry Training, 1902*. Whilst *The Times* acknowledged that all these measures were steps in the right direction, it found their scale of application still to be inadequate. The bulk of the activities aimed at fostering physical training for the British youth were still being organised by the large reservoir of patriotic voluntary associations.[122]

In the manufacturing town of Macclesfield, Liberal Unionist Sir Henry Birchenough, together with philanthropist and social reformer Thomas Coglan Horsfall, founded in 1900 the Patriotic Association 'for the encouragement of physical training and military drill among lads between the ages of ten and seventeen'.[123] Birchenough insisted that national prosperity and military efficiency hinged on the physical fitness and martial spirit of Britons. Patriotism was vital, yet a robust and disciplined nation was essential. There was no doubt that the government's military plans would falter without proper physical energies. He therefore envisioned citizens creating a potent home defence at the local level by cultivating fit, patriotic, trained and disciplined youths, primed to safeguard the nation. 'Our object', Sir Birchenough explained more specifically in an article published in *Nineteenth Century* and pointedly entitled *Local Beginning of Imperial Defence: An Example*, was 'to begin with the boys in the elementary day schools, and to follow them with a carefully organised system of drill and gymnastics until they are old enough to become members of the Volunteer Corps'. By early 1901, all twenty-six Macclesfield district schools had embraced the Patriotic Association's proposal and were adhering to the following provisions:

1. All district schools were to allocate one hour per week during school hours for military drills.
2. Only students beyond the third standard were to participate in the drills.
3. Wherever possible, a school staff member was to act as the drill instructor, receiving compensation from the Association.
4. A professional drill instructor, employed and financed by the Association, was to visit and inspect town schools once a month and country schools once a fortnight.
5. The Association was to provide a covered hall in a central location (such as the Volunteer drill hall) for the use of town schools that lacked suitable playgrounds for military drills.[124]

In a few months, the Patriotic Association was overseeing the drilling of over two thousand children. The exercises and the orderly movements seemed so 'delightful' to the girls that in some of the schools they begged to also take part in drilling, and their requests were accepted. The Patriotic Association played a role in establishing gymnastic clubs and promoting shooting clubs in the towns. Boys were also equipped with carbines and other military equipment. All these activities were financed by private generosity. Lord Roberts, Sir Maurice and many others commended the work of the Patriotic Association.[125] However, it was discontinued in 1905, primarily in response to the Report of the Interdepartmental Committee on the Model Course of Physical Exercises, which recommended local authorities implement the more sober Syllabus of Physical exercises.[126]

Some contemporaries considered physical training without some form of moral disciplining to be an unbalanced pursuit. In 1901, the Bishop of Stepney, Henry Burdett and others founded the Twentieth Century League with the aim of coordinating and supervising the efforts of the numerous voluntary associations dedicated to providing recreational opportunities for the youth of London. These included, among others, the Church Lads' Brigade, the Social Institutes Union and Federation of Working Men's Social Clubs, Oxford House, the London Playing Fields Society and the YMCA. In its programme, the League promised to mitigate the growth of hooliganism, which was becoming a cause of considerable public apprehension. In this undertaking, physical training of working boys and girls was seen as an effective preventive against 'weakness of spirit' and the 'irascibility of temper'. Predictably, the League garnered Conservative support, notably from Lord Alverstone, who served first as vice-president and then president. From its inception, the League began setting up committees in various boroughs and engaging in outreach activities, but it failed to bring its federative aspirations to fruition.[127]

The Twentieth Century League did not introduce any particularly novel elements. It merely aimed to rejuvenate tried initiatives that had suddenly seemed lacking in efficacy. The late Victorian era had been a kind of golden age for youth associations and societies.[128] The Boys' Brigade, established in 1883, was the oldest organisation of its kind. Headquartered in Glasgow, it boasted branches not only across the United Kingdom, but also globally, in places such as the United States, Denmark, India, Ceylon, China and Japan. While its central aim was to propagate Christ's teachings among boys and nurture qualities like obedience, discipline and self-respect under the banner of Christian manliness, its appeal extended beyond any single Christian denomination. The Brigade was organised along military lines and used drills to engage boys. However, it also provided religious activities, such as Bible classes and Sunday services, while a variety of athletic clubs, ambulance classes, bands, reading rooms, boys' libraries and summer camps added to its educational programme. By 1905–1906, in Britain alone the Boys' Brigade had a membership of 53,486 boys aged twelve to seventeen years distributed across 1,237 companies, while its overall headcount including officers and staff sergeants was 60,612.[129]

Another significant group was the Church Lads' Brigade with headquarters in London. Established in 1891, this body had important similarities with the Boys' Brigade in its goals. Its main objective, as set out in its constitution, was 'To advance Christ's Kingdom among boys from all walks of life, promoting reverence, discipline, self-respect, and everything that contributes to genuine Christian character'. By incorporating principles of military organisation and more orthodox religious and educational initiatives, the Church Lads' Brigade aimed to create a space for underprivileged boys, especially those who, having completed their formal education by the ages of twelve to fourteen, were compelled to seek employment. The organisation stressed the importance of discipline, camaraderie and physical fitness. Like the Boys' Brigade, it established various clubs, initiated bands and garnered popularity through summer camps. As its name implied, the Church Lads' Brigade was closely linked with the Church of England. It functioned on diocesan lines and aspired to train its members to be 'loyal Churchmen, regular churchgoers, and communicants'. By 1907, the organisation boasted 1,145 companies across Britain and 112 in the colonies.[130]

Adding to the list of organisations fostering 'steadiness of character' in boys, were the London Diocesan Church's Lads Brigade, the Catholic Boys' Brigade and the Jewish Lads' Brigade.[131] In 1899, the Reverend John Brown Paton created the Boys' Life Brigade, whose aim was:

> to lead our boys to the service of Christ; to train them for an active, disciplined, and useful manhood; and to promote habits of self-respect, obedience, courtesy, and helpfulness to others, and all that made for a manly Christian character. These objects shall be sought chiefly by means of drill – not associated with the use of arms, but with instruction and exercises in the saving of life from fire, from drowning, and from accident.[132]

The cultivation of 'healthful vigour' and moral discipline was oriented towards the preservation of lives. The Brigade was closely connected with Sunday School. Membership was open to boys aged twelve to seventeen with younger ones joining as cadets in specialised company sections. Instruction included marching and gymnastics, stretcher drills, water safety and life-saving techniques, hygiene practices and first aid. In 1902, the Girls' Life Brigade was formed. The aim of the new movement was:

> to awaken in our girls a sense of their responsibility in life, to help them to make the very best use of their powers of body and mind, and so to train them to be capable and useful women. The discipline of the Brigade will encourage habits of punctuality and promptitude, self-respect, courtesy, and helpfulness to others; physical drill of various kinds will develop the body; and lessons in first-aid, sick-nursing, and life-saving will impart knowledge requisite in times of emergency. The Bible class and the personal influence of the officers in each Company will, it is believed, induce the girls to concentrate all their powers to the service of God.[133]

Enrolment was open to girls aged ten and above. The curriculum of company instruction was the same as that of the boys, with the addition of nursing. By April 1906, the Boys' Life Brigade had a combined membership of 8,485 (7,648 members and 726 cadets on roll, and 781 officers), while the Girls' Life Brigade counted a total of 1,363 members.[134]

Despite their military trappings, all these associations were fundamentally religious. Their concern, as one historian put it, was with the 'successful transition from Christian immaturity to maturity'.[135] Unsurprisingly, by the end of the century, many conservatives pondered uneasily whether prudential virtues of self-abnegation, fortitude and chivalry might be rendered obsolete by the new social-Darwinian realities of the age. All agreed that the Boer War had awakened British men from their 'laissez-faire complacency', which seemed to have sapped their manhood, leaving them unable to confront the hostility of more vigorous adversaries.[136] In 1899, the indefatigable Lord Meath established the Lads' Drill Association, inspired by the simple goal of '[arousing] the British nation to the serious nature of the problem of Imperial Defence'. In his introduction to the 1904 annual report, Lord Meath stated that, while not endorsing conscription, the association strove 'to point out the absolute necessity and to emphasise the importance, if the Empire is to be maintained, of training to arms, during the educative portion of their lives, the entire male youth of the British race, confident that in time of real danger the great mass would voluntarily offer their services to the State'.[137] Lord Meath, who had sponsored an impressive number of 'schemes for social improvement' since the early 1880s, was convinced that the work of the new association would be of 'inestimable advantage in reforming the loafing elements to be found amongst all classes' and nurture those manly virtues essential for efficient citizenship.[138]

For Meath and many other Conservatives, the question raised by the Marquis of Salisbury – 'How long can the final disintegration of the Empire be postponed?' – continued to cast an ominous shadow. The decline of British manhood extended beyond issues of health and sanitation. It raised questions about Britain's ability to compete in the struggle for world power, and no nation could thrive if weighed down by multitudes of weaklings and 'defectives'. 'Bodily discipline' was seen as a panacea against all social maladies. The problem was how to administer this cure and the degree of compulsion that could be deemed necessary to ensure the physical regeneration of the British race. It is not surprising that amid the South African disasters, the conscription debate resurfaced with a vengeance, creating division within the Right over the potential merits of compulsory military service compared with the volunteer system.[139]

Before, during and immediately after the war, several public figures highlighted the issue of British military unpreparedness. For instance, Spenser Wilkinson called for a strengthening of the efficiency of volunteers. In 1900, Colonel Lonsdale Hale and Thomas Miller Maguire lashed out on the organisation and training of both the regular forces and volunteers.[140] Coulton praised the Swiss system as a model which would, in Douglas Haig's words, root 'the Army in the people'. In an extensive article in *The Practitioner*, Sir James Cantlie, founder and inaugural President of the Royal Society of Tropical Medicine and Hygiene, advocated compulsory military service to halt the progressive physical degeneration of the population:

> From a national health point of view compulsory military service would be a great hygienic gain to the nation. Our public school boys, that is, the youths of the classes, are given time and opportunity to indulge in out-of-door sports, but the children of the masses have no such privileges. After school life is over, at, say, thirteen, the boy of the poorer classes in town has no playground open to him; he has to look forward to close indoor employment, and his holidays are but an occasional run to the seaside or the country in Bank Holidays. Were he, however, compelled to undergo [...] military training, say from seventeen to nineteen, how much would it mean to him and to the nation! The direct physical benefit obtainable is calculated to increase the work-producing power of the nation. The discipline inculcated during these critical periods of life is potential of great good. The habits of cleanliness taught and the meaning of hygiene and sanitation insisted upon, elementary though they would necessarily be, would affect the man's future life, it may be insensibly and to but a slight degree; but a minimum of education in these matters, touching as it would all classes, means a colossal total towards betterment.[141]

In 1901, George F. Shee went as far as attributing apotropaic functions to conscription in *The Britons' First Duty*. Drawing inspiration from George Quick's *The Rush to Ruin, and the Remedy* and other books by Horsfall on physical training, Shee was of the view that universal military service, combined with a scientific system of gymnastics, would significantly improve the nation's physique and prevent the degeneration of the race so worryingly described in the Reports of the Army Medical Department. 'The training of the whole manhood of the nation', he said, 'in discipline, duty, obedience to authority, manliness, and self-mastery [would prove to be] a moral and intellectual factor of untold value in the life of the people'. By rescuing 'the moral degenerates from the slum', military training would help rein in expenses on prisons, workhouses and mental asylums, and generally improve national efficiency.[142]

The Norfolk Commission on the Militia and Volunteers, which had condemned the unpreparedness of the auxiliary forces for war and had recommended – in vain – some vague scheme of compulsory service, provided the NSL with the opportunity to promote universal military obligation as a means to cultivate and rejuvenate the nation as a whole. The Precis of Evidence, compiled by the then secretary of the NSL, Shee, and submitted to the Commission, strongly emphasised the link between military service and the health of the nation. It was argued that national service would not only significantly enhance the physical fitness of the people but would also be a potent method for disciplining hooligans and the 'disorderly elements' of the population. In considering the potential loss of national wealth resulting from diverting labourers from their civilian occupations, the document emphasised not only the brevity of the proposed training period but also the compensations, which included reductions in expenses related 'to hospitals, workhouses, prisons, and lunatic asylums to which many young men tended to gravitate'. In addition, serving together in a true national force would unite people from all social classes and instil in them the importance of 'responsible citizenship' and a sense of 'social solidarity'.[143] When questioned by chairman Aretas Akers-Douglas about accommodation for conscripts, Shee declared that 'to a great number of the working classes it would be an infinite benefit to be taken away from their slums and unhealthy quarters, and learn in barracks better cleanliness and punctuality, and get better housing, air and food, and so on'.[144]

It should come as no surprise that a social reformer like Horsfall supported mandatory national service to protect and enhance the population. Among the benefits of the 'principle of universal obligation' he saw the opportunity to conduct yearly examinations to evaluate the population's overall condition, the impetus for social reform, a boost in patriotism and the cultivation of a broad sense of camaraderie transcending social classes. In *The Relation of National Service to the Welfare of the Community*, Horsfall wrote:

> General service could not fail to improve the position of the working class as a whole greatly ... Most of these men ... would be physically unfit for service, though some ... would be fit, and the large proportion of rejections among them would compel the community to improve the conditions under which they lived, and to prevent, by good physical training in schools, by continuation classes, by the feeding of hungry children, and the discouragement of drinking the creation of any more poor creatures of the kind. By these measures, and the training in common action which all who served in the army would receive, the power of the working classes to work together for ends desired by them, and the knowledge possessed by them respecting the conditions necessary for their welfare, would be very greatly increased.[145]

Socialists such as Henry Hyndman, Robert Blatchford and Henry Quelch also supported the principle of mandatory service, citing its potential to usher in significant social improvements. However, as the socialist newspaper *Labour Leader* pointed out in response to the startling recommendations of the Norfolk Commission, the word 'conscription' sounded 'as hateful to British tradition as slavery'.¹⁴⁶ While Horsfall and some socialist dissenters were concerned with the improvement of working-class conditions, industrialists were in favour of national service in the name of productivity, efficiency and competition, especially against Germany. In the view of soap and glycerine manufacturer Captain George Rowlandson Crosfield, who played an important role in disseminating the NSL's message in northern England, a short military training programme would instil essential habits of discipline and orderly work in the community.¹⁴⁷

In *Some Objects of the League*, issued by the NSL in the summer of 1905, it was stated that universal military training for national defence would, among other effects, strengthen 'the national fibre and sense of civic duty by connecting all men with national ideals through personal service in youth'; improve 'national health through sound physical development in all schools, continued during the period of military training'; support 'industrial organization'; replace 'hooliganism and jingoism with self-control and a sense of responsibility'; and counteract 'the centrifugal tendencies natural in a democratic state, and to lead, by a common sacrifice for a great ideal, to the organisation of our national resources for national strength and efficiency'.¹⁴⁸ Once at the helm of the NSL, Lord Roberts basically reiterated the view that military training would 'solve many of our social problems, by improving the character, the morale and the physique of the race'.¹⁴⁹ However, from 1908 onwards, the concern for physical prowess, while not entirely sidelined, began to take a backseat to concerns of potential invasion and preservation of the social order. In Lord Roberts's words:

> The Army was not a perfect medium of education, but it does accomplish two things thoroughly: it demolishes class prejudices, and it teaches self-discipline. Of late years it is to be feared that the education of the nation has been singularly unsuccessful in these two respects. Apathy towards one's duties, 'envy, hatred, and malice' towards other classes, do not make for a strong, happy, and united people, nor for a durable Empire.¹⁵⁰

The prioritisation of social discipline overshadowed the pursuit of social reform. Addressing a large crowd at Victoria Halls, Lord Curzon began by citing Luke 11:21: 'When a strong man armed keepeth his palace, his goods are in peace'. He then asked, 'Is there anyone among you who would not be better off for having learned some lessons in discipline, self-sacrifice, and manly exercise on the drill ground, shooting range, or in the camp?'¹⁵¹

At the beginning of 1903, Sir Maurice published a new article entitled *National Health. A Soldier's Study*, in which he asked 'Is it or is it not true that the whole labouring population of the land are at the present living under conditions which make it impossible that they should rear the next generation to be sufficiently virile to supply more than two out of five men effective for the purposes of either peace or war?' The available figures painted a disquieting picture, revealing that 60 per cent of young men were unfit for military service due to 'defective physique' – even more so considering that the recruits being accepted for service were shorter, lighter and 'narrower chested' than in the past. In a stern judgement, Sir Maurice stated, 'no nation was ever yet for any long time great and free, when the army it put into the field no longer represented its own virility and manhood'.[152] March saw publication of the Annual Report of the Inspector-General of Recruiting for the Year 1902, which stated significantly that 'the one subject which causes anxiety in the future, as regards recruiting, is the gradual deterioration of the physique of the working classes, from which the bulk of the recruits must always be drawn'. The ideologue and secretary of the NSL, George F. Shee, comparing the physical condition of British recruits with their French and German counterparts, found the latter to have a significant advantage. 'While our national physique shows many signs of deterioration', he remarked, 'the physique of Continental nations has improved and is improving since the adoption of universal military service gave to the whole manhood of those countries a sound physical training and discipline of body and mind'. He also pointed out that during their initial six months of training, recruits typically increased their chest girth by an average of two inches. The logical conclusion drawn from this observation was that underprivileged youths in the country were suffering a severe lack of physical training.[153] Around this time, William Taylor, Director General of the Army Medical Department, wrote a memorandum on the alleged 'physical degeneration' of the British people. Addressed to the Secretary of State for War and issued as a Parliamentary Paper in the summer of 1903, the report confirmed Sir Maurice's estimates. In his attempt to determine whether 'this indictment of the nation's health' was applicable to the entire population or only a specific section of it, Taylor stressed that a considerable portion of soldiers were recruited from the unskilled labour class, the large majority of whom were living near or below the poverty line. It was not difficult to infer that that the 'impairment of physical vigour' of the urban population was the result of a combination of undernourishment, unsanitary living conditions, endemic alcoholism and the spread of tuberculosis and syphilis in densely populated areas.[154] Following the release of Taylor's memorandum, Liberals and Conservatives alike voiced their disparagement of urban life and their idealisation of the rural world in similar terms.[155]

The question of physical decadence was not only a military, but also a racial concern. On 15 February 1902 in Liverpool, Lord Rosebery reminded the advocates of efficiency that 'the Imperial principle is not merely for extending the dominions of the British Crown. The Imperial principle [reaches] right down to the bottom of our social organisation. It is no use having an Empire without an Imperial race'.[156] In *The Lancet*, Sir Lauder Brunton starkly contemplated whether these recruits, who lacked both physical robustness and mental acuity, would marry women similarly afflicted. This could set off a cycle in which the progenies would only contribute to the statistics of infant mortality, criminality and degeneracy. Brunton proposed the appointment of a commission to determine the most effective methods for addressing the 'national calamities' of dental decay, flat feet and feeble constitution.[157] The suggestion was reiterated in a letter to the *Manchester Guardian* on 2 April 1903. Sir Brunton, who is primarily remembered for being the first to use amyl nitrite to treat angina pectoris, believed that physical efficiency was the very foundation of military efficiency.[158] Brunton's interest in 'physical efficiency' was stimulated by the Italian physiologist, Angelo Mosso, who came to England to explore the general principles of 'industrial fatigue'. In his earlier campaigning, Brunton recommended that the rudiments of marksmanship be taught in schools at the earliest possible age, and that children were to play with toy guns and percussion caps. In *The Times*, he suggested turning traditional childhood games, such as 'I spy', 'French and English', and 'Prisoner's Base' into war games. This would provide young boys with basic military skills and preclude the need for any government to introduce conscription.[159] In 1901, Brunton and Colonel Pennington, one of his patients, drafted a scheme for military training in schools, 'with the object of teaching from early youth discipline, bodily activity, accuracy, the habit of observation, and the skilful handling of arms; and to develop the intelligence of individuals in the direction of thinking and acting for themselves in reference to a common object, and especially with reference to mutual action'. The course was tailored to gradually accommodate the capabilities of children and boys across different age groups. Instruction would cover physical exercises, close-order drills, range estimation, shooting, scouting and skirmishing, and would culminate in the formation of a cadet corps.[160] However, in 1902, Brunton realised that advocating the introduction of military training in schools 'in the present temper of the country' was futile, and that 'the only possible thing was to try for physical training'. In 1915, in the preface to his *Collected papers on physical and military training*, he wrote: 'Had the risks which I then pointed out been recognised, and the course I then advocated been adopted, our position in regard to this present war would have been very different'. Brunton's ideas concerning physical regeneration were attracting significant attention among conservatives and right-wingers, including Henry Craik (then president of the Scottish Commission on Physical Education), Algernon Borthwick, First Baron Glenesk and Leopold Maxse. In 1903, Brunton took steps to organise a national league which could ensure the implementation of a national 'health conscience'. The scheme, which aimed to federate the 'various agencies' committed to the advancement of physical training, was not formally initiated until the summer of 1905. Also supporting this initiative was the Bishop of Ripon, William Boyd Carpenter, who had become particularly concerned about the declining birthrate and the disproportionate propagation of 'physically inferior stocks' within the British population. As for the national physique, the Bishop agreed with the Lord of Meath that the great rural reservoir of vigour was withering away, and that urban civilisation had 'weakened the blood' of British people.[161]

Fears over the alleged physical degeneration of the British people were further heightened by publication of the Report of the Inter-Departmental Committee on the Employment of School Children (1902) and the Report of the Royal Commission on Physical Training in Scotland (1903). The Scottish report found that there was 'an undeniable degeneration of individuals of the classes where food and environment are defective, which called for attention and amelioration in obvious ways, one of which is a well-regulated system of physical training'. At this point, even the most authoritative sceptics became convinced, or claimed to be convinced, that the issue of physical fitness was not a localised, passing affliction. In July, *The British Medical Journal* (BMJ) for the first time debated the alleged physical decline of the nation. Apart from 'unsound teeth', the journal suggested that the causes of the growing physical unfitness could be ascribed to parental neglect or ill-treatment. The 1901 census of England and Wales revealed that out of a total of 1,334,688 boys aged between ten and fourteen years around 10.35 per cent (138,130) were involved in labour, while out of 1,339,279 girls of the same age, the percentage dropped to a still intolerable 5.26 per cent (70,262). It was no wonder, the journal commented, that children developed 'imperfect constitutions'. Accordingly, the BMJ warned: 'Now, more than at any time in the history of the British people do we require stalwart sons to people the colonies and to uphold the prestige of the nation'. There was hope that the Duke of Devonshire's promised Commission to inquire into the alleged degeneration of the urban population, would, if not dispel fear, then at least provide the means to arrest the phenomenon.[162]

On 3 September 1903, the Balfour government reluctantly established the Interdepartmental Commission on Physical Deterioration. Nearly eleven months later, the Committee released a ninety-three-page report containing only eight pages of recommendations. Despite the sombre accounts of misery, disease and malnutrition given by the sixty-eight witnesses examined, they concluded that there was no evidence to support the view that the British race was undergoing a general and progressive deterioration. The report highlighted the lack of appropriate housing as the most critical of the factors contributing to physical deterioration. 'This evil', it stated, 'was the greatest in one-room tenements, the over-crowding there being among persons usually of the lowest type, steeped in every kind of degradation and cynically indifferent to the vile surroundings engendered by their filthy habits, and to the pollution of the young brought up in such an atmosphere'. Another striking aspect of the report was the malnourishment of children, revealed by statistics indicating that between 16 per cent and 20 per cent of the entire school population suffered food scarcity. The Committee made fifty-three recommendations, which included establishing a permanent anthropometric survey and a sickness register, creating a new advisory health council, appointing medical officers in areas exceeding a specific population threshold, enforcing stricter laws on unsanitary and overcrowded housing, enabling local authorities to provide meals for undernourished children lacking proper nutrition at home, establishing specialised schools for 'retarded' children, promoting physical activities and exercises for students, granting funds from the National Exchequer to all clubs and cadet corps focused on physical or quasi-military training, educating mothers in prenatal care and cookery, addressing alcoholism and regulating issues like juvenile smoking and syphilis.[163] The apprehension with which degeneration was regarded had, as noted by historians, been momentarily calmed, yet the language associated with it continued to flourish.[164]

After the Report came out, new organisations surfaced, while existing ones gained renewed momentum. As a testament to his unwavering spiritual devotion to the empire, the indefatigable Lord Meath founded the Empire Day Movement. This society was primarily aimed at reinforcing among all British subjects the virtues that defined a 'model imperial citizen', including loyalty, patriotism, courage, endurance, respect for and obedience to lawful authority and the willingness to make personal sacrifices for the collective good. Its overarching goal was to instil these values in the youth, in particular, and raise their awareness of their duties and responsibilities. Empire Day was first observed in Great Britain on 24 May 1904, a date that coincided with the birthday of the late Queen Victoria. It was celebrated in all schools and consisted in a miscellany of patriotic lectures, recitations, songs, readings and other elements that exalted the grandeur of the empire. The motto of the Empire Day movement was: 'One King, One Flag, One Fleet, One Empire'. It operated autonomously and without oversight from the Board of Education. From its very inception, it drew praise from right-wing conservatives and scrutiny from those opposed to militarism. In 1908, the House of Commons rejected formal recognition of Empire Day, to the jubilation of Irish Nationalists and Labourites. Their delight was not entirely unwarranted, as Lord Meath himself later argued that the success of the Empire Movement could be gauged by the significant enlistment of young men from various parts of the Empire in 1914. It was not until 1916 that

Lord Meath successfully secured government endorsement for Empire Day, despite already enjoying the status of a statutory holiday in most of the Dominions. The Empire Day movement ultimately proved to be a resounding and enduring success.[165]

Lord Meath's fight to protect British masculinity and character from the entropy of modern society found another channel in The Duty and Discipline Movement. Instigated in 1909, at the time when Lloyd George introduced the famous Budget, the movement aimed to 'combat softness, slackness, indifference, and indiscipline, and to stimulate discipline, and a sense of duty and alertness throughout the national life, especially during the formative period of home and school training', and 'to give reasonable support to all legitimate authority'.[166] The movement disseminated its ideas through various publications, including *Essays on Duty and Discipline*, the *Patriot Series* and pamphlets. These works covered a broad array of topics, encompassing child-rearing, the nurturing of 'true manhood', moral stamina and physical culture. Special attention was paid to the modern perils of 'indulgence', 'immoderate pursuit of pleasure' and 'sentimentality', all of which were seen as factors that could undermine 'the moral fibre of children'. In hyperbolic rhetorical terms, the erosion of juvenile discipline was posited as standing as a 'serious social danger, and a peril to the permanent security of the Empire'. Unsurprisingly, while the 'Great Labour Unrest' roared, the early training of boys in responsible citizenship and the 'value of a certain hardness in education' were promoted with renewed vigour. The contributors to this 'crusade', which had amassed four thousand members by the eve of the war, included bishops, archbishops, members of the military and many conservatives. The various endorsements of the 'Duty and Discipline' series included one from Admiral Lord Charles Beresford, who praised the movement emphasising that 'The future of our race depends upon the children of today: Unless a sense of duty, self-respect, obedience, discipline, and good comradeship is practically taught and ingrained in the youthful mind, the old characteristics of our people will disappear'. William Bull added that 'it is a most timely reminder that the moral character which has made the race strong for good purposes was not acquired by indulgence and dependence on the efforts of others'. Balfour concurred, stating that the 'objects [of The Duty and Discipline Movement] were quite admirable'. The organic, motor and nervous development of the growing child converged with the deliberate and mindful cultivation of moral and social discipline.[167]

During the House of Lords debate on Lord Roberts's National Service (Training and Home Defence) Bill, Lord Meath unequivocally articulated this [unquenchable] conservative thirst and aspiration for a robust order. He affirmed his support for the voluntary principle but contended that the British people had become too soft, undisciplined and lacking in manliness, and therefore in need of some form of universal training. Consequently, he called for the integration of harmonious relations into the entire social organism:

> What we want is discipline in the upper classes, discipline in the middle classes, and discipline in the lower classes. If we had more discipline, we should not have such a large number of men and women who think nothing of the State and of the community, whose sole idea is pleasure, pleasure, pleasure; and we should not have those 'slackers' in the lower classes whose whole idea is how much money they can get out of their employers and how little work they can do.[168]

As far as Meath and right-wing conservatives were concerned, society functioned as an organism governed by the principles and processes of organic life. Ideas of patriotism, civic duty, self-discipline, self-sacrifice, punctuality and discipline counteracted the degenerating impact of modern society and cultivated resistance, immunity and physiological efficiency. Lord Meath and The Duty and Discipline Movement were not alone in advocating for social hygiene. In 1901, with the backing of the National Vigilance Association, the National Social Purity Crusade was established with the explicit aim of combatting 'the terrible and insidious spread of impurity in current literature, in schools, as well as in the cities, towns, and villages' of Britain. The 'crusaders' targeted illegitimacy, prostitution, mendicity, crime and all forms of debasing habits as factors that, in their view, 'weakened willpower, depleted the physical nature, and enervated the body'. With the threat of a continental war looming, the campaign for purity exhibited all the characteristics of apocalyptic zealotry and eugenic fatalism.[169] An often-quoted manifesto of 1911 sounded the alarm at 'the low and degrading views of the racial instinct' which were allegedly pervading society. 'Many causes, old and new', stated the manifesto, 'are contributing to the evasion of the great obligation of parenthood and the degradation of the marriage tie'. Predictably, evidence of this decline was found in the birthrate. The manifesto insisted that British youth of both sexes were 'in danger of corruption due to the circulation of pernicious literature for which no defence can be offered'. 'The situation is further aggravated', it said, 'by the fact that our education system too frequently ignores the sacred and responsible functions that confront the young upon reaching maturity. The tendencies of the age make it imperative that they should be taught to entertain high conceptions of marriage as involving duties to the future of the nation and the race'. The manifesto also declared that 'a high proportion of immorality and inebriety is due to the neglect of the incurably defective-minded, whose progeny, lamentably numerous under present conditions, too frequently resemble their parents and largely reinforce the ranks of degradation and shame. These cases must now receive permanent care separate from the community, so that they and posterity may be protected'. In conclusion, the signatories of the manifesto expressed the opinion that it is only along these lines – 'by raising the ideals of marriage, by educating for parenthood, and by intervening to prevent degeneracy' – that the demoralisation referred to can be addressed. Among the signatories of this manifesto, which effectively brought together and consolidated all the apprehensions held by conservatives, could be found peers, bishops, archbishops and reactionaries, whose inherent pessimism predisposed them to view any form of change as an indication of societal decline.[170]

In June 1905, Brunton finally established the National League for Physical Education and Improvement (NLPEI). The aims of this organisation were to kindle public concern for the physical well-being of people across the entire kingdom. It sought to create a cohesive network that would bring together all societies and individuals dedicated to countering those factors that were contributing to the national degeneration. In this task, it aimed to support existing organisations and establish new ones focused on promoting physical health and wellness in areas lacking such initiatives. The movement adhered to non-political and non-denominational principles. After the inaugural meeting at Mansion House on 28 June, where speeches were delivered by distinguished figures such as the Bishop of Ripon, the Lord Chief Justice (Lord Alverstone), William Broadbent, Richard Haldane and James Crichton-Browne, another meeting was held at the Cannon Street Hotel, where approximately thirty representatives from diverse societies dedicated to promoting 'national health' convened to align with the plan put forward by the NLPEI.[171] Shortly afterwards, the Twentieth Century League also merged with this new organisation. Over time, the NLPEI focused on ensuring the availability of pure milk and nutritious food for infants and children. They also highlighted the importance of comprehensive physical training for school children and of establishing clubs, institutes and drill associations for boys and girls in their after-school years. The NLPEI received support from conservatives such as Lord Halsbury, Lord Ashbourne, Lord Meath, Henry Craik, John Batty Tuke, John Eldon Gorst (before the Tariff Reform controversy) and many others.[172]

Early on in his efforts, Brunton had been forced to redirect his attention from military preparedness to physical preparedness, reconceptualising the latter as a medical concern and elucidating it in physiological terms. For instance, drawing on Mosso and Kronecker's research, he emphasised the potential negative effects of overexertion and the need for well-structured, graduated training programmes to ensure the fitness and health of individuals, particularly in military training. Acknowledging the wisdom of Solomon

– 'Be not righteous overmuch, neither make thyself over-wise, why shouldst thou destroy thyself?' – Brunton underscored the paramount significance of balancing the physical and mental aspects of training in efficiency. In this regard, he praised the physical training systems of Sweden and Switzerland, both of which countries, he argued, had prioritised military and physical preparedness in their educational systems. In Switzerland, military gymnastics were compulsory in elementary schools and were taught by specially trained instructors. They also offered voluntary rifle practice and military drill, both with and without arms. In Sweden, compulsory rifle practice was established in public secondary schools for boys aged fifteen to eighteen under the supervision of specialised instructors. In a short pamphlet entitled *National Physical Training. An open debate*, Brunton wrote:

> In the Swiss as well as the Swedish system the muscles are trained by position exercises either with or without light weights, and the brain by drill. Co-ordinating nerve centres are trained by games of ball, and the heart and lungs are developed by running. The attention required to act at once at the word of command in drill involves, at first at least, a considerable amount of nervous strain, and is to be reckoned as mental rather than as bodily exercise. It is very useful in training habits of prompt obedience and of combined action, but like other lessons is apt to be wearisome to the child, and should not be continued long at a time [...] The games recommended by the Swiss rules are of the same kind as those which are popular with us – tig, cross-tig, leap-frog, hide-and-seek, and games of ball. These games are carried out in the open air, and as many players as possible take part in them. According to the rules of the game, no scholar is to be idle, and the masters watch the games as much as the exercises in order to see the effect of them upon the scholars and to prevent those who are weakly being injured from overstrain.[173]

The Swiss and Swedish systems of open-air calisthenics and preparatory military instruction provided Brunton with a model for nurturing patriotism, civic responsibility, and personal development in all those aspects that contribute to the cultivation of clean, healthy, robust British manhood. It is highly likely that Brunton was acquainted with the age-old military adage that states, 'A vicious man is never an athlete, and an athlete is rarely anything but a wholesome, well-conducted man'.

In Brunton's view, preparedness conveyed the idea of being ready or equipped for any situation or contingency, whether it was related to war or peace. In November 1908, he presented a paper entitled *Physical Education and Training in Relation to National Defence* at a National Defence Association meeting at the Piccadilly Hotel. Brunton admitted that he did not foresee the need for compulsory service in Britain. However, acknowledging the need to prevent conscription, he stressed the importance of improving standards of physical fitness among potential recruits from all social classes, and the need to provide equal opportunities for physical fitness and education to underprivileged children, starting with health and fitness education in infancy and continuing with physical training beyond formal schooling. In addition, Brunton drew attention to the societal and economic benefits of improved fitness and urged collaboration between municipal organisations and the NLPEI. He concluded his speech by invoking the metaphor of Noah's Ark in foreboding tones, and cautioning against any sense of complacency he expressed his support for the thorough preparation of the younger generation to dispel the looming spectres of invasion and societal decadence. Brunton's impassioned plea for action was part of the response to an unsuccessful endeavour to incorporate military drill into the standard curriculum of schools, as mandated in Haldane's Territorial Forces Act.[174] The issue of mandatory military training in schools resurfaced time and again in the years right before (and during) the war, accompanied by proposals on how it could be efficiently structured. However, these proposals met with opposition from both Parliament and the public and as a result no definitive action was ever taken. Patriotic grassroots initiatives therefore continued to oversee the military or quasi-military instruction of students.[175]

Brunton was also a member of the Council of Boy Scouts. In 1910, he wrote in the *Daily Telegraph* that 'education in order to be complete should not only be mental and physical, but also moral [...] and this is what the Boy Scout movement supplies'.[176] The official mission of the Boy Scouts as set out by its founder, Lieutenant General Sir Robert Baden-Powell, was: 'To help boys of whatever class to become all-round men, to give them character and make them capable of looking after themselves in whatever circumstances they were placed. The movement's method was to educate the boys in a way that would greatly appeal to them, namely scoutcraft or backwoodsmanship and its manly attributes'.[177] While the Boy Scouts movement was explicitly non-military in nature, it was widely acknowledged that the qualities of character and intellect instilled in young boys through the scout system closely matched those that were highly valued in military service.[178] Certainly, those who accused Baden-Powell of grooming the next generation of British soldiers could not have been easily mollified by his injunction that 'Every boy ought to learn how to shoot and obey orders, else he is no more good when war breaks out than an old woman'.[179] The presence of serving or retired Army officers in the inaugural executive committee, some of them with affiliation to the NSL, reinforced the perception that the movement had underlying military intentions or influences. It is of particular significance that in the spring of 1921, the NSL, acknowledging that its primary objectives had become unattainable, ceased its operations. The remaining funds in its possession, a total of approximately £12,000, were donated to the Scouts as the body that 'most successfully teaches the ideals of citizenship of which Lord Roberts' scheme was a part'.[180]

Baden Powell's cry for 'character' was more than the ethical expression of a pessimistic *Weltanschauung*. In a lecture presented to the Royal United Service Institution in spring 1911, entitled 'Boy Scouts in Relation to National Training and National Service', Baden-Powell stated that 'To be a Soldier a man must be a MAN, not a sheep ... and the main aim [of the Boy Scouts] is to help the national training in character':

> Over-civilization threatens England with deterioration. Free feeding and old-age pensions, strike pay, cheap beer and indiscriminate charity do not make for the hardening of the nation or the building up of a self-reliant, energetic manhood. They tend, on the contrary, to produce an army of dependents and wasters, and this is being steadily recruited by 46 per cent. of our working boys, who are employed, so long as they are boys, in 'blind alley' occupations, which fit them for nothing when they become grown up. The best types of manliness left in our race are our colonial frontiersmen – men who, if they want to live, have to be resourceful and energetic, plucky and enduring under the difficulties of climate and surroundings, and who have to fight their way to success. These are the men whom we hold up to the boys as examples to follow. They are the true 'scouts' of the nation.[181]

The hero of the siege of Mafeking harboured conservative concerns about societal degeneration and decadence. Influenced by Elliott Mills's pamphlet *The Decline and Fall of the British Empire*, he warned in his enormously popular *Scouting for Boys*, that:

> The main causes of the downfall of Rome are similar to that which resulted in the downfall of other great empires, such as the Babylonian, Egyptian, Greek, Spanish, and Dutch, and that cause may be summed up in each case as the decline of good citizenship and the want of energetic patriotism. Each nation, after climbing laboriously to the zenith of its power, seemed then to become exhausted by its effort, and sit down in a state of repose, relapsing into idleness, studiously blind to the fact that other nations were gradually pushing up to destroy it [...] The main point is for us to take the lesson to heart, and see, before it is too late, that our Empire also be not undermined by these defects.[182]

In another passage, his crude, social-Darwinist understanding of history was linked to the quest for physical regeneration and efficiency. 'Recent reports on the deterioration of our race ought to act as a warning to be taken in time before it goes too far. One cause which contributed to the downfall of the Roman Empire was the fact that the soldiers fell away from the standard of their forefathers in bodily strength'.[183] Manhood should be nourished and shielded from the perceived dangers of welfare ('people ... being fed by the State'), idleness, luxury and 'democracy'. *Scouting for Boys* was packed with references to the importance of military readiness, with Baden-Powell asserting that 'Peace cannot be certain unless we show that we are always fully prepared to defend ourselves in England, and that an invader would only find himself ramming his head against bayonets and well-aimed bullets if he tried landing on our shores'.[184] Being prepared for war was the most reliable means of maintaining peace.

On the occasion of the thirtieth anniversary of the founding of the Boy Scouts, more than a few contemporaries were inclined to attribute the success of Kitchener's New Army to the 'boy-scout spirit'. It was said that one of the movement's greatest achievements was the mobilisation of one hundred and fifty thousand members, with ten thousand fatalities and eleven awards for the Victoria Crosses.[185] Furthermore, at the onset of the war, Baden-Powell easily shifted the emphasis of the scouting movement from tracking, woodcraft and wilderness survival to some sort of paramilitaristic training with the establishment of the Scouts Defence Corps. This initiative aimed to train all Scouts and former Scouts aged fourteen and above in military drills, marksmanship and related skills, with the overarching goal of creating a disciplined cadre of young men capable of constituting a reserve force for homeland defence.[186]

By 1909, six thousand girls had joined the scout movement under the banner of the 'Girl Guides'. The movement's prospectus acknowledged (again) that the nation faced a dual threat of moral and physical decadence, much of it stemming from 'the ignorance and supineness of mothers who have never taught themselves'. The document stressed that 'girls must be partners and comrades rather than dolls', given the significant influence they had on men's actions and character in adulthood. It recommended character training for girls on a par with boys and expressed concern about girls either idling away their time or, vice versa, pursuing excessively 'manly' activities. The new organisation therefore aimed to inspire girls to engage in useful 'woman's work with zeal', and in making themselves useful to others and themselves while preserving their 'womanliness'. The quest to escape the seemingly inescapable fate that besets empires demanded the united sacrifice of every Briton, irrespective of gender.[187]

Amongst the array of organisations that the conservative mind regarded as tools for counteracting national degeneration and promoting efficiency, the EES merits inclusion. Founded in 1907, it had three core objectives. The first was to highlight the national importance of eugenics, the goal being to shape public opinion and foster a sense of responsibility with regard to aligning all aspects of human parenthood with eugenic ideals.

Figure 3.1 Lieutenant General Sir Robert Baden-Powell, Lord Haldane, and a scout patrol leader at the Royal United Service Institution. *Daily Mirror*, 30 March 1911. Image © Reach PLC. Image created courtesy of The British Library Board

The second was to disseminate knowledge of hereditary laws, as far as they were known, in the pursuit of 'improving' the race. Lastly, it would endeavour to bring eugenic education to households and schools. The Society played an active role in advocating for the Mental Deficiency Act of 1913, a piece of English social legislation that was unprecedented in being informed by heredity.[188] While conservatives generally preferred bodily discipline to selective breeding, there were some important exceptions. Balfour agreed to become Honorary vice-president of the EES in 1913, and Joynson Hicks and the then unknown Neville Chamberlain also joined the Society. The appointment of the Malthusian and conservative Montague Hughes Crackanthorpe as President of the Eugenics Society signalled a programmatic convergence between a minority of eugenicists and proponents of conscription, which stemmed from the belief that military service was deemed 'eugenically useful' due to its promotion of physical fitness and efficiency.[189]

Eugenics undoubtedly appealed to a diehard minority. For example, Lord Willoughby de Broke was a friend of the founder of the EES, the Fabian Caleb Saleeby and a devoted eugenicist. In 1914, perhaps taking his cue from Galton, he introduced a Bill to require young men who had inherited a privileged status in society to validate their position by fulfilling their military obligations. The established aristocracy, insulated from the relentless forces of natural selection by tradition, should be preserved from 'impending extinction' and allowed to rekindle its martial spirit. However, Willoughby de Broke conceded that 'measures for the improvement of the race' could not be dictated solely by principles of hereditary, but needed to be aligned with environmentally driven social reforms.[190] In short, he firmly believed that the security of Britain rested on 'breeding from the best stocks and bringing to maturity the greatest possible number of mentally and physically sound men and women, reared among healthy surroundings, in the ideals of Religion and Patriotism, equipped with a trade education, protected by a Tariff from unfair foreign competition [and] trained to bear arms'.[191]

Aside from Willoughby de Broke and a few other diehards who had the patience to undertake statistical or biometric investigations, the Right found its most ardent advocate of eugenic methods in Arnold White. In his book *The Problems of a Great City* (1886) he emerged as a precursor of negative eugenics. Years later, he introduced the notion of 'sterilisation of the unfit', although he limited his recommendations to segregating specific 'defective' classes, stricter marriage laws and preventive detention for repeat offenders. In *The Views of Vanoc*, White wrote that 'Race-improvement to-day is not a question of philosophy, but existence [...] If the first law of life is self-preservation, England must choose between State suicide and race improvement. If the latter alternative be accepted, then the causes of deterioration must be dealt with as firmly as defects in a dam behind which is accumulated the rainfall of a county'. As Saleeby put it, the 'strength and magnitude' of the institutions and ideologies that supported empires and civilisations were insignificant if the racial foundations were in a state of degeneration.[192]

In the years preceding the war, further initiatives surfaced with the aim of reinvigorating British manhood, including Henry Page Croft's National Citizen Army. However, while right-wingers persisted in speculating on the disciplinary value of conscription, grassroots physical training movements continued to spring up throughout the country. For example, the physical culture movement, pioneered by the father of modern bodybuilding, Eugene Sandow, saw remarkable growth.[193] Since the 1890s, Sandow had recommended the adoption of some kind of State system of physical culture with the ultimate object of raising the standard of the 'race as a whole'. 'Healthier and more perfect men and women' he said, 'will beget children with better constitutions and more free from hereditary taint'. 'Surely', Sandow added, 'what has been done for the horse and the dog cannot be impossible of accomplishment in the case of man'. The launch of *Sandow's Magazine* in 1898, with its exhortations to nurture the physique in order to bring it to its utmost potential in strength and aesthetic appeal, in parallel with cultivation of the mind, appealed to a large middle-class readership. As the new century began, the expansion of physical culture societies and clubs, increasing sales of 'developers' and 'exercisers', the publication of books on various aspects of physical training and the wide dissemination of magazines such as *Health Culture and Vim, Vitality, Apollo's Magazine* and *Health and Strength*, together provided compelling evidence that concerns about degeneracy had become firmly ingrained in the British collective consciousness. In 1904, the editor of the popular *Health and Strength* explicitly wrote:

> On all sides we have signs of a great awakening on the part of the British people to the fact that the nation is in a quick state of degeneration ... 'Health & Strength' have fought the battle of the standard (physical culture standard) of the nation alone, but now their ranks are being daily swelled, and their cause strengthened. They are only waiting for further reinforcements where they make an advance all along the lines and all those social evils which so long have bred deterioration will then be swept away.[194]

In 1906, *Health and Strength* contributed to the establishment of the Health and Strength League, whose motto was 'Sacred thy body even as they soul'. The new League, which had acquired thirteen thousand members by 1911, focused on physical and mental improvement, purity and honour. Although it does not appear to have had any direct political affiliation, the Health and Strength League's pronounced emphasis on physical and moral efficiency aligned harmoniously with right-wing visions of a robust and vigorous nation.

In the minds of right-wingers and many conservatives, the celebration of physical efficiency was closely intertwined with combat sports and martial arts. These disciplines were viewed as a means not only to promote manhood and health, but also to instil values of discipline, temperance and self-control. For instance, Lord Meath saw boxing as an avenue for young individuals to channel and release their aggression in a structured and supervised way, and as offering an environment conducive to constructive pursuits that at the same time discouraged the destructive behaviours often associated with hooliganism. Similarly, Baden Powell voiced his support for ju-jitsu, which had gained popularity following Japan's victory over Russia in 1905. In addition, Conan Doyle played a role in popularising Bartitsu, a hybrid martial art that incorporated elements of boxing, *savate* (French kickboxing) and stick fighting. The aim of Bartitsu was to equip urban dwellers with practical self-defence skills against street crime.[195]

On the eve of the war, questions such as 'Are we losing our national resilience?' or 'Can we raise children with a more Spartan-like upbringing?' remained unanswered. Within the British Right, there was only one certainty, as articulated by Lord Milner: '(1) Whatever happens & whoever may be the ultimate enemy, a people who can fight will prevail in the long run over a people that can't. & (2) even if they never fought, the trained people would still prevail in peace by virtue of its greater grit and all-round efficiency'.[196] They could not know that the greatest test of 'the survival of the fittest' was right around the corner, and that the virile bodies, which they did so much to strengthen, were destined to be ravaged by the dreadful weapons of modern warfare.

The Edwardian Right's emphasis on physical fitness, military discipline and martial aesthetics persisted into the postwar years. Some historians argue that British fascists, responding to the physical trauma, emasculation and deep alienation experienced by men after the First World War, revived the ideals of imperial manliness associated with the late Victorian and Edwardian eras. Others, however, contend that these efforts did not signify a genuine restoration but rather the imposition of a brutalised hypermasculinity – one that prioritised regimentation and obedience while undermining the ethos of 'patriotic volunteerism' that had once defined British manhood before 1914.[197]

Notes

1. Arthur James Balfour, *Decadence*, Henry Sidgwick Memorial Lecture (Cambridge, 1908).
2. Marquis of Salisbury, 'Disintegration', *Quarterly Review* 156 (July–October 1883), pp. 559–595.
3. Lloyd P. Gartner, *The Jewish Immigrant in England, 1870–1914* (London: Allen & Unwin, 1960); John A. Garrard, *The English and Immigration: 1880–1910* (London: Oxford University Press, 1971); Bernard Gainer, *The Alien Invasion: The Origins of the Aliens Act of 1905* (London: Heinemann, 1972); Colin Holmes, *Anti-Semitism in British Society, 1876–1939* (London: Routledge, 2015); Johnson, 'Trouble is Yet Coming!', pp. 137–156.
4. Arthur Henry Lane, *The Alien Menace* (London: Boswell Publishing Co., Ltd, 1934), p. 212.
5. Jill Pellew, 'The Home Office and the Aliens Act, 1905', *The Historical Journal* 32, no. 2 (1989), pp. 369–385; Sam Johnson, '"A Veritable Janus at the Gates of Jewry": British Jews and Mr. Arnold White', *Patterns of Prejudice* 47, no. 1 (2013), pp. 41–68.
6. 'Mr. Chamberlain's Reply to Lord Rosebery', *Yorkshire Gazette*, 9 June 1894.
7. See, in general, Garrard, *The English and Immigration: 1880–1910*.
8. Gartner, *The Jewish Immigrant in England*, p. 47.
9. William Evans-Gordon, *The Alien Immigrant* (London: W. Heinemann, 1903). See also Cecil Bloom, 'Arnold White and Sir William Evans-Gordon: Their Involvement in Immigration in Late-Victorian and Edwardian Britain', *Jewish Historical Studies* 39 (2004), pp. 153–166.
10. 'Britain for the British: To Discourage Alien Paupers', *Star of Gwent*, 15 March 1901.
11. Ibid. See also 'British Brothers' League', *Tower Hamlets Independent and East End Local Advertiser*, 4 May 1901.
12. [No title], *East London Observer*, 11 May 1901.
13. 'The Great Alien Question in East London: "British Brothers" Up in Arms', *East London Observer*, 11 May 1901.
14. 'The British Brothers League: Important Letter from Colonel Sir Howard Vincent', *East London Observer*, 25 May 1901.
15. 'British Brothers' League', *East London Observer*, 25 May 1901.
16. 'To the Editor of the East London Observer', *East London Observer*, 25 May 1901.
17. John Brown, 'The Alien Immigration: A Word on the Other Side', and 'Plain Words to the British Brothers' League', *Tower Hamlets Independent and East End Local Advertiser*, 25 May 1901 and 22 June 1901. John Brown was president of the Stepney Liberal and Radical Association.
18. 'The Alien Movement', *East London Observer*, 1 June 1901.
19. A BBL manifesto issued 'to the working men of East London' was reproduced in the *East London Observer*, 8 June 1901.

20 'The British Brothers' League and Mr. John Brown', *Tower Hamlets Independent and East End Local Advertiser*, 13 July 1901.
21 'British Brothers and Mr. J. Brown', *Tower Hamlets Independent and East End Local Advertiser*, 29 June 1901.
22 'A Stepney Rip Van Winkle', *Tower Hamlets Independent and East End Local Advertiser*, 6 July 1901.
23 'Londoners' League', *East London Observer*, 3 August 1901.
24 'The Anti-Alien Crusade', *East London Observer*, 17 August 1901.
25 'British Brothers' League: Important Manifesto', *East London Observer*, 24 August 1901.
26 'The Alien Invasion', *East London Observer*, 31 August 1901.
27 'News in Brief', *East London Observer*, 14 September 1901.
28 'London Letter', *Manchester Evening News*, 16 September 1901.
29 'British Brothers' League: Resignation of Mr. Shaw', *Tower Hamlets Independent and East End Local Advertiser*, 21 September 1901.
30 'The British Brothers' League', *East London Observer*, 5 October 1901.
31 'The British Brothers' League', *East London Observer*, 12 October 1901.
32 'British Brothers in Arms', *East London Observer*, 19 October 1901.
33 'Eastern Counties', *The Times*, 23 November 1901.
34 'The British Brothers' League', *East London Observer*, 26 October 1901.
35 'The British Brothers' League', *East London Observer*, 16 November 1901.
36 'To Check Alien Immigration', *Pall Mall Gazette*, 19 November 1901.
37 'Overcrowding in Stepney', *Tower Hamlets Independent and East End Local Advertiser*, 2 November 1901.
38 'The Alien Question', *East London Observer*, 16 November 1901.
39 'Alien Immigration', *East London Observer*, 9 November 1901.
40 'The Alien Invasion', *Tower Hamlets Independent and East End Local Advertiser*, 23 November 1901.
41 'The Alien Invasion', *Pall Mall Gazette*, 12 December 1901.
42 'British Brothers' League', *East London Observer*, 14 December 1901.
43 'Bethnal Green Conservatism', *East London Observer*, 28 December 1901.
44 See, for instance, *Manchester Courier*, 15 January 1902.
45 'The British Brothers' League: Letter from Miss Corelli', *Morning Post*, 10 January 1902.
46 'Alien Immigration', *East London Observer*, 21 December 1901. Article originally published in the *Daily Chronicle*.
47 'The Alien Question: Opinions of Public Men', *East London Observer*, 6 September 1902.
48 Garrard, *The English and Immigration*, p. 39.
49 'The Pink Ribbon League', *Pall Mall Gazette*, 29 November 1901.
50 Quoted in Garrard, *The English and Immigration*, p. 62.
51 'Special Notice', *Justice*, 4 January 1902.
52 See, for instance, *East London Observer*, 4 January 1902.
53 'The Anti-Alien Crusade', *East London Observer*, 18 January 1902 and 'England for the English', *Tower Hamlets Independent and East End Local Advertiser*, 18 January 1902.

54 'A Son of an Alien', *East London Observer*, 25 January 1902.
55 'Eastern Notes', *East London Observer*, 25 January 1902.
56 'Mr John Brown's Views', *East London Observer*, 18 January 1902.
57 'Letter to the Editor', *East London Observer*, 25 January 1902.
58 'The Government and the Aliens', *East London Observer*, 25 January 1902.
59 'Topical Tattle', *Justice*, 25 January 1902.
60 'Among Trade Unions', *Justice*, 6 September 1902.
61 'Aliens on the War Path', *Tower Hamlets Independent and East End Local Advertiser*, 20 September 1902.
62 'Jews in London', *Manchester Courier*, 28 January 1902.
63 The correspondence between the BBL and the President of the Board of Trade, Gerald Balfour was published in the *East London Observer*, 25 January 1902.
64 'No English Need to Apply', *East London Observer*, 25 January 1902.
65 'Citizen of No Mean City', *East London Observer*, February 8, 1902.
66 'The Great Alien Problem', *East London Observer*, 8 February 1902.
67 'The Great Alien Problem: Letter from Mr. S. M. Samuel M.P.', *East London Observer*, 15 February 1902.
68 'The Great Alien Problem: More Correspondence', *East London Observer*, 22 February 1902.
69 'The Anti-Alien Movement', *East London Observer*, 8 March 1902.
70 'The Anti-Alien Movement', *East London Observer*, 15 March 1902.
71 Quoted by T. Dundas Pillans in a letter to the *Pall Mall Gazette*, 26 February 1902.
72 See, for example, 'The Royal Commission & Alien Immigration', *East London Observer*, 21 June 1902.
73 'The Shrieking Brotherhood', *East London Observer*, 1 March 1902.
74 For a general overview of immigration in England, see Panikos Panayi, *An Immigration History of Britain: Multicultural Racism since 1800* (Harlow: Pearson, 2010).
75 'The Alien Commission and The British Brothers' League', *East London Observer*, 5 July 1902. The former president Shaw criticised the leaflet and referred to antisemitism as a departure from the original character of the League.
76 'Parliament and the Aliens', *East London Observer*, 3 May 1902.
77 William Stanley Shaw, 'Alien Immigration and the British Brothers' League', *East London Observer*, 27 September 1902.
78 'The British Brothers' League', *Tower Hamlets Independent and East End Local Advertiser*, 16 August 1902. See also 'The British Brothers' League: First Annual Report and Balance Sheet', *East London Observer*, 16 August 1902.
79 Report of the Royal Commission on Alien Immigration with minutes of evidence and appendix, Vol. 1, p. 286.
80 'Exciting Contest at Stepney', *Daily News* (London), 6 August 1902.
81 Viscount Mountmorres, 'The Foreign Invasion of London, Impressions on the Spot', *Daily Mail*, 18 September 1902.
82 See Johnson, 'Trouble is Yet Coming!', pp. 151–152.

83 'The British Brothers', *Tower Hamlets Independent and East End Local Advertiser*, 6 December 1902.
84 'The Position of the British Brothers League', *East London Observer*, 13 December 1902. 'The British Brothers' League', *Tower Hamlets Independent and East End Local Advertiser*, 20 December 1902.
85 'The British Brothers' League', *East London Observer*, 20 December 1902.
86 'The British Brothers League', *East London Observer*, 21 March 1903.
87 'Alien Immigration', *East London Observer*, 27 June 1903.
88 'Undesirable Immigrants', *Manchester Evening News*, 22 May 1903.
89 'Alien Immigration', *East London Observer*, 4 July 1903.
90 'Alien Immigration', *East London Observer*, 11 July 1903.
91 Report of the Royal Commission on Alien Immigration: With Minutes of Evidence and Appendix. Vol. 1, 1903, p. 40.
92 Ibid., pp. 40–43
93 'The British Brothers' League. Development of the movement', *East London Observer*, 5 September 1903.
94 'Labour Topics', *Mid-Lothian Journal*, 18 September 1903.
95 'The British Brothers' League: Forthcoming Meeting', *East London Observer*, 26 September 1903.
96 'British Brothers' League', *East London Observer*, 30 January 1904.
97 'Alien Immigration: Meeting in East London', *London Evening Standard*, 11 November 1903; 'East London's Scourge', *Tower Hamlets Independent and East End Local Advertiser*, 14 November 1903.
98 'The British Brothers' League', *East London Observer*, 24 October 1903.
99 'Alien Immigration', *London Evening Standard*, 12 January 1904; 'Great Anti-Alien Demonstration', *Tower Hamlets Independent and East End Local Advertiser*, 16 January 1904.
100 'British Brothers' League, *East London Observer*, 30 April 1904.
101 'The Aliens Bill and The Home Office', *The Times*, 3 May 1904.
102 William Evans-Gordon, 'The Attack on the Aliens Act', *The National Review* 285 (November 1906).
103 Garrard, *English and Immigration*, p. 43.
104 'The Aliens Bill: How It Was Killed', *Tower Hamlets Independent and East End Local Advertiser*, 20 August 1904.
105 'British Brothers' League', *East London Observer*, 3 December 1904.
106 'The Mile End Contest', *London Evening Standard*, 10 January 1905.
107 Myer Jack Landa, *The Alien Problem and Its Remedy* (London: King & Son, 1911), p. 34.
108 *Jewish Chronicle*, 15 December 1905. Quoted in Garrard, *The English and Immigration*, p. 103.
109 'The Aliens Act Made Useless: Our Ports Reopened to Criminal, Pauper and Diseased Aliens', Handbill published by the British Conservative Party in 1906.
110 Quoted in Larry L. Whiterell, *Rebel on the Right: Henry Page Croft and the Crisis of British Conservatism, 1903–1914* (Newark, NJ: University of Delaware Press and Associated University Presses, 1997), p. 79.

111 'British Brothers' League', *Tower Hamlets Independent and East End Local Advertiser*, 14 January 1911.
112 Kenneth Lunn, *The Marconi Scandal and Related Aspects of British Anti-Semitism, 1911–1914* (PhD diss., University of Sheffield, 1978). The work provides an in-depth insight into the use of antisemitism during the affair.
113 William Stanley Shaw, 'A New British Brothers' League', *East London Observer*, 7 September 1918.
114 'The Alien Question', *East London Observer*, 14 September 1918.
115 Robert Benewick, *Political Violence & Public Order: A Study of British Fascism* (London: Allen Lane, 1984), pp. 25–27.
116 Hynes, *The Edwardian Turn of Mind*, pp. 15–52. See also Bentley B. Gilbert, 'Health and Politics: The British Physical Deterioration Report of 1904', *Bulletin of the History of Medicine* 39, no. 2 (1965), pp. 143–153.
117 Arnold White, *Efficiency and Empire* (London: Methuen & Company, 1901), pp. 102–103 and 106.
118 Benjamin Seebohm Rowntree, *Poverty, A Study of Town Life* (London: Macmillan, 1901), pp. 216–221. The recruitment criteria included a minimum height of five feet seven inches for Cavalry Dragoons and Lancers, five feet six inches for Hussars and Infantry, a minimum chest measurement of thirty-four inches for all and a uniform minimum weight of 115 lb (8 stone 3 lb) across branches.
119 'Weights and Measurements of Our Children', *The Times*, 26 November 1901.
120 'Miles' (Major General Sir John Frederick Maurice), 'Where to Get Men', *Contemporary Review* (January 1902), pp. 78–86.
121 'National Training and National Defence', *The Times*, 29 March, 5 April and 10 April 1902.
122 'National Training and National Defence', *The Times*, 29 March 1902.
123 On the Patriotic Association, see Penn, *Targeting Schools*, pp. 106–107.
124 Henry Birchenough, 'Local Beginning of Imperial Defence: An Example', *The Nineteenth Century* 279 (May 1900), pp. 728–733.
125 See, among others, 'Military Drill for Macclesfield Schoolboy', *Cheshire Daily Echo*, 17 January 1901.
126 Penn, *Targeting Schools*, pp. 101–117.
127 Christopher Prior, *Edwardian England and the Idea of Racial Decline* (Basingstoke: Palgrave, 2013), pp. 91–98.
128 See, generally, Springhall, *Youth, Empire and Society*.
129 John Springhall, Brian Fraser and Michael Hoare, *Sure and Steadfast: A History of the Boys' Brigade 1883–1983* (London: Collins, 1983).
130 Pat Brooklyn, 'The Church Lads' Brigade: Its Work and History', *The English Illustrated Magazine* 17 (1904), pp. 511–519.
131 Richard A. Voeltz, '"A Good Jew and a Good Englishman": The Jewish Lads' Brigade, 1894–1922', *Journal of Contemporary History* 23, no. 1 (1988), pp. 119–127.
132 Quoted in Michael Sandler, *Continuation Schools in England & Elsewhere: Their Place in the Educational System of an Industrial and Commercial State* (Manchester: University of Manchester Publications, 1907), p. 89.

133 Ibid., p. 91. On the construction of middle-class female identity, Joan N. Burstyn, *Victorian Education and the Ideal of Womanhood* (Lanham, MD: Rowman & Littlefield, 1980); Carol Dyhouse, *Girls Growing Up in Late Victorian and Edwardian England* (London: Routledge, 2012).

134 Dan Frederick Adonis, *'Today's Boys, Tomorrow's Men': A Short History of the Boys' Brigade of Britain, with Further Reference to the Boys' Brigade in South Africa (circa 1880s–1980s)* (Master's thesis, University of Cape Town, 1995).

135 J. A. Mangan and James Walvin, 'Introduction', in Mangan and Walvin (eds), *Manliness and Morality*, p. 1.

136 On the Victorian ideal of manliness, Norman Vance, *The Sinews of the Spirit: The Ideal of Christian Manliness in Victorian Literature and Religious Thought* (Cambridge: Cambridge University Press, 1985). See also J. A. Mangan, 'Social Darwinism and Upper-Class Education in Late Victorian and Edwardian England', in Mangan and Walvin (eds), *Manliness and Morality*, pp. 135–159.

137 In 1906, the Lads' Drill Association was incorporated with the National Service League. John O. Springhall, 'Lord Meath, Youth, and Empire', *Journal of Contemporary History* 5, no. 4 (1970), pp. 97–111; James A. Mangan, '"The Grit of Our Forefathers": Invented Traditions, Propaganda, and Imperialism', in John M. Mackenzie (ed.), *Imperialism and Popular Culture* (Manchester: Manchester University Press, 2017), pp. 113–139.

138 Both quotes in Sandler, *Continuation Schools in England & Elsewhere*, p. 87.

139 Adams and Poirier, *The Conscription Controversy*, pp. 16–32.

140 Spencer Wilkinson, *The Volunteers and the National Defence* (London: A. Constable & Co., 1896); T. Miller Maguire, 'Surprise in War, from a Military and a National Point of View', *The National Review* 31, no. 183 (1898), pp. 361–373; Lonsdale Hale, 'The Unreadiness of the Volunteers', *The National Review* 31, no. 185 (1898), pp. 683–693.

141 James Cantlie, 'The Health of the People', *The Practitioner*, March 1902, pp. 259–283. Quote at p. 276.

142 Shee, *The Briton's First Duty*, pp. 174–208.

143 Precis of Evidence to Be Offered on Behalf of the National Service League, pp. 22–23.

144 Report of the Royal Commission on the Militia and Volunteers, p. 246.

145 Thomas Coglan Horsfall, *The Relation of National Service to the Welfare of the Community* (Manchester: Simpkin, Marshall, Hamilton, Kent & Company Limited, 1904), pp. 28–32.

146 'Conscription', *Labour Leader*, 3 June 1904.

147 George F. Shee, 'The Story of the National Service League', *The British Dominions Year Book* (1922), pp. 108–118.

148 *National Service Journal* 2 (November 1905).

149 Quoted in Farr, *The Development and Impact of Right-Wing Politics in Britain*, p. 26.

150 Earl Roberts, 'Imperial and National Safety. How to Restore Our Military Efficiency: A Reply to the Duke of Bedford', *The Nineteenth Review and After* 439 (September 1913), p. 458.
151 'Lord Curzon On Imperial Defence', *The Times*, 22 October 1910.
152 Major General Sir John Frederick Maurice, 'National Health; A Soldier's Study', *Contemporary Review* 83 (January 1903), pp. 41–56.
153 George F. Shee, 'Deterioration in National Physique', *The Nineteenth Century and After* 315 (May 1903), pp. 797–805.
154 The memorandum is entirely reproduced in the *Journal of the Royal Army Medical Corps* (London: John Bale, Sons & Danielsson Ltd., 1903), pp. 224–230.
155 Daniel Pick, *Faces of Degeneration: A European Disorder, c. 1848–1918* (Cambridge: Cambridge University Press, 1989), pp. 212–216. On the language of 'degeneration' across the entire political spectrum see also Richard A. Soloway, *Demography and Degeneration: Eugenics and the Declining Birthrate in Twentieth-Century Britain* (Chapel Hill, NC: UNC Press Books, 2014).
156 [nN title], *Manchester Evening News*, 17 February 1902.
157 Sir Lauder Brunton, 'National Health and Physical Education', *The Lancet*, 14 February 1903.
158 Sir Lauder Brunton, 'National Defence and Physical Education', *Manchester Guardian*, 2 April 1903.
159 'War Games for Children', *The Times*, 7 January 1902.
160 'Letter on Military Training in Schools, to Col. Pennington (July 2nd, 1901)', 'Military Training in Schools with Col. Pennington (1901)', and 'Physical and Military Training in Schools with Col. Pennington (1901)', in Sir Lauder Brunton, *Collected Papers on Physical and Military Training* (London: privately published, 1915).
161 Hansard, HL Deb Vol. 124, Cols. 1324–1356 (6 July 1903).
162 'National Health and Military Service', *British Medical Journal* 2 (25 July 1903), pp. 207–208.
163 Report of the Interdepartmental Committee on Physical Deterioration (1904), pp. 84–93.
164 Hynes, *The Edwardian Turn of Mind*, pp. 23–24.
165 Springhall, 'Lord Meath, Youth, and Empire', pp. 105–111; Jim English, 'Empire Day in Britain, 1904–1958', *The Historical Journal* 49, no. 1 (2006), pp. 247–276.
166 Reginald Brabazon Meath, *Memories of the Twentieth Century* (London: John Murray, 1924), pp. 23–24.
167 *Essays on Duty and Discipline: A Series of Papers on the Training of Children in Relation to Social and National Welfare* (London: Cassell and Company, Ltd, 1913).
168 Hansard, HL Deb Vol. 2, Col. 329 (12 July 1909).
169 Hynes, *The Edwardian Turn of Mind*, pp. 33 and 281.
170 'National Social Purity Crusade', *The Times*, 4 April 1908.
171 *The Times*, 29 June 1905. Article reprinted in Brunton, Account of Inauguration of the League at the Mansion House (28 June 1905) *Collected Papers*, art. 21.

172 See, for instance, 'Physical Education', *The Times*, 24 and 26 April 1909.
173 Sir Lauder Brunton, 'National Physical Training: An Open Debate' (Reprinted from the *Manchester Guardian*, 2 June 1903).
174 Sir Lauder Brunton, 'Physical Education and Training in Relation to National Defence' (Proceedings of the National Defence Association, Paper read at the Evening Meeting of the National Defence Association, at the Piccadilly Hotel, 25 November 1908, Sir George Taubman-Goldie in the Chair, Reprinted from National Defence, March, 1909).
175 Penn, *Targeting Schools*, pp. 146–159.
176 'Boy Scouts', *Daily Telegraph*, 4 June 1910.
177 Baden Powell, 'The Boy Scout', *The Times*, 25 September 1909.
178 John O. Springhall, 'The Boy Scouts, Class and Militarism in Relation to British Youth Movements 1908–1930', *International Review of Social History* 16, no. 2 (1971), pp. 125–158.
179 Robert Baden-Powell, *Scouting for Boys* (London: Horace Cox, 1908), p. 11.
180 Quoted in Michael Rosenthal, *The Character Factory: Baden-Powell and the Origins of the Boy Scout Movement* (New York: Pantheon, 1986), p. 206.
181 Lieutenant General Sir Robert Baden-Powell, KCB, KCVO, 'Boy Scouts: In Connection with National Training and National Service', *Journal of the Royal United Service Institution* 55 (1911), pp. 581, 595.
182 *Scouting for Boys*, p. 338.
183 Ibid., p. 208.
184 Ibid., p. 313.
185 Martin Middlebrook, *The First Day on the Somme* (London: Allen Lane, 1971), pp. 10, 14, 217, 236.
186 Springhall, 'The Boy Scouts', p. 152.
187 Baden Powell, *Girl Guides: A Suggestion for Character Training for Girls* (London: Bishopsgate Press, 1909), p. 7.
188 See, in general, Soloway, *Demography and Degeneration*, pp. 31–37; Donald MacKenzie, 'Eugenics in Britain', *Social Studies of Science* 6, no. 3–4 (1976), pp. 499–532; Daniel J. Kevles, *In the Name of Eugenics: Genetics and the Uses of Human Heredity* (Cambridge, MA: Harvard University Press, 1995), chapter 5.
189 Geoffrey R. Searle, *Eugenics and Politics in Britain, 1900–1914*, Vol. 3 (Leiden: Noordhoff International Publishing, 1976), pp. 36–37.
190 Phillips, *The Diehards*, p. 109.
191 Willoughby de Broke, 'The Tory Tradition', *National Review* 58 (1911), p. 211.
192 Arnold White, *The Views of 'Vanoc': An Englishman's Outlook* (London: K. Paul, Trench, Trübner, 1911), p. 285.
193 Ina Zweiniger-Bargielowska, *Managing the Body: Beauty, Health, and Fitness in Britain, 1880–1939* (Oxford: Oxford University Press), pp. 62–104.
194 Zweiniger-Bargielowska, 'Building a British Superman', pp. 600–601.
195 Godfrey, 'Urban Heroes versus Folk Devils', pp. 13–23.
196 Quoted in Adams, 'The National Service League', pp. 63–64.
197 Julie Gottlieb, 'Fascism in Britain: Building the Blackshirt in the Inter-War Period', *Contemporary European History* 20, no. 2 (May 2011), pp. 111–136; Zweiniger-Bargielowska, 'Building a British Superman', pp. 595–610.

4

'The revolt of the good citizens': Free Labour and practices of patriotic strikebreaking, 1901–1914

Here's a hand from me and mine,
Gie's a hand from thee and thine,
The Grip the world go round,
This thought should fly o'er land and sea,
Where'er the heart and voice are free:
GOOD CITIZENSHIP AND LIBERTY
The bond by which we're bound.[1]

A few months after the passage of the *The Defence of the Realm Consolidated Act* (1914), the notorious professional strikebreaker, William Collison, categorically wrote 'Patriotism has killed Socialism'. He went on to predict that 'the Special Constables, the Civic Guards, the City Train Bands, and all those organizations which have enabled that Issachar of the Nation – the middle class – to so strongly assert its patriotism, have created a spirit of unity in that body which augurs ill for the future fomenter of industrial unrest'. There was no doubt, according to the self-styled 'king of the blacklegs', that this patriotic citizenry would prove to be a lasting and powerful bulwark in defence of 'Freedom for Labour and Security for Property'.[2] Collison, who had shepherded 'free labourers' for over twenty years, had obstinately regarded trade unionism as 'an accursed thing, a greater enemy of this country [Britain] than any foreign power'.[3] With the growing political strength of the labour movement, especially after the outraged reaction to the Taff Vale case, Collison had come to the view that closer cooperation between groups of employers and citizens was necessary in order to protect the free market and free society. With this in mind, he looked at the techniques which American employers and their organisations had adopted to deal with 'the labor problem'. The first part of this chapter deals specifically with Collison's unsuccessful attempts to establish a Citizens' Industrial Alliance of Great Britain, along the lines of the Citizens' Industrial Association of America (CIAA). It reconstructs the encounters Collison had with the main representatives of the open-shop movement and the guidance he was given by anti-union employers in the industrial heartlands of the United States. The general premise behind the Alliance was that the protection of individual freedom and private property, the pillars on which the very existence and wealth of the British economic order depended, constituted a basic tenet of the principle of good citizenship and a test of patriotic zeal. The second part of the chapter focuses on these right-wing, conservative organisations, which assumed, or sought to assume authority without legal sanction in order to protect the 'public interest' during the Great Unrest (1911–1914). In particular, it focuses on those upper- and middle-class institutions, such as the Liverpool Civic Service League, the London Volunteer Police Force and the Leeds Citizens' League, which took a manifestly belligerent attitude towards organised labour and engaged in strikebreaking activities. The overall goal of the chapter is to reveal the inclination of certain conservative sectors of British society to respond to the advance of political and industrial democracy with violence in the name of patriotism.

'Free Labour joins hands with Free Citizenship': William Collison and the Citizens' Industrial Alliance of Britain

'I did the work that my soul and brain ached to do. I broke their strikes. I am a blackleg, my Lord God Almighty. I was called the king of the blacklegs. And if I ever in Thy divine and infinite wisdom it pleases Thee to trust my soul into a human mould once more, I will rise up a blackleg and break their strikes again – so help me, God'.[4] With this prayer, amply illustrating his flamboyant character, Collison closed his singularly candid autobiography, *The Apostle of Free Labour*. As a defector from trade unionism, Collison had founded the National Free Labour Association (NFLA) in 1893, with the purpose of protecting 'the right of every working man to do what he pleases with his own labour'.[5] Structured around a network of free labour offices, the association became the preeminent supplier of strikebreakers to British industries up until the First World War. At its peak, according to French journalists Paul Mantoux and Maurice Alfassa, who travelled to England in 1902 to study British trade unionism, the NFLA had about eighty thousand members, the numbers having been swelled by soldiers returning from the Boer War.[6] Over the years, the association broke a few hundred strikes, mostly in the unskilled and semi-skilled trades. Replicating the Pinkerton Detective Agency, a special unit was established with the task of protecting strikebreakers from pickets.[7] If a chief constable or a local Watch Committee denied protection to 'free labourers', Collison wrote, 'I would send my emergency men, arm them, and meet organized violence with organized violence'.[8] The NFLA's services were not limited to labour replacement, but also included lobbying, defamatory press campaigns and lawsuits against trade unions. In 1900, Collison played an important role in the rail strike that led to the momentous Taff Vale judgment, which removed the unions' immunity from legal action for damage caused during a strike. The decision made unionism ever more vulnerable to hostile employers, and also threatened to crush the civil liberties and industrial rights that had been guaranteed for over a quarter of a century.

As dire as the situation appeared for unionism at the time, the sense of repression and intimidation inherent in the Taff Vale decision was a blessing in disguise for British Labour. More than any other circumstance or factor, it gave new impetus to the movement for the political representation of labour, which had its origins in a resolution passed by the Trades Union Congress in 1899. The following year, numerous trade unions and trade councils joined the Fabian Society and the Independent Labour Party in the newly formed Labour Representation Committee with the aim of reversing the court's decision and restoring the security of the trade unions as embodied by the legislations of 1871 and 1875. Under continual pressure from Labour representatives, the Conservative government finally resorted to the dilatory expedient of appointing a Royal Commission to enquire into the status of the law on trade disputes and trade unions. Labour's political strength was seriously misjudged by the Conservatives, who remained opposed to any modification of the law as it had been interpreted by the courts. While the Conservative government proved obdurate, Collison responded to Labour's political agitation and propaganda with his typical vigour and vitriolic rhetoric. After each parliamentary session in which Labour members attempted to introduce a bill to restore the rights of the trade unions, the *Free Labour and Industrial Review* – the official organ of the NFLA – denounced the proposed legislation as an attempt to legalise illegalities and coercion. At the beginning of 1904, the association's paper, which was edited by the journalist, John Charles Manning, warned that there were signs in the industrial world of a 'coming storm'.[9] The need to protect the security of property and the right to buy and sell labour in a market governed by forces of supply and demand had suddenly acquired a new sense of urgency.

Around this time, perhaps unsurprisingly, Collison and his associates began to show a keen interest in the methods and weapons that advocates of the open-shop movement were employing to deal with the 'labour problem' in the United States. As early as the last quarter of the nineteenth century, the United States, which had seen the growth of a vast market in security in the field of industrial relations, had provided militant employers and anti-unionists in Britain with a fertile terrain for the study of labour oppression.[10] A few years earlier, for instance, the spectre of a society paralysed by large-scale, coordinated strikes prompted the prominent economic philosopher William S. Jevons to review the American experience of settling 'industrial emergencies'. 'It is worthy of notice', Jevons wrote, 'that the great railway strike [of 1877] in the United States, which was, in fact, an industrial insurrection, was brought to an end not by any legal process, but by the arbitrary exhibition of force'.[11] Jevons's point implied that the Conspiracy and Protection of Property Act of 1875, which had defined the position of British organised labour in relation to criminal law, only punished actions leading to loss of life, injury or damage to property when these effectively involved a breach of contract. The law did not provide for emergency measures that prohibited, or at least restricted stoppages in essential industries and transport. 'If any very large proportion of the colliers of the kingdom were to leave work, even after due legal notice', Jevons observed, 'they might bring the industry of the country to a standstill. Not only industry, indeed, but the sustenance and health of millions of their fellow citizens would be imperilled'.[12] In order to pre-empt the disruptive effects of strike action, he advocated pioneering methods of labour conscription for discharging the duties essential to the good of the national community.[13]

Over time, and in particular after the emergence of 'new unionism', the search for a strategy to both prevent a reduction in output and protect the general welfare of the consumer public went as far as threatening to emulate American industrial vigilantism and labour espionage.[14] Furthermore, the series on 'American Engineering Competition and Progress' and 'The Crisis in British Industry' in *The Time*s emphatically condemned the unions' hampering of British industries by reducing productivity and discouraging investment, and very likely causing their decline in the face of aggressive competition from abroad. By implication, the 'unreasonable and pernicious' influence of labour militancy should be suppressed, including by imitating the crudest instruments of industrial defence devised by American capital.[15]

Of course, Collison shared the belief that trade unions were inflicting severe damage on British industry and, unless checked, on the nation as a whole. He severely criticised the unions for their ca'canny (go-slow) policy and other methods of passive sabotage. Under these circumstances, the intransigent anti-union stance of American employer associations, such as the National Association of Manufacturers, the National Metal Trades Association and the National Founders Association, appeared to him and his associates to be a pursuable strategy for restoring industrial discipline and efficiency. 'The Free Labour Association', historian Richard H. Heindel wrote in his classic study on the American influence on Britain between 1898 and 1914, 'harkened with cheers to America where the quick, go-ahead man was allowed to push forward, and resolved to ask Carnegie to publish pamphlets on the subject of free labor'.[16] At the end of February 1904, the *Free Labour Press* wrote that 'One of the most important developments in the United States during the past year has been the gradual and steady organization of capital'. The formation of the CIAA, which aimed to fight any outside interference, restriction or limitation placed upon industries, 'made it apparent that 1904 may witness one of the greatest conflicts that the industrial world has known'. The main issue was naturally the 'open shop question'.[17]

At the inaugural meeting of the CIAA, which took place in Chicago on 29 October 1903, over one hundred organisations, including local employers' associations, manufacturers' organisations and citizens' alliances, had sounded the tocsin against union organisation by declaring their unyielding antagonism to the principles of collective bargaining. In December 1903, the executive committee of the CIAA declared that union shops and union shop contracts were a means 'to overthrow individual liberty and property rights' and urged the 'rapid organization of those who believe in the maintenance of law and order and the perpetuation of our free institutions, to the end that they may wield their full and proper influence upon the destinies of the nation'.[18] American employers and the parties of law and order closing ranks persuaded Collison that such a movement should be emulated in Britain. At the twelfth congress of the NFLA, which was held in London at the end of October 1904, a resolution was passed which gave:

> unqualified approval for the aims and objects of the National Association of Manufacturers and the Citizens' Industrial Association of America as organisations with the potential for great public good, as powerful factors in the formation of good citizenship, and important in their possibilities for wisely educating public opinion on vital questions pertaining to the relations of capital and labour, employer and employee.[19]

In defence of those social and industrial institutions under which Britain had prospered, Free Labour had to join hands with traditional principles of responsible and efficient citizenship. A short time later, the official magazine of the Manufacturers Association, *American Industries*, published an article by an unnamed correspondent from the NFLA. The author, perhaps Collison himself, praised American employers for their hostility to the labour organisation and for opposing any legislation aimed at limiting proprietorial and managerial prerogatives. The National Association of Manufacturers, which had taken the leadership in protecting corporate interests in America and publicly supported vigilante violence against union organisers, was particularly commended for its staunch opposition to the eight-hour day and to any attempt to remove the power of the Federal Courts to issue injunctions in labour disputes. The NFLA correspondent noted that the industrial defence movement was not confined to the narrow circle of employers in larger industries but involved a myriad state-based and small employer associations, citizens' alliances, community associations, and other suchlike groups. While the employers' association was the most common form of organisation in the east of the country, the citizens' alliance, 'which more nearly resemble[d] the vigilance committee' constituted the most effective form of organised resistance in the west. Given this situation, those opposing the unions had demanded closer collaboration between manufacturers and ordinary citizens:

> The clergyman and the professional men of all kinds, the clerks, the citizens generally, and in innumerable instances non-union men, or free and independent workmen – who realize that their great desire (namely to keep out of the unions or to break away from them), surely required the cooperation of the employer, who must stand back of them at all hazards if they would do so, and who could do this only by concerted and united action.

All these avowed enemies of labour came together to form the CIAA, whose methods in the spheres of both government and economics were 'hitting unionism where it hurt'. As a result, groups of employers who had taken the middle ground on the 'labor problem' or had made some concessions to the workers were becoming increasingly aware that solidarity was 'essential for their protection and even for their self-preservation'. The NFLA correspondent came to the conclusion that 'the most valuable lessons of the last two years of controversy in the United States has been, not only to teach the value of organization, but to teach what kind of organization is the best', and added that the threat of unionism and labour politics transcended national boundaries and that the abiding sentiment of 'Hands across the sea' should grow into a common front for the open shop.[20]

At the end of 1904, British interest in union-busting in the United States was not confined to the anti-labour fringes. In view of the rapid progress of the CIAA, William Warrand Carlile, an expert in monetary theory, asked in *The Times*: 'if resolutely organized opposition on the part of employers can achieve what has been achieved in America, why should not similarly organized opposition achieve as much among ourselves?'.[21] When the second reading of the Trade Union and Trade Disputes Bill was passed by a large majority in the House of Commons in the parliamentary session of 1905, the *Daily Mail* raised the spectre of strikebreaking and labour espionage by hailing the professional strikebreaker James 'The Boss' Farley as 'the man who always wins'.[22] Likewise, the American correspondent of *The Times*, George Washburn Smalley, discreetly invited British employers and authorities to look at the strikebreaking tactics that Farley had adopted in breaking urban transport strikes 'for educational purposes'.[23] The sudden increase in attention that the conservative press was according the notorious American strikebreaking entrepreneur sent the message that British employers and their allies would fight to the last to prevent any reversal of the system of industrial relations that had emerged from the Taff Vale judgement. Later on, this combative attitude may have been exacerbated by irrational fears that the contemporaneous Russian revolutionary crisis was contagious or at least influential.[24]

Ultimately, a Conservative-controlled Standing Committee on Law made so many amendments to the Trade Disputes Bill that in May its proponents were obliged to withdraw it. Nonetheless, anti-labour forces knew that it was, at best, a Pyrrhic victory. Indeed, on 18 May before the Council of the National Liberal Federation at Newcastle-upon-Tyne, the Liberal leader Sir Henry Campbell-Bannerman declared that his party shared the view of Labour and the Trades Union Congress on the need to revise trade union laws.[25] As expected, after the general election of 1906 the new Liberal government lost no time in tackling the issue and a new Bill was introduced in March by the Attorney General, John Lawson Walton. The most intransigent sectors of British industry reacted by accusing the government of raising trade unions above the law and made repeated allusions to forms of self-defence. In an interview in the *Daily Mail*, Cuthbert Laws, manager of the Shipping Federation, stated that 'If things go on as they seem to be shaping up, we in this country may be compelled in our own defence, from the sheer necessity of the case, to form some such force as the Pinkerton police in America'.[26] George Livesey also declared: 'Perhaps if this Bill becomes law employers must have to establish a force such as the Pinkerton police of America for the protection of men who wish to work in face of strike'.[27] The *London Evening Standard*, owned by newspaper magnate and ardent protectionist Arthur Pearson, also wrote that it was unlikely that 'employers will sit down while their possible adversaries are being provided with new weapons of offence. They will form organisations on the American model'.[28]

Before the Bill was submitted for a second reading in early November 1906, Collison sent a circular letter with the title 'A Vital Question for all Free Citizens' to the principal open-shop associations of America. Published in the official organ of the National Metal Trades Association, *The Open Shop*, the letter stated that the 'collusion of Trade Unionism and Socialism with the openly-avowed object of capturing the Electoral and Legislative machinery of the Country for partizan [sic] and factioned ends, have made manifest the absolute necessity of an organised and more comprehensive effort to meet the exigencies of the situation'. To protect the rights of individuals and communities from subversion, a counter-movement was needed along the lines of the anti-labour bodies in America. Thus, in the name of free citizenship, Collison proposed the formation of a Citizens' Industrial Alliance for 'securing to citizens the full force of their Electorate rights, exercised by them to the industrial advantage of the country as a whole instead of for the exclusive benefit of restricted sectional parts to the obvious detriment of others'. For this purpose, he sought advice from those American employers who were waging a relentless war on the trade union movement.[29] In mid-November, Collison announced in *The Times* that he had accepted an invitation from James A. Emery, president of the CIAA, to attend the organisation's fourth annual convention. In the United States, Collison was expected to scrutinise the organisational and operational characteristics of the open-shop movement.[30]

At the CIAA convention, which was held in Chicago on 3–4 December, Collison presented labour unrest and mounting state interventionism in industrial relations as the main problems facing British industrial firms.[31] He argued that, beginning with the emergence of 'the new trade unionism' and the permeation of the labour movement with socialist principles, the ensuing strikes, boycotts, unlawful picketing and violence against persons and property had driven manufacturers out of the country, closed down factories and left people unemployed. In such circumstances, government attempts to introduce bilateral methods of dispute resolution posed a serious threat to the principles of individual liberty and freedom of contract, and an incentive to industrial insubordination:

> A prominent feature in labor troubles in Great Britain has been arbitration [...] Arbitration boards, civic federations, religious faddists, notoriety hunting politicians, and more often still, civic functionaries, form the material from which amateur arbitrators are usually recruited. Dire is the havoc which such persons have played in trades with which they have interfered [...] We are not afraid of Democracy. With Hamilton, one of the framers of your Constitution, we believe that 'the disease upon us is democracy', and that it is our business to checkmate it.[32]

The increasing representation of labour in legislative and governmental bodies and the advance of industrial democracy had to be countered by a 'revolt of the good citizens'. 'The men whose patron saint is St. George need not fear even socialism', Collison proclaimed. He then announced that the NFLA had decided to establish a Citizens' Alliance. The primary object of his mission to America was therefore 'to study the CIAA's ways of working, and to go back and tell a great meeting which we are going to convene in London early in the new year, what I have found out and the way you have worked your business and the big success you have achieved. We hope to go on and do likewise'.[33]

While in Chicago, Collison paid a visit to the Union Stock Yard & Transit Co. at the invitation of the meatpacking magnate Jonathan O. Armour. He walked around the 320 acres of the meatpacking district and examined the highly innovative meat processing and packaging techniques that were in operation, and was favourably impressed by the organisation of the stockyards. He bluntly declared Upton Sinclair's recently published novel, *The Jungle*, which detailed the miserable work conditions in the meatpacking industries in Chicago and had caused a sensation in both the United States and Britain, to be a string of 'ridiculous statements, sophistries (sic), and barefaced exaggerations from beginning to end'. According to the leader of the NFLA, the book had been written for the purpose of 'creating class hatred and destroy[ing] the dignity of honest work'.[34]

On 6 December 1906, in the company of the assistant secretary of the CIAA, William E. Alexander, Collison visited the Cleveland Twist Drill Company upon invitation of its President and General Manager, Francis F. Prentiss. The Ohio company, which was the first to replace tungsten with molybdenum in the development of high-speed steels and became one of the leading manufacturers of drilling and milling tools in America, had not tolerated any outside interference in management and advocated an open-shop policy. During the visit, Collison took an interest in the matter of employee welfare: changing rooms, toilet facilities, dining rooms and recreational spaces were provided for the company's employees in order to create a working environment conducive to 'industrial peace' and hence higher productivity.[35] On the southern shore of Lake Erie, Collison spoke at a lunch given for him by the members of the Builders' Exchange.[36] From there he moved on to Battle Creek in Michigan where he was guest of Charles W. Post, pioneer and manufacturer of processed food products, such as the coffee substitute, Postum, and Grape Nuts.[37] Collison then visited Roycrofters in East Aurora, where he hoped (without success) to meet the colony's founder, writer and philosopher Elbert G. Hubbard.[38] After a brief stopover at Niagara Falls, he travelled to Pittsburgh where he again spoke on labour conditions in Great Britain at a banquet given in his honour by the local Builders' Exchange. In the 'Steel City', Collison visited the Westinghouse Electric and Manufacturing Company's recently built plant. 'I need not add', Collison wrote 'that this great Company flies the flag of the Open Shop'. One of the precepts of this philosophy, as told to Collison by one of the corporation's managers, was 'The Trade-union Smelting Pot versus Industrial Freedom will boil until only the dross of the smelting will be left therein'.[39]

On 15 December, Collison sailed from New York to Liverpool. Ironically, his return to England coincided with the passing of the Trade Disputes Act, which eliminated the tort of civil conspiracy in trade disputes and legalised

THE SQUARE DEAL

working classes, that none of us desire to reduce their standard of comfort, that none of us would like to see their labor more arduous or less remunerative, and that if we thought socialism or trades unionism could do for labor half of what they claim to do, not one of us would raise a voice or hand except in the way of bidding them Godspeed. (Applause.) It is because we do not believe this, because we believe that even with their aims are good, their methods of promoting these aims are foolish, barbarous, and nearly always suicidal, that we take issue with them.

I am not without sympathy with the working classes. I am a workingman myself, know their struggles and have shared them. I am not

WILLIAM COLLISON.

Biographical Sketch.

COLLISON, WILLIAM ("Free-Labor Bill"), born Stepney, 1865. Apprenticed to tea merchant's, 1879. Joined the Army, 1881; purchased his discharge, 1883. At work riverside wharves and wool warehouses, and for some time as bricklayer's laborer. On the Executive Council of the Amalgamated Laborers' Union, 1885. Elected on the Mansion House Relief Committee, 1886, and placed in charge of relief works. Received letter breathing warmest approval and commendation for his untiring zeal and powers of organization from the late Cardinal Manning, Omnibus driver and conductor, 1887-88-89. Worked 119 hours per week. Organized Busmen's Union, which led for its object, mainly, a reduction of the excessive hours of labor. Later, the Union was captured and subsidized by Mr. Sutherst, of company-promoting fame, who engineered the strike of the London General Omnibus men. This strike originated from the masters wishing to impose a check upon dishonest conductors. Collison admitted the justice of this—the Union did not—and hence that disastrous strike, the result of which was most clearly set forth by Mr. Collison in his celebrated "Manifesto against Strikes." Unfortunately at that time the men were lost to all reason, but previous to this Mr. Collison declined to have anything further to do with the Union. His connection with the inner circle of Trade Unions, however, did one thing. It proved beyond a doubt that the new Unions were captured by political adventurers and Socialistic notoriety hunters. Founded the National Free-Labor Association, 1893; Free-Labor Gazette, 1894; published "On the Trail of the Agitator," and the celebrated "Wilson" pamphlet, described by the press as "the most scathing exposure of a labor mis-leader ever printed." Sued for libel by J. H. Wilson, M. P., who claimed £5,000 damages. Case heard before Mr. Justice Hawkins and a special jury on March 14th and 15th, 1896. After fifteen months' delay Wilson absolutely refused to enter the witness box. Jury reluctantly awarded him one farthing damages. Collison is described by the press as "an energetic worker and one of our ablest industrial organizers;" "has the fearlessness and energy essential to the struggle against Trade Union tyranny." "He possesses in an eminent degree the essential qualities of a leader of men—resource, resolution, the habit of authority, and intense earnestness of purpose."]

opposed to any reasonable and honest efforts to improve their condition; I rejoice at the immense progress that has been made in this direction during the last forty years, and I am as anxious as any trades unionist can be to see the good work go on. But it is because I am anxious for this, and because I am certain that modern trades unionist claims and methods are fatal to all chances of national progress, even for the worker, that I oppose them.

I propose to give you some idea of the state of labor in England in 1889, showing how socialism joined hands with trade unionism at that date and promulgated a general strike, and how the National Free Labor Association was called into existence to protect workers willing to work, and to enforce the right of workingmen to follow their employment without intimidation or molestation from adverse influences.

The London dock strike in 1889 brought into existence a large number of the new labor unions, whose leaders in most instances were mere outsiders, unconnected with the particular trade and industry they professed to lead, but who possessed the qualification of being prominent members of the socialist party. In a word, the socialist party captured the new unions, and determined to run them for the propagation of their own peculiar and anti-English ideas. The weapons which the leaders of the new trade unions elected to use were strikes, intimidation, boycotting, and unlawful picketing, and for more than three years they employed these detestable agencies, with more or less success, until the indignation of the great body of workingmen throughout the country, unconnected with trade and labor unions, was fairly and honestly aroused.

Among the new unions the most active in promoting strikes here, there, and everywhere, were the Dockers' Union, the Sailors' and Firemen's Union, the Gas Workers' Union, and the National Coal Porters' Union. These organizations were assisted in their suicidal policy by a body calling themselves "the Federation of Riverside and Carrying Trades." The first declaration of policy on the part of the combined unions was to declare in favor of a national strike on a given day, which was to dislocate the entire trade of the country, and place "the whole of the implements of production and industry in the hands of the workers." This desperate stroke of policy on the part of the leaders of the new unions alarmed their supporters in the ultra radical press, who stated that, in the event of a national strike, they could not enlist public sympathy "by the influence of bands, banners, and begging-boxes." Then the idea was reluctantly abandoned, only to be followed by a series of unprovoked and senseless strikes, fomented entirely by the new union leaders, such as never before occurred in the industrial history of the British Empire.

I could pursue this distressing topic ad infinitum, and could demonstrate the folly, the wickedness and incapacity of the leaders who have constituted themselves the champions of the new trade union movement. However, I am content to point out that the strikes, fomented by these agitators, at the Royal Albert and Victoria Docks, London; at the ports of Cardiff, Southampton, Barry, Swansea, Bristol and Hull; the gas-workers' strikes at Leeds, Manchester, and the South Metropolitan Gas Works, were all unnecessary and abortive. The strike of the London coal porters in 1892 was a disastrous failure. The strike of the unfortunate London postmen (fomented entirely by socialist agitation) led to wholesale dismissals from the service by the Postmaster-General, bringing ruin and starvation to the wives and children of these ill-advised men, which will not be readily forgotten by the public at large. Also the contemplated revolt of the London police, and of the soldiers in the various barracks in and around the metropolis. These strikes, commenced in one form or another, all ended in disaster to their socialist promoters, not adding to the respect and esteem with which a number of indispensable national servants have always been regarded by the Empire at large.

All these strikes were conducted with extraordinary violence, setting every vestige of common law at defiance. Picketing and watching and besetting were pursued with extraordinary virulence. Men were watched and followed miles away from their residences and places of employment, and in many cases brutally ill-used. Bands were hired to play the "Dead March" outside the houses or lodgings of free labor men. Willing workmen had to be escorted to and from their work by police and soldiers. Shopkeepers, saloon men, and landladies were intimidated in order to prevent them serving the free labor men with food, or refreshment, or to give them lodgings. The children of the free labor men were reviled, ill-used, and spat upon by their schoolmates, at the instigation of trade union fathers.

Not only was the liberty of a man to work during a strike interfered with, but no man was allowed to go to work without being in possession of a trade union ticket, and in the case of the Sailors' and Firemen's Union so much as £10 to £15 ($50 to $75) was extorted from "poor Jack" before he was allowed to become a member of this tyrannous Sailors' Union and made eligible to follow his legitimate employment.

At this time the Dock Laborers' Union, led by Burns, Mann and Tillett, who claimed to be the originators of what they are pleased to describe "the new trade unionism," decreed that their books should be closed, that no new members were to be enrolled, that they were now sufficient in numbers to perform the work at the docks, and that any addition thereto would but impede their progress, by being brought into competition with the accredited members of the Dockers' Union. Thousands of workmen in the port of London declined to be boy-

Figure 4.1 William Collison in Chicago. *The Square Deal* 2, no. 6, January 1907

peaceful picketing. At the beginning of January 1907, in a column published in the *Free Labour Press and Industrial Review* titled 'Notes from America', Collison presented some of his findings:

> The trade-union leaders in America are much more powerful, unscrupulous, and aggressive than their brothers in England, and until recently have been able, in most trades, to enforce the 'closed shop' [...] and they resort to every crime to enforce these conditions – even murder. But the tide has turned. The movement for the 'open shop' is growing, and in all the American cities I visited, I found a strong, well-organized body of level-headed, determined employers and good citizens, banded together in Citizens' Industrial Associations for this object ... [The CIAA] has some of the keenest intellects among businessmen connected with it [...] 'We fly the flag of the open shop', they say, 'and we challenge organized labor to pull it down'.[40]

At about the same time, the St. Louis-based monthly magazine, *The Exponent*, published by the local Citizens' Industrial Association (CIA), congratulated Collison for founding an organisation whose declaration of principles was remarkably similar, if not identical, to that of the Missouri organisation.[41] It does not seem unreasonable to assume that James W. Van Cleave, President of both the St. Louis CIA and the National Association of Manufacturers, and chairman of the National Council for Industrial Defense, provided Collison with advice and guidance. In *The Apostle of Free Labour*, Collison eloquently praised Von Cleave as the 'representative of all that is best and energetic in American enterprise'.[42]

Despite the fanfares that accompanied Collison's tour of America, the project of federating national and local employers' associations and citizens' committees into one powerful anti-labour alliance met with little interest and faded away, and was perhaps forgotten by early 1908. *The Free Labour and Industrial Review* continued to publish the CIAA's bulletins until the spring of 1907. Sometime later, during his tour of Europe to examine industrial relations and labour legislation there, James A. Emery spoke at the eighteenth annual congress of the NFLA in London, reaffirming the need to preserve at any cost every principle and institution of liberty against 'the festering wedge' of unionism and socialism.[43] Thereafter, extracts from the annual reports of the NFLA occasionally appeared in *The Square Deal* until 1915.

Plans for a Citizens' Industrial Alliance of Britain failed, due in part or perhaps entirely to the NFLA's services having gradually fallen into disrepute over the years and having indeed been more or less rejected in certain industries. However, the importance of these encounters between Collison and the leading representatives of the open-shop organisation in the United

States do not lie in what they accomplished, but rather in the way they reflect the disquiet that Collison and his patrons felt in the face of the rise of Labour as a political power.[44] 'The Labour Party', Collison nervously wrote in *The Square Deal* in the spring of 1911, 'having intimidated a weak-kneed Government into passing the "The Trade Disputes Act", we now see in all strikes, in this boasted land of freedom, honest non-society workmen ... hunted like rabbits'.[45]

'Patriotic' strikebreaking during the Great Unrest, 1911–1914

In the years preceding the war, the danger of a general strike, which would have 'placed the country in rigor of death' and precipitated a political revolution, haunted conservative and nationalist ranks almost unceasingly.[46] It is hardly surprising that public debates on how to prevent a potential paralysis of society and on how the public as citizens and consumers should protect their rights and should assist law enforcement officials in safeguarding them, regularly unfolded in conjunction with serious stoppages at home and abroad. Much praise, for instance, was heaped on those Swedish citizens who had joined the *Frivilliga Skyddskåren* – voluntary security brigade – during the general strike of 1909. T. H. Penson, lecturer in modern history and economics at the University of Oxford, commented in *The Economic Journal* that 'it was clearly demonstrated that when threatened the upper and middle classes could rise to the occasion and do all that was necessary to keep the social machine at work and in perfect order'. In his view, the general strike was not a labour dispute, but an attack upon the community itself. The need to defend property and maintain 'the various services which the conditions of modern life have rendered almost indispensable', brought together citizens from very different classes, upbringings and professions:

> it was something of an anomaly to see noblemen and officers of the highest rank driving cabs, merchants and stockbrokers doing ambulance work, civil engineers working in the stoke-hole of a steamer or attending to the gas, water, and electric lighting machinery, civil servants and undergraduates acting as tram conductors or unloading the ships bringing wood, coal and provisions to the capital.[47]

The *Frivilliga Skyddskåren* and the defection of those workers who had organised themselves into the 'yellow union' *Svenska Arbetareförbundet*, which had initially participated in the industrial action, contributed to breaking the strike. The correspondent for *The Times* openly commended the Swedish strikebreaking experiment, which appeared to substantiate the impression that all strike contingencies would inevitably be met with counter-mobilisation by the public.[48]

An important implication of this was that 'loyal citizens' should take upon themselves the task of defending the security and welfare of the community, and at the same time it was evidence of the growing contempt held by most conservative sectors of British society for the Liberal government's assertion of neutrality in industrial disputes. In 1907, the Amalgamated Society of Railway Servants (ASRS) approached the railway companies, which continued to refuse both recognition of the union and any form of negotiation. A strike ballot was held in September that year, yielding an overwhelming majority in favour. This prompted Lloyd George, then President of the Board of Trade, to intervene. Under his pressure, the railway companies agreed to establish a Conciliation and Arbitration Scheme. Similarly, the government intervened in various other disputes, including those in the cotton industry and shipyards, often pressing employers to negotiate with workers. In May 1910, workers employed by Messrs. Houlder at the Newport docks went on strike. In response, Messrs. Houlder arranged to bring in replacement workers ('free labourers') and requested police protection for them. The situation quickly escalated, prompting the Home Secretary to suggest that the Board of Trade act as an arbitrator between Messrs. Houlder and the striking workers. A Board of Trade representative informed Messrs. Houlder that force might be necessary to prevent the 'free labourers' from working if they were brought to the docks, and that the company could be held responsible for any breach of the peace. Despite this warning, Messrs. Houlder asserted their legal right to employ 'free labourers', citing *Beatty v. Gilbanks* [1892], which established that individuals cannot be prevented from engaging in lawful activities, even if those activities provoke unlawful responses. However, authorities failed to provide adequate protection for the company and its replacement workers, forcing the 'free labourers' to leave town under the escort of a hostile crowd. Ultimately, the Home Secretary assumed full responsibility for the actions of the local authorities, alongside the Home Office and the Secretary for War (acting as his *locum tenens*). By this point, Messrs. Houlder had agreed to enter arbitration.[49]

For right-wingers, 'old established' anti-socialist societies, and 'reactionary' industrialists, the Trade Disputes Act of 1906, state-sponsored conciliation, and the wave of social reforms from 1906 to 1909 – including the amendment of the Merchant Shipping Acts, the Workmen's Compensation Act, relief works for the unemployed under the Unemployed Workmen Act of 1905, Old Age Pensions and the Coal Mines (Eight Hours) Act – were all seen as evidence of a 'Lib-Lab conspiracy' against private and proprietorial rights. Additionally, government attitudes towards industrial relations – particularly the timidity or indecision in providing unconditional protection for strikebreakers – were blamed for encouraging renewed disturbances that in turn ran counter to the national economic interest.[50]

These accusations of cowardice against the government and sensationalised accounts of violent strike disturbances, especially in the Belfast Dock and Carters Strike of 1907 and the prolonged South Wales coal strike of 1910, incited vigilante action. In March 1911, the future leader of the Labour Party, George Lansbury, denounced in parliament 'the practice of associations of employers to employ private police during strikes and lock-outs'. He referred specifically to those London printing firms that had hired special guards to protect their premises during the dispute between the Typographical Association and the Printing Trades Employers' Associations in Great Britain and Ireland.[51] At the same time, the Liberty and Property Defence League, which had taken over the Free Labour Protection Association (FLPA), were offering private security services to employers and property owners against the aggressive actions of militant trade unionism. The League's scheme stemmed from the failure of the police to provide proper protection, especially when its actions were challenged by Labour members of local government bodies.[52]

The great transport strikes of summer 1911 gave a tremendous new impetus to the organisation of self-defence by the 'bourgeois class'. In June, a seaman's strike broke out in Southampton then spread to other seaports of the United Kingdom, 'and passed on to the transport workers of the inland cities, with the contagious quickness of conflagration'.[53] In August, the country came to a worrying standstill. 'Communications were held up', the *Board of Trade Labour Gazette* reported, 'food supplies ceased, traffic was regulated by 'passes' issued by strike committees, railway stations were occupied by troops carrying the ball cartridge, the man in the street found the stable security of his life vanishing in a moment'.[54] There was no doubt in the minds of many contemporaries that the gravity of the industrial unrest in conjunction with the controversy surrounding the Parliament Act of 1911, the women's militant suffrage movement and rising tensions over Home Rule reflected the ongoing division of British society into irreconcilable camps. 'There is no King in Israel', *The Times* lamented, 'every man is a law unto himself'.[55]

In this atmosphere of foreboding, there were reports of private citizens spontaneously making preparations for vigilante violence and labour replacement. The manager of H. L. Raphael's Refinery in London notified the Home Office that he had made 'complete preparations against any attack on this place, that our men are fully armed and we shall not sit still and watch our property being looted as did the owners of property at Newport, Tonypandy, Hull, Manchester, Cardiff and other towns'.[56] In Liverpool, rumours circulated that ordinary citizens had started arming themselves to protect their property after riots broke out in the days following 'Bloody Sunday'.[57] Meanwhile, employers were rushing to have their male employees sworn in as special constables to ensure their own premises would receive police protection. A letter written on behalf of the 'middle classes', who were feeling the brunt of the transport strike, petitioned Home Secretary Winston Churchill to deport the trade unionist Tom Mann. The letter added that there were many men ready to take the law into their own hands to get rid of the radical labour leader.[58]

As the ASRS seemed prepared to call a national strike, the anti-Liberal Middle Class Defence Organisation urged 'all members of the middle classes, and in particular strong, healthy young men' to organise themselves into teams for 'the maintenance of the food supply'.[59] Similarly, newspapers were flooded with letters from ordinary citizens recommending the organisation of volunteer corps in order to prevent the paralysis of transport and trade. 'There must be thousands of young men', a theatre owner wrote to the *Daily Telegraph*, 'who could be useful as guards, engine firemen, 'flag men'&c., and they would have the satisfaction of knowing that they were actually taking part in the defence of the county, as much as though a foreign army had invaded it'.[60]

When the national railway strike started on 18 August, sparking rioting and disturbances in many parts of the country, the already overstretched police resources were put under severe strain. The circumstances were grave enough to warrant the contentious use of military forces to maintain essential services and supplies. Apart from the extensive use of troops, which was a dramatic reversal of previous attempts to demilitarise protest policing, the government gave much importance to enrolling special constables.[61] Since the passing of the Special Constables Act of 1831, the appointment of temporary officers had been the quickest and most convenient means of supplementing law enforcement in case of actual or impending riots or other serious disruptions or disturbances of the public peace. However, over the years, as journalist Tony Bunyan noted in his book on the political police in Britain, the special constables had changed from 'a volunteer force drawn from the whole community for limited periods to a smaller, permanent and loyal body recruited largely from the petit-bourgeoisie'. Therefore, when major protests erupted, the special constabulary provided 'a rallying point for those committed to perpetuating the prevailing order'.[62]

It is no wonder, then, that the engagement of special constables in industrial disputes had become an increasingly contentious political issue. If Conservatives and moderate Liberals generally praised it as a healthy form of civic patriotism, labour representatives viewed it as deliberate provocation and a sanctioning by public authorities of strikebreaking measures.[63]

'The revolt of the good citizens' 191

Figure 4.2 1. Badges, hats, truncheons and armlets being served out to special constables at the Guildhall, London; 2. soldiers working as porters in Liverpool; 3. 'unable to get supplies': a butcher's shop in Liverpool. *The Illustrated London News*, 26 August 1911. Image © Mary Evans Picture Library

At the outbreak of the railway strike, thousands of 'men of trustworthy character and good physique' responded to the Home Office's appeal for special constables.[64] As expected, the middle classes constituted the largest recruitment pool. According to the annual report on the constabulary and police forces in England and Wales, 4,142 citizens were sworn in by magistrates in Liverpool to deal with the August riots. The majority of these men were 'employed as a night watch at different premises; but over one thousand two hundred did actual street duty in the disturbed areas, and rendered valuable service to the city'.[65] In London, more than six thousand 'patriotic citizens' volunteered for special constable duties, as their predecessors had done during the Chartist disturbances or in connection with the Clerkenwell outrages and the Trafalgar Square riots.[66] In Sheffield, the rapid response of citizens to the Lord Mayor's appeal for special constables was regarded as a noble expression of patriotic sentiments. The men exercising such responsible citizenship were provided with a truncheon, a whistle, a pair of handcuffs and a black and white badge to be worn on the arm.[67]

In many places, there were plenty among those who volunteered their services as special constables who were eager to use their truncheons on strikers. Their zeal caused the very breaches of public peace that they had been assigned to protect, and left lasting, bitter memories.[68] For instance, during a parliamentary debate in 1923, the Labour MP John Joseph (Jack) Jones reminded the House that 'In 1911 we had Bluebottles on top of the meat vans, and they were special constables, and very special constables. They were not used to break the strike, but to break people's heads'.[69]

The anger of strikers was further, and perhaps even more, exacerbated by the spontaneous or apparently spontaneous formation of corps of volunteer workers. In Liverpool, a number of university students stoked the turbines of electric power stations to supply the energy needed for street lighting and to run tramway services. Meanwhile, other 'upstanding citizens' helped with cleaning the streets and with driving horse-drawn carriages, carts and other such vehicles laden with merchandise from train stations to markets. In York, the trains of the NER were manned by volunteers,[70] while in London, volunteers and Euston station clerical staff acted as signalmen, porters, shunters and goods guards.[71]

Although short-lived, the railway strike made a deep impression on the public and raised an unprecedented interest in methods that could counteract or mitigate the effects of serious disputes. Certainly, there was gloomy and unrealistic talk of class war, revolution and a headlong descent into anarchy and social breakdown. In a frenzied letter to the *Pall Mall Gazette*, a member of the Conservative Junior Constitutional Club wrote that the railway strike had unequivocally demonstrated that it was time for the middle classes to unite and prevent the 'band of agitators from sowing the evil seed':

> Let us raise a strong force of men from the ranks of the middle classes and upper classes, taking those who are acquainted with the use of arms; each district or county to undertake enrolment, binding themselves to serve on emergency, and subscriptions for arms and equipment raised, and ex-Army officers or Territorials invited to organize each county or district; and these forces in time of trouble to be placed under the command of the military in each district of the country.
>
> The great middle class, the backbone of this country, who have been bled by taxation, reviled by demagogues as the despoilers of the poor man, must now, if ever, show their determination to check the vile growth of anarchy in this country. Before such forces as this country could raise drawn from the best of our middle classes, anarchy and mobs would have no headway should civil war ensue, the protection of property and the lives of our women be secured from attack.[72]

In vehement, declamatory tones, Sir Arthur Clay asserted in his then recently published 'Syndicalism and Labour' that only a vigorous response of the middle classes could save society from the attacks of its enemies, i.e., socialists, syndicalists and anarchists. 'In the social organism', Clay significantly wrote, 'the action of the middle class, when peril threatens the community, is similar to that of the phagocytes in the blood of a man, who, when the organism of which they are part is attacked by bacilli hostile to its well-being, stream to the point of intrusion and engulf the enemies'.[73] In his Darwinian perspective, he was dumbfounded by the apathy with which the middle classes were regarding the threat of collectivism and the various 'social diseases' which had accompanied the process of democratisation. Clay explained that this passive attitude could be attributed to the diffusion of modern humanitarian influences and a certain naive belief that the country's economic and social system was unassailable. In addition, growing state interventionism and the abundant crop of social legislation that had followed the Progressive Alliance and the rise of Labour had induced a sort of hypnotic state in the middle classes. However, the time had now come for them – as the protective army of phagocytes – to awaken from their lethargy and escort the 'nation along the path of true civilization'.[74]

Underlying the astonishingly brazen threats of middle-class reaction was a widespread feeling that further industrial unrest, perhaps wider and more enduring, might break out at any moment and that the arrangements made by the government to respond to strikes appeared to be ineffective, if not downright detrimental. Virtually everyone objected to military intervention in industrial disputes, except where the provision of essential supplies and services was disrupted. At the same time, it seemed that the use of special constables would be insufficient to alleviate the worst effects of a serious strike. At the end of August, *The Times* began to publish letters advocating the enrolment of ordinary citizens in new volunteer organisations that could assist the civil authorities in maintaining law and order and relieve the army of the embarrassment of strike policing. The secretary of the Yeomanry Old Comrades' Association, L. M. Musgrove, judged the industrial crisis to be so acute that former Yeomen should be immediately called up and placed at the disposal of the civil authorities as mounted special constables.[75] Proposals for using ordinary citizens as strikebreakers or labour replacements abounded. The editors of *The Times* endorsed the establishment of a national standing volunteer corps, whose organisational logic and practices explicitly echoed those of the *Frivilliga Skyddskåren*.[76]

Meanwhile, Lord Montagu of Beaulieu advanced the idea of a motor-vehicle organisation to minimise transport disruption caused by a nationwide rail strike. He pointed out that there were about one hundred and twenty thousand vehicles in the country, of which fifty thousand were registered with the Royal Automobile Club and the Automobile Association and Motor Union. In addition, there were at least ten thousand commercial vehicles, comprising lorries, vans and omnibuses. Assuming that the major automobile organisations of Great Britain would support the organisation, Lord Montagu declared that private motor vehicles could transport milk, meat, fruit, vegetables and other perishable goods; medical supplies; troops or police; even passengers, although on a limited basis; and also deliver mail. The government should ensure the protection of motorists when loading, driving and unloading vehicles.[77] The plan put forward by Lord Montagu was, at least initially, welcomed in motoring circles. In a letter to Winston Churchill, the Conservative politician William Joynson-Hicks offered to raise a voluntary motor service that could be mobilised by the government to transport food and other essentials in case of stoppages on the railways. In case of emergencies, this organisation of 'private motors' could help the authorities transport troops or policemen, and in this regard, Joynson-Hicks recalled that between four and five hundred members of the Automobile Association and Motor Union had by way of an experiment undertaken to transfer a battalion of Guards from London to Hastings and back in 1909.[78]

The idea of concerted action on the part of patriotic motorists to complement or replace railway services during strikes received the support of a number of merchants, shopkeepers and tradesmen. Arthur Walter Gamage, the owner of a renowned department store in central London, thought that Montagu's scheme could be effective if the government provided allowances and tax benefits for the firms and individuals joining the association. In addition, he suggested that the government should stipulate a contract with oil companies 'to allow them first call on an agreed quantity of petrol, and that the contractors should be bound to have a fixed quantity always at call'. Drivers, Gamage wrote, should be recruited under similar criteria to those for the Army Reserve. In conclusion, he said that by assembling a large fleet of motor vehicles belonging to delivery companies such as Carter-Paterson, Pickford and Thompson, and to department stores such as Gamages, Harrods and Whiteley's, as well as LGOC omnibuses, 'any railway strike would be shorn of many of its terrors'.[79] Despite the endorsements from well-known wealthy figures, many argued that the proposal was impracticable due to the threat of violence by pickets on the roadway and elsewhere.[80] In light of these objections, the 'antidote' proposed by Lord Montagu for future transport strikes appears to have fallen through.

Around the same time, an article in *The Spectator* uncompromisingly titled 'Picketing and Counter-Picketing' commented that society was bound to protect itself against syndicalist methods. In particular, employers were urged to deal with the problem of picketing by forming corps of counter-pickets who would keep the pickets under continuous surveillance and take legal action against them for any breach of the law. If deemed necessary, these corps should also use 'physical force to prevent a breach of the peace'. It was, in the writer's view, as much the responsibility of ordinary citizens as of the police to stop a crime from being committed. Needless to say, *The Spectator* insisted – controversially – that it was 'a scandal that private persons should have to organize such a system of mutual defence; but since the present Ministry obviously attaches more importance to keeping the Socialist vote in the House of Commons than to keeping the King's peace, private individuals are driven back upon self-protection'.[81]

In drawing a disturbing picture of what would occur if the railway strike were to go to extremes, W. T. Stead drew a parallel between the regulations of the Hague Convention (on the general laws and customs of war) and the legislative enactments relating to the prevention of strikes in force in Britain. He pointed out that while the signatory powers to the 1907 Hague Conference had admitted the principle of arbitration and made their court the statutory tribunal for the resolution of conflicts between States, the government's policy for settling industrial disputes remained unreservedly permissive and voluntary. Unfortunately, the arbitration boards' jurisdiction extended only to cases brought jointly by both contending parties. The chief victim of this lack of a permanent formal body for settling industrial disputes was the public. As a general strike or a lockout harmed ordinary people, Stead suggested adopting the provisions of the 1907 Hague Convention regarding the protection of civilians in order to mitigate the effects of serious industrial disputes. The result would be legislation that treated picketing or any interference with normal production as intimidation or restriction of liberty. At the same time, certain legal provisions would be enacted to adequately safeguard services held to be essential to the general welfare of the community. A higher tribunal, Stead went on, would consider whether a strike or lockout was an offence against the State, in which case it would mean that those who called the strike could be tried for the crime of treason. Pending the passage of this legislation, Stead acknowledged that civilian self-defence might be necessary and justifiable:

> In every community there may have organised a volunteer force of men willing and ready to take the places of strikers whose abstention from work threatens the whole community with the loss of the indispensable services of public utility represented by those who supply food, drink, light, sanitation, and the transmission of raw materials. There is an irreducible minimum of necessaries of life without which human society cannot hold together. If the Government and the legislature will not guarantee this irreducible minimum, the citizens will have to take their own measures.[82]

Among the various possibilities of industrial defence, Stead mentioned the organisations of strikebreakers in the United States, which had been 'recognised as a necessary check upon the exorbitant demands of the unions'. Stead warned, however, that such extreme measures were more likely to escalate disputes rather than prevent them. A possible solution to the labour problem, Stead concluded with a sudden moderation of his views, may lie in 'some system of profit sharing and co-partnership, or some kind of State Socialism, which may or not may not be reached by the road of municipal ownership of services of public utility'.[83]

The practice of professional strikebreaking and company police systems that was characteristic of the most militant sectors of American capital continued to exert its fascination on all those who preached the gospel of industrial defence. *The Nation*'s commentators brought the wrath of their readers upon their heads when they argued that employers would be justified if they decided to take the law into their own hands. In a letter to the editors, former Liberal MP and socialist convert R. B. Cunninghame Graham wrote that 'One of your correspondents goes so far as to regret that employers had not been left alone to deal with the strikers outside the law. One sees a vision of a force of British Pinkertons, and of railway stations surrounded by barbed-wire entanglements charged with electricity, after the fashion that certain employers have adopted in the United States'.[84]

While anti-strike schemes and speculation abounded, the government urged every police district to continue enrolling trustworthy citizens as special constables and to record their names in a classified register as being available for immediate employment. To ensure a consistent organisational structure, two types of reserve police were recommended. The first would comprise retired policemen prepared to rejoin the ranks should the need arise, while the second would consist of citizens ready to serve as special constables under the 1831 Special Constables Act.⁸⁵ These arrangements did not impinge on the initiatives for civilian self-defence. In Liverpool, at the end of a meeting convened by the Lord Mayor, the Earl of Derby, resolutions were passed authorising the formation of a Civic Service League (CSL).⁸⁶ The Lord Mayor was appointed president *ad interim*, while a managing committee consisting of prominent business and civic leaders, including J. F. Rodgers (President of the Fruit Brokers' Association), H. R. Robertson (Chairman of the Mersey Dock Board), J. H. Verson (President of the Corn Trade Association) and the shipowner Sir William Bowring, was appointed to oversee the league.⁸⁷ In the words of its first chairman, F. J. Leslie, the CSL was an 'organisation of Citizens willing to assist the Authorities in preserving the health, safety and well-being of the City in time of need'.⁸⁸ Its membership was to be drawn from among the men who had volunteered at the Lister Drive power station, and those who had served as special constables during the recent strikes. A women's branch of the league was also created.⁸⁹ Before long, the CSL was receiving criticism from law enforcement officials. The Head Constable of Liverpool, Sir Leonard Dunning, complained that the league had no authority to call upon the King's subjects to help the authorities in cases of tumult or riot. The responsibility for calling for their assistance as special constables rested with Justices of the Peace rather than private or class interests. There was also the natural and legitimate suspicion among unions and workers that the league was nothing more than a strikebreaking body. Even within the ranks of the CSL, many believed that its avowed neutrality was a just a specious pretence to hide its anti-union bias. Leslie peremptorily rejected these accusations, arguing that the league would not take a side in any dispute between labour and capital where the services of its volunteers might be required. By the same token, in explaining why he had undertaken the presidency of the league, the Lord Mayor said that as a public official he was charged with the duty of impartiality in industrial disputes, but he could not escape the responsibility of enforcing law and order in the city and ensuring the continuation of all essential services, in particular the distribution and sale of the necessities of life. Establishing a properly organised 'band of citizens', ready to be called upon as the need arose, should therefore be considered a beneficial and salutary endeavour.⁹⁰ As of winter 1911, the CSL was actively recruiting and training individuals for various positions: electrical, steam and marine engineers, motor vehicle drivers, horseback riders, stokers, ambulance and medical staff, street cleaners and general clerical workers.⁹¹ On the eve of the war, two thousand five hundred volunteers had been registered and allotted functions.⁹²

The CSL was immediately imitated around the country. The Mayor of the Metropolitan Borough of Chelsea proposed forming a Civic Service League 'with a view to the ratepayers assisting the [Borough] Council in the event of future strikes'.[93] Meanwhile, Conservative MP Gershom Stewart's prediction that citizens would 'organise themselves into committees of self-defence' if the government did not effectively deal with the issue of peaceful picketing, became reality.[94] At the end of the summer, London-based art dealer William Mailes Power initiated a movement for a civilian force that he envisioned would supplement regular law enforcement operations in cases of emergency, but without being formally attached to any auxiliary or part-time volunteer branch of the police organisation. Power had long been a fine example of upper-middle-class patriotism and devotion to the cause of Britain. He had joined the Volunteers as early as 1878, and in 1906 as a member of the 13th Middlesex (Queen's Westminster) Volunteer Rifle Corps he had competed with them in a rifle match against the Seventh Regiment of the National Guard of New York for the Howard Vincent Challenge Shield.[95] During the London Dock Strike in August 1911, when London was threatened with extensive shortages of food and raw materials, Power had personally offered Scotland Yard his services in raising a company of 'special constable cyclist patrols'.[96] Following the announcement by the Commissioner of Police, Sir Edward Henry, that a register was to be kept of the men who had enrolled as special constables during the railway strike, Power conceived the idea of a civilian organisation for use in strike emergencies. In a letter dated 16 September, he informed the Home Secretary, Winston Churchill, that his scheme for a volunteer police force was 'still in its embryo stage', but had already received 'strong support not only from gentlemen of position ... but, what is more important still, from very large numbers of private citizens who have expressed their desire [...] to prevent the recurrence of the disorders which accompanied the recent strikes'. The expenses of the force would, at least in its initial stages, be met by private means. In the memorandum attached to the letter, Power further explained the whys and wherefores of the 'voluntary auxiliary body'. He argued that the procedures and modes of enrolment of special constables under the 1831 Special Constable Act did not always secure sufficient recruits in all areas of responsibility. Special constables were sworn in at a moment's notice, when the time pressures of the emergency made it difficult or impossible for magistrates to perform proper checks of the volunteers' backgrounds and credentials. The new force, instead, was permanent and composed of citizens of proven loyalty and ability to volunteer their services. These men would be summoned when needed and placed under the orders of the Chief Commissioner and the various Chief Constables. Finally, Churchill was asked permission for his name to appear among the vice-presidents of the

Council, over which the Duke of Argyll had been asked to preside.[97] The Home Office, which had grown suspicious of Power's intentions, declined any support whatsoever for a private organisation that appeared to misinterpret Churchill's proposals for the establishment of Police Reserves.[98]

Despite the government's hostility, the Volunteer Police Force (VPF) was established in London on Trafalgar Day (21 October) with the Duke of Abercorn as its first president. Viscount Templetown, who presided over the inaugural meeting at the Crystal Palace, declared that the movement was apolitical, made no demand for State aid and was intended as a supplement rather than a replacement for the regular police forces. Arnold Statham, barrister at law, explained the legal foundation of the VPF, arguing that it sprang directly from 'one of the mainsprings of the British Constitution – the right of the public to combine for self-defence':

> It does not require an Act of Parliament to enable British citizens to fly to the rescue of human life. It does not require Statutory authority to justify Englishmen in protecting the liberty of the subject and the inviolability of property. The right to maintain law and order is the natural heritage of British subjects.[99]

While the army should be the last resort in civil disturbances, every respectable citizen had the right to 'take a firm stand against anarchy'. This, Statham claimed, was because the 'destiny of the nation, the very security of the lives of the persecuted men, women and children are primarily in the hands of the people themselves'. Consequently, the VPF's existence did not, and could not, depend upon the passage of any proposed legislation. 'If any change in the law is wanted at all', Statham said, 'it is that it should be made a misdemeanour not to go to the rescue when the call for help is made in case of riot'. There was no law which could thwart the will of the individual to defend his own community. 'If scoundrels begin setting fire to houses as they did recently in Swansea and elsewhere', Statham rhetorically asked, 'are stalwart men to sit still and watch the bonfire because no authority was invited to interfere?'. Naturally, Statham's outspoken criticism was sustained by the feeling that the government was weak and ineffectual when it came to dealing with nationwide labour stoppages. It was therefore of absolute importance that citizens should be ready to deal with the 'enemy that lurk[ed] within our midst'. This enemy was Labour, which Statham accused of coercing the nation into submission through the ominous threat of a general strike. Sympathetic strikes, picketing and disorders were just 'a mere cloak for class warfare' and harbingers of revolution. Faced with this dismal prospect, the public authorities' dithering was viewed as criminal negligence. 'What Britain wants-to-day', Statham shouted to a roaring crowd, 'is not weak-kneed local authorities, but a Bismarck with a Will of Iron'. Given the situation, the VPF should be regarded as a cost-free form of 'national insurance' against uncertainty and a true symbol of democratic participation and direct popular rule. Following this combative speech, Statham moved the first resolution:

> that this Mass Meeting of citizens from all parts of the United Kingdom, impressed with the urgent necessity of quelling lawlessness and disorder from time to time in case of need, resolves to form, without casting any additional burden upon the taxpayer, a Volunteer Police Force of private citizens to cooperate with the Regular Forces in the protection of life, property and liberty, where the same are assailed, and for the maintenance of general transport, whensoever the public carriers of the people's food are threatened with violent interference.[100]

The resolution was passed unanimously by the meeting. F. C. Morgan, President of the Central Association of Accountants, then moved the second resolution, which provided for the general constitution of the VPF. In fourteen points, it stated that the force would have no ties with political parties or business interests; it would operate with a decentralised structure that encouraged and recognised local direction; its resources and revenue would depend entirely on private donations. In addition, it was stressed that the VPF would cooperate with the police forces while remaining free to act in order to protect 'public methods of locomotion, transport or private property, without awaiting the intervention of absentee officials'. This second resolution was also carried unanimously and it was announced that branches of the VPF would also be formed in Scotland and Ireland. The meeting ended with readings of the congratulatory telegrams and letters sent by Earl Lonsdale, Viscount Churchill, the Venerable Archdeacon Sinclair, Lord George Hamilton and Conservative MPs George Parker, William Bull and Arnold Ward, all of whom endorsed the force as a necessary bulwark of freedom and property. Two metropolitan police magistrates, John De Grey and Albert de Rutzen also in opportunely welcomed what appeared to them 'the most simple and most sensible method of meeting a national want'.[101]

The press gave the formation of the VPF wide coverage and published lengthy excerpts from the inaugural proceedings. Before long, a large number of applications for enrolment arrived at the VPF's headquarters in Victoria Street. The majority of applicants were upper-class young men imbued with a narrow elitism, snobbery and a lack of empathy for workers' grievances. The opportunity to defend the community from strikes that were presumed would threaten the safety and health of people may have offered them a physical outlet for their adrenaline and a stage on which to project their 'patriotic' masculinity'.[102] In a satirical article in the left-wing weekly newspaper *The Eye-Witness* titled 'The Honorary Strikebreakers', the radical Josiah Wedgwood wrote that the VPF was a 'call to the idle rich young men to stamp on the restless workers and keep them in their place'. Just as they volunteered to fight the Boers, they now swore to stand side by side with artisans, clerks and petty shopkeepers in the fight 'against a new and more terrible enemy – the enemy who only folds his arms'. Far from being a mere new version of the NFLA, Wedgwood saw the VPF as the 'British edition of the Pinkerton's detective'. Such a body, he added, could be spelled in only one way: 'CLASS WAR'.[103] Similarly, an anonymous commentator for the Bournemouth-based *Christchurch Times* spoke of 'a number of busybodies, almost entirely prominent Tories' who were travelling around the country to establish a Pinkerton-type private police force:

> This new body is to have a uniform and it is quite certain that it will be composed of men who are strongly anti-trade unionist. Thus, if such a force were to become numerous, there is all the material for class antagonism of the worst kind.[104]

Meanwhile, railway companies announced their intention of making use of the services of Abercorn's force if circumstances demanded it.[105] A provisional list of directions to commanding officers of the VPF in case of new labour troubles on the railways was published in *The Times*. The document stated that each commanding officer should remain in close contact with railway officials and keep his men in a constant state of readiness, so that they could be rapidly deployed to terminals, stations, depots and interchange facilities for passengers and freight. Aside from protecting railway property, the men would escort through the picket lines those enginemen, shunters, firemen, signalmen and other railway employees who refused to strike. If necessary, anyone with expertise in railway rolling stock should be on hand to lend their services. Each man should wear a uniform and be 'served with a weapon for self-defence of approved design'. The list forthrightly stated that: 'The men are not to wait for orders from any authority but are to use under their own Officers, their force and the entire weight of their organisation to immediately crush any exhibition of brutality to which their attention may be called'.[106]

By then, it was obvious that such a uniformed force, which had no connection whatsoever with the special constable scheme and took upon itself the right to safeguard proprietorial prerogatives, represented a potential danger to British labour and democracy. The weekly newspaper of the Social-Democratic Federation, *The Justice*, contentiously wrote:

> There are two movements now going on by which the master class are now endeavouring to ensure themselves against any dislocation of business in the event of a strike, especially a strike of railway men. One is the Home Office movement for the enrolment of special constables [...] and the other is the organization of a 'volunteer police force' by the capitalists themselves. In connection with the former it appears that the Home Office is making a census, by means of inquiries among manufacturers and others, of employees between the ages of 25 and 40 physically capable of acting as special constables. These, it is understood, will be enrolled and called upon as required – a sort of civil conscription in the interests of capitalism. With regard to the other, they are organized on the lines of the infamous Pinkertons of America. They are to be used as police or strike-breakers indiscriminately as occasion serves.[107]

Not surprisingly, when newspapers reported the founding of new VPF branches in Yorkshire, local trade unionists set about organising their own security plans and forces. The Bradford branch of the ASRS passed a resolution in favour of a Physical Protection League, 'whose objects shall be the training and equipment of selected Trade Unionists in order [...] to meet on equal terms the bullies of organised capital'.[108] An identical resolution was put forward by railwaymen in Huddersfield, but met with opposition.[109] Proposals for workers' defence were subsequently dropped when the Bradford and District Trades and Labour Council agreed that any response by violent means on the part of workers would frighten employers and probably help build a wider consensus on the VPF. At the same time, it was recommended that political pressure should be put on the government to have Abercorn's organisation of strikebreakers promptly disbanded.[110]

In the House of Commons, Wedgwood and others repeatedly questioned the new Home Secretary, Reginald McKenna, about the precise nature of the VPF and the steps the government intended taking against a private venture that was arming its own members with bludgeons 'to break people's heads'. McKenna replied that the government had no knowledge of the VPF beyond what had recently appeared in the press. He knew that the organisers of the force had proposed forming companies of volunteers and providing them with uniforms and equipment, and that they were committed to raising funds for that purpose. He was not aware that any railway or mining company was supporting the movement, although he had been informed that some had been approached by Mr. Power. It was obvious, McKenna argued, that such a private force did not have any authority or power until its members were enrolled as special constables in conformity with the Special Constables Act of 1831. Therefore, if they attempted to physically interfere with pickets exercising their rights, the pickets would be entitled to police protection. He went on to say that it was a statutory offence to wear a uniform or any badge, patch or insignia as a designation of rank. In conclusion, while recognising that it was the duty of all citizens to assist the ordinary police forces in emergencies, McKenna warned Abercorn and his men that no government could permit the establishment of an independent organisation that usurped the functions of the State and whose conduct was likely to cause a serious breach of the peace.[111]

The government's frosty, if not hostile, response stirred the indignation of conservative and right-wing opinion. *The Morning Post*, for instance, disparagingly accused McKenna of caring more about keeping Labourites quiet than of taking the necessary precautions to protect the general welfare of the people. As such, the trumped-up accusations against the VPF of being an organisation 'whose methods inevitably become open to suspicion', constituted a deplorable denial of the right of every citizen to assist the police at all times of crisis.[112] In *The Times*, Statham in his capacity as secretary of the Grand Council summarily denied that the 'patriotic movement' had any intention of usurping and exercising the functions of the regular police.[113] In an attempt to dispel any misapprehension, both in and out of parliament, the Central Office issued a pamphlet titled 'Aims and Objects of the Volunteer Police Force'. The document pointed out that the force was an attempt to organise all law-abiding citizens for the purpose of assisting 'in the maintenance of Law and Order' in the event of strikes, riots or national emergencies. More precisely, the VPF would supplement the police when they were outnumbered and unable to contain lawlessness and disorder; guard railway stations, junctions and signal boxes; prevent arson and the looting of warehouses, shops and houses; prevent the disruption of public utilities, such as water, gas and electricity supplies; escort vans, carts and other vehicles transporting food and other essentials of life; defend women, children and vulnerable citizens from being harassed or unduly disturbed by rioters; ensure the health of livestock; prevent intimidation of and violence against non-unionist workers; and, finally, provide a Reserve Force in time of war.[114]

The new pamphlet – a copy was sent to all MPs – with its lofty aims and promises of high standards of conduct predictably failed to convince government authorities that the sponsors of the VPF were engaged in a lawful endeavour. Renaming it the Civilian Force was equally unhelpful in dispelling the impression that the organisation embraced elements that would inevitably lead to serious disorder and violence in the streets. Without resort to legal subtleties and refinements, Permanent Under-Secretary Sir Edward Troup considered it inadmissible 'for a Government which stands for law, order and impartiality, and not for punching the heads of strikers, to have anything to do with it'.[115] There was no doubt among Labour ranks that the Civilian Force had been devised as a strikebreaking agency for use in maintaining transport and public utilities whenever a strike was threatened or imminent. To the anarcho-syndicalist, Madame Sorgue, at the time touring the United Kingdom, Abercorn's organisation ominously resembled the squads of *lavoratori volontari* (voluntary workers) that landowners in the province of Parma had employed to crush the 1908 general agrarian strike. The 'most dangerous woman in Europe', as a State Prosecutor in Milan designated her, predicted that the force would cause workers 'grave trouble'.[116]

These fears were not unfounded. Members of the Civilian Force had contacted anti-labour organisations and employers in search of funds. For example, at the beginning of 1912, a deputation of the Civilian Force met with representatives of the Shipping Federation, perhaps the most militant employers' association in the United Kingdom, to offer them their strike-breaking services. The powerful association of shipowners agreed to donate £500 to the force and pledged to increase it to £1,000 or possibly more if it was able to deliver on its promises. At the annual General Meeting of the Shipping Federation in May of that year, the president of the Special Committee, Charles Harrison, justified the decision to rely on private security to protect freedom of labour as follows:

> Unless we can get some protection other than we can get at present, under the Trade Disputes Act, it will be necessary for ship owners and for other employers to constitute a force which will give their men protection when they are willing to work and not allowed to work by other influences. We shall have to take that step sooner or later, unless we can get the Trade Disputes Act repealed.[117]

Despite the Federation's donation, the Duke of Abercorn reassured McKenna that there was 'no idea of the Civilian Force as being a privately controlled or directed organization'.[118] In a new booklet, titled *The Civilian Force*, it was ambiguously stressed that the members or supporters of the force were 'in no way "strike breakers" as they do not take the part of any particular employer or Trade Union, but voluntarily assist in carrying on Transport and other services of vital importance to the distribution of necessities of life to the Community at large'. It also offered 'its protection to men who desire to work from being compelled by force or threats unwillingly to abandon their employment'. The members of the Civilian Force would be sworn in as special constables before going on duty in the streets or in public places to carry out these tasks. On private property, as permitted by the precedent of *R. v. Bishop of Bangor* (Shrewsbury Summer Assizes, 1796), there was no need for members of the Civilian Force to be sworn in as they would be acting lawfully 'on behalf of the Proprietor as his friends or servants for the purpose of protecting his property from forcible trespass'. After this preamble, the pamphlet set out the general aims and policies of the force and described in greater detail the system of administration, the functions of commanders and staff, and how all the branches of the Civilian Force were organised and potentially mobilised. For the purposes of immediate deployment in case of emergency, service members were organised into district companies of 120 men under the command of a captain appointed by headquarters. Each company included technical personnel to assist with railways, ships, tramways and other means of transport, and to operate power plants, gas works and other public utilities. The uniform of the Civilian Force was grey with fawn facings, and, in anticipation of violence, their equipment included a helmet, an armlet, a whistle, a numbered shoulder badge and a weapon of defence. Much along the lines of the old volunteer clubs, training in boxing, wrestling and *canne* fencing was expected to be provided.[119]

In anticipation of a resumption of industrial unrest, the Duke of Abercorn attempted to enlist in the Civilian Force officers of the Indian Services who were home on leave. The plan, which raised serious doubts at the India Office over its legality and wisdom, was quickly abandoned.[120]

Around this time, the threat of a combined mining and railway strike prompted the Civilian Force to issue a pamphlet in which 'the extremists in the Labour Party' were accused of hatching a revolutionary plan. It was, therefore, of paramount importance that 'every patriotic citizen should hasten to the assistance of the only body (the Civilian Force) that has been organised to assist the Forces of the Crown to cope with such an INSURRECTION IN THE LABOUR WORLD'.[121]

The first major test for the Civilian Force came during the 1912 London Dock Strike. Hundreds of its members were engaged by the shipowners for 'protective purposes'. At Greenhithe and Northfleet Dock, they violently clashed with pickets, with many injuries on both sides.[122] The General Manager of The Shipping Federation, Cuthbert Laws, confirmed to *The Times* that 'the Federation has assisted the authorities by the employment of members of the civilian force for the more immediate protection of the men on their way to the docks and while at work'.[123] Accusations of 'Pinkertonism' were immediately hurled at the Civilian Force. The *Daily Herald* wrote that the 'existence of this "wholly unauthorized horde" is a direct challenge to militant democracy'. Accordingly, the Left-oriented paper, which had become the platform for syndicalists and 'rebellious minds' warned that this 'slave guard' should be disbanded so that British employers would be discouraged from emulating their American counterparts and 'garrisoning their work with armed hooligans'.[124]

The progress of the Civilian Force suffered a severe setback with the death of the Duke of Abercorn in early 1913. William M. Power, who had been expelled from the force for alleged administrative malfeasance, set up

CLOTHED IN THE MAJESTY OF THE LAW; MEMBERS OF THE CIVILIAN POLICE, IN THEIR NEW UNIFORMS, ON DUTY DURING THE DOCK STRIKE.

The Civilian Police Force came into being after the great strike last autumn, when a scheme for the protection of London's food supply was drawn up by the War Office and Scotland Yard. The new force has proved its value during the recent trouble on Thames side. On May 28, for instance, on an urgent call, a fully equipped company of about 120 was sent down within a few hours, and successfully escorted 600 workers to the docks. Later some of the force assisted in loading an emigrant-steamer due to leave for Australia.

Figure 4.3 Members of the Civilian Force in uniform and armed with sticks. *Illustrated London News*, 8 June 1912. Image © Mary Evans Picture Library

Figure 4.4 The Civilian Police before deployment to the docks. *Daily Herald*, 31 May 1912. Image © The British Library Board. All Rights Reserved

a Volunteer Civil Force, precipitating a legal dispute over the new body's name. Thereafter, all the Civilian Force's activities and operations gradually wound down then ceased altogether. While the force faded from the public eye – surviving only in the imagination of the science fiction writer Twells Brex, who depicted the struggle between orderly volunteer citizens and their *bête noire*, socialism, in his novel *The Civil War of 1915* – the Shipping Federation intervened in the Dublin lockout.[125] Initially, when the most significant industrial dispute in Irish history began, the Federation resisted calls for assistance. This hesitation stemmed partly from the fact that a large number of its strikebreakers were engaged elsewhere and partly from the belief that Dublin employers lacked the resolve to prevail. However, the resolute opposition of William Martin Murphy – a former nationalist MP, chairman of the Dublin Tramways Company, and owner of the *Irish Independent* – to the Irish Transport and General Workers' Union (ITGWU) and its leader, Jim Larkin, along with the growing support of the TUC and its affiliated unions for Dublin workers, reversed the shipowners' stance.[126] By the end of the year, the Shipping Federation had deployed one thousand one hundred 'free labourers' to Dublin, transporting them on depot ships. The *Ella* was frequently used to ferry men and supplies from Merseyside, while the *Paris* served as their accommodation.[127] The importation of strikebreakers, the arming of loyal employees by employers and the violent repression of strikers by the Dublin Metropolitan Police and the Royal Irish Constabulary (RIC) led the ITGWU to establish the Irish Citizen Army. Meanwhile, the Shipping Federation's Emergency Committee, acting on a recommendation from its Clyde District Committee, resolved to contribute up to £5,000 – later increased to £10,000 – to support Dublin employers 'on the brink of collapse'. The reason adduced for this 'Fund' was:

> The committee is of opinion that if the Dublin employers were allowed to succumb to the forces arrayed against them, the method of co-operative financial support by the British Trade Unions of the system of Syndicalism, which at present obtains in Dublin, would become established as a permanent factor in industrial warfare, and furthermore, that the system would rapidly be extended to this country in a more aggravated form that which has hitherto obtained.[128]

Larkinism – and its doctrine of mass organisation in 'One Single Union' and sympathetic strikes – was ultimately defeated. However, these events sowed the seeds for the more militant and revolutionary Irish nationalism that would come to define the years that followed.[129]

In the rest of the United Kingdom, although trade union leaders disowned Larkin and succeeded in preventing widespread sympathetic action, the

Dublin dispute had a profound impact on workers' minds. Industrial action continued, prompting the emergence of other anti-Labour and anti-strike civilian groups, which positioned themselves once more as defenders of society against its perceived internal foes. On the eve of the Leeds Corporation strike (11 December 1913–13 January 1914) William W. MacPherson, former managing director of the Wellington Foundry branch of Fairbairn Lawson Combe Barbour Ltd., urged the formation of a local Citizens' League of Law and Order. Modelled on the Liverpool Service League, the new body would provide volunteers to take over public services and prevent their imminent paralysis. At the beginning of the strike, MacPherson announced that a 'body of independent citizens prepared to back up by practical action those who bear the burden of responsibility' had responded to its appeal. 'The object of this movement', he stated, 'is to give expression to a strong and widespread feeling which exists among all sections of the community, that a city of 450,000 inhabitants is not to be held up at the dictates of the leaders of a few trade unions'.[130] When the tramwaymen came out in sympathy with the corporation employees, offers of assistance in one way or another began to pour in, which led to the Citizens' League being established. It was also reported that a number of students from Leeds University had volunteered their services at the New Wortley and Meadow Lane gasworks and at the electric power station.[131] The conservative press lavishly praised the popular response and held it up as an example to be followed throughout the United Kingdom. *The Manchester Courier*, owned by Viscount Northcliffe, argued that: 'There are different types of strikes, and there are striking differences in the way of meeting them. It does not seem probable that Leeds will allow itself to be terrorized as in the case with Dublin'.[132] A London correspondent went so far as to say that it was recognised in official quarters that the citizens of Leeds 'have not merely saved their own town from the designs of the most Syndicalist of trade unions, but have performed a real service to the whole country'.[133]

After thirty-three days, the strike ended in defeat for the workers. Besides the obstinacy of the Emergency Committee of the Corporation, which was backed by important industrial interests, the intervention of university students as strikebreakers added another layer of bitterness to the dispute and its immediate aftermath. Student hostility to labour was not uncommon and certainly not unforeseen since universities were the exclusive domain of the upper and middle classes. More surprising was the indignant and unanimous condemnation of the trade union movement by the University of Leeds administrators.[134] The Pro-Chancellor (A. G. Lupton) and the Vice-Chancellor (M. E. Sandler) had received requests for assistance from council departments at the onset of the strike and communicated these to staff, students and other members of the university, 'a considerable number of whom, seniors and juniors, volunteered immediately'.[135] When a deputation from the Leeds Trade Council laid before the university's executive officers their objection to the use of student labour to fill union jobs, Sandler replied that the strike was not an ordinary dispute between employer and employees, but an attack on the 'health, safety, and well-being of the whole community'. There were some services that were essential to the community and needed to be maintained. The disruption of these services was tantamount to sabotage. Accordingly, Sandler argued, the university felt it was its duty to put the skills and knowledge of its members at the service of the Corporation in order 'to prevent the city from being ... held up'. In a subsequent press statement by university officers, they maintained that they 'took action in the belief that the failure of certain municipal services would have consequences disastrous to all classes of the community'.[136] Predictably, official university statements which unrepentantly denied any accusation of favouring 'students blacklegging' enraged Labour representatives and raised a certain dissent among university staff. *The Yorkshire Post* contemptuously railed against those who had disapproved of the university's actions: 'we are surprised, and somewhat disgusted, to find there are Professors in the University in receipt of public money from the ratepayers and from endowments provided by wealthy citizens, who think it wrong that certain students in the university should have come to the rescue of the City to whom they owe so much'.[137] The *Post* went on to urge the heads of the university to exercise adequate supervision over those of its employees who held revolutionary syndicalist views.

The opposition of Leeds citizens to the Corporation employees strike – which was viewed by conservative pundits as a potential forerunner of similar protests in Manchester and other northern cities if successful – spawned imitations. When fourteen thousand coal porters and carmen went on strike in London, medical students transported coal for hospitals, in part using cabs and private cars.[138] Vague talk of organising groups of citizens to prevent the interruption or suspension of essential services began or resumed throughout the country.[139] The situation appeared to substantiate American socialist John Spargo's belief that 'So long as there exists sufficient armed force to preserve the essentials of public order, the middle class in every country has sufficient skill and power to prevent the complete paralysis of society'. And nowhere, in his view, were there better chances for establishing bodies of citizen-strikebreakers than in the major industrial countries, such as Britain, Germany and the United States.[140]

When the war broke out, anti-labour vigilante pressure was immobilised, although only temporarily. The 'martial ardour of the zealot patriots', who appointed themselves as enforcers of social order and industrial efficiency, was rapidly redirected to providing assistance in essential or primary war services. The Russian Revolution of 1917 brought new fears and the dark foreboding of coming troubles to Britain. The postwar upsurge in industrial militancy and concerns over the Triple Alliance of dockers, railwaymen and miners prompted the government to draw up extensive plans for handling industrial emergencies.[141] At the beginning of 1919, faced with a bus and tube strike and a strike of electricity workers, the War Cabinet set up an Industrial Unrest Committee, which eventually became the Supply and Transport Committee. The committee also considered it necessary to form a 'Citizen Guard' to assist the police in 'meeting all contingencies' and to avoid the 'distasteful' use of troops in strikebreaking activities. The formation of this new body was prudently halted in favour of strengthening the special constabulary. In 1920, the Emergency Powers Act was rushed through Parliament, allowing the government, when faced with any action likely to 'deprive the community, or any substantial portion of the community, of the means of life by interfering with the supply and distribution of food, water, fuel, or light, or with the means of locomotion', to declare a 'state of emergency'. Meanwhile, a myriad of strikebreaking formations (e.g., the NCU, the British Empire Union etc.) emerged, echoing some of the organizational principles of the VPF and other anti-strike leagues of the prewar years.

By the early 1920s, the government had made it clear that all loyal, responsible and patriotic citizens would need to play their own part in averting 'national starvation and the ruin of industry'. The government of Stanley Baldwin reactivated the Supply and Transport organization, which had been largely inactive since 1921, and passed the 1923 Special Constables Act. One month after Red Friday (31 July 1925), the government's confidence in civilian volunteers was such that Joynson-Hicks, now Home Secretary, stated that the Fascists and Crusaders were trustworthy and could be relied upon in handling nationwide strikes. At the end of 1925, the Organisation for the Maintenance of Supplies (OMS) suddenly arose, uniting all anti-labour forces and placing itself at the government's disposal before vanishing as a separate entity at the outbreak of the 1926 General Strike.[142]

In conclusion, this chapter has explored how right-wing certitude that the Liberal government was unable or unwilling to enforce the law and protect the safety of the British public led to the formation of alliances, civic leagues and parapolice groups that endeavoured to assist the community at large by containing disorder and preventing the disruption of essential public services during major strikes. Particularly in the years immediately preceding the First World War, the appearance of these self-appointed vigilantes put considerable pressure on and even created some minor fissures in the State's monopoly of force. At the same time, it showed a certain propensity among conservative upper-middle and middle classes to respond to disruption and protect the social order by violent means. This mobilisation, according to some contemporary observers, arose from certain paranoid attitudes and prejudices that in due proportion later characterised the formative stages of fascism.[143]

Notes

1 'Notes from America', *Free Labour Press and Industrial Review*, 5 January 1907.
2 William Collison, 'Patriotism Has Killed Socialism'. Extract from the Report Accompanying the Twenty-second Annual Balance Sheet of the National Free Labour Association of Great Britain, for the Year Ending 31 Dec 1914, *The Square Deal* 16 (March 1915), pp. 165–167.
3 William Collison, *The Apostle of Free Labour: The Life Story of William Collison, Founder and General Secretary of the National Free Labour Association* (London: Hurst and Blackett, 1913), p. 84. On the National Free Labour Association, Geoffrey Alderman, 'The National Free Labour Association', *International Review of Social History* 21, no. 3 (1976), pp. 309–36; John Saville, 'Trade Unions and Free Labour: the Background to the Taff Vale Decision', in Asa Briggs and John Saville (eds), *Essays in Labour History: In Memory of G. D. H. Cole* (London: Palgrave Macmillan, 1967), pp. 317–350.
4 Collison, *The Apostle of Free Labour*, p. 328.
5 'Our Policy and Programme in Brief', *Free Labour Gazette*, 7 November 1894, p. 1.
6 Paul Mantoux and Maurice Alfassa, *La Crise du Trade-Unionisme* (Paris: Arthur Rousseau 1903), p. 224. For a case of veterans being sent to the Mond Chemical Works by Collison, see Annual Report, *Free Labour Press and Industrial Review*, October 1903, p. 24.
7 Allen Hutt, *British Trade Unionism: A Short History* (London: Lawrence & Wishart, 1962), p. 42.
8 Collison, *The Apostle of Free Labour*, p. 221.
9 '1903–1904', *The Free Labour Press and Industrial Review*, 2 January 1904, p. 5.
10 On strikebreaking and union-busting in the United States, Sidney Howard, *The Labor Spy* (New York: Republic Publishing Company, 1924); Leo Huberman, *The Labor Spy Racket* (New York: Modern Age Books, 1937); Anthony J. Lukas, *Big Trouble* (New York: Simon and Schuster, 1997); Robert M. Smith, *From Blackjacks to Briefcases: A History of Commercialized Strikebreaking and Unionbusting in the United States* (Athens, OH: Ohio University Press, 2003); Frank Morn, *'The Eye That Never Sleeps': A History of the Pinkerton National Detective Agency* (Bloomington, IN: Indiana University Press, 1982); Stephen H. Norwood, *Strikebreaking and Intimidation: Mercenaries and Masculinity in Twentieth-Century America* (Chapel Hill, NC: University of North Carolina Press, 2002).

11 Stanley W. Jevons, *The State in Relation to Labour* (London: Macmillan, 1882), p. 137.
12 Ibid., p. 135.
13 Ibid., p. 137.
14 See, for instance, the strikebreaking and anti-labour policies of the Shipping Federation. On the organization of shipowners, see Leslie H. Powell, *The Shipping Federation* (London: The Shipping Federation 1950). More recently, my article 'Strikebreaking and Anti-Unionism on the Waterfront: The Shipping Federation, 1890–1914', *European History Quarterly* 49, no. 4 (2019), pp. 570–596. See also the case of the FLPA. The organisation, under the direction of the great champion of libertarianism Lord Elcho, aimed 'to test systematically the efficiency, or otherwise, of existing laws for the protection of non-unionists, and, if necessary, to obtain an amendment of such laws'. Although the FLPA was not an out-and-out strikebreaking agency, it was said to have its own private police for the surveillance and counter-picketing of strikers. On the FLPA, TNA: RAIL 92/67/66.
15 *American Engineering Competition: Being a Series of Articles Resulting from an Investigation Made by 'The Times' London* (New York: Harper & Brothers Publishers, 1901); *Trade Unionism and British Industry*, a reprint of the 'The Times' articles on the 'Crisis in British Industry' with an introduction by Edwin A. Pratt (London: Murray, 1904).
16 Richard Heathcote Heindel, *The American Impact on Great Britain, 1898–1914: A Study of the United States in World History* (New York: Octagon Books, 1968; originally University of Pennsylvania, 1940), p. 203.
17 'The Open Shop', *Free Labour Press and Industrial Review*, 20 February 1904.
18 Quoted in Frank Tenney Stockton, *The Closed Shop in American Trade Unions* (PhD diss., Johns Hopkins University, 1910), p. 48. On the CIAA, see, generally, Selig Perlman and Philip Taft, *History of Labor in the United States, 1896–1932* (New York: Macmillan, 1935), Vol. IV, pp. 129–137; Jerome L. Toner, *The Closed Shop* (Washington, DC: Labor's Non-Partisan League, 1942), pp. 75–79 and 115–127. More recently, Chad Pearson, *Reform or Repression: Organizing America's Anti-Union Movement* (Philadelphia, PA: University of Pennsylvania Press, 2016).
19 'Free Labour Congress', *The Free Labour Press and Industrial Review*, 8 October 1904.
20 'Industrial Defense in the United States as Seen by a Traveling Correspondent of the Free Labour Association of Great Britain', *American Industries*, 1 November 1904. See also 'Congress Resolutions', *The Free Labour Press and Industrial Review*, 29 October 1904.
21 William Warrand Carlile, 'The Open Shop Movement in America', *The Times*, 24 December 1904.
22 'Farley, the Strike Breaker: The Man Who Always Wins', *Daily Mail*, 9 March 1905.
23 [From an American Correspondent], 'James Farley, Strikebreaker', *The Times*, 12 May 1905.

24 On British responses to the Russian Revolution of 1905–1907, see W. S. Adams, 'British Reactions to the 1905 Russian Revolution', *The Marxist Quarterly* 3 (1955), pp. 173–185; Charles E. Holt, *English Liberals and Russia 1895–1907* (PhD diss., University of Kentucky, 1976); William Harrison. 'The British Press and the Russian Revolution of 1905–1907', *Oxford Slavonic Papers* (New Series) 7 (1974), pp. 75–95.
25 Carlton Hayes, *British Social Politics: Materials Illustrating Contemporary State Action for the Solution of Social Problems* (Boston, MA: Ginn and Company, 1913), p. 15.
26 'Shall Trade Unions Be Placed above the Law?', *Daily Mail*, 5 April 1906.
27 'South Metropolitan Gas Company: Sir George Livesey on the Tar Market', *The Gas World*, 11 August 1906.
28 [No title], *London Evening Standard*, 26 April 1906.
29 'A Vital Question to All Free Citizens', *The Open Shop*, October 1906.
30 'National Free Labour Association', *The Times*, 15 November 1906; J. W. Emery's letter to W. Collison is reprinted in the *Free Labour Press and Industrial Review*, 17 November 1906.
31 The complete speech of Collison is reprinted under the title 'Good Work Being Done by Our Kin across the Sea', in *The Square Deal* 2, no. 6 (January 1907) (Convention Number), pp. 18–22.
32 Ibid., p. 20.
33 Ibid.
34 'Notes from America: The Truth about Chicago Stockyards', *Free Labour Press and Industrial Review*, 25 January 1907.
35 'Notes from America – Open Shop in the United States: The Cleveland Twist Drill Company', *Free Labour Press and Industrial Review*, 19 January 1907.
36 'Labor Conditions in England – Wm. Collison', *The Ohio Architect and Builder*, December 1906, pp. 19–23.
37 'Notes', *The Square Deal* 2, no. 6 (January 1907), p. 38.
38 'Notes from America – Roycrofters of East Aurora', *Free Labour Press and Industrial Review*, 2 February 1907.
39 'Notes from America – Gigantic Industries: The Westinghouse Electric and Manufacturing Company: A Visit to the East Pittsburgh Plant Philosophy of the "Open Shop"', *Free Labour Press and Industrial Review*, 12 January 1907.
40 'Notes from America – On the Path of Industrial Peace Free Labour Joins Hands with Free Citizenship', *Free Labour Press and Industrial Review*, 5 January 1907.
41 'Citizens' Industrial Association of the British Empire', *The Exponent*. Citizens' Industrial Association of St. Louis, January 1907, p. 22.
42 Collison, *The Apostle of Free Labour*, p. 311.
43 'Mr. Emery to the English'. Remarkable Address by the American Industrial Investigator Before the Free Labour Conference in Britain, *The Square Deal*, February 1911, pp. 29–31.
44 Alderman, 'The National Free Labour Association', pp. 318–319.

45 William Collison, 'England's Free Labour Followers Are Being Harassed on All Sides: Political Party in House of Commons Trying to Capture All Labour', *The Square Deal* 3 (May 1911), pp. 329–330
46 Quotation in Victor Griffuelhes, *L'Action Syndicaliste* (Paris: Librairie des sciences politiques and sociales, 1908), Bibliothèque du mouvement socialiste, no. 4, p. 33.
47 T. H. Penson, 'The Swedish General Strike', *Economic Journal* 19, no. 76 (December 1909), pp. 602–609.
48 'The Swedish "General" Strike', *The Times*, 1 September 1909.
49 T. C. Tobias, 'Newport Dock Dispute', *L. Q. Rev.* 26, no. 377 (1910).
50 On government neutrality and employers' reaction, see Barbara Fletcher, 'The Government Were Determined to Make the Men as Strong as the Masters: The Experience of the Shipping Federation, 1906 to 1910', *Maritime Policy and Management* 11, no. 4 (1984), pp. 261–268.
51 Hansard, HC Deb Vol. 22, Cols. 1862–1863 (Strikes and Lock-outs ('Private Police')), 13 March 1911.
52 'Trade Union Tyranny: League for the Protection of Free Labour', *Nottingham Evening Post*, 4 March 1911.
53 'Strikes', *Board of Trade Labour Gazette*, August 1911, reprinted in *The Fortnightly Review*, no. DXLII, New Series, 1 February 1912.
54 Ibid.
55 'The Strikes', *The Times*, 8 August 1911.
56 General Manager of H. L. Raphaels's Refinery to the Home Office, 11 August 1911, in TNA: HO 144/5491/212342/28.
57 'Troops Clear Liverpool Streets with Bayonets', *Daily Mirror*, 16 August 1911.
58 TNA: HO 45/1065A/212470/68. Letter from W. Davil (?) to Churchill, 16 August 1911.
59 'Protecting the Food Supply', *Evening News*, 17 August 1911.
60 'Railway Volunteers', *Daily Telegraph & Courier*, 19 August 1911.
61 On policing the 'Great Unrest', see Clive Emsley, *The English Police: A Political and Social History* (London: Harvester Wheatsheaf, 1991); Roger Geary, *Policing Industrial Disputes: 1893–1985* (Cambridge: Cambridge University Press, 1985); Jane Morgan, *Conflict and Order: The Police and Labour Disputes in England and Wales, 1900–1939* (Oxford: Oxford University Press, 1987); Barbara Weinberger, *Keeping the Peace? Policing Strikes in Britain, 1906–1926* (Oxford: Berg, 1991).
62 Tony Bunyan, *The History and Practice of the Political. Police in Britain* (London: Quartet Books, 1977), p. 98.
63 For a comprehensive history of the special constabulary and its public perception, see Claire Katherine Leon, *Special Constables: An Historical and Contemporary Survey* (Ph.D. diss., University of Bath, Bath, 1973).
64 TNA: HO 45 10659/212856.
65 Report of H.M. Inspector of Constabulary on the County and Borough Police Forces for the Year ended 29th September 1911, made to His Majesty's

Principal Secretary of State, under Section 15 of the County and Borough Police Act, 1856, p. 22.
66 'The London Special Constables', *Evening Mail*, 21 August 1911.
67 'Civic Patriotism', *Sheffield Daily Telegraph*, 21 August 1911.
68 'Special Constables in Fight Corner', *Sheffield Daily Telegraph*, 25 August 1911.
69 Hansard, HC Deb Vol. 163, Cols. 1973–2010 (7 May 1923).
70 'N.E.R Men Involved', *Hartlepool Northern Daily Mail*, 18 August 1911.
71 'Amateur Mail Porters', *Daily Mirror*, 21 August 1911.
72 'Lessons of the Strike', *Pall Mall Gazette*, 21 August 1911.
73 Sir Arthur Clay, *Syndicalism and Labour: Notes Upon Some Aspects of Social and Industrial Questions of the Day* (New York: E. P. Dutton & Company, 1911), p. 211.
74 Ibid., p. 220.
75 L. M. Musgrove, 'Yeomanry Old Comrades' Association', *The Times*, 19 August 1911.
76 'General Strikes and General Strike-Breakers', *The Times*, 26 August 1911.
77 Montagu of Beaulieu, 'Road Transport During Strikes', *The Times*, 23 August 1911.
78 Letter reprinted in 'Our Food Supply: Voluntary Motor Service', *Brecon County Times*, 8 September 1911. The 1909 experiment of transporting a battalion by private cars is also mentioned in Ernest Llewellyn Woodward, *Great Britain and the German Navy* (London: Clarendon Press, 1935).
79 'Road Transport during Strikes', *The Times*, 25 August 1911.
80 'Motoring Notes', *The Graphic*, 2 September 1911.
81 'Picketing and Counter-Picketing', *The Spectator*, 11 November 1911.
82 W. T. Stead, 'What We Have Learned from the Railway Strike: Hints from the Hague for the Regulation of Industrial War', *The Review of Reviews* 44 (September 1911), pp. 249–255.
83 Ibid., p. 255.
84 'Letters to the Editor', *The Nation*, 9 September 1911.
85 Home Office Circular 214312 of the 15th of September 1911.
86 The Liverpool Athenaeum Archives, CSL, Minute Book Vol. 1 (29 August 1911–19 September 1913).
87 'Civic Service Corps', *Liverpool Evening Express*, 22 August 1911.
88 'Permanent Civic Service', *Liverpool Daily Post*, 30 August 1911.
89 'For Emergencies in Liverpool: League of Civic Service', *Liverpool Daily Post*, 30 August 1911.
90 'Liverpool's Civic Service League: Lord Derby on the Duties of Mayor', *Yorkshire Post and Leeds Intelligencer*, 23 February 1912.
91 'Liverpool Civic Service League', *Liverpool Daily Post*, 15 September 1911; 'Day to Day', *Liverpool Daily Post*, 16 September 1911; *The Charity Organisation Review* 30 (1911), pp. 341–342.
92 The Liverpool Athenaeum Archives, CSL, CSL 4 [1911]-1920.
93 'The Metropolitan Boroughs', *Shoreditch Observer*, 11 November 1911; 'West London Press', *Chelsea News and General Advertiser*, 19 January 1912.

94 Hansard, HC Deb Vol. 29, Cols. 2282–2378 (22 August 1911).
95 For biographical information on William Mailes Power, see TNA: WO 339/93876. Also, see his profile in *The Business World: Men & Methods of the New Georgian Era: Imperial Interests, Pen Sketches and Illustrations* (London, 1913), pp. 130–131.
96 'A Volunteer Police Force', *The Standard*, 8 September 1911.
97 Letter from W. M. Power to Home Secretary Winston Churchill, 16 September 1911, in TNA: HO 45.10666.216733, Volunteer Police Force, 1911–1914.
98 Letter from (Sd) E. Blackwell to W. M. Power, 2 October 1911, in Ibid.
99 The proceedings of the inaugural meeting were printed and circulated in a booklet titled 'The Volunteer Police Force'. Copy of the booklet is in TNA: HO 45.10666.216733.
100 Ibid.
101 Ibid.
102 Cicely V. Wedgwood, *The Last of the Radicals: Josiah Wedgwood, M.P.* (London: Cape, 1951), pp. 88–91.
103 Josiah Wedgwood, 'The Honorary Strikebreakers', *The Eyewitness*, 21 December 1911, pp. 16–17.
104 [By a Trade Unionist], 'The Labour Movement', *Christchurch Times*, 2 December 1911.
105 'Unrest Among Railway Employees', *The Railway Times*, 18 November 1911.
106 'Volunteer Police and a Railway Strike: Directions to Commanding Officers', *The Times*, 13 November 1911.
107 'A British "Pinkertons" Organization', *Justice*, 18 November 1911.
108 'The Railway Situation: Men in Militant Mood', *The Manchester Guardian*, 4 December 1911.
109 [No title], *Leeds Mercury*, 21 December 1911.
110 'Bradford Weekly Telegraph', *Bradford Weekly Telegraph*, 5 January 1912.
111 Hansard, HC Deb Vol. 32, Cols. 1009–1010 (4 December 1911).
112 'The Volunteer Police Force', *Morning Post*, 2 December 1911.
113 'The Volunteer Police Force: A Reply to Criticism', *The Times*, 6 December 1911.
114 A copy of 'Aims and Objects of the Volunteer Police Force' in TNA: HO 45.10666.216733, Volunteer Police Force, 1911–1914.
115 Letter from Edward Troup to Russell Scott, 12 March 1912, in Ibid.
116 'London Letter', *Irish News and Belfast Morning News*, 29 December 1911.
117 Modern Record Centre, Shipping Federation, General and Executive Council Meetings, Proceedings at General and Executive Council Meetings. Bound volume. May 1912–November 1914, Annual General Meeting, 17 May 1912, p. 8.
118 Letter of the Duke of Abercorn to the Home Secretary, 8 March 1912, in TNA: HO 45.10666.216733, Volunteer Police Force, 1911–1914.
119 The Civilian Force. Founded on Trafalgar Day as the 'Volunteer Police Force', 7–8. A surviving copy of the booklet is in TNA: HO 45.10666.216733, Volunteer Police Force, 1911–1914.

120 TNA: HO 45.10666.216733/12, Volunteer Police Force, 1911–1914. For the proposal of the Duke of Abercorn to raise an 'Indian Service Company' in connection with the Civilian Force, see also 'The Civilian Police: An Appeal to Indian Officers', *The Times*, 7 March 1912.
121 'Civilian Force: The Danger of a National Strike', in TNA: HO 45.10666.216733/15.
122 Modern Record Centre, Shipping Federation, Policy and Administration, Grey Books, Transactions of the Federation, 1911–1914, Report of the General Purposes Committee to the Executive Council, 29 November 1912.
123 'The Civilian Force', *The Times*, 6 June 1912.
124 'The New Slave Guards', *Daily Herald*, 28 August 1912.
125 On the 1913 Dublin lockout, see Francis Devine (ed.), *A Capital in Conflict: Dublin City and the 1913 Lockout* (Dublin: Dublin City Council, 2013); 'Lockout 1913: Special Issue', *History Ireland* 21 (2013); Emmet O'Connor, *A Labour History of Ireland, 1824–2000* (Dublin: University College Dublin Press, 2011), pp. 92–95; Donal Nevin (ed.), *James Larkin: Lion of the Fold* (Dublin: Gill and Macmillan, 1998); Padraig Yeates, *Lockout: Dublin 1913* (Dublin: Gill and Macmillan, 2000), and 'The Dublin 1913 Lockout', *History Ireland* 9, no. 2 (Summer 2001), pp. 31–36.
126 On the TUC and the Dublin Lockout, Ralph Darlington, 'British Labour Movement Solidarity in the 1913–14 Dublin Lockout', *Labor History* 57, no. 4 (2016), pp. 504–525.
127 Modern Record Centre, Shipping Federation, Central Labour Office, Annual Report, 23 April 1914.
128 Ibid., Report of the General Purposes Committee to the Executive Council, 14 November 1913, report 303, p. 146.
129 See, for example, Niall Whelehan, 'The Irish Revolution, 1912–23', in Alvin Jackson (ed.), *The Oxford Handbook of Modern Irish History* (Oxford: Oxford University Press, 2014), pp. 504–525.
130 'The Right to Work: Proposed League of Law and Order', *Yorkshire Evening Post*, 12 December 1913.
131 'What Is Being Done at Gasworks', *Yorkshire Evening Post*, 18 December 1913.
132 'The Strike Mania', *Manchester Courier and Lancashire General Advertiser*, 16 December 1913.
133 Quoted in J. E. Williams, 'The Leeds Corporation Strike of 1913', in Asa Briggs and John Saville (eds), *Essays in Labour History*, 1886–1926 (London: Macmillan, 1971), p. 73.
134 Arthur Greenwood, 'The Leeds Municipal Strike', *Economic Journal* 24 (March 1914), pp. 138–145.
135 M. E. Sadler, 'Note on Mr. Greenwood's Article on the Leeds Municipal Strike', *Economic Journal* 24 (March 1914), pp. 146–152.
136 'Shook for Leeds Citizens', *Daily Citizen*, 30 December 1913.
137 'A Rush to Work', *Yorkshire Post and Leeds Intelligencer*, 27 December 1913.
138 'The Coal Strike', *Framlingham Weekly News*, 31 January 1914.

139 'The Lesson of Leeds', *Kilkenny Moderator*, 20 December 1913.
140 John Spargo, *Syndicalism, Industrial Unionism and Socialism* (New York: Huebsch, 1913), pp. 124–129.
141 Ralph H. Desmarais, *The Supply and Transport Committee, 1919–1926: A Study of the British Government's Method of Handling Emergencies Stemming from Industrial Disputes* (Madison, WI: University of Wisconsin, 1970); Keith Jeffery and Peter Hennessy, *States of Emergency: British Governments and Strike Breaking since 1919* (London: Routledge & Kegan Paul, 1983).
142 R. C. Maguire, 'The Fascists … Are … to Be Depended Upon: The British Government, Fascists and Strike-Breaking during 1925 and 1926', in Nigel Copsey and Dave Renton (eds), *British Fascism, the Labour Movement and the State* (Basingstoke: Palgrave Macmillan, 2005), p. 8.
143 For a definition of the VPF as a precursor of fascism, Wedgwood, *The Last of the Radicals*, p. 89.

5

The arming of Ulster: the Home Rule crisis and the British League for the Support of Ulster and the Union

> What is the wage the faithful earn?
> What is a recompense fair and meet?
> Trample their fealty under your feet.
> That is a fitting and just return. (William Watson, *Ulster's Reward*, 1912)

Amid the Home Rule crisis (1912–1914), the most radical advocates of Union openly embraced the language of rebellion and 'anarchy'.[1] Thousands of Ulstermen took part in military drills in broad daylight, while arms were procured openly and in an often buccaneering spirit. They provocatively supported the Kaiser and took a defiant stance against the forces of the Crown, seducing army commanders away from their sworn allegiance. Distinguished dignitaries of the Protestant Church in Ulster publicly bestowed their solemn blessing upon seditious political rites. Astonishingly, the dissidents faced no legal repercussions, and equally perplexingly they assumed the guise of paragons of lawfulness by presenting themselves as guardians of the Constitution and Empire. Importantly, this mobilisation extended beyond the geographical confines of Ulster. Explicit support from Conservative leader Bonar Law and his party gave firm reassurance to Ulsterites that they would not stand alone in their resistance to the law. Furthermore, popular conservative opposition to granting Ireland self-government manifested in the form of leagues and covenants.[2] This chapter traces the right wing's flirtation with paramilitary violence through the activities of the UVF and the BLSUU.[3] To do so, it first explores the formation, structuring and consolidation of the UVF and its relationship with Tory extremism.[4] Secondly, it reconstructs the history of the BLSUU, showing how it channelled the British Right's propensity to stir up sectarian tensions and reignite latent reservoirs of violence that could be mobilised for political purposes. The analysis presented in this chapter also has the aim of elucidating the specific operational connection between the UVF and the BLSUU, with the latter undertaking the recruitment of military expertise, weapon procurement and the acquisition of financial resources for their brethren in Northern Ireland.

The Home Rule crisis and the formation of the Ulster Volunteer Force

The composition of the second parliament under King George V, elected in December 1910, was very similar to its lately dissolved predecessor. With Conservatives and Unionists holding 272 seats, Liberals 271, Irish Nationalists 84 and Labour 42, the result was a hung parliament. In this precarious state of affairs, the Irish Nationalists held the balance of power, and this, coupled with the impending Parliament Act of 10 August 1911, paved the way for the enactment of a law granting Ireland a measure of home rule. In the King's Speech in February 1912 the government announced its intention to amend Gladstone's 'Government of Ireland Bill 1886'. On 11 April, just three days before the Titanic sank on its maiden voyage, Prime Minister Asquith fulfilled his political obligations to Irish Nationalist leader John Edward Redmond by introducing 'A Bill to Amend the Provision for the Government of Ireland'. This Bill outlined the establishment of an Irish Parliament, which included a Senate of forty members appointed by the Imperial Executive, and a House of Commons consisting of 164 members elected by the existing Irish constituencies. The Irish Parliament would operate under triple control: the Lord Lieutenant's veto, the right of appeal to the Privy Council on matters of law validity and the overriding authority of Imperial legislation. Provisions were also made to protect religious equality. The Irish Parliament would be responsible for funding most Irish services. Financial arrangements were put in place to set up the new government, including an annual gift of £500,000 from the Imperial Exchequer, later reduced to £200,000. Although Irish revenue fell short of expenditure by about £1,500,000, plans were included to readjust the financial arrangements once Ireland achieved self-sufficiency. Lastly, the Bill provided for a reduction in Irish representation in the Imperial Parliament from 103 to 42 members.[5]

Despite proposing only moderate legislative devolution, the Bill profoundly polarised public opinion and saw the conservative Right skilfully wielding the language of violence and threat. Evidently, Lord Randolph Churchill's cry of 'Ulster will fight, and Ulster will be right', uttered a generation before, were still echoing loudly among the defenders of the Empire. With startling regularity, Unionist extremists conjured up vivid and unnerving scenarios of civil war, grave disorder and bloodshed in their efforts to exorcise the spectre of Home Rule. In January 1912, the future High Lord Chancellor of Britain, Frederick Edwin Smith, who was then serving as MP for Liverpool Walton, declared that 'Ulster, in refusing to submit to Nationalist domination under a trick, would be right in resisting', and added that 'there was no length to which Ulster would not be entitled to go, however desperate or unconditional, in carrying the quarrel if the quarrel was wickedly fixed upon them'.[6] At Baldock, in February, Lord Cecil candidly stated that 'if he lived in Belfast he would seriously consider whether rebellion was not better than Home Rule'.[7] Meanwhile, Ulster Unionist leader Lord Carson continued to commend physical force and gave promises of marches from Belfast to Cork. In Belfast, he reminded his audience that 'We are not out for a holiday-making. We are here to meet a revolution in the only way a revolution can be met by realizing our responsibilities and not caring about the consequences determined that we shall defeat it'. Later he would 'solemnly' reject the authority of parliament, adding that he '[did] not care twopence whether it [was] treason or not'.[8]

After the Bill had passed its second reading on 9 May by a vote of 372 to 271, and had reached the committee stage in mid-June, Bonar Law joined in with the incendiary and reckless language and even contended that the government was in danger of mob lynching. At Blenheim Palace, as one historian eloquently wrote, his admonition reverberated in language unheard since the era of the Long Parliament:

> We regard the Government as a revolutionary committee which has seized by fraud upon despotic power. In our opposition to them we shall not be guided by the consideration, we shall not be restrained by the bonds which would influence us in an ordinary political struggle. We shall use any means – whatever means seem to us likely to be the most effective. This is all we shall think about. We shall use any means to deprive them of the power which they have usurped, and to compel them to face the people they have deceived.[9]

As for the Ulster resistance, he stated 'I can imagine no length of resistance to which Ulster will go which I shall not be ready to support, and in which they will not be supported by the overwhelming majority of the British people'. This outbreak of hysteria, or 'Ulsteria', as certain contemporaries punningly called it, was given lyrical treatment by Rudyard Kipling in a poem published in the *Morning Post*, part of which reads:

> The dark eleventh hour
> Draws on and sees us sold
> To every evil power
> We fought against of old
> Rebellion, rapine, hate,
> Oppression, wrong and greed
> Are loosed to rule our fate,
> By England's act and deed.[10]

Alarmed by the aggressive tenor of the Conservative discourse, Churchill started to wonder whether the Unionist leadership had any policy for Ireland apart from rendering it ungovernable.[11] Undoubtedly, the Ulster question had reached paroxysmal levels, with the 'imperishable memories of the Battle of the Boyne' acquiring renewed vividness. On 14 September, a football match held at the Celtic Park stadium in Belfast between Belfast Celtic (Roman Catholic) and Linfield (Protestant) culminated in a riot, leaving more than one hundred injured. The confrontation seems to have been initiated by the Orangemen. Over several tense days, a series of demonstrations unfolded across Ulster, specifically in Enniskillen, Derry, Ballymena, Coleraine, Dromore, Portadown, Crumlin, Ballyroney and Belfast, reaching its peak on Ulster Day (28 September). Large crowds rapturously invoked the sacrosanct right to resist a 'despicable sovereignty'. The divine Being was frequently called upon. The cry 'we will not have Home Rule' resounded mightily and unchallenged. In Derry, Carson announced, 'Don't imagine we are out for fun. We are almost driven to despair by the Government. They wage war upon us. Well, they will face the consequences just as we will'.[12] This 'gospel of irresponsibility' failed to deter prominent Unionist leaders from proffering messages of support and even taking part in one or more of these demonstrations. In Derry, F. E. Smith made a solemn pledge to support British unionism: 'I say, under God we are with you in the fight that lies in front of you'.[13] In Dromore, Lord Willoughby de Broke reaffirmed that promise, belligerently declaring that the Unionists of England were going to help the Ulstermen 'not just through speeches'. Peaceful methods would be tried first, 'but if the last resource were forced upon them by the Radical Government in their desire to keep place and power, they would find they not only got the Orangemen against them, but every white man in the British Empire would be giving not only their moral, but [...] their active support to one of the most loyal populations that ever lived under the Union Jack'.[14]

In each of the places he visited, 'General Carson', as he was mockingly referred to by his critics, was escorted by mounted guards brandishing dummy wooden rifles and occasionally dressed in khaki uniforms. In Portadown, the entourage somewhat bizarrely included two dummy cannons and a replica ambulance along with hospital nurses. In Coleraine, Carson was presented with a blackthorn stick decorated with orange and purple ribbons.[15] A few days later, at Ulster Hall in Belfast he had the honour of being conferred with the yellow banner under which 'the great apostle of civil and religious liberty', King William, had marched to victory at the Boyne.[16]

The quasi-royal honours accorded to the 'General' led a correspondent for the *Daily Mail* to pointedly suggest that 'it might be well to omit from the receptions of their leader [Carson] some of the ceremonial which

Figure 5.1 1. Parade in honour of Carson in Portadown. Men with a dummy cannon, dummy rifles and uniform caps. 2. Carson, Smith, Lord Londonderry and J. B. Lonsdale at the saluting post. *The Sketch*, 2 October 1912. Image © Mary Evans Picture Library

is usually reserved for the Sovereign'. First Viscount Rothermere's emissary added 'Apart from this lapse, which, after all, is intended to be nothing more than an expression of loyalty to the Crown, the military character of these gatherings is natural and symbolical'.[17] The 'lapse' was repeated in Ballyroney and then became a habit.

While it is debatable whether Carson merited the title of 'General', he was undoubtedly gaining a reputation as one of the finest showmen on earth. On 25 September 1911, resolutions were passed at the Conference of Unionist Clubs and Orange Lodges in Belfast aimed at making preliminary arrangements for a Provisional Government for Ulster. Three days later, on Ulster Day, scores of people pledged their unwavering opposition to Home Rule by signing a solemn Covenant. The whole affair took on the highly choreographed appearance of a ritual. In a melodramatic display of fanaticism, one individual demanded to sign the document using a pen dipped in his own blood.[18] Anyone hesitating to take the pledge ran the risk of being seen as the heir of Robert Lundy. The text, which was made public a few days beforehand, ran thus:

> Hereby pledge ourselves in Solemn Covenant in this our time of threatened calamity to stand by one another in defending, for ourselves and our children, our cherished position of equal citizenship in the United Kingdom, and in using all means which may be found necessary to defeat the present conspiracy to set up a Home Rule Parliament in Ireland; and, in the event of such a Parliament being forced upon us, we further solemnly and mutually pledge ourselves to refuse to recognise its authority. In sure confidence that God will defend the right, we hereto subscribe our names, and, further, we individually declare that we have not already signed this Covenant.

In a spirit of general mobilisation, a women's Covenant, identical to the men's, was also drafted and signed *en masse*. The Covenant was reported to have been endorsed by 218,206 men and 228,991 women in Ulster. In the rest of Ireland and Great Britain, 19,162 men and 5,055 women signed, bringing the total number of endorsements to an impressive 471,414.[19]

Ulster Day was celebrated with particular religious fervour and solemnity. As on holy days, hundreds of special services were held, in which the sermons predictably incorporated passages such as Isaiah 26:1–9, Ephesians 6:10–18 or Psalm 46. Reverend William McKean, preaching at a special service in Ulster Hall, roared that 'They were standing that day in the face of a great religious and political issue which might involve the destruction of their liberties, and even the peace of their country'. The Protestant Bishop of Down, Connor and Dromore, Charles D'Arcy, at a service in Belfast Cathedral asserted that the Covenant rested upon 'the principle that when life and liberty are threatened, men are bound to risk all [...] true men, must be prepared to hold together in defence of their altars and their hearths, and to face all dangers'. After a military parade of Unionists, the Protestant Bishop of Derry and Raphoe, George Alexander Chadwick, speaking at Glendermot Parish Church gave Christian legitimisation to violence. Recalling the teachings of Aurelius Augustine and Thomas Aquinas on the doctrine of the *bellum iustum*, he said: 'There were causes which no Christian was at liberty to fail to defend, even to the uttermost. To be tame, to be submissive always, when great things were at stake – that was not the Christian temper'.[20]

The Ulster Covenant made a profound impression in Great Britain and the South of Ireland. It was widely signed in London, Liverpool and various English towns, and in Edinburgh the ceremony took place on the same gravestone in Greyfriars Churchyard on which the National Covenant had been signed in 1638. As Sir Edward Carson set sail from Belfast on the ferry ship 'Patriotic', seen off by seventy thousand well-wishers and later met with an equally enthusiastic reception in Liverpool, the Unionist press hastily speculated on the demise of Home Rule. While the Nationalists maintained a prudent silence, the Liberals derided the pageantry.

The commitment to protect their 'cherished position of equal citizenship' in the United Kingdom, employing any means necessary to thwart the conspiracy, was not made lightly. Ulster Unionists had been drilling and arming themselves even before the huge gathering at James Craig's house, Craigavon, in September 1911, where the martial efficiency exhibited by a contingent of Orangemen from the counties of Tyrone and Armagh drew praise and was subsequently emulated around the country. These men were said to have 'learned drill in the Yeomanry, Militia, or Boys' Brigades'.[21] Prior to this event, in the latter part of 1910, the Ulster Unionist Council (UUC) openly expressed its inclination to resort to armed resistance. Although they had small stores of old rifles dating from 1886 and 1893, these were far from sufficient. A 'secret' defence committee therefore established connections with arms dealers in Britain and on the continent to bolster their stocks.[22] In this they were facilitated by the lapse of the Peace Preservation Act of 1881 in 1906, which meant there was no longer a statutory authority to restrict the importation and sale of arms and ammunition in Ireland. The Gun Licence Act of 1870 remained in effect, granting authorities the power to impose licence duty on individuals carrying firearms, yet no serious efforts were made to enforce it. Meanwhile, two statutes – the Customs Laws Consolidation Act of 1876 (39 & 40) and the Customs and Inland Revenue Act of 1879 (42 & 43 Vict. Ch. 21) – which could have effectively halted the distribution of arms, remained in force as provisions for emergencies, but the government prudently downplayed the urgency of the situation.²³ Consequently, throughout 1911 several thousand pieces of weaponry were procured and transported to Belfast. In September 1911, ten cases labelled 'Spelter' and containing two hundred rifles and bayonets were brought ashore in Leith from Hamburg, intended for delivery to Belfast. However, the Customs authorities confiscated the cases citing misdescription and imposed a fine of £10, which the consignee paid. After months of being shifted from depot to depot, the cases were finally sent back to Hamburg. In the meantime, scores of 1887 pattern Vetterli-Vitali rifles (.41 calibre), previously discarded by the Italian army, made their way to Ulster, where they were used by drill instructors in Unionist clubs.²⁴

At the dawn of 1912, passions were running deep in Ulster's political landscape. When the First Lord of the Admiralty, Winston Churchill, attempted to address a meeting at Ulster Hall, he encountered angry resistance. Around the same time, Unionists had meticulously examined the laws on public order, breaches of the peace, and unlawful assembly in order to clarify the problematic issue of whether drilling and training in military exercises were legal. As was to be expected, they discovered a loophole. A statute of 1819 (the Unlawful Drilling Act) 60 Geo. III. 1 Geo. IV. C. I, which applied to Ireland, prohibited drilling as a danger to His Majesty's subjects and the government. However, this statute could easily be evaded with reference to Section I, which allowed meetings for training and drilling to be held with the approval of any two Justices of the Peace – and in Ulster there were plenty of JPs who trusted that drilling was directed at inculcating in men that subconscious obedience that was essential to defending the Constitution of the United Kingdom.²⁵

As a result, Orange Lodges, Unionist clubs, Protestant youth military organisations and those unaffiliated associations that were committed to popularising the ideals of 'efficient citizenship', started organising basic drills for volunteers in halls, rooms or the open fields – at first discreetly, then more openly and more boldly.²⁶ By the spring of 1912, the police, who were closely monitoring this grassroots phenomenon, acknowledged that drilling was widespread and involved thousands of men.²⁷ Numerous clubs received drill instruction from ex-soldiers. The drill was typically basic and only occasionally involved the use of dummy rifles. Marksmanship, instead, was practised without any restriction, at least until 1913, under the guise of miniature rifle clubs.²⁸

The impact of military training was unmistakable at the Balmoral Show Grounds on 9 April, Easter Tuesday, as club contingents marched through the streets of Belfast to the gathering place. Approximately three hundred thousand people attended the demonstration, during which Bonar Law pledged the Unionist Party's staunch support to Ulster. He then eloquently proclaimed that once the crisis had passed, Ulster would be hailed with Pitt's

228 *The lure of violence*

Figure 5.2 Sir Edward Carson and E. T. Smith inspecting Ulster volunteers *Illustrated London News*, 14 March 1914. Image © Mary Evans Picture Library

famous words: 'You have saved yourselves by your exertions, and you will save the Empire by your example'.[29]

At the end of 1912, pursuing what it called the 'forward policy', the Ulster Unionist Council's Executive Committee took the decision to form a unified organisation out of this 'paramilitary craze'. In January 1913, the UVF

Table 5.1 Number of drill practices held by Unionist clubs and the number of people taking part in drills between November 1912 and December 1913

Month		Number of drill practices held	Drill participants
	1912		
November		219	4,062
December		216	3,349
	1913		
January		209	5,341
February		289	5,062
March		300	5,305
April		326	5,016
May		402	7,811
June		442	8,603
July		396	11,152
August		456	10,470
September		757	15,262
October		1,038	25,302
November		1,412	23,497
December		1,742	29,979

Source: Intelligence Notes, 20

was officially established and elaborate military arrangements were made. In its early stages, the UVF replicated the organisational framework of the Volunteer Force. Each county was divided into companies, sub-divisions or sections. According to RIC reports, the organisation's progress was spearheaded by the country gentry, a significant number of whom were retired military officers. The amalgamation of the existing 297 Unionist clubs and then the Orange Lodges into a 'new army' met with resistance in some places, but on the whole it progressed in a sufficiently orderly way. Drill practices showed varying trends throughout the year, with notable surges in February, May and September, interspersed with temporary setbacks in the periods of spring sowing and summer harvesting. Similarly, drill participants displayed varying levels of engagement, with notable increases in attendance in January, May and September, and minor declines in February and November. The search for rifles became frantic. In August 1913, the police lamented 'an abnormal business in the sale of arms that was carried out in Belfast'.[30] In the autumn, they noted that 'Rifles, mostly of an old Italian pattern, were used for instructional purposes at outdoor parades, but many modern rifles of English make are believed to be in the possession of individuals'.[31] Small shipments of Martini-Enfield rifles, imported from Birmingham and 'processed' by Belfast firearms dealers, were distributed among the force's ranks.[32] At the end of 1913, the police estimated that the UVF had amassed the numbers of arms per county given in Table 5.2.

On 4 December, a Royal Proclamation finally enforced the restrictions outlined in section 43 of the Customs Consolidation Act, 1876, and section 8 of the Customs and Inland Revenue Act, 1879, which specifically forbade the importation of arms and ammunition into Ireland, and the coastal transport of military arms and ammunition. Despite the Proclamation, the influx of arms showed no signs of abating, and in light of the conspicuous display of firearms at public meetings, the unrepealed Statute of Northampton (3 Edw. 3, c. 3) was evoked. The Statute, which had languished in obscurity during the eighteenth and nineteenth centuries, reappeared in a prosecution in the early twentieth century: in the case of *R. v. Meade* (1903) the accused was charged with discharging a firearm in a public street. The judge informed the jury that 'the offence [was] charged ... [not only] under the Statute of Edward III, but also under Common Law', and that the defendant was liable to punishment for 'firing a revolver in a public place, with the result that the public were frightened or terrorized'. Consequently, during the Ulster Winter Assizes, indictments were served and trials were conducted under a centuries-old statute.[33] Nevertheless, legal sanctions turned out to be no deterrent. In August, the police reported that Ulster shopkeepers had had to replenish their revolver stocks as a result of the prosecution of certain Unionists in the Newry district for unlawful assembly.[34]

With the tumultuous growth of the force – by the end of April forty-one thousand individuals had joined – came a pressing the need for formal procedures and internal bureaucratisation. In September 1913, a General Staff (or Advisory Board) was appointed, with their headquarters at the Old Town Hall in Belfast. Lieutenant General Sir George Richardson, who

Table 5.2 Quantity of arms believed to be in the possession of the Ulster Volunteer Force by December 1913 according to police reports

County	Total arms
Antrim	4,490
Armagh	1,799
Belfast	3,781
Cavan	1,681
Donegal	50
Down	2,330
Fermanagh	98
Londonderry	466
Monaghan	395
Tyrone	1,951

Source: *Intelligence Notes*, 33

had previously served in the Indian Army, assumed the role of General Officer Commanding (GOC) of the force. Among the English Army officers selected by Richardson to assist him in reorganising the force were Colonel Couchman, Captain J. D. Scriven, Colonel J. H. Patterson, Major Tempest Stone and Captain W. A. Malone.[35] While the Commander-in-Chief was allowed a large measure of latitude and discretion over matters of discipline and 'good order', the appointment of officers was under strict political guidance. The axiom that armed groups are at risk of forfeiting their ability to engage in political action when military strategies become dominant could have been coined by the Unionist leadership.

The UVF was reorganised on the lines of the regular army and structured on a strictly territorial basis, reflecting the geographical distribution of Unionist associations. The military committee aimed to keep centralisation to a minimum, with the county serving as the basic organising unit. Each county division comprised a number of regiments that varied according to the number of local volunteers. Each regiment was then divided into various battalions, companies, half-companies, sections and squads. A special service force was formed consisting of three thousand men selected from the battalions of the Belfast division. Regiments also established a transport section and asked industrialists to sign agreements to provide trucks, while farmers contributed horses, carts and wagons. Each county established a committee to oversee operations with representatives designated at the divisional, district and local levels. The UVF, as Lord Castlereagh wrote, was an infantry army with no significant cavalry presence except for the Enniskillen Horse. Nonetheless, numerous regiments had mounted infantry sections, primarily comprised of yeoman farmers.[36]

Like any armed group, the UVF lacked funds. Acquiring equipment involved substantial costs, especially given the need to go through illicit channels. Continuous financing was also needed to recruit experienced officers, provide training and secure other essential resources for the development and maintenance of the UVF. Various fundraising initiatives were launched, with the announcement of Sir Edward Carson's Union Defence Fund in February 1913 being the most significant attempt to obtain financial contributions from businesses and individuals. In addition to this support, an Indemnity Fund was established to provide compensation to UVF members and their dependents in the event of personal injury or loss of life incurred while performing official duties. By January 1914, the fund had accumulated over £1,000,000, primarily in the form of pledged commitments.[37]

To meet the challenging demands of an 'imagined war', training camps were organised. The first of these was held at Baronscourt, County Tyrone, on the Duke of Abercorn's estate, under the watchful eye of Sir Edward Carson and F. E. Smith. The camp accommodated over four hundred

Table 5.3 Estimates of the number of arms in possession of the UVF, the number of drilling practices and the number of participants in drills according to police reports

Police estimates on 31 March 1914

Est. of no. arms in possession of the UVF		No. of drilling practices		No. of participants
Lee-Enfield	3,276	January	1,672	30,852
Martini-Enfield	6,580	February	2,006	35,520
Mixed modern rifles	12,018	March	1,939	38,220
Miniature rifles	81			
Italian rifles	2,732			
Other old models	201			
Total	24,879			

Source: *Intelligence Notes*, 34

officers and non-commissioned officers from the UVF's Tyrone Regiment. Repurposed stables served as sleeping quarters, while the former coalhouse was transformed into a mess room. The estate itself provided space for activities such as revolver shooting, concentrated fire practice and tactical demonstrations of attack and defence.[38] Other camps followed at Ormiston Park (Belfast), Loughgall Demesne (Co. Armagh), Knockballymore (Co. Fermanagh), Templepatrick (Co. Amtrin), Magilligan (Co. Derry) and so on. War simulation exercises were staged with the aim of testing the volunteers' military readiness, capabilities and decision-making skills. At the end of July 1913, a mock scenario of the outbreak of hostilities between the Ulster Provisional Government and the Irish Nationalist Government was acted out in Drogheda. The Irish Nationalists were allotted an estimated force of around twenty thousand men, who were advancing northwards with the intention of crossing the River Boyne to invade Ulster. A section of the UVF, comprising motorcyclists, engineers and mechanics, was assigned the task of slowing the enemy's advance by demolishing bridges, sabotaging the railway and seizing rolling stock. Following the successful 'operation', the Union Jack was hoisted on the Boyne obelisk, accompanied by a card confidently stating, 'Rebel hands may tear down the flag, but they will never tame the lion hearts of Ulster'.[39]

Several days later, on the anniversary of the Relief of Derry (12 August), sectarian tensions erupted in Derry resulting in the widespread use of firearms. At the same time, military preparations began to extend beyond the narrow boundaries of Ulster. In Dublin, a well-trained corps of two thousand men was established with volunteers receiving training three nights a week at different centres in the city from retired non-commissioned army officers, and with a musketry course also being offered. The purpose of this UVF reserve force was to stand ready to safeguard the civil and religious liberties of Protestants in Dublin and the southern regions of Ireland in case the Home Rule Bill was passed. Arrangements were also made for the wives and families of the men employed in the Dublin Volunteer Corps to be sent to homes in England at the outbreak of hostilities.[40]

Yet behind its impressive facade, the UVF struggled to conceal some of the problems associated with military improvisation, including friction in the chain of command, lack of trained officers and a supply of arms that relied more on audacious inventiveness rather than routine efficiency. Only the charisma of 'General' Carson seemed to provide the legitimacy needed to overcome these weaknesses. 'The genuine prophet, like the genuine military leader and every true leader in this sense', Max Weber wrote, 'preaches, creates, or demands new obligations'. In this regard, and despite his assertions of delegating command of the UVF to a professional soldier, Carson persisted in touring, inspecting, reviewing, recruiting, awarding decorations and participating in battalion and ceremonial formations. Between 17 September and 4 October, Carson inspected twenty-three thousand volunteers. His arrival in Banbridge was greeted with the firing of a small cannon salute, using guns similar to those kept on the decks of steamers for use in foggy conditions. He arrived in Ballyclare by car escorted by twenty 'dispatch riders' on motorcycles.[41] At Carney Hill, Carson declared 'I like to get nearer the enemy [...] I like to see the men are preparing for what I call the Great Day'.[42]

The real strength of the UVF lay in its numbers rather than its military proficiency. In the summer of 1913, Carson, who might have appreciated the legacy of Gerhard von Scharnhorst on military theory, wrote to all the Unionist clubs in Ulster that 'as leader my responsibility compels me to point to the danger of anyone holding aloof at this juncture, when it is necessary to perfect the final arrangements. My request is that all our men should join the Ulster Volunteers. Even old men can help guard their property, their hearths, and their homes, and thus release the younger and more active for whatever work may be necessary'.[43] By the end of the year, membership had reached 56,651, and grew even further to 84,865 by May 1914, although it is likely that there was a considerable discrepancy between 'total strength' and actual 'fighting strength', particularly in large formations. The ranks comprised men of all classes – country gentlemen, professional men, artisans, workers, farmers – and all Protestant creeds (Episcopalians, Methodists and Presbyterians). In the great scheme of preparing and maintaining the fighting machine, Unionist mothers, wives and sisters did their bit. As part of this effort, over four thousand women were engaged in the Ambulance and Nursing Corps. At Randalstown, twenty-four women of the local Women's Ambulance Association wearing white uniforms, and boys bearing stretchers paraded before 'General' Carson'.[44] At the beginning of 1914, *The Times* reported

> that during all these months ... the preparations of this grim, determined community have been steadily pushed ahead ... Night after night, after days of toil in farm and shipyard and in weather which has often reproduced the worst discomforts of a campaign, they have been assembling to drill in every parish of Protestant Ulster. Sections have grown into companies, companies into battalions, battalions into regiments and brigades.[45]

To Colonel Repington, *The Times*'s respected military correspondent, the UVF appeared to be a 'democratic community in arms'. The men who enlisted and underwent training were organised into squads of twelve with a squad leader elected by the members. Two squads formed a section and elected their own section leader. These sections, in turn, elected their company officers, who were then responsible for selecting the commanding officer, subject to approval from headquarters.[46] The 'democratic element' was weaker in the rural areas where some units were formed along patron-client relations, resembling the 'private armies' of a bygone era.[47] In the finest traditions of British military volunteering, UVF units assumed the financial responsibility for procuring clothing, equipment and, in some cases, firearms. The Unionist press consistently focused on the united efforts of men from all walks of life and occupations to shape themselves into effective soldiers. Furthermore, the work of training cemented a disciplined bond that transcended simple military affairs. Lord Castlereagh, unperturbed by his position as both paramilitary commanding officer and MP, wrote significantly that: 'In the Belfast regiments are representatives of all classes of a big industrial and commercial community. Men stand shoulder to shoulder with employers in the ranks. Workman drills master; managers on parade salute clerks. The class distinctions of civil life vanish before the necessities of discipline'.[48]

The assumption that Ulsterites who armed themselves and proclaimed their belief in the Union were necessarily of the 'Right' should not be applied without exception. Participation in rebellion was not solely motivated by loyalty to the Crown or Empire, nor by fear of Catholic domination. While many volunteers may have found in marching and drilling an outlet for militaristic tendencies – particularly as the Rifle Volunteer movement had never been extended to Ireland, and the Haldane reforms of 1908 similarly failed to establish Territorial Force units there – others joined the UVF out of concern that Home Rule would lead to economic hardship for Ulster. The largest UVF regiment, raised in East Belfast, included significant numbers from the Belfast shipyards, one of the most heavily unionised workforces in the British Isles. It is reasonable to suggest that many on the Left also preferred to remain within the United Kingdom, as it appeared evident that a Home Rule parliament would face financial difficulties and might be tempted to abandon the National Insurance Act. This Act, which incorporated distinct health and unemployment insurance schemes, had proven beneficial to many. Indeed, in 1918, several candidates stood on an Ulster Unionist Labour Association ticket, underscoring the subsumption of the labour movement within Ulster Unionism.[49]

Emerging in Belfast in 1912, the Young Citizen Volunteers of Ireland (YCV) became a major component of the Belfast UVF, although their constitution initially stated that they were 'apolitical'. The YCV arose partly as a response to growing class militancy – Larkin's ITGWU had developed out of the Belfast dock strike of 1907 – and partly as a pathway for young men who had aged out of organisations like the Boys' Brigade, Church Lads' Brigade and Boy Scouts to continue their involvement in military-style activities. The YCV's commitment to fostering civic pride and responsibility among young men from a strictly non-sectarian and non-political stance was gradually eroded by financial dependence on Unionist figures and the 'paramilitaristic inclinations' of Colonel R. Spencer Chichester, the YCV's Commanding Officer, ultimately culminating in the YCV's merger with the UVF in 1914.[50]

Ulster identity, although not monolithic, also served as a potent rallying cry for many UVF members and was reinforced through 'choreographies of force', including commemorative events, the presentation of colours, inspections and reviews, and funerals. Large parades, with volunteers marching in formation, conveyed a spectacle of unity and readiness.[51] Reporting on a parade of the Enniskillen Horse in the summer of 1913, the *Fermanagh Times* wrote: 'The discipline of the men, their upright, smart, soldierly bearing and the ready unhesitating way in which they immediately obeyed commands were all subjects of favourable criticism throughout the day and spoke well for the regular and systematic training which, we understand, every troop and squadron is receiving from experienced instructors'.[52] Regimental colours and the vast panoply of Unionist symbols were also powerful representations of faith. Religious ceremonial elements added a further layer of solemnity, with invocations, benedictions and prayers for the protection of the cause of Ulster. Finally, and perhaps most importantly, parades were intended to inspire awe in enemies and defy authority. Four days after plans had been announced for a 'Provisional Government' of Ulster, over ten thousand Belfast Volunteers paraded at the Royal Ulster Agricultural Society grounds at Balmoral in an imposing display of martial pomp. These armed parades, as Attorney General John Moriarty counselled, were 'absolutely illegal and the parties advising and openly encouraging them as well as those taking part in the drilling, marching and other military operations [were] guilty of felony of the 11 and 12 V., s. 3'. In other words, it was treason. However, for the sake of political prudence, the Attorney General recommended that 'prosecution should not be commenced without the express authority of the Executive'. The government refrained from taking any immediate action.[53]

At the end of November 1913, in response to the growing momentum of the Ulster movement against Home Rule, the Irish National Volunteers (INV) was established. This new entity brought together members of the Gaelic Athletic Association, Sinn Féin, the Irish Republican Brotherhood, the Gaelic League and all those who had little sympathy for the Irish Parliamentary Party. The inaugural gathering of the INV also saw a strong representation from the ITGWU, which, under the leadership of James Larkin, was involved in one of the most bitter industrial disputes in the nation's history – the Dublin Lockout. The declaration on the volunteers' enrolment form read: 'I, the undersigned, wish to join the Irish Volunteers, established to safeguard and uphold the rights and freedoms shared by all the people of Ireland, regardless of social class, religious belief, or political persuasion'.[54]

While the South was arming, plans had begun to materialise on English soil for the recruitment of volunteers to be transported across the North Channel to provide assistance to Ulster. Before the House of Commons, Lord Claud Hamilton, Chairman of the Great Eastern Railway, openly declared:

> I am a member of a family brought up in Ulster, but no longer resident there. I have three brothers, all of whom have had the honour of being members of this House. Do you suppose that we will allow our brethren in Ulster to have this measure forced upon them? No. We shall go over and take our stand by their side. I say more. I had the honour of being a member for Liverpool for eight years. I have merely to go to the quay of Liverpool and ask for volunteers, and they will come to me, not in hundreds, but in thousands, to go to the succour of their brethren in Ulster.[55]

This kind of rebellious discourse became reality in March 1913, when the BLSUU took on the task of channelling subversive enticements into a cohesive organisational framework.

The Overseas Army[56]

At the end of January 1914, the future Governor-General of the Irish Free State, Tim Healy, wrote to his brother that 'An Englishman (nephew of a peer) said to me there would be a civil war in England as well as in Ireland,

and that Willoughby de Broke and his men would ride up to London and attack Asquith, and that the soldiers would not resist! I never heard such dire threats'.[57] The anonymous 'nephew of the peer' might have been pulling Healy's leg, but the threats remained symptomatic of the level of bellicosity that the rhetoric around the crisis had taken on.

Several months earlier, while Willoughby de Broke was travelling across Ulster alongside Carson, his lieutenant Thomas Comyn Platt proposed to the Second Earl of Selborne the formation of a 'League of British anti-Home Rulers'.[58] The establishment of this new organisation, Platt suggested, could potentially sound 'the note of Civil War, should the government continue its devilish policy'.[59] In advocating his scheme, he insisted that the era of mere Unionist rhetoric had come to a close, to give way to a period of resolute action. Selborne's response was a testament of Conservative 'rancorous restraint' and ochlophobia (an intense fear of crowds) recently exacerbated by the industrial unrest in Britain:

> I will never say that is always wrong to take arms. I should myself take up arms without any hesitation for the monarchy against a republic, and I have already said that I think Ulster is wholly justified in her present attitude. But civil war is the ultima ratio and the last party in the world that ought to turn to arms if it can possibly avoid it or go outside legal and constitutional forms is the Conservative and Unionist party. If they did so lightly, it is likely that it would mean the breaking up of society and the end of the nation, for it would remove all restrictions on radicals and socialists who are blind to the value of tradition and authority. Finally, it is not really the United Kingdom alone which would be affected but the whole empire.[60]

Undeterred by Selborne's misgivings, and perhaps spurred on by Carson's umpteenth 'praise of irresponsibility', Comyn Platt and his diehard mentor continued to explore the fertile terrain of Conservative revolt. At the close of 1912, Willoughby de Broke penned a letter to Bonar Law angrily asserting that Toryism should be liberated from 'the morass compounded by [...] years of hucksterism, wire pulling, and opportunism'. He championed the unwavering embrace of 'a few national ideas', and resolutely repudiated Home Rule as a mortal peril to the very existence of the empire.[61] It was in this rebellious state of mind that Willoughby de Broke envisaged an organisation able to provide military expertise and recruitment services to the incipient UVF. On 27 March 1913, a letter to *The Times* bearing the signatures of one hunded Unionist Peers and one hundred and twenty Unionist Members of Parliament, citing the urgent need to carry the battle against Home Rule from Westminster to the constituencies, announced the formation of the BLSUU:

> The Government have announced their determination to take full advantage of the Parliament Act in order to establish a Parliament and Executive in Dublin, in spite of the sworn intention of the men of Ulster to resist this measure by every means in their power. We desire to point out to our countrymen that this determination does not affect Ulster alone. We believe that the repeal of the Union would be fatal to the prosperity of Ireland, to the safety of the United Kingdom, and the consolidation of the Empire. We also believe that the force of the Home Rule Bill into law while the Constitution is in suspense and without a General Election would be a gross violation of the right of the electors of the United Kingdom to be consulted before grave changes are effected by Parliament. It is quite clear that the men of Ulster are not fighting only for their own liberties. Ulster will be the field on which the privileges of the whole nation will be lost or won. We therefore appeal to all British citizens who sympathize with Ulster, and who value their own freedom, to join the above League that has been formed to support the men of Ulster in the great struggle that lies before them.[62]

The defence of Ulster's liberties, which was considered a matter of national strength and security, reinforced the call to duty of sympathisers in England and Scotland. Carson promptly thanked Willoughby de Broke, adding that he always 'felt certain that in our determination to resist Home Rule we would have behind us all those who were not prepared to sacrifice their friends for the purpose of placating their enemies'.[63] A few days later, the Standing Committee of the UUC also approved the establishment of the new body, which promised to rally the best, and if necessary the worst, instincts of patriotism.[64]

The distractions caused by the First Lord's statement on the Navy, the proceedings before the Marconi Committee and the disorderly scenes that took place during the Committee Stage of the Consolidated Fund Bill, drew attention away from the announcement of the establishment of the BLSUU. To those who were taking note, the League seemed like just another addition to the embarrassingly long list of Unionist leagues. However, there were other observers who, aware that the line between tawdry melodrama and sordid tragedy in politics is remarkably thin, began to wonder if the BLSUU might be taking Ulster's plea for 'rifles rather than pamphlets' a little too seriously. These conjectures were not without justification, not least because during the period in question, two patricians, Lord Leitrim and Lord Farnham, were involved in gun smuggling from England to Donegal, the latter even going as far as using his own yacht and chauffeur for the task.[65]

Among those gathered at the inaugural meeting of the Committee of the BLSUU, which took place on 11 April under the chairmanship of Lord Willoughby de Broke, were Lord Charles Beresford MP, Viscount Lewisham

MP, Colonel T. E. Hickman MP, Basil Peto, Thomas Comyn Platt (the honorary Secretary) and Hugh Ridgway (assistant secretary). The committee announced that a large number of letters of support had been received from across the nation and that a steady influx of donations ranging from five shillings to fifty pounds was coming in.[66] A month later, Basil Peto wrote to *The Times* that the work of the BLSUU had generated the 'liveliest interest' from the Union Defence Fund. He added that 'It was in the belief that there were in this country many men who did not desire to see Ulster fight her battle alone, if the Government carry the Home Rule conspiracy to the bitter end. [...] the BLSUU already possesses agents all over the country, and more are wanted'.[67] Gerald H. T. Madden, a prominent Co. Monaghan Unionist and veteran of the Boer War (Sixteenth Lancers), was appointed the 'major agent' in South-East England. In the press he appealed to 'the men of the Windsor and East Berkshire constituencies who value their freedom to join the league [...] and not to allow their loyal fellow countrymen in Ireland to be handed over to a disloyal Nationalist government'.[68] Additional agents were announced in Leeds and Sheffield, tasked with identifying individuals with military training and command experience.[69]

An exemplary BLSUU agent was Major C. H. Tippet. He began his military career as a private in the First V.B. Lincolnshire Regiment and rose through the ranks to become a lieutenant in the South Wales Borderers in 1886, then a captain in the Bristol Rifles in 1894 and subsequently transferred to the Fourth Battalion Royal Dublin Fusiliers as a captain in 1896. In 1900, he was awarded the officers' extra certificate at the School of Musketry in Hythe, and became a qualified instructor on the Maxine machine gun. After passing the field officer examination he was promoted to Major in October 1900. During the Boer War, Tippet served under the command of General Sir John French and was awarded the South African War Medal with five clasps. In early 1903, he was gazetted as an honorary Lieutenant Colonel in the Fourth Royal Dublin Fusiliers. Apart from his military service, Major Tippet was an experienced political agent for the Conservative Party, taking part in contests in Lincolnshire and South Monmouthshire. He served as the chief agent for the Unionist Party in North Somerset and, later, in South Suffolk. Tippet was also a Freemason and became a Worshipful Master in November 1912. In 1914, he was the leading agent of the Suffolk Branch of the BLSUU. At the outbreak of the First World War, he volunteered for service again and lost his life at Gallipoli in August 1915.[70]

Another BLSUU agent was Evelyn Milnes-Gaskell, a cousin of Edward Wood, the future Lord Irwin and later Viscount Halifax. He was educated at Eton and Trinity College, Cambridge, and in 1904 became a Justice of the Peace for the West Riding of Yorkshire. On 12 September 1906, he was awarded the rank of Major in the Queen's Own Yorkshire Dragoons

Yeomanry and completed his training at the School of Musketry. Milnes-Gaskell actively served as a Representative and Member of the West Riding of Yorkshire Territorial Force Association. From 1901 to 1904, he was also Aide-de-Camp to the Governor of Tasmania. From 1907, he was a dedicated member of the West Riding of Yorkshire County Council.[71] At the Dungannon Rifle Club, in the presence of Captain William Tillie Dickson, Milnes-Gaskell stated that he had recruited 'the services of several army officers with seven- or eight-years' experience'.[72]

Predictably, the recruitment of agents focused on 'captains of venture' on half-pay and 'brutalized' veterans of the Boer War. One prominent example was none other than Frank Percy Crozier, future British general and leader of the 'Black and Tans'. He was born in Bermuda in 1879 to an officer father, spent his childhood in Gibraltar and later attended Wellington College in England. Initially rejected from the army due to his short height, he worked in a stockbroker's office, but obtained his military training by joining a volunteer corp. In 1898, Crozier moved to Sri Lanka (then Ceylon) and worked on a tea plantation while maintaining his military ties by joining the Ceylon Light Infantry. When the Boer War broke out, he quickly made his way there by signing on as a ship's cook. Enlisting as a private in a colonial corps in Durban, he participated in the Natal campaign, including the battle of Spion Kop and the relief of Ladysmith. Within five months, he received a regular commission. Towards the end of the war, he volunteered for service in West Africa, where he took part in the Ashanti campaign and later engaged in operations against the Hausas in Nigeria. In 1905, he participated in operations in Zululand before retiring from the army three years later and relocating to Canada. In 1913, Crozier joined the BLSUU. 'Having drifted onto half-pay and then into the Reserve', he recalled years later, 'I became involved in a movement which originated in Conservative circles and then later extended throughout the country and calling itself [...] the British League for the Support of Ulster'.[73] Upon enlisting, the League provided him with a carbine.[74] In Ulster, Crozier raised the Special Service Section of the West Belfast Regiment. During the First World War, he became Commander of the Ninth Royal Irish Rifles and served throughout the conflict, rising to the rank of Brigadier General. He was mentioned in dispatches seven times, was awarded the Distinguished Service Order (DSO) and the *Croix de Guerre*, and was appointed Companion of the Order of St. Michael and St. George (CMG). In the final stages of the war, he was a military adviser to the Lithuanian Government. Following a special mission to Latvia and Estonia in 1920, he resigned his commission and returned to Ireland, where he raised the infamous Auxiliary Division of the RIC. Appalled by the atrocities committed by his own men in Cork, Crozier publicly resigned his commission on 19 February 1921 and joined the crowded ranks of disillusioned soldiers turned pacifists.[75]

Other BLSUU recruits had experience of the South African veldt. Lieutenant Colonel J. H. Patterson, soldier, big game hunter and author of *The Man-Eaters of Tsavo* and *In the Grip of the Nyika: Further Adventures in British East Africa*, was assigned a commanding role in West Belfast. He had previously served in South Africa with the Seventy-Sixth Company Imperial Yeomanry and had been awarded the Distinguished Service Order by King Edward VII. During the First World War, Patterson led the Zion Mule Corps at Gallipoli and fought with the Jewish Legion. The strong desire of some veterans to return to duty or to seek adrenaline-inducing environments might also have been the motivation for Charles St. Aubyn Wake to accept the BLSUU's offer. In Ulster, he became associated with the South and West Belfast Regiments. In some cases, the need to provide for themselves or their families appears to have been the motivating factor for some veterans to accept officer positions in the UVF. Mathematician and future MP for Windsor, Annesley Ashworth Somerville offered J. C. Madden, Commanding Officer of the Monaghan Regiment, the services of a South African veteran with financial difficulties and pledged to cover the veteran's pay for one year.[76] In his meticulous scrutiny of UVF officers, Timothy Bowman has established that the BLSUU enlisted the aid of at least seven, and possibly nine, officers who had expressed their willingness to serve either at the UVF HQ or in the Belfast Regiments. Most of these officers had had entirely conventional army careers, while a minority had followed more unorthodox trajectories.[77]

There was an implicit expectation that BLSUU agents would develop a synergistic relationship with the UVF command. However, gun-runner Major Frederick H. Crawford expressed dissatisfaction with the 'operational plan' put forward by the BLSUU, which he dismissively referred to as the 'long name' society. He considered their offer to dispatch unarmed men to Ulster to be useless, arguing that Ulster did not need a 'rabble of unarmed men to house and feed and look after'. Crawford insisted that what they really required were weapons and ammunition. If the League was unable to provide arms, they could at least provide financial assistance to purchase them. Otherwise, Crawford peremptorily concluded, 'Put up the shutters in your Society'.[78] Shortly afterwards, Crawford made contact with William Bull, who helped secure a warehouse in Hammersmith for arms storage. The depot would be a temporary repository for arms acquired in Hamburg until their safe transfer to Ulster could be ensured. Although the scheme enjoyed initial success, it was cut short when the London Metropolitan Police raided the depot and confiscated several thousand Vetterli-Vitali rifles. The government had to justify the seizure by invoking the Gun Barrel

Proof Act of 1868, which stipulated that the barrels of small arms imported into England without proper proof and marking had to undergo testing at either the Proof House in Birmingham or the Gunmakers' Company in London within twenty-eight days of arrival. Noncompliance with this law carried a fine of £2 per barrel, resulting in a substantial penalty of £12,000 to £14,000 for the intercepted cargo. As Crawford reluctantly accepted the setback, suspicions were roused regarding the possible involvement of the BLSUU in the smuggling operation.[79]

When the government reintroduced the Home Rule Bill in the new session in May 1913, bringing the Parliament Act into operation for the very first time, Willoughby de Broke wrote in *The Times* that it was evident to anyone not deliberately turning a blind eye that the situation was approaching 'a state of extreme danger'. The House of Lords had no power under the Parliament Act to refer the Home Rule Bill to the people, while Ulstermen would not comply with a Dublin-based Parliament and were prepared to resist with force. The most effective way to avert disaster, according to Willoughby de Broke, was to demonstrate to the government that opposition extended well beyond Ulster. He again asserted the duty of Unionists across Britain to demonstrate commitment to the cause until they had the opportunity to vote against the repeal of the Union. It was under these circumstances that the BLSUU had been specifically formed to take concrete measures to ensure that Ulster would not stand alone in its hour of 'supreme crisis', should it unhappily arise.[80]

In early June, during an interview with a representative from the *Pall Mall Gazette*, a 'prominent and active' member of the BLSSU shed light on the organisation. When asked about the Parliamentary situation, he unequivocally declared that 'the time for speaking is past. We do not want men to speak for us, but to shoot for us'. The interviewer probed further into their activities, and the League member disclosed that they had nearly 150 agents deployed throughout England. These agents were tasked with recruiting men willing to stand with Ulster and the Union, regardless of the consequences. 'We are' he declared, 'preparing for the worst, and nothing else matters at all'. When asked if the BLSSU was preparing for armed resistance, he candidly replied 'Certainly. For this Ulster has quite made up its mind and is facing the situation with dauntless courage. So are our English Unionists'. He revealed that they had received assurance from one source that 'a troop of fully equipped mounted men' was ready to follow BLSUU orders and had also had encouraging reports from various places, such as Berkshire, Brighton, Bournemouth, Cheltenham, Portsmouth and elsewhere. Each enlisted man had committed his 'unwavering support' and it was noteworthy that 75 per cent of those enlisted were retired army personnel. Within three months, the interviewee stated, the League anticipated having seven thousand well-organised, armed men prepared to serve under orders. The inclusion of the Duke of Bedford, Viscount Castlereagh, Ronald McNeill, MP for St. Augustine's and Mr. Charles Carlos Clarke, a distinguished presence on the London Stock Exchange, enhanced the prestige of the BLSUU's executive committee.[81]

On 3 June, as the Customs in Belfast apprehended eight large cases containing bayonets and rifles, apparently dispatched from Manchester, a private meeting was held between Carson, Captain James Craig and other Ulster leaders, and the committee of the BLSUU at Londonderry House to discuss how the League could assist the UVF in their search for military expertise.[82] A few weeks earlier, Colonel Hickman had started looking for a senior officer willing to become the UVF's commander-in-chief. He approached Lord Roberts, who in turn recommended Lieutenant General George Richardson for the position. At this time, Colonel Hickman was also heavily involved in gun-running operations.[83] Another individual involved in the illegal arms trade was Major Francis T. Tristram, who was the BLSUU agent for Darlington. As managing director of Casebourne & Company Ltd., Tristram controlled several cement plants in the North of England, which provided excellent cover for the 'packaging' and transportation of firearms and ammunition. At West Hartlepool, for instance, the Ulster gun-runners concealed five hundred cartridges within each bag of cement. These 'enriched bags' were then transported to Belfast through a privately owned harbour at Haverton Hill.[84]

Following the debate on the second reading, which was primarily focused on the issue of Ulster, and agreement to the Bill by a vote of 368 to 270 on 10 June, the BLSUU intensified its campaign. In this context, Carson's declaration that Ulster had the certain support of the entire Unionist Party in its determination to resort to arms greatly helped to remove the last rhetorical inhibitions. Addressing the House of Commons, Lord Beresford bellowed: 'I say, and I honestly think, that it is deplorable that a man who has worked the whole of his life in the British service, who has been loyal to the Union Jack, should have to stand up in the House of Commons and say that he is prepared, knowing his responsibility, to go and be one of the first to be shot down if troops are sent to Ireland. That is not swagger. That is what I intend to do if you send troops to Ireland'.[85] Soon after, the BLSUU issued a new press statement declaring that 'there can be no doubt that the question of Home Rule for Ireland can only be settled either (a) by the surrender of the Government, or (b) by the surrender of Ulster, or by a civil war ... and the third is staring us in the face'. It was against this background that the BLSUU had been formed 'for the purpose of organising those of our fellow countrymen who will reinforce the Ulstermen in their armed resistance to the tyranny of the

Government'.⁸⁶ A month later, Willoughby de Broke caused a sensation when he declared in the House of Lords that since 'a trial of physical force' seemed inevitable, 'some of my friends and I, among whom I am proud to number the Duke of Bedford, and several members of Parliament, have instituted a League [...] In case the noble Lords opposite do not know the address of this League I will tell them that it is No. 25 Ryder Street, curiously enough next door to a gunmaker's shop'. Amidst the general amazement, he added, 'If Lord Crewe would like to come round to the office of the League ... I will tell him what we are doing. I shall not tell him how many men I have on my side [...] I think noble Lords on the Front Bench opposite would be astonished if they knew the amount of influential support this movement is receiving from all classes of our fellow-countrymen in England, Scotland, and Wales'.⁸⁷

In July, as the Home Secretary, Reginald McKenna, acknowledged that there was insufficient evidence to initiate legal action against the BLSUU at that particular moment, forty-two delegates of the League made their way to Belfast to participate in The Twelfth celebrations. Before an enormous crowd at Craigavon, Carson 'insulted' the King by advising him to refuse to give his assent to the Home Rule Bill until there had been a general election. Following this invocation to commit a 'revolutionary act', a message from Willoughby de Broke was read out, which proclaimed that the League 'was going strong [and] getting new volunteers every day. You may be assured that when your supreme struggle comes, Englishmen, Scotchmen, and Welshmen will stand by your side. The preservation of the British Constitution is our battle as well as yours, and we shall not allow you to fight it alone'.⁸⁸

The following day, the City and District Unionist Club held a special church parade at Belfast Cathedral. Members attended the service, which began with the processional hymn 'Onward Christian Soldiers' and concluded with a rendition of 'Rock of Ages', a hymn that had a significant symbolic association, as it had also been played at Gladstone's funeral. During the service, the Lord Bishop of Derry delivered a belligerent address, drawing inspiration from passages in the Bible, such as Luke 22:36 ('he that hath no sword, let him sell his garment, and buy one') and Matthew 26:52 ('for all they that take the sword shall perish with the sword'). Any exhortation to turn the other cheek would not have gone down well with the Ulsterites. The Cathedral was filled to capacity, with thousands more unable to enter. Delegates from the BLSUU, wearing armlets bearing the motto 'For Union and Empire', were among the early arrivals.⁸⁹ In the meantime, Colonel Hickman assured the members of the Cliftonville

The arming of Ulster 245

Figure 5.3 The photo was taken in the office of the BLSUU at 25 Ryder St., St. James's, London for propaganda purposes. *Evening Herald* (Dublin), 11 June 1913. Image © The British Library Board. All rights reserved

Unionist Club that if the need for action arose, the people of Ulster would receive strong support.[90]

At the end of the summer, after the Home Rule Bill had been defeated in the Lords for the second time, the League boasted hundreds of honorary agents operating throughout the country, with a notable presence in London,

Lancashire and Yorkshire. Of the five thousand enlisted volunteers, 70 per cent were said to be retired army personnel.[91] In Scotland, Ulster's appeal to religious brethren was a potent catalyst for recruitment. On the day that Sir Edward Carson and all the other Irish Unionists addressed meetings in Edinburgh, *The Scotsman*, published a letter, effectively a statement of the writer's militant enthusiasm:

> Dear Sir, – Referring to the notice in Unionist papers, I trust you will kindly add my name to the British League for the Support of Ulster. I enclose P.O.O [postal office order for] £1 as my subscription and wish I could make it more. I will give my active support to the League, and, when called upon, am prepared to proceed to Ulster with a rifle or revolver and ammunition, to maintain myself while there, and to submit to the discipline enforced by authorities of the League.[92]

The letter aimed to inspire thousands of fellow Scotsmen who were eagerly seeking guidance to join the ranks of those prepared to make sacrifices for Ulster, and to alleviate the tension stemming from inaction. At the time, a prominent feature of the League was the assistance it received from women, who were willing to form nursing corps and arrange accommodation for refugees. In Warwickshire, Mrs. M. L. Adderley circulated appeals on behalf of the BLSUU to all landowners and residents for their support in providing temporary homes for the thousands of people who might be displaced in Ulster and across Ireland if the Home Rule Bill were passed. The appeals highlighted the potential bloodshed, famine and peril facing women, children and old men. The League proposed taking up vacant houses in Leamington or offering shelter under individual roofs. Mrs. Adderley drew attention to the importance of being prepared for the 'fateful day'.[93]

As other conservative groups made preparations to host 'imaginary' refugees, Willoughby de Broke repeatedly underscored the seriousness of the BLSUU's endeavours to actively recruit the 'right sort' of men to assist Ulster's armed resistance. On the anniversary of the signing of the Ulster Covenant, he engaged in a spirited conversation with a large crowd gathered at the Philharmonic Hall in Liverpool. He posed a critical question: 'But what I want to know is – what are we going to do?' The audience replied with determined shouts of 'Help!' and 'We are going to fight!'. Willoughby de Broke then further ignited the crowd's fervour by asking how many among the two hundred and fifty thousand who paraded before Sir Edward a year ago in Liverpool would be willing to risk their lives, property, and means for the cause. They replied unanimously with resolute shouts of 'All!' accompanied by loud cheers. Lord Willoughby de Broke was unequivocal: 'Demonstrations are not going to kill Home Rule. In the last resort we shall have to meet force with force and coercion with coercion'. Again, the crowd responded with enthusiastic cheers. Further fanning the flames, he concluded by declaring that the League had a larger number of volunteers signed on in Liverpool than in any other city in the Kingdom [...] and warned that unless the British Government met their political demands, 'it will be civil war, and it will be civil war to the knife. And the responsibility will not be ours; it will be the responsibility of those in high places who have chosen to disregard the feeling of the country'.[94] Alderman Archibald Salvidge's advice to Willoughby de Broke to refrain from exacerbating sectarian divisions on Merseyside was woefully disregarded.[95]

Willoughby de Broke continued to allude to the spectre of civil war also in private communications. He openly admitted to Bonar Law the necessity of resorting to 'physical force', and that his 'Blenheim pledge has chrystallized [sic]' in the presence of BLSUU agents in every constituency in England, Scotland and Wales.[96] While continual talk of armed resistance might have been a tactic to pressurise the government into agreeing to call a general election, it was causing concern even among some fervent anti-Home Rulers. Lord Robert Cecil, for instance, confessed to Willoughby de Broke that BLSUU's publications 'rather frighten[ed] him at first glance'. He added that the threat of violence had to be met with appeals to reason since 'Civil war, if it failed, would be disastrous to Ulster, and if it succeeded, it would probably be fatal to the United Kingdom'.[97] When Lord Cecil acknowledged Lord Loreburn's plea for an interparty conference on the Irish question, Willoughby de Broke responded that his intention was to prevent escalation rather than prepare for violence. 'Those who are acting with me', he wrote, 'think that the stronger the forces arrayed against Home Rule, the more likely the government is to avoid the extreme touch, and to appeal to the constituencies'.[98] This clarification did little to alter Lord Cecil's view that sometimes prudence is the highest wisdom.

Unfazed by Lord Cecil's moderate stance, Willoughby de Broke invited the fourth Marquess of Salisbury to join the BLSUU's executive committee. In a letter to the Marquess, he expounded on the League's dual objectives, which were, firstly, to draw public attention in England to the fact that the English were as concerned with the question of the repeal of the Union as the Ulstermen were; and, secondly, to ascertain whether or not the English consented to the repeal of the Union, and if they did not, whether, if worse came to worst, they deemed it worth fighting for alongside the Ulstermen. Willoughby de Broke restated the BLSUU's role as a 'deterrent', arguing that if a significant contingent from England were deployed to Belfast, it would shake the 'government's morale' and probably compel Asquith to abandon

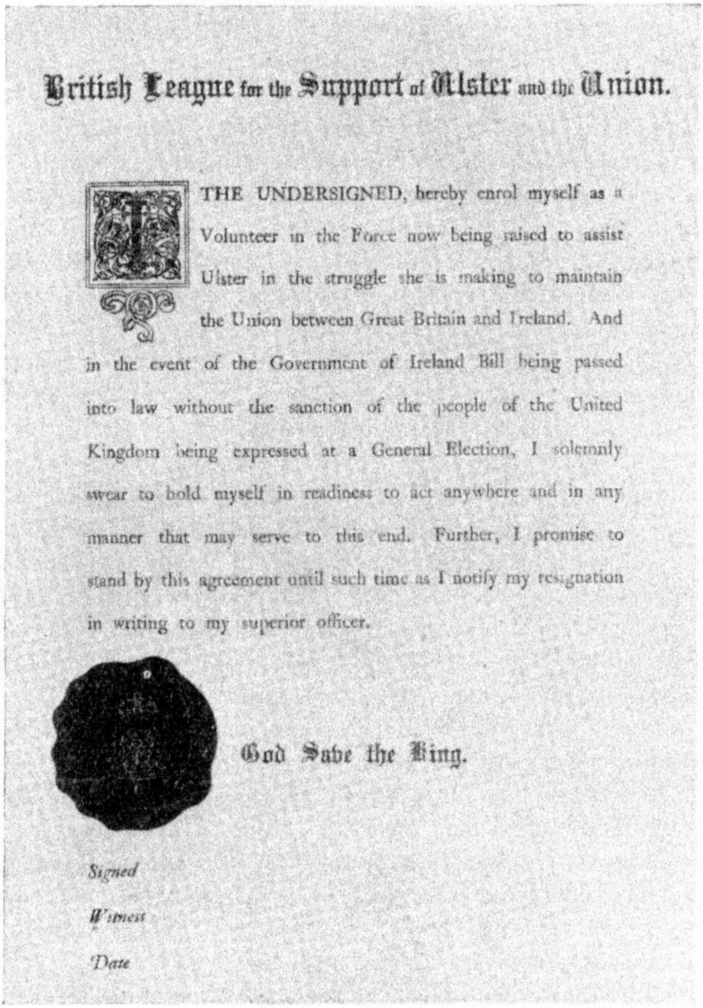

British League for the Support of Ulster and the Union.

THE UNDERSIGNED, hereby enrol myself as a Volunteer in the Force now being raised to assist Ulster in the struggle she is making to maintain the Union between Great Britain and Ireland. And in the event of the Government of Ireland Bill being passed into law without the sanction of the people of the United Kingdom being expressed at a General Election, I solemnly swear to hold myself in readiness to act anywhere and in any manner that may serve to this end. Further, I promise to stand by this agreement until such time as I notify my resignation in writing to my superior officer.

God Save the King.

Signed
Witness
Date

HAVE YOU SEEN THIS—AND WHAT DO YOU THINK OF IT? A FORM ISSUED BY THE "BRITISH LEAGUE FOR THE SUPPORT OF ULSTER AND THE UNION."

Figure 5.4 BLSUU Form, *The Sketch*, 3 December 1913. Image © Mary Evans Picture Library

Home Rule.⁹⁹ Salisbury was cold to Willoughby's proposal to 'back Ulster in deeds as well as words' and left the BLSUU's pledge unsigned.

A few weeks later, Austen Chamberlain, who considered extra-parliamentary efforts to resolve the Ulster problem nothing short of madness, warned Willoughby de Broke that:

> Civil war is an awful thing, not to be lightly encountered, but it is not the greatest evil which confronts us if the coercion of Ulster is tried. For if that is done, the House of Commons v. the Army will break in the process ... If officers throw up their commissions and troops refuse to fire, Home Rule is dead, but a great deal else is dead too. I won't dwell on the dangers of foreign complications, real though they be, but how will you meet another general strike on the railways or in the mines? It is not civil war that is the greatest peril but anarchy'.[100]

Chamberlain was evidently acquainted with the incontrovertible truth that violence was akin to chaos, as it had the potential for unpredictable and potentially catastrophic outcomes. In more colourful language, the 'diehard' Duke of Northumberland told Willoughby de Broke that 'those who are preparing it [armed resistance] are hatching a brood of chickens which will some day – and probably at not distant date – come very awkwardly home to roost in England'.[101] The unsettling forecast of a civil war that would not be confined to Ulster, but instead would have the capacity to engulf the whole of Britain, weighed heavily on the minds of some Conservatives.

Willoughby de Broke's inability to attract prominent Unionists to join the League neither tempered his extremism nor hindered the BLSUU's relentless activities. Perhaps because several other 'diehards' were also expressing their belief in the inevitability of civil war. The Earl of Winterton recalled that a notable contingent of young MPs was willing to provide 'physical assistance' to Ulster – and in greater numbers and with more significant levels of commitment than initially known or later disclosed. Moreover, he personally formed a command, in which he enlisted South African veterans, to stand prepared to support the Ulster volunteers.[102] Lord Saltoun, a respectable Scottish peer, wrote to Willoughby de Broke that 'Civil Wars up to this have been against the Supreme Authority, The King. This if it comes will be on our side for the King & Constitution and against the government of the country'.[103] The ease with which the prospect of bloodshed was contemplated was both astonishing and concerning. The Duchess of Somerset wrote to Carson assuring him that 'The day that the first shot is fired in Ireland – I shall have my complete ambulance started and ready [...] I have also undertaken to house 100 women and children from Ulster – The Duke and I will both come over to give all the help we can'.[104] Apart from these fantasies, the 'overseas army', as George Peel sardonically called the BLSUU, was also benefiting from the enthusiasm it was garnering in Ulster. The Irish Unionist Alliance Yearbook noted that 'such a British movement [was] inspiriting to all Irish unionists at the present time', while James Craig was delighted by Willoughby's uncompromising devotion.[105]

Undoubtedly, the BLSUU's visibility greatly increased over the autumn of 1913 and its mantra 'Until the Home Rule Bill is torn up and a General Election has taken place, the works must go on' became all the more familiar. Hugh B. Ridgway, assistant secretary of the BLSUU, explained to the *Pall Mall Gazette*'s correspondent that the movement had widespread reach, with over three hundred agents operating across the country. Favourable reports had been received from cities such as Liverpool, Glasgow, Manchester and Wrexham, with Liverpool alone enrolling over a thousand men. In many places, volunteers were being taught drills or given training. Ridgway pointed out that 'The majority of [them] are retired Army men, and a very large percentage of the agents are retired Army officers; but there are also some still on the active list'. Other volunteers hailed from diverse backgrounds, with professionals, large manufacturers, stockbrokers and businesspeople all volunteering their services for Ulster. The recruitment process was quickly progressing, with a hundred men joining daily. The establishment of a Provisional Government for Ulster further inspired many who until then had been uncertain whether to step forward and offer their assistance. Ridgway also pointed out that the objective was to create an efficiently organised, well-equipped force that would act as a reserve and be ready to respond to the demands of the Ulster movement's leaders when needed. 'We are in deadly earnest', he concluded, 'All talk of conference and compromise may go on, but we shall prepare for what we regard as inevitable'.[106]

The suspicion that Ridgway and other members of the BLSUU were prone to exaggeration was not entirely unfounded. However, in October 1913, the honorary agent in Birmingham, W. H. Nightingale, informed Willoughby de Broke that volunteers with prior military experience, including a corporal from the Warwickshire Yeomanry, had begun drilling new recruits. Nightingale was convinced that 'nothing but a strong display of force in Great Britain will influence Mr. Redmond in the least'. He therefore planned to form several companies and to muster '1,000 soldiers of civil and religious liberty' within a few weeks, asserting that 'the time for mere talk is over'.[107] Besides the West Midlands, the BLSUU's recruitment drive was also making swift progress in Scotland. Efforts were underway by J. G. Jameson, the prospective Unionist candidate for East Edinburgh, to enlist workers in the Canongate.[108] Captain R. W. MacLeod of the Seventy-Ninth (The Queen's Own Cameron Highlanders) Regiment of Foot was seeking recruits in Ross-shire.[109] The BLSUU's influence extended to Port Glasgow where 'fifty loyalists' had already joined Carson's army.[110] Furthermore, signs that the BLSUU was pushing recruitment among Southern Unionists were also apparent.[111] Another important recruitment pool, as Henry Machu Imbert-Terry revealed to Bonar Law, was the Conservative youth organisations.[112]

In November 1913, during a meeting of the Primrose League in Slough, Charles C. Clarke proudly declared that the League had enlisted ten thousand men. Some time later, it was announced that, with the impending incorporation of new battalions from Romford and East Ham, the force was expected to reach a total of twenty thousand men.[113] In Norwich, on the occasion of the forty-seventh annual conference of the National Unionist Association of Conservative and Liberal Unionist organisations, Willoughby de Broke confidently stated: 'We are enlisting, and enrolling, and arming a considerable force of volunteers, who are going to proceed to Ulster to reinforce the ranks of Captain Craig and his brave men when the proper time comes'.[114]

As the latter part of 1913 unfolded, there was no indication of a reduction or a weakening in the 'warlike preparations'. At the beginning of November, the BLSUU gathered at a luncheon at the Hotel Cecil, with notable attendees including Rudyard Kipling and Arnold White. The speeches delivered during the event shared a common thread: a firm stance against any compromise or agreement. Willoughby de Broke reiterated that they must be 'prepared for the worst to get the best' and 'to meet violence with violence'. Offers of assistance were given. One landowner, who had served in Rhodesia, made a commitment to sell his last acre of land to finance a troop from his own district. An elderly, middle-class Ulsterman volunteered to take charge of twenty-five men and cover their necessary expenses. The founder of White, Allom & Co., Sir Charles Allom, committed to equip one hundred men, should the need arise, to aid Ulster in its resistance against Home Rule. The League's official motto, 'One King, one Flag, and one Parliament', resounded with unwavering clarity.[115]

On 11 November, *The Times* published a new BLSUU appeal:

> We call upon all able-bodied fellow-countrymen who think the Ulstermen are arming in a righteous cause to enrol themselves and prepare to reinforce the ranks of the men who are going to risk their lives for the integrity of the Empire as well as their own civil and religious liberties secured to them by the British Constitution.[116]

In an interview with the *Daily Mirror*, the outspoken Ridgway stated, 'We are out to shoot instead of to speak'. He revealed that thousands of men in England were actively gearing up to support Ulster in a potential conflict by drilling three to four times a week. Three hundred and twenty-five agents were enrolling almost two hundred men a day from all classes. Support for the League was gaining momentum in key towns such as Bath, Birmingham, Bradford, Bristol, Davenport, Glasgow, Halifax, Huddersfield, Leeds, London, Manchester, Plymouth, Portsmouth and York. 'Something is going to happen', declared Ridgway.[117]

In November, Unionist women formed the 'Help the Ulster Women Committee' with the Duchess of Abercorn serving as chairwoman and Mr. Harold Smith MP as vice-chairman. The organisational work was undertaken by Miss Graham Hope from the Women's Amalgamated Unionist and Tariff Reform Association, along with Mr. Arbuthnot from the Primrose League. Miss Hope explained that 'Our aim, in brief, was to provide houses over here for invalids or sick wives and the children of those who would be fighting in Ulster. We were fully expecting all able-bodied wives to stay by their husbands' sides and to help, for example, in loading their rifles during actual fighting'.[118]

Inevitably, F. E. Smith joined the BLSUU Committee towards the end of that month. On 20 September in Ballyclare, he ranted:

> I have refused to believe that the occasion will ever arise in which even this Government, corrupt and guilty as it is, will dare to attempt to march upon Ulster. But if that unhappy moment in the history of empire arrives, I tell you this, on the behalf of the Unionist party in Great Britain – from that moment we hold ourselves absolved from all allegiance to the government. From that moment, we on our part will say to our fellows in England 'To your tents, O Israel!' From that moment we shall stand side by side with you, refusing to recognize any law, and prepared with you to risk the collapse of the whole body politic to prevent this monstrous crime.[119]

The threat echoed Carson's notorious Antrim speech on the 'pledges and promises of the generals to keep the old flag flying'. In Dublin, Bonar Law made another ominous reference to the Army, inviting Asquith to recall the fate of King James. Some Unionists somewhat recklessly suggested that the Army's refusal to intervene against Ulster might ultimately contribute to the defeat of the Home Rule Bill.

The festival of seditious speeches and tirades continued without respite. Colonel Hickman told his Wolverhampton constituents that nine thousand men were drilling in the country in preparation for the 'Ulster campaign':

> You may be quite certain that these men are not going to fight with dummy muskets. They are going to use modern rifles and ammunition, and they are being taught to shoot. I know because I buy the rifles myself. I won't tell you where I get them from, but you can take it from me that they are the best, and if the men will only hold them straight, there won't be many Nationalists to stand up against them.[120]

Figure 5.5 'New Fighting force for Ulster', *Daily Mirror*, 12 November 1913
Image © Reach PLC. Image created courtesy of The British Library Board

Not caring for the consequences, Hickman also revealed that he had interviewed twenty-six officers in London who were willing to serve in the UVF. Only later, and after an embarrassing delay, he explained that he had meant 'retired officers'.[121] A few weeks earlier, a *Pall Mall Gazette* correspondent had reported that the League was recruiting primarily from commissioned and non-commissioned Army ranks, and from members of the

Territorial Army. Moreover, there were individuals with prior experience in the Imperial Yeomanry during the South African campaign who were more than willing to offer their services. It was announced that retired generals, colonels and majors were included on the list.[122] Although these statements appeared to be gross exaggerations or outright fabrications, the fact that certain members of the BLSUU committee held commissions in the Army or the Navy while advocating armed resistance against the forces of the Crown caused widespread outrage. More than one voice began to be heard urging the government to suppress the League or, at the very least, have the Criminal Investigation Department at Scotland Yard investigate it.[123]

In December, a confidential circular was issued bearing the emblem of the BLSUU as well as a Royal crown along with the rose, thistle and shamrock. The document outlined the recruitment process and the incentives offered. The BLSUU aimed to enlist 'suitable men to assist the loyalists of Ulster if necessary in their armed resistance to home rule'. Enrolled individuals were expected to pay for their journey to and from Ulster themselves, while everything they needed during their stay would be provided. They were expected to be able to carry out a 'number of drills', and would be required to sign an attestation form. The need for utmost confidentiality regarding organisational matters was impressed upon them. The men were selected carefully, ensuring they were unwavering Unionists, fully committed to the cause regardless of the costs or risks. It concluded by stating, 'I am particularly anxious to establish a Branch in your town immediately. Therefore, I would appreciate it if you could provide me with one or two names of individuals I could personally contact'.[124] The document was also disseminated in North America where recruiting was reported to be taking place in Ontario, Winnipeg and Minnesota. Upon receiving the circular, a wealthy British landowner visiting New York expressed his perplexity: 'I am a patriotic Britisher, but this attempt to incite rebellion appals me. I do not know what the country is coming to'.[125]

While 'the red-blood-will-flow' rhodomontade continued and the nephew of John Edward Redmond publicly announced his decision to fight for Ulster, a Royal proclamation was issued on 4 December prohibiting the importation of arms into Ireland. The following day, Lieutenant Colonel Sir John Robert Pretyman Newman, MP for Enfield, made a rather wild suggestion: 'If Mr. Asquith did employ the British Army, he would break the back of the Army, and if by any chance he should bring bloodshed in Ulster by means of Imperial troops, then, to his mind, any man would be justified in shooting Mr. Asquith in the streets of London'. In the same vein, A. M. Samuel declared at Old Trafford that 'When the first shot of civil war was fired in Ulster, as sure as they stood there, one of the Cabinet Ministers would be hanged on a lamppost in Downing Street'. In a remarkable outburst during a Unionist demonstration in Warrington, Joynson Hicks roared 'The people of Ulster have behind them the Unionist party. Behind them was the Lord God of Battles. In His name and their name, I said to the Prime Minister, "Let your armies and batteries fire. Fire if you dare! Fire and be damned!"'[126]

Realisation was beginning to dawn that persistent exposure to violent and aggressive language was leading to desensitisation. Informal talks between Asquith and Bonar Law, which had been promised at the end of 1913, seemed to aggravate the malaise. In unexpected Sorelian language, Leo Amery told the Conservative leader that 'what is wanted is what the French call *un geste*, the significant act which arrests attention and illuminates the whole situation'.[127] Speaking at a Junior Constitutional Club, Willoughby de Broke promised that, if necessary, the BLSUU would dig trenches in Ulster.[128] In an interview with *The Globe*, the increasingly verbose Ridgway brazenly admitted that the weapons that had been sent out were short carbines. Drilling took place two or three days a week, the largest centres being in Liverpool and Yorkshire. The BLSUU was only accepting men who could cover their own expenses and were 'prepared to go ahead and risk everything'. To back up his assertions, Ridgway cited a letter from a captain in the Reserve, who had served in South Africa and was prepared to support the Loyalists of Ulster 'in the last extremity'. The BLSUU assistant secretary bragged that 'this spirit animates thousands' of law-abiding citizens prepared to assist Ulster in resisting by force an unconstitutional act.[129]

At the end of 1913, Lord Milner 'discovered' the existence of the BLSUU. On 3 December, the former High Commissioner to South Africa wrote to Carson, asking 'whether there is not something which men like myself, who disbelieve in mere talk at this juncture, can do to help you'. Anticipating the Home Rule Bill's imminent third and final reading, he predicted that a rebellion would take place in Ulster within a year. Milner voiced deep concern that the success of such an uprising, the epitome of 'unshakable principles and devoted patriotism – of loyalty to the Empire and the Flag', was perilously dependent on external support. Consequently, he advocated for the establishment of a strategically placed organisation capable of 'paralysing the arm' that might be raised against Ulsterites.[130] To pursue his vision of resistance, Milner needed to recruit a cohort of steadfast men, and among the most promising prospects was 'W. de B. & his merry men'.[131] Subsequently, Carson made Milner's intentions known to Willoughby de Broke, who then contacted Milner inviting him to join the BLSUU committee. In his attempts to persuade the great 'proconsul' of the empire, de Broke explained that 'the object of this league [was] to arm all Unionists on this side of the water who wish to fight with the Ulstermen', while warning him that without proper armed preparedness Unionist leaders might 'produce some compromise'. Milner, who shared de Broke's pessimism, accepted an invitation to attend a BLSUU meeting as a 'sympathetic outsider'. However, in agreement with his aide-de-camp Leo Amery, Milner recognised the need for a less bellicose, but no less resolute organisation, that was truly capable of appealing to a wider audience. It was therefore decided to establish a British Covenant, modelled on the Ulster example. Long's Union Defence League (and later Lord Robert's League of Covenanters) was entrusted with coordinating the drive for signatories. At a meeting on 12 January 1914, according to Amery, Willoughby de Broke gave his 'passive' approval to the scheme, and thereby the BLSUU became *de facto* absorbed within the British Covenant movement. The new arrangement required the League to scale back some of its more martial aspects and utilise its over four hundred agents for propaganda and signature collection.[132]

The BLSUU's apparent loss of operational autonomy proved to be more illusory than real. A memorandum found in the Milner papers indicates that armed preparation had not been halted. 'In the last resort', it stated, 'the same organization which has been created for the purpose of demonstration could be used to furnish a really effective resistance to the action of the Government, and [stir up] an organised and immediately successful national uprising'.[133] The BLSUU was thus proving to be an invaluable reserve of militaristic instincts and ambitions, and its appeal extended far beyond appearances. Amery, for instance, was taken aback to learn that even his dentist harboured a fervent desire to join the League and fight in Ulster.[134] Even H. A. Gwynne, editor of the *Morning Post*, wrote to Carson expressing his weariness of men who merely advocated decisive action from the comfort of their office chairs, which prompted him to volunteer his own services.[135]

At the beginning of 1914, the BLSUU made a press announcement boasting an enrolment of over thirteen thousand men – a large enough number to allow the organisation to reject those found 'unsuitable' for service. Lord Claud Hamilton, as well as several peers, MPs, military and naval officers, medical professionals, soldiers, sailors, aviators, wireless telegraphists and mechanics had signed the attestation form and joined the ranks. In Liverpool, Birmingham, London and other cities men were carrying out drills. Enthusiasm in Scotland was on the rise daily, and people were drawing parallels with the cause of the Old Covenanters. Anonymous donations poured in.[136] In a newspaper article, Comyn Platt stated that 'we are arming them with the service rifle as quickly as we can. The great difficulty is that so many rifles are wanted in Ulster that we find it difficult to get all we require over here. Some of the biggest manufacturers of arms are full up with orders to Ulster and we naturally can only take the second place'.[137] In response to the BLSUU's announcement, the *War Office Times and Naval Review* wrote:

> if we are to take the League at its face value, it exists for the purpose of fomenting and promoting rebellion in a part of the United Kingdom, it seeks to seduce officers and men of the Army and Navy from their allegiance to the Crown, and it is engaged in procuring and exporting to Ireland rifles, not only wooden, but Martini-Henry, which are intended to be used in resistance to the forces of the Crown detailed by the Executive to enforce the Law. If such a League is a not a criminal organization, then we do not know what criminality means.[138]

Despite the sacrosanct tone of the article, it seems that it failed to rouse the law enforcement and investigative authorities from their apathy. Remarkably, the BLSUU premises at 25 Ryder Street remained untouched. According to historian Charles Townshend, the Asquith government's calm approach to the threat of a civil conflict testified to the pervasive resilience of Liberal assumptions. This *habitus* of trust in the 'absorptive capacity of English consensualism' drove the government perilously close to the brink of catastrophe.[139]

In early February 1914, just before the opening of parliament, Willoughby de Broke, along with Ampthill, Arran and Stanhope, dispatched letters to all the peers, urging them not to accept any compromise to avoid what they deemed 'an act of betrayal'.[140] They asserted that the only genuine alternative to civil war was the dissolution of Parliament. A few days later, Willoughby de Broke proposed amending the Army Annual Act, which governed the discipline and regulation of the Army, as a means to prevent the government from deploying troops to coerce Ulster. The idea was not entirely unprecedented. In 1783/1784, Charles James Fox considered using this strategy as a final resort to overthrow Pitt the Younger's 'mince-pie' administration, and threats to adopt it were made during the reform crisis of 1830–1832. Despite being rarely invoked and its potential subversive implications, amending the Army Annual Act was constitutionally viable. To the dismay of Willoughby de Broke and Milner, Bonar Law decided to abandon his initial 'wicked temptation' and refused to disable the army.[141]

While tampering with the Army Annual Act was the most 'scandalous' strategy, it was not the only one invoked to incapacitate or at least to undermine the military. At the end of 1913, James L. Garvin proposed that 'every Unionist ought to prepare to leave the Territorials. The whole of the Unionists' influence throughout the country ought to be used to prevent recruits from joining it as long as there is the slightest threat of coercion of Ulster'.[142] In January, the Duke of Bedford went so far as to point out that the government lacked enough force to crush the UVF in the 'extremely probable civil war'. The RIC numbered only ten thousand compared with the UVF's hundred thousand members. As a result, Asquith had no choice but to depend on the Army, but there were still significant challenges:

> [since] the greater part was always away, the men on foreign service, while the recruits were at home [...] it was quite easy to calculate that the final figures of the strength of the army would be less than 100,000 in May, and the greater part of it would be boys, far too young for the ghastly work which must go on in Ulster before the Prime Minister had seen this thing through. They could not send the whole British Army into Ireland. They would have to keep above half of it in England and Scotland, and even the force in Ireland would not all be in Ulster, but a big part of it would be elsewhere. The Government would not have a force of more than 15,000 for Ulster [...] It was surely common sense to imagine that Ulster, with 90,000 men and many more in reserve, was not going to confine her resistance to riots in Belfast. It would be a campaign between large, disciplined bodies in the field. It would be a campaign of Civil War.[143]

Around that time, BLSUU military preparations were continuing. Units were being established in Kent and East Sussex, and as part of this effort 'drill instructors and chauffeurs' were being actively sought.[144] 'In the spirit of Lord Carson', the City Companies of Ulster Volunteers in London – enrolled under the auspices of the BLSUU – held their first parade at Chelsea in mid-March.[145] Colonel Hickman, accompanied by Major A. A. C. Nelson and Mr. Hugh B. Ridgway, inspected the BLSUU recruits in Liverpool and Glasgow. In Everton, the majority of the men, many of whom were Army Reservists sporting medals, were equipped with rifles.[146] In Glasgow, where eight volunteer clubs with a total of one thousand members had been established, five companies under the command of Captain George Webb were selected for a display of drill manoeuvres at Protestant Hall, with the leading company equipped with rifles. Volunteers were also inspected in the South Lanarkshire town of Hamilton.[147] Several new clubs were started in Airdrie and Kilmarnock. Meanwhile, Captain William Tillie Dickson, commander of C Company of the Dungannon Battalion thanked Willoughby de Broke for his 'earnest' support.[148]

On 5 March 1914, Augustin Birrell introduced the Home Rule Bill for the third and final time. Four days later, during its second reading, Asquith presented the government's concessions to Ulster. Under the proposed scheme, the electorate in each of the nine counties of Ulster would be able to vote on whether their county should be excluded from the arrangement for six years from the first meeting of the Irish parliament.

Redmond agreed to this scheme. Bonar Law, instead, expressed concerns that if the government insisted on the excluded counties joining the arrangement after six years, the Unionists could not accept the plan. He once again urged an election to address the entire question. Asquith stood firm: the government had no intention of making any additional concessions. At this point, the crisis entered a new phase. On 14 March, the War Office instructed the Commander-in-Chief in Ireland, Sir Arthur Paget, to protect military depots in Ulster from potential raids. At the Curragh barracks, General Hubert P. Gough, Brigadier of the Third Cavalry Brigade, and another fifty-seven officers of his command saw the orders as a move towards coercing Ulster and resigned their commissions. On 21 March, the government gave assurances that the movements ordered were not for repressive purposes but were merely precautionary. Two days later, Colonel J. E. B. Seely, Secretary of War, informed the House of Commons that an inquiry conducted by the Army Council had established that the incident was a misunderstanding. As a result, the officers were directed to rejoin their units and their resignations were formally withdrawn. On the following day, it was disclosed that an Army Council had convened in London and a memorandum had been given to General Gough to take back to Ireland. Signed by Seely, Field Marshal Sir John French, Chief of the Imperial Staff and others, the memorandum stated that while the government retained the right to use all the Crown's forces to maintain order in Ireland or elsewhere, they had 'no intention whatever of taking advantage of this right in order to crush political opposition to the policy and principles of the Home Rule Bill'. Colonel Seely took all the blame for this 'guarantee' and tendered his resignation, which Asquith declined to accept, although he also rejected the 'guarantee', saying that the government would never yield to demands for such assurances 'which, if allowed, would place the Government and the country at the mercy of the Army'. Field Marshal French and Sir John Spencer Ewart, the Adjutant-General, tendered their resignations and stood by their decision, while Colonel Seely resigned from the cabinet. To prevent future misunderstandings, a new Army order was issued explicitly stating that 'An officer or soldier [was] forbidden in the future to ask for assurances as to orders which he may be required to obey'. On 30 March, Asquith announced that he would personally assume the post of Secretary of War. For this to be possible, as mandated by the Place Bill of 1705, he resigned from the House of Commons and sought re-election.[149]

The Curragh incident increased the confidence of Ulster Unionists and further galvanised the BLSUU's activism. The events in Ireland, wrote an *Evening Standard* correspondent, gave a 'great fillip to the Ulster

Volunteer force which [was] being enrolled in England'. This was confirmed by Comyn Platt: 'we cannot possibly deal with all the correspondence that we are receiving from every part of England. Those who have been enrolled want to get off at once for Ulster. All the men in one county are under the county committee, and we shall in due course advise them as to their action. Everything has been considered, and we shall only have 'to give the word'. Drilling is going on night after night'.[150] On 21 March, Willoughby de Broke somewhat bizarrely volunteered his services to General Richardson, telling him that he would 'serve in the ranks or do any duty you wish'. In presenting his credentials, he wrote 'I am a retired Yeomanry Officer, aged 45. I can ride and shoot and have commanded a Squadron of Yeomanry'. Richardson tactfully rejected the offer, and with the assistance of his aide-de-camp, Captain Frank Hall, he let the peer know that his expertise in political matters could be of potentially greater use than his contribution in military affairs. The episode did not bode well for the reputation of the BLSUU, and left some UVF commanders scornfully regarding 25 Ryder Street as a dwelling place of fools.[151]

At the end of March, the new colours of the Glasgow city section of the BLSUU were consecrated. The principal club marched from its headquarters in Cowcaddens to George Square 'headed by a brass band and cheering crowds'. They were joined by five more sections from other districts of the city. The entire battalion, under the command of Captain Webb, proceeded to George Street and High Street, where they gathered at the City Halls' Grand Hall. The front portion of the hall was reserved for the volunteers and one of the sections made an appearance on the stage with rifles shouldered. The Marquis of Graham declared that 'The Volunteers were men of the right stuff [...] All right-thinking people admired those soldiers who had put their consciences before their careers'. Mrs. S. Brown then presented Union Jacks to representatives of the companies. Reverend Professor Cooper, who consecrated the colours, expressed the wish that they might never be unfurled save in a righteous cause. Captain Webb replied that if they were ever called upon to fight for the Protestants of Ulster, they would bring honour and glory to the colours presented to them. A telegram of support was sent to Sir Edward Carson. The volunteers on the platform then presented arms and afterwards marched off bearing the colours aloft while the national anthem was sung. The following day, the various contingents assembled in Blythewood Square and marched to a church service in the City Halls, where Reverend James Brisbie delivered an 'appropriate sermon'.[152] The BLSUU's recruitment efforts in Scotland also benefitted from the formation, from at least the spring of 1913, of 'athletic clubs' for union sympathisers who were training to serve in Ireland. The *Daily Record* estimated the 'strength of the Scottish contingent' as follows:

Glasgow: 1,500
Clydebank: 150
Hamilton and District: 350
Kilmarnock: 120
Coatbridge: 180

In addition to these two thousand three hundred volunteers, Edinburgh was said to have six clubs with a membership of three thousand, while Aberdeenshire had raised three hundred members. Volunteers from Greenock and Ayr and other parts of the country had purportedly enlisted.[153]

During these hectic days, nearly two million British citizens were reported to have signed the Covenant at around ten thousand locations. The declaration of the British Covenant, much diluted from its original draft, was as follows:

> I, ..., shall hold myself justified in taking or supporting any action that may be effective to prevent it (the Home Rule act) being put into operation, and more particularly to prevent the armed forces of the Crown being used to deprive the people of Ulster of their rights as citizens of the United Kingdom.

Many distinguished figures were among the signatories of the 'tempered and guarded' document.[154] On 4 April, the 'British Covenanters' held a massive demonstration in Hyde Park to protest against the use of the armed forces against the people of Ulster. They arranged for several prominent figures, including Carson, Milner, Austen Chamberlain, Long, the Marquess of Londonderry, F. E. Smith, Lord Charles Beresford, Lord Robert Cecil and others, to address the crowd from fourteen platforms strategically positioned in a wide semicircle between the Serpentine and the Bayswater Road. During the event, several processions converged on the centre of the rally from twenty-two different rendezvous points. One of these consisted of members from the Carlton, Junior Carlton, Conservative, Constitutional and Junior Constitutional Clubs, while another comprised members of the Ladies' Imperial Clubs, each of whom carried the national flag. Representatives of the City followed. Then, as *The Times* wrote, 'with soldierly tread, arrived the men of the British League for the Support of Ulster, a serviceable force which divided itself into guards for the each of the platforms'.[155]

Patriotic songs were sung and an abundance of signs, banners and posters were brandished bearing the following inscriptions: 'Why not put these grave matters to the proof by ballots?' 'The hero of Sydney Street wants battleships and bullets', 'Irish Terriers of purest pedigree at the Curragh versus Rats of Whitehall and Patrick Fords of Waterfords', 'An Irish soldier and gentleman saved the Cabinet of Cowards from becoming a Cabinet of Assassins', 'Ulster is right, Ulster will fight', 'God Save the King from domestic traitors, from foreign enemies, above all from the machinations of their ministers'. 'The men who once tried to sell the lion's skin while the beast was still alive were eventually killed while hunting it'.[156] Estimates of the crowd's size varied, with some sources suggesting it reached around two hundred thousand, while the police estimated it to be approximately one hundred thousand. The success had exceeded even 'the most sanguine anticipations' of the British Covenanters.[157]

Following the Curragh incident, the second reading of the Home Rule Bill resumed in a more conciliatory manner. However, Parliament's efforts at compromise seemed to have had no influence on the prevailing sentiment in Ireland. Organisation of the UVF proceeded steadily and instructional camps were set up for the Belfast regiments. On the morning of 25 April, they received information that significant quantities of arms along with ample supplies of ammunition had landed clandestinely at Larne, Bangor, Donaghadee and Belfast during the previous night.[158] Meanwhile, after languishing for several months and alarmed by the government's conciliatory overtures, the Irish Volunteers received a significant boost with a formal endorsement from the Irish Parliamentary party. The organisation's membership subsequently rose to approximately one hundred and ten thousand by the end of May. In June, the Irish Parliamentary party 'usurped' control of the Irish Volunteers and proceeded with an organisational restructuring of the force. With generous contributions from the United States, a considerable fund was raised to purchase arms and equipment, and gun-running operations in the South quickly gained momentum, rivalling those of the UVF.[159]

The acquisition of rifles in both the North and the South gave a substantial new impetus to the BLSUU's recruitment efforts, creating a new heightened sense of urgency among agents and commanders. A manifestation of this zeal was seen in Glasgow, where a mobilisation exercise drew two thousand participants.[160] In Manchester, advances were reported in the organisation of a force predominantly comprising junior Unionists, members of Conservative and Unionist clubs and Orangemen. A notable proportion of these men had soldiering experience, which facilitated the organisation of drilling. The League was structured into companies and sections, each led by a commander, who was also entrusted with the safe keeping of arms, ammunition and equipment.[161] In Leeds, the BLSUU was reportedly making 'considerable progress' and pro-Ulster demonstrations were held.[162] Two days after the Home Rule Bill passed in the House of Commons for the third time, Earl Winterton declared to the Kingston, Surbiton and District Branch of the BLSUU that the League now boasted over sixteen thousand well-trained riflemen ready to embark on a journey to Ulster. Given the improbability of the government allowing such a sizable group to leave the country, he hinted that alternative means would be sought. He also warned that, if necessary, tens of thousands could gather around the House of Commons to exert pressure on the Government to resign.[163]

In early July, Lord Willoughby de Broke made a visit to the Wealdstone camp in London, which was in the No. 1 (West London) area of the BLSUU, where he presented colours to the five hundred enrolled men comprising the group. Most of the men had travelled there to participate in drills and training exercises. The camp was under the command of Colonel A. C. Holland, with Majors Hogg and Hannan serving as company officers, Captain Duke as Adjutant and C. H. Allberry (honorary agent for the area) as Quartermaster Sergeant. During his visit, Lord Willoughby de Broke was accompanied by Lieutenant General Sir Reginald Pole-Carew, Colonel Nicholson and Colonel T. E. Hickman. The enrolled men proudly paraded as Broke presented the colours, which featured a Union Jack and the words 'For King and Union' on a yellow background, and which were blessed by Reverend H. R. Collum. Sir Reginald Pole-Carew took the opportunity to address the men and stress the importance of honing their shooting skills.[164]

At this time, the League boasted twenty thousand members, with about two thousand five hundred in Glasgow, two thousand in Liverpool, eight hundred in Birmingham, eight hundred in Manchester and between three and four thousand in London, while scores of retired officers had signed the BLSUU attestation form. It was made known that the force would be called upon to replace 'the wastages of war'. The new 'supreme commander' was Lieutenant General Sir Reginald Pole-Carew, Liberal Unionist MP for Bodmin with a long military career behind him.[165] He had been commissioned into the Coldstream Guards in 1869 and first saw active service under Lord Roberts in the Afghan campaign of 1879–1880, when he joined the march to Kandahar. In the Egyptian campaign he served as A.D.C. to the Duke of Connaught, and during the Burmese War of 1886 he was military secretary to Lord Roberts and was subsequently made a Companion of the Order of the Bath. For his services during the Boer War, he was awarded the Medal with five Clasps, promoted to Major-General and made a KCB (Knight Commander of the Order of the Bath). He retired from the army in 1906. His appointment as Commander of the BLSUU responded to the League's need to coordinate and control a force that was expanding beyond its initial projections and to establish its prestige. In mid-July, General Pole-Carew inspected the Glasgow Volunteers and told the men that 'the time was now past for talking' and asking them, as he had in London, 'to learn to hit the mark with the rifle'.[166]

264 *The lure of violence*

On 14 July, as the House of Lords unanimously approved the Amending Bill, the BLSUU placed the force in a state of readiness. During the period between the Bill's approval by the Lords and its consideration by the House of Commons, an unsuccessful attempt to find a mutually agreeable solution was made by a conference of party leaders convened by the King at Buckingham Palace. The situation became even more tense when, forty-eight hours later, confrontations erupted between the military and Irish Volunteers during an arms smuggling operation at Howth, resulting in the deaths of two soldiers, a policeman and three volunteers. Upon their return to Dublin, the troops faced hostility from a crowd, which led to three fatalities and thirty-two wounded. The stark contrast between the bloodshed in Dublin and the leniency shown towards the UVF, who regularly paraded with arms, deeply troubled Redmond. In response, on 27 July he made an urgent call to the government to take decisive and drastic measures to address the actions of the troops.

However, the following day, with the UVF and the Irish Volunteers appearing equally unyielding and convinced that civil war was imminent, Austria declared war on Serbia and thus began the conflict into which Britain would be drawn a week later. Domestic disputes were put on hold and at the end of July the House of Commons unanimously agreed to suspend indefinitely debate on the Amending Bill. The BLSUU committee immediately issued a letter to their six hundred agents throughout England, Scotland and Wales urging them to help recruit as many men as possible for the Great War, stating that 'A national emergency is upon us [...] The Ulster and Irish question is dormant for the present'.[167] In the meantime, 'imprisoned by their patriotism' members of the UVF enlisted in Kitchener's army, forming the basis of what historians later referred to as the Covenanting Army: the Thirty-sixth (Ulster) Division.[168] During the war, the UVF rapidly declined but underwent a brief revival in 1920. The BLSUU, instead, fell into oblivion, a poignant testament to the Unionists' loss of composure during the prewar years. As Henry Page Croft recalled, suddenly 'Ireland was forgotten, tariffs were forgotten, all was forgotten, for a cloud hung over the world and the greatest storm of all history was about to break'. All had been for naught.[169]

Notes

1 For a comprehensive collection of political records including speech excerpts, commentary on current politics, parliamentary divisions, highlights from newspapers and speeches, government reports and summaries of magazine contents from the years 1912–1914, refer to *Liberal Magazine* and *Conservative*

Gleanings and Memoranda. Additionally, see John Joseph Horgan, *The Complete Grammar of Anarchy* (Dublin: Maunsel & Company Limited, 1918).

2 See, for example, on the Ulster Defence League, Walter Long, *Memories* (London: Hutchinson & Company, 1923); Sir Charles Petrie, *Walter Long and His Times* (London: Hutchinson & Company, 1936); John Kendle, *Walter Long: Ireland and the Union, 1905–1920* (Montreal: McGill-Queen's University Press, 1992).

3 On the BLSSU, Jackson, *Popular Opposition to Irish Home Rule*; Alan F. Parkinson, *Friends in High Places: Ulster's Resistance to Irish Home Rule, 1912–14* (Belfast: Ulster Historical Foundation, 2012), pp. 193–197; Phillips, 'Lord Willoughby de Broke and the Politics of Radical Toryism, 1909–1914', *Journal of British Studies* 20, no. 1 (1980), pp. 205–224; Thomas C. Kennedy, 'Tory Radicalism and the Home Rule Crisis, 1910–1914: The Case of Lord Willoughby de Broke', *Canadian Journal of History* 37, no. 1 (Spring 2002), pp. 23–40; William S. Rodner, 'Leaguers, Covenanters, Moderates: British Support for Ulster, 1913–1914', *Éire-Ireland* 17, no. 3 (1982), pp. 68–85. More generally, on British perceptions and reactions to Home Rule. G. K. Peatling, *British Opinion and Irish Self-Government, 1865–1925: From Unionism to Liberal Commonwealth* (Dublin: Irish Academic Press, 2001).

4 On the UVF, see Timothy Bowman, *Carson's Army*; Timothy Bowman, 'The Ulster Volunteer Force, 1910–1920: New Perspectives', in Boyce and O'Day, Alan (eds), *The Ulster Crisis*, pp. 247–258; Timothy Bowman, '"The North Began" … But When? The Formation of the Ulster Volunteer Force', *History Ireland* 21, no. 2 (2013), pp. 28–31; Michael Thomas Foy, *The Ulster Volunteer Force: Its Domestic Development and Political Importance in the Period 1913 to 1920* (PhD diss., The Queen's University of Belfast, 1986); Viviana Marsano, *Those Who Wish for Peace Must Prepare for War': The Ulster Volunteer Force and the Home Rule Crisis of 1912–14* (PhD diss., University of California, Santa Barbara, 1997).

5 On the Home Rule Bill, Patricia Jalland, *The Liberals and Ireland: The Ulster Question in British Politics to 1914* (New York: St. Martin's Press, 1980); Jeremy Smith, *The Tories and Ireland, 1910–1914: Conservative Party Politics and the Home Rule Crisis* (Dublin: Irish Academic Press, 2000). For an historical contextualisation, Eugenio F. Biagini, 'The Third Home Rule Bill in British History', in Doherty (ed.), *The Home Rule Crisis*, pp. 412–442.

6 Quoted in *The Liberal Magazine* 20 (1913), p. 29.

7 'Why Not Rebellion', *Belfast Weekly Telegraph*, 17 February 1912.

8 'Ulster's Position Defined', *Belfast Telegraph*, 10 April 1912.

9 The speech is often quoted. See, for example, Dennis Gwyn, *The History of Partition (1912–1925)* (Dublin: Browne and Nolan, 1950), p. 46.

10 Rudyard Kipling, *Rudyard Kipling's Verse* (London: Hodder and Stoughton, 1919), p. 306.

11 Smith, *The Tories and Ireland*, p. 73.

12 'The Ulster Campaign', *Northern Whig*, 21 September 1912.

13 'Not Standing Alone', *Sheffield Daily Telegraph*, 21 September 1912.

14 'The Home Rule Fight', *Belfast News-Letter*, 25 September 1912.
15 *Portadown News*, 21 September 1912.
16 Stewart, *The Ulster Crisis*, p. 63.
17 'Yesterday's Scenes at Portadown', *Daily Mail*, 26 September 1912.
18 'The Ulster Covenant', *Daily Mail*, 30 September.
19 Stewart, *The Ulster Crisis*, pp. 61–66. On the role of women in the UVF, see Marsano, 'Those Who Wish for Peace Must Prepare for War', pp. 304–342.
20 'Address of the Bishop of Derry', *Belfast News-Letter*, 30 September 1913. Previous quotes were reproduced by numerous newspapers. For convenience, refer to Horgan's *The Complete Grammar of Anarchy*, pp. 15–16.
21 Brendan Mac Giolla Choille (ed.), Chief Secretary's Office, Dublin Castle: *Intelligence Notes 1913–16*, preserved in the State Paper Office (Dublin: State Paper Office, 1966), p. 18.
22 On the establishment of a secret UUC defence committee and their early contacts with foreign arms dealers, see Alvin Jackson, *Ireland 1798–1998: War, Peace and Beyond* (Chichester: Wiley-Blackwell, 2010), p. 233. For gun-running activities in 1910–1911, see also Bowman, *Carson's Army*, pp. 140–141.
23 TNA: CO904/182, 'City of Belfast Importation of Arms' by John F. Moriarty, 23 August 1913. For the legal situation on owning and carrying firearms in Britain before the First World War, as well as the importation of arms in Ireland, see Bowman, *Carson's Army*, pp. 135–138; Marsano, 'Those Who Wish for Peace Must Prepare for War', pp. 343–417.
24 *Intelligence Notes 1913–16*, p. 21.
25 Bowman, *Carson's Army*, pp. 34–38. For an outline of the legislation on the whole question of public meetings, private armies, breach of the peace, unlawful assembly, and riot, see Joseph Baker, *The Law of Political Uniforms, Public Meetings and Private Armies* (London: H. A. Just & Co., 1937).
26 In retracing the origins of Ulster Unionist militancy, Bowman emphasises the role of the Young Citizens Volunteer of Ireland (YCVI) in the grassroots 'militaristic' mobilisation that took place right after the Home Rule Bill became a concrete possibility, Bowman, *Carson's Army*, pp. 24–31.
27 Report received from the Deputy Inspector General of the RIC entitled 'Drilling in Ulster'. Lloyd George Papers. House of Lords Record Office (HLRO), C/19/3/5, February 1912.
28 *Intelligence Notes*, p. 25. On the miniature rifle movement, see Chapter 1.
29 Quote in Robert Blake, *Unrepentant Tory* (New York: St. Martin's Press, 1955), p. 129.
30 *Intelligence Notes*, p. 22.
31 Ibid., p. 28.
32 Ibid., p. 32.
33 Ibid., p. 34. On *R v. Meade*, Baker, *The Law of Political Uniforms*, p. 125.
34 *Intelligence Notes*, p. 25.
35 Stewart, *The Ulster Crisis*, p. 122. For a comprehensive analysis of UVF command and control, Bowman, *Carson's Army*, pp. 76–115; Timothy Bowman,

'The Ulster Volunteer Force', in Doherty (ed.), *The Home Rule Crisis*, pp. 312–319.
36 Viscount Castlereagh, 'The Ulster Volunteer Force', *British Review*, July 1914, p. 7.
37 Bowman, *Carson's Army*, pp. 155–157.
38 'Ulster Volunteer Force', *Northern Whig*, 7 October 1913.
39 'Ulster Volunteer Force: Mimic Warfare', *Belfast Telegraph*, 28 July 1913.
40 'The Ulster Volunteers', *The Times*, 10 November 1913.
41 *Intelligence Notes*, p. 28.
42 'Anti-Home Rule Campaign', *Belfast News-Letter*, 4 August 1913.
43 PRONI, D. 1414/12, Herdman papers, letter Carson to Fellow Covenanters.
44 *Intelligence Notes*, p. 29. The Ulster Volunteer Nursing Corps, see Marsano, 'Those Who Wish for Peace Must Prepare for War', p. 176.
45 'Reopening the Campaign', *The Times*, 16 January 1914.
46 'The Volunteers of Ulster', *The Times*, 18 March, 1914.
47 On the social composition of the UVF, Bowman, *Carson's Army*, pp. 45–75.
48 Viscount Castlereagh, 'The Ulster Volunteer Force', p. 4.
49 Bowman, *Carson's Army*, p. 68.
50 Ibid., pp. 24, 30–31.
51 On armed organisation and propaganda, Foy, *The Ulster Volunteer Force*; Foy, 'Ulster Unionist Propaganda against Home Rule 1912–14', *History Ireland* 4, no. 1 (1996), pp. 49–53.
52 Quoted in Bowman, *Carson's Army*, p. 126.
53 *Intelligence Notes*, pp. 30–31, Document signed by John F. Moriarty on 15 September 1913.
54 On the formation of the Irish Volunteers, see F. X. Martin, *The Irish Volunteers, 1913–15* (Dublin: James Duffey, 1963).
55 Hansard, HC Deb Vol. 37, Col. 1938 (1 May 1912).
56 The title of this section is inspired by George Peel, who, in *The Reign of Sir Edward Carson* (London: P. S. King, 1914), referred to the British League for the Support of Ulster and the Union as 'the overseas army'.
57 T. M. Healy, *Letters and Leaders of My Day*, Vol. II (New York: Frederick A. Stokes Company, 1929), p. 535.
58 Comyn Platt to Selborne, September 1912, BLO, Selborne Papers, 77/14–17.
59 Thomas Comyn Platt was the son of vicar. He had entered the Diplomatic Service as an honorary attached in 1894. He was at the British embassy in Istanbul for three years, after which he was employed at the Foreign Office for a year, being subsequently appointed honorary attaché at Athens. In 1897, Platt returned to the Foreign Office, where he was employed on various committee, including the China committee until 18989, in which year he was appointed secretary to the Commissioner of Uganda. After a year in this capacity, he returned to the Foreign Office, where he acted as secretary to the South African Plains Committee, and also temporarily as assistant private secretary to Lord Lansdowne. In 1901, Platt left the Foreign Office and took up politics. He contended the Louth Division of Lincolnshire in

1906 and was defeated by Sir Robert Perks. Platt initiated and organised the Chamberlain Shilling Fund and the Chamberlain annual dinner. He was one of the chief organisers of the Confederacy. Comyn Platt published several books, including *The Turks in the Balkans*. See also Witherell, *Rebel on the Right*, p. 217.

60 Selborne to Comyn Platt, 19 September 1912, in Selborne Papers, 177/18–22. See also Kennedy, 'Tory Radicalism and the Home Rule Crisis', pp. 30–31.
61 Willoughby de Broke to Bonar Law, 19 November 1912, in House of Lords Record Office (HLRO), Andrew Bonar Law Papers, 27/4/74.
62 'Ulster and the Union: The Formation of a New League', *The Times*, 27 March 1913.
63 'Ulster and Home Rule', *The Times*, 28 March 1913.
64 'The British League', *Belfast News-Letter*, 2 April 1913.
65 Stewart, *The Ulster Crisis*, p. 95.
66 'Court Circular', *The Times*, 12 April 1913.
67 'Ulster To-Day and To-Morrow', *The Times*, 9 May 1913.
68 'British League', *Berkshire Chronicle*, 11 April 1913.
69 'To Help Ulster', *Sheffield Daily Telegraph*, 4 April 1913.
70 'One King! One Flag! One Parliament!', *East Anglian Daily Times*, 23 March 1914. See also 'Major C.H. Tippet Killed in Action', *South-West Suffolk Echo*, 21 August 1915.
71 *Yorkshire Who's Who: The County Series of Who's Who in the United Kingdom* (London: Westminster Publishing Company, 1912), p. 278.
72 'Dungannon Rifle Club', *Strabane Weekly News*, 14 February 1914.
73 Frank P. Crozier, *Ireland Forever* (London: Jonathan Cape, 1932), p. 34.
74 Frank P. Crozier, *Impressions and Recollections* (London: T. W. Laurie Limited, 1930), p. 142.
75 See, generally, Charles Messenger, *Broken Sword: The Tumultuous Life of General Frank Crozier 1897–1937* (Barnsley: Pen and Sword, 2013).
76 Bowman, *Carson's Army*, pp. 58–60 and 62.
77 Ibid., p. 59.
78 The Arming of Ulster. Crawford's Account [n.d.]. Craig Papers. PRONI, D 1415/B/36, 27.
79 Stewart, *The Ulster Crisis*, pp. 94–95. Marsano, 'Those Who Wish for Peace Must Prepare for War', pp. 188–190.
80 'Unionists and Ulster', *The Times*, 27 May 1913.
81 'Ulster Will Ffight', *Pall Mall Gazette*, 2 June 1913.
82 'Our London Letter', *Belfast News-Letter*, 4 June 1913. During a parliamentary debate, Chief Secretary for Ireland, Birrell, was queried about the suspected connection between the BLSUU and confiscated rifles in Belfast. He denied having official information about any such link, including inquiries about Lord Farnham's role. Though Irish authorities had conducted their own inquiries, no specific actions were disclosed.
83 Stewart, *The Ulster Crisis*, pp. 132–133.
84 Ibid., pp. 100–102.

85 Hansard, HC Deb Vol. 53, Cols. 1501 (10 June 1913).
86 'Ulster's Armed resistance. A hundred British recruiting centres', *Northern Whig*, 12 June 1913.
87 Hansard, HL Deb Vol. 14, Col. 925 (14 July 1913).
88 'At Craivogan', *Belfast News-Letter*, 14 July 1913.
89 'Belfast Unionist Clubs', *Belfast News-Letter*, 14 July 1913.
90 [title], *Belfast News-Letter*, 15 July 1913.
91 'Progress of Enrolment', *Belfast Weekly News*, 11 September 1913.
92 'Support for Ulster', *The Scotsman*, 14 June 1913.
93 'British League for the Support of Ulster and Union', *Warwick and Warwickshire Advertiser*, 27 September 1913. On the diverse plans of Conservative associations to provide shelter to Ulster refugees, Jackson, *Popular Opposition to Irish Home Rule*, pp. 173 and 234.
94 'Volunteers Meet in Liverpool', *Birmingham Mail*, 30 September 1913.
95 Jackson, *Popular Opposition to Irish Home Rule*, p. 137. On Liverpool during the Home Rule crisis, Dan Jackson, '"Friends of the Union": Liverpool, Ulster and Home Rule, 1910–1914', *Transactions of the Historic Society of Lancashire and Cheshire* 152 (2003), pp. 101–132.
96 Letter from Lord Willoughby de Broke to Andrew Bonar Law, 11 September 1913, in HLRO, Andrew Bonar Law Papers, BL 30/2/10.
97 Letter from Cecil to Willoughby de Broke, 18 September 1913, in HLRO, Willoughby de Broke Papers, WB 6/1.
98 Letter from Willoughby de Broke to Cecil, 21 September 1913, British Library, Cecil Papers, Add Mss 51161.
99 Letter from Willoughby de Broke to the fourth marquess of Salisbury, 29 October 1913, Hatfield House, Salisbury Papers, 73/187. See also Rodner, 'Leaguers, Covenanters, Moderates', pp. 71–72.
100 Letter from Chamberlain to Willoughby de Broke, 23 November 1913, in HLRO, Willoughby de Broke Papers, WB 6/8.
101 Quoted in Phillips, *The Diehards*, p. 154.
102 The Earl Winterton, *Orders of the Day* (London: Cassell, 1953), p. 38.
103 Letter from Saltoun to Willoughby de Broke, 16 January 1914, HLRO, Willoughby de Broke Papers, WB 7/10.
104 Quoted in Buckland, *Irish Unionism*, p. 52.
105 Jackson, *Popular Opposition to Irish Home Rule*, p. 136.
106 'Ulster's Defence', *Pall Mall Gazette*, 10 October 1913.
107 The letter is quoted in Jackson, *Popular Opposition to Irish Home Rule*, p. 155 and Parkinson, *Friends in High Places*, p. 195.
108 'Unionism in East Edinburgh', *The Scotsman*, 7 November 1913.
109 'British League for the Support of the Ulster and the Union', *North Star and Farmers' Chronicle*, 23 October 1913.
110 'The Home Rule Question', *Port-Glasgow Express*, 29 October 1913.
111 Bowman, *Carson's Army*, p. 62.
112 Letter from H. M. Imbert Terry to Andrew Bonar Law, 29 August 1913, in HLRO, Andrew Bonar Law Papers, 30/1.

113 *Daily Telegraph*, 11 December 1913. See also Peel, *The Reign of Sir Edward*, p. 30.
114 'Lord Willoughby and Ulster', *Leamington Spa Courier*, 14 November 1913.
115 'Support Ulster', *The People*, 9 November 1913.
116 'The Irish Crisis', *The Times*, 11 November 1913.
117 'British Ulster Army Forming', *Daily Mirror*, 12 November 1913.
118 'Women to Help Ulster', *Daily Mirror*, 13 November 1913.
119 'Imposing Parade of Volunteers', *Belfast Weekly News*, 25 September 1913.
120 'Arming for the Defence of Ulster', Newcastle *Daily Chronicle*, 25 November 1913.
121 Stewart, *The Ulster Crisis*, pp. 132–133.
122 'Englishmen for Ulster Army', *Pall Mall Gazette*, 19 November 1913.
123 See the compilation of articles published by *The War Office Times and Naval Review*. The journal emphasised the concerning link between the 'Carson movement' and individuals holding commissions. Consequently, the journal recommended discontinuing their payments. It was suggested that if Lord Charles Beresford had realised that engaging in seditious rhetoric could lead to the forfeiture of his £850 annual stipend, as well as his rank and decorations, his enthusiasm for the Ulster cause might have diminished.
124 Circular published in *Daily Mail*, 2 December 1913.
125 'Ulster war call for Britishers here: league, headed by Lord Willoughby de Broke, sends out a startling circular. Wants only fighting men wealthy landowner, here on a visit, is amazed at rebellious tone of the letter', *New York Times*, 1 December 1913.
126 Quotes are respectively in *Liberal Magazine* 21 (1914), pp. 782 and 783; 22 (1915), p. 52.
127 Quoted in Rodner, 'Leaguers, Covenanters, Moderates', p. 76.
128 'Speech by Lord Willoughby de Broke', *Belfast News-Letter*, 18 December 1913.
129 'Arming in England', *Globe*, 6 December 1913.
130 The Letter is printed in Ian Colvin, *The Life of Lord Carson*, vol. II, pp. 241–242, and Stewart, *The Ulster Crisis*, pp. 130–131.
131 Kennedy, 'Tory Radicalism and the Home Rule Crisis', p. 33. The quote from Lord Cecil's letter to Amery, dated 18 January 1914, in Bodleian Library, Milner Papers, Add Mss 689–10.
132 The entire episode has been detailed in Rodner, 'Leaguers, Covenanters, Moderates', pp. 72–77; Kennedy, 'Tory Radicalism and the Home Rule Crisis', pp. 34–35; Gregory D. Phillips, 'Lord Willoughby de Broke and the Politics of Radical Toryism, 1909–1914', *Journal of British Studies* 20 (1980), pp. 209–220; Stewart, *The Ulster Crisis*, pp. 133–135; Thackeray, *Conservatism for the Democratic Age*, pp. 75–76, 78. While there are minor variations, all sources concur with the account of the alliance between Milner and the British League, as outlined by Leo Amery in Leo S. Amery, *My Political Life, Vol. I: England Before the Storm 1896–1914* (London: Hutchinson, 1953).
133 'Memorandum', n.d., unsigned, BLO, Milner Papers (MP), Milner Dep, Add Mss Eng Hist C.689, 178–185.

134 Jackson, *Popular Opposition to Irish Home Rule*, p. 175.
135 Letter from H. A. Gwynne to Sir Edward Carson, 18 February 1914, in PRONI, D/I 507/A/5/1 0.
136 'Support for Ulster', *Northern Whig*, 9 June 1914.
137 'Ulster's Peril', *Pall Mall Gazette*, 14 January 1914.
138 'Wooded Heads and Wooded Guns', *War Office Times and Naval Review*, 15 January 1914.
139 Charles Townshend, *Making the Peace: Public Order and Public Security in Modern Britain* (Oxford: Oxford University Press, 1993), p. 51.
140 Letter circulated to peers, 4 February 1914 in HLRO, Willoughby de Broke Papers, WB 8/5.
141 Jeremy Smith, '"Paralysing the Arm": The Unionists and the Army Annual Act, 1911–14', *Parliamentary History* 15, no. 2 (1996), pp. 191–207.
142 [No title], *Observer*, 30 November 1913.
143 'The Duke of Bedford on "Civil War"', *Bedfordshire Times and Independent*, 16 January 1914.
144 [No title], *Kent & Sussex Courier*, 27 February 1914.
145 'Help for Ulster', *Belfast News-Letter*, 18 March 1914.
146 'Help for Ulster', *Luton Times and Advertiser*, 13 February 1914.
147 'Scottish Support for Ulster', *The Scotsman*, 13 February 1914.
148 'Ulster Volunteer Force: Enthusiastic Proceedings at Dungannon', *Belfast Weekly News*, 12 February 1914.
149 Ian F. W. Beckett (ed.), *The Army and the Curragh Incident, 1914* (London: Army Records Society, 1986).
150 'Ulster's Army: Boom in Recruiting in England', *London Evening Standard*, 24 March 1914.
151 Parkinson, *Friends in High Places*, pp. 95–196.
152 'Consecration of New Colours', *Belfast News-Letter*, 30 March 1914.
153 'The Volunteers: Strength of the Scottish Contingent', *Daily Record and Mail*, 25 March 1914.
154 Rodner, 'Leaguers, Covenanters, Moderates', pp. 78–85.
155 'Great Demonstration in Hyde Park', *The Times*, 6 April 1914.
156 'The Coercion of Ulster', *Belfast News-Letter*, 6 April 1914.
157 For a detailed description of the demonstration in Hyde Park, see Jackson, *Popular Opposition to Irish Home Rule*, pp. 188–195.
158 On the Larne gun-running, see Stewart, *The Ulster Crisis*, pp. 202–207.
159 On the arming of Irish Volunteers, William Henry Kautt, *Arming the Irish Revolution: Gunrunning and Arms Smuggling in Ireland, 1911–1922* (Lawrence, KS: University Press of Kansas, 2021), pp. 20–24.
160 'Ulster Volunteers: Glasgow's Response to Midnight Mobilisation', *London Evening Standard*, 11 May 1914.
161 'Manchester Volunteer for Ulster', *Manchester Courier*, 12 May 1914; 'Ulster's Support: 500 Manchester Recruits Enrolled', *Huddersfield Daily Examiner*, 19 May 1914.
162 [No title], *Exeter and Plymouth Gazette*, 16 June 1914.

163 'The Home Rule Crisis', *Belfast News-Letter*, 27 May 1914.
164 'London Volunteers in Camp: Presentation of Colours at Wealdstone', *Evening Mail*, 3 July 1914.
165 '20,000 Britons Ready', *Weekly Dispatch* (London), 12 July 1914.
166 'Glasgow's Volunteers Parade', *Daily Record*, 11 July 1914.
167 [No title], *Daily Citizen* (Manchester), 7 August 1914.
168 Philip Orr, *The Road to the Somme: Men of the Ulster Division Tell Their Story* (Belfast: Blackstaff Press, 1987). For a critical interpretation of the continuity between UVF and the 36th (Ulster) Division, see Timothy Bowman, 'The Ulster Volunteer Force and the Formation of the 36th (Ulster) Division', *Irish Historical Studies* 32, no. 128 (2001), pp. 498–518.
169 Croft, *My Life of Strife*, p. 84.

Conclusions

Warlike strength of a people is the true reflex
of their moral and mental vigour ...
war is the supreme test of national value. (H. P. Wyatt)[1]

The year 1900 saw the publication of Kenelm D. Cotes's *Social and Imperial Life of Great Britain*. Coming as it did amid the early failures of the Boer War, the book questioned whether decisive battles and 'fortuitous' military genius alone determined a nation's destiny, or whether deeper societal forces were inexorably driving empires towards a ruin that would be ultimately consummated on the battlefield. Embracing French general Louis-Jules Trochu's axiom that '*L'esprit d'une armée est l'esprit même de la nation dont elle sort*' (The spirit of an army is the spirit of the nation from which it springs), Cotes rejected the theory that 'decisive battles' were the primary causes of national disaster. He argued that empires collapsed not merely due to external forces, but because they had already begun to decay from within, eroded by the pernicious effects of internal discord, moral degeneration and corrupted civic virtue and by the perils of complacency and excessive luxury. In nearly seven hundred pages, Cotes contended that the laws of history demonstrated that only martial communities 'where every citizen must be a soldier, and every soldier a citizen' truly preserved their freedom. Yet such freedom, he argued, could only be sustained through unceasing vigilance and a perpetual readiness to defend it. The modern idea of 'national solidarity' had given rise to mass armies of citizen-soldiers, elevating the 'connection between war and the national character' to unprecedented importance. War had therefore become 'an index of the state of the country'. At the same time, Cotes argued that, despite its many evils, war was a necessary force in the 'advancement of civilisation' and that for most societies of the past peace had meant stagnation. War awakened minds from lethargy and spurred ingenuity, it destroyed the 'worn out and effete' and wrought a 'religious' cohesion that transcended egoism and social feuds. In England, he wrote, 'each stage in arming the people is a stage of industrial and constitutional progress'.[2]

The British Right accepted the Darwinist postulate that 'military races' inevitably extinguished their 'less militarised' counterparts. Consequently, history imposed on societies the existential imperative to improve the 'art of war' in order to survive. This implied the preservation of the instincts of self-defence, physical vigour and pugnacity and the cultivation of patriotic virtues and moral strength. The 'fighting qualities of the race' emerged as the definitive criteria by which the vitality of the nation might be judiciously assessed. From this perspective, it is not surprising that the Right reframed the chagrin, astonishment and distress caused by the 'regrettable incidents' of the Boer War into a more comprehensive critique of British modernity. The starting (and central) point for 'national revival' was the rearticulation of a 'higher conception of citizenship'. Since the Right interpreted the relationship between individuals and the nation in 'organicist' terms, this 'higher citizenship' essentially meant the 'consciousness of a common destiny', 'the ideal of social solidarity' and the 'filial obligation of service to the State'.[3]

Higher (or patriotic) citizenship represented the full realisation of an individual's duty to the national community. The employment of force by citizens in defence of the realm was both a legal right and a moral obligation, in line with the overarching principles of self-defence in English law. While the law prohibited assault, it acknowledged that when a person's life, freedom or property was threatened, the law could be temporarily suspended. This right of self-defence was on a par with the concept of national or imperial self-defence. Legally speaking, the latter was simply an extension of the former, meaning that in order to protect the realm, every 'loyal citizen' was not only justified in using force but was indeed bound to do so, even if, under extraordinary circumstances, it might result in death. Following the principle laid down in Rex v. Pinney, the neglect of this duty was considered criminal to the highest degree. Moreover, in addition to invoking the fundamental principle of self-defence, which authorised the use of force in the face of insurrection, riot or any violent challenge to the law, the Right pushed the 'voluntary' principle – already in effect in the Volunteers – to its limit.[4]

The South African military crisis evoked the spectre of military unpreparedness. Well before the Norfolk Commission declared that the militia and Volunteers lacked 'the strength or the military efficiency required to enable them to fulfil the functions for which they exist[ed]', and that it was 'the duty of every citizen of military age and sound physique to be trained for national defence', the debate on the 'military obligations' of citizenship had already been reignited.[5] Although public opinion was that conscription, at least in the form familiar to the continental nations, was 'out of the field of practical politics', the Right insisted that the British had to become a 'race of sharpshooters'. Victory in the impending 'battle for world supremacy' hinged on superior arms and skills in weaponry, and proficiency with the rifle – the primary weapon for the individual soldier – was therefore a duty, one too important to ignore or delegate without exposing the national community to 'manifest danger'. Consequently, the safety, if not the future survival of Britain, did not depend on what laws the government might pass, but on the will of each man to acquire technical knowledge of the rifle, to become skilled in sighting and aiming, in directing and adjusting fire and in all those elements of marksmanship that would enable him to shoot with deadly accuracy. In light of this premise, the 'civilian rifle movement', urged on by Lord Roberts, the Dukes of Norfolk and Westminster, various army officers and a significant portion of the Conservative Party's *jeunesse dorée*, set out to establish miniature rifle ranges in every town and village across Britain. These smaller ranges, intended as substitutes for full-sized or service ranges, would provide citizens with the opportunity to learn the rudiments of rifle shooting. 'By perfecting themselves in the use of the rifle', Lord Roberts wrote in *The Rifleman*, 'They are performing one of the most important duties that pertain to patriotism. It should come as natural to man to shoot as to walk or to run, and as congenial as to play games'.[6] Only through this 'efficient arming' of democracy could the empire be safeguarded. Contrary to previous historical assumptions, the spring and summer of 1905 did not mark the climax of Roberts's obsession with rifle shooting, but rather its beginning. The popularisation of rifle shooting came at the same time as the Right's strenuous appeals to set up extensive marksmanship training in all schools. Headmasters were mostly in favour of making miniature rifle shooting mandatory for all boys aged sixteen and above. The Right viewed the teaching of marksmanship as a 'tolerable' alternative to, though not an equal substitute for universal military training, believing it would cultivate expertise in the grim yet unavoidable art of killing among future generations. While the assertion that the NSL 'carried its propaganda into every nook and corner of England' may seem exaggerated to many historians, there is little doubt that the 'cult of the rifle' – as decried by pacifists – had, by 1914, become an expression of popular militarism and a symptom of a new brand of right-wing activism.[7]

The pressing imperative of national defence imposed on men and boys the practical duty of acquiring marksmanship skills, which would test their 'vocation for killing'. However, as this study has shown, the Right was concerned that the British nation had become 'over-civilised' and was condemned to degeneracy and decline having failed to preserve the 'martial instincts of the race'. In the aftermath of the Boer War, Captain Charles Ross of the Norfolk Regiment remarked, 'Civilization is the triumph of the principle of sentiment [...] over the savage instincts of the human animal. But love and sentiment are out of place in the struggle for existence'. He contended that war signified a regression to nature, where victory was solely determined by 'the exercise of the sterner barbaric qualities'. Ross denounced the 'castrating' effects of modern existence and supported all those organisations that gave 'thought to war, and to the necessity of exercising its thews and sinews'.[8] One of those bodies was the Legion of Frontiersmen, which brought together men hardened at sea, in battle or in the 'remotest outposts of the empire'. These individuals symbolised the attainment of mature manhood – self-sufficient, resilient, courageous, robust, patriotic and resolute. As the product of stern necessity, the frontiersmen displayed all the qualities necessary to secure victory in battle between man and man or nation and nation. The Legion aimed to cultivate among British youth military and quasi-military skills: pathfinding, horsemanship and pack transport, canoe and raft building, boat sailing, motor vehicle operation and maintenance, scouting and reconnaissance, stalking, marksmanship, signalling and first aid. In addition, it popularised 'war games' designed to enhance physical fitness in ways that would benefit future soldiers. The Frontiersmen's reverence for voluntary service and opposition to conscription, rather than marking them as apostates from right-wing orthodoxy, revealed their fundamental alignment with the Right's ideals of duty, sacrifice and military readiness. Not surprisingly, they played an important role in the development of the Boy Scouts, with many Legion members becoming scoutmasters.

Pocock and his fellow frontiersmen insisted on their duty to serve the country in any emergency and frequently offered the War Office their espionage and 'spy hunting' services. They intensified fears of a German invasion – a veritable nightmare in conservative minds. In this respect, the Legion of Frontiersmen was another, perhaps more eccentric symptom of Edwardian society's militarisation. However, this study has demonstrated that the links between the Legion and the political organisations of the 'radical right', particularly after 1910, were stronger than previously thought. The Frontiersmen responded to Leo Maxse's appeal to form an organisation 'to smash up the roving band of turbulent and rowdy Radical Socialists, who have been in the habit of breaking up Unionist and Imperial Meetings now for some years'.[9] In this capacity, they acted as strong-arm security guards at meetings of the Imperial Pioneers or Pioneers of Empire. At the same time, some Frontiersmen were ready 'to take the field' in defence of Ulster and the Union at the perilous peak of the Home Rule Crisis. Although the Legion's aims were initially apolitical – with the leadership prohibiting members from attending political meetings in uniform and distancing the organisation from mercenary activities – there is clear evidence that over time many Frontiersmen adopted a more militant, radical stance.

The Right believed that the survival or death of a nation depended on the extent to which the physical, mental and moral stamina of the people had degenerated. Amidst the early disasters of the Boer War, the controversy over the 'deterioration of the national physique' reached its zenith, and the findings of the Inter-Departmental Committee did little to allay fears that Britain was dying for lack of exertion. One of the factors that the Right identified as undermining the nation's vitality and moral strength was immigration. Immigrants, especially poor Jews from Eastern Europe, were accused of introducing nervous disorders, insanity, feeble-mindedness and an 'excessive amount' of venereal disease into Britain. Purported to be especially prone to criminality and pauperism, immigrants were also said to possess 'inferior' hereditary traits that could potentially weaken the national stock. For the Right, the 'dilution of the race' caused degeneration, and degeneration would, in turn, doom the country to ultimate failure. Taking this perspective, some right-wingers accused German-Jewish financiers of plundering the country, while others stirred the populace's 'instinctive' hatred of Jewish immigrants in the East End of London and other parts of the country. The BBL was the product of these antisemitic and xenophobic expressions. The League's gatherings – regularly attended by prominent right-wing and conservative figures – erupted in scenes of hysterical uproar that some historians have compared to the tumultuous rallies of Oswald Mosley in the late 1930s and the National Front in the 1970s.[10] There were assaults on 'groups of foreigners' and persistent threats of violence. The names of Kishinev, Yekaterinoslav, Kamenetz-Podolsk, Romny, Kremenchug, Chernigov and other cities where anti-Jewish pogroms had occurred, were ominously evoked, and someone even went so far as to hope to witness similar horrors in the streets of England.

The preservation of the 'race' did not only rest on demonising Jews and foreigners and inciting violence against them, it also required the cultivation of what contemporaries called 'physical efficiency'. Research on the NSL, as also confirmed by this book, has indicated that the campaign for 'national service' may have been part of a broader and more widespread movement to secure a general improvement in the 'health of the nation'. According to many right-wing politicians and journalists, whose social analyses drew on theories of evolution and degeneration, the British people had grown weak: their muscles were untrained, their senses were dulled and their attitude to physical exertion was one of distaste. The nation was ageing, while younger, more vigorous powers loomed on the horizon. Military training was seen as a powerful antidote to physical deterioration. The movement for military conscription also had the aim of strengthening national cohesion and efficiency. For the Right, it offered a means to steer the attitudes, aspirations and 'energies' of young Britons along patriotic lines, particularly during a period of heightened social and cultural tensions. In 1912, Lord Milner stated that 'national service' would provide 'a better physique and a more alert mind, discipline, self-control, self-reliance and the habit of orderly cooperation with one's fellows. It would be a form of not only military, but also social reform of the very highest character'.[11] In the spring of 1914, commenting on Willoughby de Broke's quixotic proposal to make military service compulsory for the 'comfortable classes' – generally defined as persons earning over £400 a year – the Duke of Bedford candidly admitted: 'I don't think it would be prudent for me to speak in support of arming and training the classes against the masses, [though] I am strongly in favour of so doing'. What the country needed was a single-minded military efficiency and self-sacrificing discipline.[12]

That part of the Right which was opposed to compulsory universal training for home defence – both because it viewed compulsion as 'an infringement of the rights of free-born Britons' and because of its loyal ties to the reserve forces (militia, yeomanry, volunteers and, later, Haldane's Territorial Force), where it maintained an active involvement – sought to demonstrate the existence of vast untapped 'human capital' that could be mobilised through existing voluntary organisations. It was argued that a strong, well-trained citizenry was fundamental to a healthy national defence, but this would require focussing on the physical and moral development of, in particular, working-class boys. The Boy Scouts, the Girl Guides, the Church Lads' Brigades, the Boys' Brigades and kindred institutions were lauded for teaching discipline, obedience, self-respect, patriotic responsibility and athleticism – all qualities necessary for the interests and safety of Britain. Lord Roberts further advocated a comprehensive plan for training boys in the Cadet Corps. Others on the Right proposed a holistic approach to physical education and military training – one that began with prenatal and early childhood development and progressed systematically through each stage of male physiological maturation. This approach aimed to create a robust national reserve of trained individuals able to contribute to the defence of the nation. The cultivation of martial habits and physical vigour was also manifested in the promotion of wrestling, boxing, martial arts, fencing and combative physical training. The Right exalted the value of hand-to hand-fighting which helped reinforce 'manly' qualities, including aggressiveness, fitness, grit and 'general toughness', and prepared young men for the rigours of combat. In this context, the pacifists were presented as weak, cowardly, unworthy and, most importantly, un-British. To some extent, the British Union of Fascists (BUF) was to reveal itself as the 'natural heir' to these Edwardian codes, practices and aesthetics of hyper-masculinity.[13]

As the book has shown, if the Right believed in the old adage *si vis pacem, para bellum* (if you want peace, prepare for war), it also believed that there were adversaries *intra muros* – these being the 'socialists' who put selfish material and class interests above the sacred rights of the organic whole and threatened to cripple the Nation's economy and society through the weapon of the general strike. After the Liberal landslide and recognition that the new government would strengthen the position of trade unions, strikebreaker William Collison – who had been a tool of employers in their offensive against new unionism since the 1890s – travelled to the United States to learn about methods of industrial espionage and union-busting. His attempt to import these practices to Britain failed, yet the episode reveals how the advance of political and industrial democracy triggered 'authoritarian reflexes' among those 'salaried' defenders of capital who aspired to Pinkertonism and those capitalists whose managerial authority and vested interests were threatened. While employers who denied workers their rights to organise and to collective bargaining made various efforts to deal with unionism – either by forming yellow or company unions or by intensifying their recourse to strikebreakers, court injunctions and lobbying – the general public began displaying an increasing disposition to assert its rights and called upon the government to defend them. The wave of strikes of 1911, with the accompanying intimidations, disorders and riots caused general concern among the property-owning upper and middle classes, who were intensely sensitive to the issue of 'law and order' and particularly receptive to the self-sacrificing qualities of patriotism. The Right seized upon these 'bourgeois' anxieties and the growing disillusionment with the State's ability (or even willingness) to protect life and property and establish industrial peace. Analogies between strikes and warfare emerged naturally. Predictably, instances of 'active' and 'responsible' citizenship devolved into vigilantism. The VPF was, to a certain extent, a paradigmatic example of ultra-nationalists who were not so much reacting to the transgression (or imputed transgression) of social norms or offering assurances of public security, but were rather combatting what they saw as the inherently 'treasonous' nature of strike action. The VPF did not view its violence as illegal or immoral, but rather as an expression of civic patriotic duty.

The VPF and the numerous parapolice corps that emerged in the Edwardian era were a precursor to the form and practices of postwar anti-labour and antisemitic organisations. The frequent overlapping of the leadership and membership of the pre- and post-war groups significantly strengthens this thesis. For instance, having suggested in 1913 that 'any man would be justified in shooting Mr. Asquith', Colonel Sir John Robert Pretyman Newman played a prominent role in forming the Middle Class Union, which was subsequently rebranded as The NCU. On the eve of the 1926 General Strike, a National Guard was formed, which copied almost verbatim the aims and objectives of the VPF. And, much as thirteen years earlier, when Abercorn and his associates refused to tolerate government inactivity in repressing industrial unrest, Colonel Tudor Fitzjohn, one of the founders of the organisation, threatened that, if necessary, his men would take matters into their own hands to prevent the destruction of property and would assume control of the railways, power stations and mining pumps.[14] The continuity between Edwardian forms of right-wing mobilisation and those 'bottom-up' organisations that rallied to quell the 'spirit of sovietism' either constrained the potential growth of fascism or shaped its development by imbuing it with distinctly nativist characteristics.[15]

On the eve of the war, all factions of the Right coalesced around the battle against Irish Home Rule. Ulster resistance had been armed and trained by retired British army officers, and had mustered over one hundred thousand men who had sworn to resist Home Rule to the last man. The Right (along with many radicalised conservatives) embraced what Asquith called 'a complete grammar of anarchy'. It fostered rebellion and sedition at levels unseen for generations. It sabotaged all efforts by party leaders to reach an understanding and a peaceful solution. It dragged the King into party politics and meddled with the army. It endorsed the use of force by facilitating the acquisition of arms and ammunition, and military training. It attempted to raise an army under the distinguished auspices of Lord Willoughby de Broke, which would, upon mobilisation, embark from English and Scottish ports to cooperate with the UVF. This general 'para-militarisation' of politics had no equivalent in Western Europe prior to 1914. When the Southern Irish also began arming and drilling in defence of Home Rule, most Englishmen and foreign observers believed civil war was inevitable. Given all this, it would be far too simplistic to claim that the British Right was in some sense more 'liberal' than its continental counterparts. Moreover, without accounting for the magnitude and far-reaching effects of the First World War, it remains 'incomprehensible' how the question of Home Rule for Ireland – which had 'dazzled, almost blinded' the Conservative leadership before the war – was later embraced by much of the same leadership through the approval of a fourth Home Rule Bill (1920) and the Anglo-Irish Treaty (1921).[16]

In summary, the British Right was convinced that the nation was succumbing to decadence. Britain appeared to have lost faith in its military instincts, its sense of discipline and its solidarity. It had ceased to be attentive to manliness and racial robustness and had, in turn, become oblivious to its imperial destiny. The Right responded to this 'crisis' with measures that were directed not only at challenging the party's traditional policies and attitudes with a more 'radical' vision of conservatism, but also at injecting into society a renewed 'spirit of national consciousness'. This 'palingenetic thrust' included campaigns for military and marksmanship training, the testing of 'racial efficiency', intolerance of the 'enemies' of the organic community and a more general enticement to violence. This effort did not constitute 'proto-fascism', but it certainly led to a suspension of British political civility, the virtues of which had been apparent in public life since the mid-nineteenth century.

Notes

1 Harold Frazer Wyatt was the joint founder and honorary secretary of the Imperial Maritime League. He stood as a National Party candidate in North Leeds in 1918.
2 K. D. Cotes, *Social and Imperial Life of Britain, Vol. I: War and Empire* (London: Grant Richards, 1900), pp. 427–428, 642.
3 Some of these concepts expressed with Hegelian arguments in Arthur Boutwood, *National Revival: A Restatement of Tory Principles* (London: H. Jenkins, 1913). On Boutwood and his influence on Willoughby de Broke, see E. H. H. Green, *Ideologies of Conservatism: Conservative Political Ideas in the Twentieth Century* (Oxford: Oxford University Press, 2002), pp. 46–56.
4 On *Rex v. Pinney*, A. V. Dicey, *Introduction to the Study of the Law of the Constitution*, 4th ed. (London: Macmillan and Co., 1893), in particular 'Note IV – The Right of Self-Defence', pp. 489–497.
5 Report of the Royal Commission on the Militia and Volunteers, pp. 16–19.
6 Quoted in the *Journal of the Royal United Service Institution* 54, no. 54 (July–December 1910), p. 1001.
7 Paul Laity, *The British Peace Movement 1870–1914* (Oxford: Clarendon Press, 2001), pp. 201–206. See also Harry Shaw Perris, *The Cult of the Rifle and the Cult of Peace* (London: T. S. Clark & Company, 1907).
8 Charles Ross, *Representative Government and War* (London: Hutchinson, 1903), pp. 6–7.
9 West Sussex Record Office, Chichester, Maxse Papers 463/t40, W. H. Fisher to Maxse, 20 March 1911, 'Private'. Quoted in Hutcheson, *Leopold Maxse*, p. 390.
10 Cecil Bloom, 'Arnold White and Sir William Evans-Gordon: Their Involvement in Immigration in Late-Victorian and Edwardian Britain', *Jewish Historical Studies* 39 (2004), pp. 153–166.
11 Quoted in Evelyn Wrench, *Alfred, Lord Milner, the Man of No Illusions, 1854–1925* (London: Eyre & Spottiswoode, 1958), p. 278.
12 Quoted in Phillips, *The Diehards*, p. 151.
13 Gottlieb, 'Fascism in Britain', pp. 114–115.
14 Labour Research Department, 'Strike Breaking Organisations', November 1925, pp. 241–245.
15 For a survey of postwar anticommunist and antisocialist organisations, Linehan, *British Fascism*, pp. 38–60.
16 Blake, *The Unknown Prime Minister*, p. 174. On the historical significance and subsequent neglect of the Third Home Rule crisis in British history, see Eugenio Biagini, 'The Third Home Rule Bill in British History', in Gabriel Doherty (ed.), *The Home Rule Crisis, 1912–1914* (Cork: Mercier Press, 2014), pp. 412–442.

Select bibliography

Primary sources

Archives

Bodleian Library, Oxford

Asquith Papers.
Birrell Papers.
Conservative Party Archive.
Gwynne Papers.
Milner Papers.
Primrose League Papers.
Selborne Papers.
Winterton Papers.

British Library

Balfour Papers.
Campbell-Bannerman Papers.
Cecil of Chelwood Papers.
Halsbury Papers.
Long Papers.

House of Lords Record Office

Bonar Law Papers.
Willoughby de Broke Papers.

Liverpool Athenaeum Archive

Civic Service League, Minute Book, Vol. 1 (29 August 1911–19 September 1913).

Select bibliography

National Archives (TNA)

Cabinet Papers

CAB 37/109/30, Drilling in Ulster. [Report of the Deputy Inspector-General of the Royal Irish Constabulary]. Printed or circulated 28 February 1912.
CAB 37/117/82, Illegalities in Ulster (November 1913).
CAB 37/117/85, Further notes from Ulster: [Importation of arms] (December 1913).
CAB 37/117/87, Position of the Army with regard to the situation in Ulster (December 1913).

Colonial Office (CO)

CO 903/17, Chief Secretary's Office, Judicial Division, Intelligence Notes, 1912–1913.
CO 903/18, Chief Secretary's Office, Judicial Division, Intelligence Notes, 1914.
CO 904/27, Ulster Unionists.
CO 904/28/1, Illegal importation and distribution of arms and reports of seizures of arms (1886–1913).
CO 904/28/2, Illegal importation and distribution of arms and reports of seizures of arms (1911/1914).
CC 904/29/1, Gun-running – reports, returns, statements etc. (1914).
CO 904/30–33, Reports, returns and opinions of legal advisors.
CO 904/119, Précis of information received by the Special Branch, Royal Irish Constabulary (RIC) (January–March 1910; June–November 1911; November 1913).
CO 904/120/1, Précis of information received by the Special Branch, Royal Irish Constabulary (RIC) (January–October 1914).
CO 904/122, Drilling of volunteers – Enniskillen Horse.
CO 904/182, Armed meetings, agrarianism, street preaching, drilling, importation of arms – reports, returns and opinions of legal advisors.

Foreign Office

HD 3/139, Secret service funds; gun-running; purchase of presents; payments to agents.
FO 800/111, Miscellaneous S.

Home Office (HO)

HO 45/10666/216733, Volunteer Police Force against strikes including Indian Services Company and for internal duty (1911–1912, 1914).
HO 144/1157/212342, Disturbances: London strikes. Transport and Docks (1911–1912).
HO 144/1211/223877, London Dock and Transport Strike (1912).

HO 144/5491, Intimidation, picketing, etc., during industrial disputes (1911–1926).
RAIL 1057/1643, National Free Labour Association and Free Labour Protection Association (1897–1914).

War Office

WO 32/9087, General and Warlike Stores: Small Arms (Code 45(J)): Proceedings of Miniature Rifle Committee Permission to manufacture.
WO 32/10426, Army organization, Legion of Frontiersmen (Code 14(S)): Recognition of Legion of Frontiersmen. WO 35/209, Military aid to civil powers: Curragh incident: reports and correspondence (March 1914 July 1914).
WO 339/93876, Captain William Mailes POWER Labour Corps (1914–1922).

Modern Record Centre, University of Warwick

The Shipping Federation, Central Executive minutes (1890–1914).
The Shipping Federation, General and Executive Council Meetings (1901–1914).
The Shipping Federation, Emergency committee minutes (1907–1932).
The Shipping Federation, Printed transactions of the Federation, committee agendas and reports (1908–1914).

Public documents: Parliament

Parliamentary Debates, 4th Series (1903–1909).
Parliamentary Debates, Commons, 5th Series (1909–1914).
Parliamentary Debates, Lords, 5th Series (1901–1914).

Parliamentary Papers (Reports of Commissioners et al.)

Report of His Majesty's Commissioners Appointed to Inquire into the Military Preparations and Other Matters Connected with the War in South Africa, Cd. 1789. London, 1903.
Report of the Royal Commission on Alien Immigration, Cd. 1741. London, 1903.
Report of the Royal Commission on Physical Training (Scotland), Cd. 1507, 1508. London, 1903.
Report of the Inter-Departmental Committee on Physical Deterioration, Cd. 2175, 2210, 2186. London, 1904.
Report of the Royal Commission on the Militia and Volunteers …: [and Minutes of Evidence and Appendices], Cd. 2061. London, 1904.
Employment of Military during Railway Strike: Correspondence between Home Office and Local Authorities. London, 1911.
Report on Certain Disturbances at Rotherhithe on June 11th 1912, and Complaints against the Conduct of the Police in Connection Therewith, Cd 6367. London, 1912–1913.
Report upon the present disputes affecting transport workers in the Port of London and on the Medway, Cd, 6229. London, 1913.

Newspapers

Belfast News-Letter
Birmingham Gazette
Birmingham Post
Daily Chronicle
Daily Dispatch
Daily Express
Daily Graphic
Daily Herald
Daily Mail
Daily Mirror
Daily News
Daily Telegraph
Dundee Advertiser
East London Observer
Eastern Daily Press
Eastern Morning News
Edinburgh Evening Dispatch
Edinburgh Evening News
Evening News
Evening Standard
Glasgow Herald
Globe
Irish Times
Leeds Mercury
Liverpool Courier
Liverpool Daily Post and Mercury
Manchester Courier
Manchester Evening News
Manchester Guardian
Morning Advertiser
Morning Post
Newcastle Daily Chronicle
Northern Daily Telegraph
Northern Whig
Pall Mall Gazette
Scotsman
Sheffield Daily Telegraph
South Wales Daily News
Sporting Life
Sportsman
Staffordshire Sentinel
Standard
Times

Western Daily Press
Western Mail
Westminster Gazette
Yorkshire Daily Observer
Yorkshire Post

An important number of London and local newspapers have been surveyed through https://www.britishnewspaperarchive.co.uk/

Selected journals and magazines

The Anti-Socialist
Army and Navy Gazette
British and Tariff Reform Journal
British Medical Journal
Bystander
Clarion
Conservative Agents' Journal
Contemporary Review
Empire Illustrated
Fortnightly Review
Free Labour Gazette
Free Labour Press and Industrial Review
Gleanings and Memoranda
Graphic
Illustrated London News
Justice
Labour Leader
Liberal Magazine
Liberty
Nation
The Nation in Arms
National Review
National Service League Journal
Navy League Journal
The Nineteenth Century and After
Primrose League Gazette
Quarterly Review
Review of Reviews
Spectator
Volunteer Service Gazette and Military Dispatch

Secondary sources

Books

Adams, R. J. Q., and Philip Poirer, *The Conscription Controversy in Great Britain, 1900–1918* (London: Macmillan, 1987).

Allen, W. E. D., *Fascism in Relation to British History and Character* (London: BUF Publications, 1933).

Amery, Julian, *The Life of Joseph Chamberlain*. Vol. IV: *1901–1903: At the Height of His Power* (London: Macmillan, 1951).

Amery, Leopold S., *My Political Life*, 3 vols (London: Hutchinson, 1953–1955).

Askwith, Lord, *Industrial Problems and Disputes* (London: John Murray, 1920).

Baker, Joseph, *The Law of Political Uniforms, Public Meetings and Private Armies* (London: H. A. Just & Co., 1937).

Ball, Stuart R., *The Conservative Party and British Politics, 1902–1951* (London: Longman, 1995).

Ball, Stuart R., and Anthony Seldon, *Conservative Century: The Conservative Party since 1900* (Oxford: Oxford University Press, 1994).

Ball, Stuart R., and Anthony Seldon, *Recovering Power: The Conservatives in Opposition since 1867* (Basingstoke: Macmillan, 2005).

Beckett, Ian F. W. (ed.), *The Army and the Curragh Incident* (London: Army Records Society, 1986).

Beckett, Ian F. W. (ed.), *Citizens Soldiers and the British Empire, 1837–1902* (London: Routledge, 2012).

Beckett, Ian F. W., *Riflemen Form: A Study of the Rifle Volunteer Movement 1859–1908* (Havertown: Pen and Sword, 2007).

Belchem, John, *Class, Party, and the Political System in Britain in Britain, 1867–1914* (Oxford: Oxford University Press, 1990).

Benewick, Robert, *Political Violence & Public Order: A Study of British Fascism* (London: Allen Lane, 1984).

Beresford, Admiral Lord, *The Memoirs of Admiral Lord Beresford*, 2 vols (London: Methuen, 1914).

Bernstein, George L., *Liberalism and Liberal Politics in Edwardian England* (London: Allen & Unwin, 1986).

Biagini, Eugenio F., and Alastair Reid, *Currents of Radicalism: Popular Radicalism, Organised Labour and Party Politics in Britain; 1850–1914* (Cambridge: Cambridge University Press, 1991).

Blake, Robert, *The Conservative Party from Peel to Churchill* (London: Eyre & Spottiswoode, 1970).

Blake, Robert, *The Unknown Prime Minister: The Life and Times of Andrew Bonar Law 1858–1923* (London: Eyre & Spottiswoode, 1955).

Blake, Robert, and Hugh Cecil (eds), *Salisbury: The Man and His Policies* (London: Macmillan, 1987).

Blewett, Neal, *The Peers, the Parties, and the People: The General Elections of 1910* (London: Macmillan, 1972).

Bourke, Joanna, *Working Class Cultures in Britain, 1890–1960: Gender, Class, and Ethnicity* (London: Routledge, 1994).
Bowman, Timothy, *Carson's Army: The Ulster Volunteer Force, 1910–22* (Manchester: Manchester University Press, 2017).
Boyce, David George, *The Irish Question and British Politics, 1868–1986* (Basingstoke: Macmillan, 1988).
Boyce, David George, and Alan O'Day (eds), *Defenders of the Union: A Survey of British and Irish Unionism, since 1801* (London: Routledge, 2001).
Boyce, David George, and Alan O'Day (eds), *The Ulster Crisis 1885–1921* (Basingstoke: Macmillan, 2006).
Briggs, Asa, and John Saville (eds), *Essays in Labour History* (London: Macmillan, 1971).
Brown, Kenneth D. (ed.), *Essays in Anti-Labour History: Responses to the Rise of Labour in Britain* (London: Macmillan, 1974).
Brown, Raymond, *Waterfront Organization in Hull, 1870–1900* (Hull: University of Hull, 1974).
Brunton, Sir Lauder, *Collected Papers on Physical and Military Training* (published privately, 1915).
Buckland, Patrick, *Irish Unionism: Ulster Unionism and the Origins of Northern Ireland 1886–1922* (Dublin: Gill and Macmillan, 1972).
Bunyan, Tony, *The History and Practice of the Political. Police in Britain* (London: Quartet Books, 1977).
Burgess, Keith, *The Challenge of Labour* (London: Croom Helm, 1980).
Burgess, Keith, *The Origins of British Industrial Relations* (London: Croom Helm, 1975).
Butler, Lord (ed.), *The Conservatives: A History from Their Origins to 1965* (London: George Allen & Unwin, 1977).
Campbell, John, *F. E. Smith: First Earl of Birkenhead* (London: Jonathan Cape, 1983).
Cannadine, David, *The Decline and Fall of the British Aristocracy* (New York: Anchor Books, 1992).
Chamberlain, Austen, *Politics from the Inside: An Epistolary Chronicle* (London: Cassell, 1936).
Clarke, Ignatius F., *Voices Prophesying War: Future War 1763–1984* (Oxford: Oxford University Press, 1966).
Clarke, Peter F., *Lancashire and the New Liberalism* (Cambridge: Cambridge University Press, 1971).
Clegg, Hugh A., *A History of British Trade Unions Since 1889, Vol. 11: 1911–1933* (Oxford: Clarendon Press, 1985).
Clegg, Hugh A., Alan Fox and Arthur F. Thompson, *A History of British Trade Unions since 1889, Vol. 1: 1889–1910* (Oxford: Clarendon Press, 1964).
Coates, Ken, and Anthony Topham (eds), *The Making of the Labour Movement: The Formation of the Transport and General Workers' Union, 1870–1922* (Nottingham: Spokesman, 1994).

Coetzee, Frans, *For Party or Country: Nationalism and the Dilemmas of Popular Conservatism in Edwardian England* (Oxford: Oxford University Press, 1990).
Coleman, Bruce, *Conservatism and the Conservative Party in Nineteenth-Century Britain* (London: Edward Arnold, 1988).
Collison, William, *The Apostle of Free Labour* (London: Hurst and Blackett, 1913).
Colls, Roger, and Phillip Dodd (eds), *Englishness: Politics and Culture 1880–1920* (London: Croom Helm, 1986).
Colvin, Ian, *The Life of Lord Carson*, Vol. II (London: Victor Gollancz, 1934).
Cornfield, Susie, *The Queen's Prize: The Story of the National Rifle Association* (London: Pelham Books, 1987).
Croft, Henry Page, *My Life of Strife* (London: Hutchinson, 1948).
Cronin, James E., and Jonathan Schneer (eds), *Social Conflict and the Political Order in Modern Britain* (London: Croom Helm, 1982).
Crossick, Geoffrey (ed.), *The Lower Middle Class in Britain 1870–1914* (London: Croom Helm, 1977).
Crouzet, François, *The Victorian Economy* (London: Methuen, 1982).
Cunningham, Hugh, *The Volunteer Force: A Social and Political History, 1859–1908* (London: Croom Helm, 1975).
Dangerfield, George, *The Strange Death of Liberal England* (New York: Capricorn, 1961).
Darlington, Ralph, *Labour Revolt in Britain 1910–14* (London: Pluto Press, 2023).
Davidson, Roger, *Whitehall and the Labour Problem in Late-Victorian and Edwardian Britain* (London: Croom Helm, 1985).
Dicey, Albert V., *England's Case against Home Rule* (London: John Murray, 1886).
Doherty, Gabriel (ed.), *The Home Rule Crisis 1912–14* (Cork: Mercier Press, 2014).
Duncan, Robert, and Arthur J. McIvor (eds), *Militant Workers: Labour and Class Conflict on the Clyde, 1900–1950* (Edinburgh: John Donald, 1992).
Dutton, David, *'His Majesty's Loyal Opposition': The Unionist Party in Opposition, 1905–1915* (Liverpool: Liverpool University Press, 1992).
Emsley, Clive, *The English and Violence since 1750* (London: A&C Black, 2005).
Emsley, Clive, *The English Police: A Political and Social History* (London: Harvester Wheatsheaf, 1991).
Ensor, Sir Robert C. K., *England 1870–1914* (Oxford: Oxford University Press, 1936).
Farr, Barbara Storm, *The Development and Impact of Right-Wing Politics in Britain, 1903–1932* (New York: Garland, 1987).
Fleming, Neil, *Britannia's Zealots, Vol. 1: Tradition, Empire and the Forging of the Conservative Right* (London: Bloomsbury Publishing, 2020).
Francis, Martin, and Ina Zweiniger-Bargielowska (eds), *The Conservatives and British Society, 1880–1990* (Cardiff: University of Wales Press, 1996).
Fraser, Sir Thomas, *The Military Danger of Home Rule for Ireland* (London: Murray, 1912).
Friedberg, Aaron L., *The Weary Titan: Britain and the Experience of Relative Decline, 1895–1905* (Princeton, NJ: Princeton University Press, 1989).

Gainer, Bernard, *The Alien Invasion: The Origins of the Alien Act of 1905* (London: Heinemann, 1972).
Garrard, John A., *The English and Immigration: 1880–1910* (London: Oxford University Press, 1971).
Gartner, Lloyd P., *The Jewish Immigrant in England, 1870–1914* (London: Allen & Unwin, 1960).
Garvin, James L., and Julian Amery, *The Life of Joseph Chamberlain*, 6 vols (London: Macmillan, 1932–1969).
Geary, Roger, *Policing Industrial Disputes: 1893–1985* (Cambridge: Cambridge University Press, 1985).
Gillis, John R., *The Militarization of the Western World* (New Brunswick, NJ: Rutgers University Press, 1989).
Gollin, Alfred M., *Balfour's Burden: Arthur Balfour and Imperial Preference* (London: Anthony Blond, 1965).
Gollin, Alfred M., *Proconsul in Politics: A Study of Lord Milner in Opposition and in Power* (London: Anthony Blond, 1964).
Grainger, J. H., *Patriotisms: Britain, 1900–1939* (London: Routledge, 1986).
Gray, John, *City in Revolt: James Larkin and the Belfast Dock Strike of 1907* (Belfast: Blackstaff Press, 1985).
Green, E. H. H., *The Crisis of Conservatism: The Politics, Economics and Ideology of the Conservative Party, 1880–1914* (London: Taylor and Francis, 1995).
Green, E. H. H., *Ideologies of Conservatism: Conservative Political Ideas in the Twentieth Century* (Oxford: Oxford University Press, 2002).
Halevy, Elie, *Imperialism and the Rise of Labour 1895–1905* (London: Ernest Benn, 1929).
Halevy, Elie, *The Rule of Democracy 1905–1914* (London: Ernest Benn, 1934).
Hamilton, Lord George, *Parliamentary Reminiscences and Reflections*, 2 vols (London: John Murray, 1917–1922).
Hattersley, Roy, *The Edwardians* (London: Little Brown, 2004).
Hearnshaw, F. J. C., *Conservatism in England* (London: Macmillan, 1933).
Heathcote Heindel, Richard, *The American Impact on Great Britain, 1898–1914: A Study of the United States in World History* (New York: Octagon Books, 1968).
Heffer, Simon, *The Age of Decadence: Britain 1880 to 1914* (New York: Random House 2017).
Hendley, Matthew, *Organized Patriotism and the Crucible of War: Popular Imperialism in Britain, 1914–1932* (Montreal: McGill-Queen's University Press, 2012).
Hobson, J. A., *The Psychology of Jingoism* (London: Grant Richards, 1901).
Hobson, J. A., *Traffic in Treason: A Study of Political Parties* (London: T. F. Unwin, 1914).
Holmes, Colin, *Anti-Semitism in British Society 1876–1939* (London: Edward Arnold, 1979).
Hutcheson Jr., John A., *Leopold Maxse and the National Review* (New York: Garland, 1989).

Hynes, Samuel, *The Edwardian Turn of Mind* (Princeton, NJ: Princeton University Press, 1968).
Jackson, Alvin, *Home Rule: An Irish History, 1800–2000* (London: Phoenix, 2004).
Jackson, Alvin, *Ireland, 1798–1998* (Oxford: Oxford University Press, 1999).
Jackson, Alvin, *Sir Edward Carson* (Dublin: Dundalgan Press, 1993).
Jackson, Alvin, *The Ulster Party: Irish Unionists in the House of Commons, 1884–1911* (London: Oxford Historical Monographs, 1988).
Jackson, Daniel M., *Popular Opposition to Irish Home Rule in Edwardian Britain* (Liverpool: Liverpool University Press, 2009).
Jalland, Patricia, *The Liberals and Ireland: The Ulster Question in British Politics to 1914* (Brighton: Harvester Press, 1980).
Jeal, Tim, *Baden-Powell* (London: Hutchinson, 1989).
Jeffery, Keith and Peter Hennessy, *States of Emergency: British Governments and Strike Breaking since 1919* (London: Routledge & Kegan Paul, 1983).
Johnson, Matthew, *Militarism and the British Left, 1902–1914* (Basingstoke: Palgrave Macmillan, 2013).
Jones, Karen, Giacomo Macola and David Welch (eds), *A Cultural History of Firearms in the Age of Empire* (Farnham: Ashgate, 2013).
Kennedy, Paul M., *The Rise of the Anglo-German Antagonism 1860–1914* (London: Allen & Unwin, 1980).
Kennedy, Paul M., and Anthony Nicholls (eds), *Nationalist and Racialist Movements in Britain and Germany Before 1914* (London: Macmillan, 1981).
Knowles, K. G. J. C., *Strikes: A Study in Industrial Conflict* (Oxford: Basil Blackwell, 1952).
Langford, Paul, *Englishness Identified: Manners and Character 1650–1850* (Oxford: Oxford University Press, 2000).
Laurie-Fletcher, Danny, *British Invasion and Spy Literature, 1871–1918* (London: Palgrave Macmillan, 2019).
Lawrence, Jon, *Speaking for the People: Party, Language and Popular Politics in England, 1867–1914* (Cambridge: Cambridge University Press, 1998).
Laybourn, Keith, *A History of British Trade Unionism, c. 1770–1990* (Stroud: Sutton, 1992).
Leng, Phillip J., *The Welsh Dockers* (Ormskirk: G. W. and A. Hesketh, 1981).
Linehan, Thomas, *British Fascism, 1918–1939: Parties, Ideology and Culture* (Manchester: Manchester University Press, 2000).
Linz, Juan J., and Alfred Stepan (eds), *The Breakdown of Democratic Regimes* (Baltimore, MD: Johns Hopkins University Press, 1979).
Long, Walter, *Memories* (London: Hutchinson, 1922).
Lovell, John, *Stevedores and Dockers: A Study in Trade Unionism in the Port of London, 1870–1914* (London: Macmillan, 1968).
Lunn, Kenneth (ed.), *Hosts, Immigrants and Minorities* (Folkestone: Dawson, 1980).
Lunn, Kenneth, and Richard C. Thurlow (eds), *British Fascism: Essays on the Radical Right in Interwar Britain* (London: Croom Helm, 1980).
Malmesbury, Lord (ed.), *The New Order: Studies in Unionist Policy* (London: Francis Griffiths, 1908).

Mangan, J. A., 'Manufactured' Masculinity: Making Imperial Manliness, Morality and Militarism (London: Routledge, 2012).

Mangan, J. A., and James Walvin, Manliness and Morality: Middle-Class Masculinity in Britain and America, 1800–1940 (New York: St. Martin Press, 1987).

Mantoux, Paul, and Maurice Alfassa, La Crise du Trade-Unionisme (Paris: Arthur Rousseau 1903).

MacDonald, Robert H., The Language of Empire: Myths and Metaphors of Popular Imperialism, 1880–1918 (Manchester: Manchester University Press, 1994).

MacKenzie, John M. (ed.), Imperialism and Popular Culture (Manchester: Manchester University Press, 1986).

Marsh, Peter, The Discipline of Popular Government: Lord Salisbury's Domestic Statecraft 1881–1902 (Hassocks: Harvester, 1978).

Mates, Lewis, The Great Labour Unrest: Rank-and-File Movements and Political Change in the Durham Coalfield (Manchester: Manchester University Press, 2016).

Mayer, Arno, The Persistence of the Old Regime: Europe to the Great War (New York: Pantheon, 1981).

McCarthy, Terry, The Great Dock Strike 1889 (London: Weidenfeld and Nicholson, 1989).

McDowell, Robert B., British Conservatism 1832–1914 (London: Faber & Faber, 1959).

McIvor, Arthur J., Organised Capital: Employers' Associations and Industrial Relations in Northern England, 1880–1939 (Cambridge: Cambridge University Press, 1996).

McKibbin, Ross, The Evolution of the Labour Party 1910–24 (Oxford: Oxford University Press, 1974).

McKibbin, Ross, Ideologies of Class: Social Relations in Britain, 1880–1950 (Oxford: Oxford University Press, 1990).

McNeill, Ronald, Ulster's Stand for Union (London: John Murray, 1922).

Messenger, Charles, Broken Sword: The Tumultuous Life of General Frank Crozier 1897–1937 (Barnsley: Pen and Sword, 2013).

Middlemas, Keith, Politics in Industrial Society: The Experience of the British System Since 1911 (London: Andre Deutsch, 1979).

Miller, Stephen M., Volunteers on the Veld: Britain's Citizen-Soldiers and the South African War, 1899–1902 (Norman, OK: University of Oklahoma Press, 2007).

Mommsen, Wolfgang J., and Hans-Gerhard Husung (eds), The Development of Trade Unionism in Great Britain and Germany 1880–1914 (London: Allen and Unwin, 1985).

Morgan, Jane, Conflict and Order: The Police and Labour Disputes in England and Wales, 1900–1939 (Oxford: Oxford University Press, 1987).

Morgan, Kenneth, The Age of Lloyd George: The Liberal Party and British Politics, 1890–1929 (London: Allen and Unwin, 1978).

Morris, A. J. A., The Scaremongers: The Advocacy of War and Rearmament, 1896–1914 (London: Routledge & Kegan Paul, 1984).

Ommundsen, Harcourt, and Ernest Herbert Robinson, *Rifles and Ammunition and Rifle Shooting* (London: Cassell, 1915).
Neal, Frank, *Sectarian Violence: The Liverpool Experience, 1819–1914* (Liverpool: Newsham, 2003).
Nowell-Smith, Simon (ed.), *Edwardian England 1901–1914* (Oxford: Oxford University Press, 1964).
O'Day, Alan (ed.), *The Edwardian Age: Conflict and Stability 1900–1914* (London: Macmillan, 1979).
O'Gorman, Frank, *British Conservatism: Conservative Thought from Burke to Thatcher* (London: Longman, 1986).
Offer, Avner, *Property and Politics, 1870–1914: Landownership, Law, Ideology, and Urban Development in England* (Cambridge: Cambridge University Press, 1981).
Palme Dutt, Rajani, *Fascism and Social Revolution* (London: Martin Lawrence, 1934).
Palmer, Stanley H., *Police and Protest in England and Ireland, 1780–1950* (Cambridge: Cambridge University Press, 1988).
Pearson, Chad, *Reform or Repression: Organizing America's Anti-Union Movement* (Philadelphia, PA: University of Pennsylvania Press, 2016).
Peatling, G. K., *British Opinion and Irish Self-government, 1865–1925: From Unionism to Liberal Commonwealth* (Dublin: Irish Academic Press, 2001).
Peel, George, *The Reign of Sir Edward Carson* (London: P. S. King, 1914).
Pelling, Henry, *The Origins of the Labour Party 1880–1900* (London: Macmillan, 1954).
Pelling, Henry, *Social Geography of British Elections 1885–1910* (London: Macmillan, 1967).
Penn, Alan, *Targeting Schools: Drill, Militarism and Imperialism* (Portland, OR: Woburn Press, 1999).
Phelps Brown, Henry, *The Growth of British Industrial Relations: A Study from the Standpoint of 1906–1914* (London: Macmillan, 1959).
Phelps Brown, Henry, *The Origins of Trade Union Power* (Oxford: Oxford University Press, 1986).
Phillips, Gordon, and Noel Whiteside, *Casual Labour: The Unemployment Question in the Port Transport Industry, 1880–1970* (Oxford: Clarendon Press, 1985).
Phillips, Gregory D., *The Diehards: Aristocratic Society and Politics in Edwardian England* (Cambridge, MA: Harvard University Press, 1979).
Pick, Daniel, *Faces of Degeneration: A European Disorder, C.1848–1918* (Cambridge: Cambridge University Press, 1989).
Playne, Caroline, *The Pre-War Mind in Britain* (London: George Allen & Unwin, 1928).
Pocock, Geoffrey A., *For Adventure and for Patriotism: 100 Years of the Legion of Frontiersmen* (Chichester: Phillimore, 2004).
Pocock, Geoffrey A., *Outrider of Empire: The Life and Adventures of Roger Pocock (1865–1941)* (Edmonton: University of Alberta Press, 2007).
Powell, David, *The Edwardian Crisis: Britain, 1901–1914* (Basingstoke: Macmillan, 1996).

Powell, Leslie H., *The Shipping Federation: A History of the First Sixty Years, 1890–1950* (London: Shipping Federation, 1950).
Price, Richard N., *An Imperial War and the British Working Class* (London: Routledge & Kegan Paul, 1972).
Price, Richard N., *Masters, Unions and Men: Work Control in Building and the Rise of Labour, 1830–1914* (Cambridge: Cambridge University Press, 1980).
Prior, Christopher, *Edwardian England and the Idea of Racial Decline* (Basingstoke: Palgrave, 2013).
Pugh, Martin, *The Making of Modern British Politics 1867–1939* (Oxford: Basil Blackwell, 1982).
Pugh, Martin, *The Tories and the People 1880–1935* (Oxford: Basil Blackwell, 1985).
Ramsden, John, *The Age of Balfour and Baldwin 1902–1940* (London: Longman, 1978).
Read, Donald (ed.), *Edwardian England* (London: Groom Helm, 1982).
Reid, Alastair, *Social Classes and Social Relations in Britain, 1850–1914* (Basingstoke: Macmillan, 1992).
Richter, Donald C., *Riotous Victorians* (Athens, OH: Ohio University Press, 1981).
Rosenthal, Michael, *The Character Factory: Baden-Powell and the Origins of the Boy Scout Movement* (New York: Pantheon, 1986).
Russell, Alan K., *Liberal Landslide: The General Election of 1906* (Newton Abbot: David & Charles, 1973).
Scally, Robert J., *The Origins of the Lloyd George Coalition: The Politics of Social Imperialism 1900–1918* (Princeton, NJ: Princeton University Press, 1975).
Searle, Geoffrey R., *Eugenics and Politics in Britain, 1900–1914* (Leiden: Noordhoff International Publishing, 1976).
Searle, Geoffrey R., *The Quest for National Efficiency* (Oxford: Basil Blackwell, 1971).
Semmel, Bernard, *Imperialism and Social Reform: English Social-Imperial Thought 1895–1914* (Cambridge, MA: Harvard University Press, 1960).
Shadwell, Arthur, *Industrial Efficiency* (London: Longmans, 1913).
Shee, George Richard Francis, *The Briton's First Duty: The Case for Conscription* (London: Grant Richards, 1901).
Smith, Jeremy, *The Tories and Ireland, 1911–1914* (Dublin: Irish Academic Press, 2001).
Smith, Paul (ed.), *Lord Salisbury on Politics* (Cambridge: Cambridge University Press, 1972).
Spargo, John, *Syndicalism, Industrial Unionism and Socialism* (New York: Huebsch, 1913).
Springhall, John O., *Youth, Empire and Society: British Youth Movements, 1883–1940* (London: Croom Helm, 1977).
Springhall, John O., Brian Fraser and Michael Hoare, *Sure and Steadfast: A History of the Boys' Brigade 1883–1983* (London: Collins, 1983).
Stewart, A. T. Q., *The Ulster Crisis: Resistance to Home Rule, 1912–1914*, first published 1967 (London: Blackstaff, 1997).

Strachan, Hew, *The Politics of the British Army* (Oxford: Oxford University Press, 1997).
Sykes, Alan, *The Radical Right in Britain: Social Imperialism to the BNP* (Basingstoke: Palgrave, 2005).
Sykes, Alan, Tariff Reform in British Politics 1903–1913 (Oxford: Oxford University Press, 1979).
Tanner, Duncan, *Political Change and the Labour Party, 1900–1918* (Cambridge: Cambridge University Press, 1990).
Thackeray, David, *Conservatism for the Democratic Age: Conservative Cultures and the Challenge of Mass Politics in Early Twentieth Century England* (Manchester: Manchester University Press, 2013).
Thompson, Paul, *The Edwardians: The Remaking of British Society* (London: Weidenfeld & Nicholson, 1975).
Townshend, Charles, *Making the Peace: Public Order and Public Security in Modern Britain* (Oxford: Oxford University Press, 1993).
Townshend, Charles, *Political Violence in Ireland: Government and Resistance since 1848* (Oxford: Clarendon Press, 1984).
Vance, Norman, *The Sinews of the Spirit: The Ideal of Christian Manliness in Victorian Literature and Religious Thought* (Cambridge: Cambridge University Press, 1985).
Wedgwood, Cicely V., *The Last of the Radicals: Josiah Wedgwood, M.P.* (London: Cape, 1951).
Weinberger, Barbara, *Keeping the Peace? Policing Strikes in Britain, 1906–1926* (Oxford: Berg, 1991).
Wheatcroft, Geoffrey, *The Strange Death of Tory England* (London: Penguin, 2005).
Wilkinson, Glenn R., *Depictions and Images of War in Edwardian Newspapers, 1899–1914* (Basingstoke: Palgrave, 2003).
Wilkinson, Spenser, *Thirty-Five Years: 1874–1909* (London: Constable, 1933).
Williams, Rhodri, *Defending the Empire: The Conservative Party and British Defence Policy, 1899–1915* (New Haven, CT: Yale University Press 1991).
Willoughby de Broke, Lord, *The Passing Years* (London: Constable, 1924).
Winterton, Lord, *Pre-War* (London: Macmillan, 1932).
Witherell, Larry L., *Rebel on the Right: Henry Page Croft and the Crisis of British Conservatism, 1903–1914* (Newark, NJ: Associated University Press, 1997).
Wrigley, Chris J. (ed.), *A Companion to Early Twentieth Century Britain* (Oxford: Blackwell 2003).
Wrigley, Chris J. (ed.), *A History of British Industrial Relations*, Vol. 1, 1875–1914 (Hassocks: Harvester, 1982).
Zebel, Sydney H., *Balfour: A Political Biography* (Cambridge: Cambridge University Press, 1973).
Ziblatt, Daniel, *Conservative Parties and the Birth of Democracy* (Cambridge: Cambridge University Press, 2017).
Zweiniger-Bargielowska, Ina, *Managing the Body: Beauty, Health, and Fitness in Britain 1880–1939* (New York: Oxford University Press, 2010).

Book chapters and articles

Adams, R. J. Q., 'The National Service League and Mandatory Service in Edwardian Britain', *Armed Forces & Society* 12, no. 1 (1985): 53–74.
Adams, W. S., 'British Reactions to the 1905 Russian Revolution', *The Marxist Quarterly* 3 (1955): 173–185.
Alderman, Geoffrey, 'The National Free Labour Association', *International Review of Social History* 21 (1976): 309–336.
Auld, John W., 'The Liberal Pro-Boers', *Journal of British Studies* 14, no. 2 (1975): 78–101.
Auspos, Patricia, 'Radicalism, Pressure Groups, and Party Politics: From the National Education League to the National Liberal Federation', *Journal of British Studies* 20 (1980): 184–204.
Bean, Ron, 'Employers' Associations in the Port of Liverpool, 1890–1914', *International Review of Social History* 21 (1976): 358–376.
Best, Geoffrey, 'Militarism and the Victorian Public School', in Brian Simon and Ian Bradley (eds), *The Victorian Public School* (Dublin: Gill & Macmillan, 1975), 129–146.
Best, Geoffrey, 'The Militarization of European Society, 1870–1914', in John R. Gillis (ed.), *The Militarization of the Western World* (New Brunswick, NJ: Rutgers University Press, 1989), 13–29.
Blanch, Michael, 'British Society and the War', in Peter Warwick (ed.), *The South African War* (London: Longman, 1980), 210–238.
Blanch, Michael, 'Imperialism, Nationalism and Organized Youth', in John Clarke, Charles Critcher, and Richard Johnson (eds), *Working-Class Culture* (London: Hutchinson, 1979), 103–120.
Blewett, Neal, 'Free Fooders, Balfourites, Wholehoggers: Factionalism Within the Unionist Party, 1906–10', *Historical Journal* 11 (1968): 95–124.
Boyce, George, 'British Conservative Opinion, the Ulster Question, and the Partition of Ireland 1912–21', *Irish Historical Studies* 65 (1970): 89–112.
Boyle, Thomas, 'The Liberal Imperialists 1892–1906', *Bulletin of the Institute of Historical Research* 52 (1979): 48–82.
Bristow, Edward J., 'The Liberty and Property Defence League and Individualism', *Historical Journal* 18 (1975): 761–789.
Brown, Kenneth D., 'The Trade Union Tariff Reform Association 1904–1913', *Journal of British Studies* 9 (1970): 141–153.
Burgess, M. D., 'Lord Rosebery and the Imperial Federation League 1884–1893', *New Zealand Journal of History* 13 (1979): 166–181.
Clarke, Peter F., 'The Electoral Position of the Liberal and Labour Parties 1910–1914', *English Historical Review* 90 (1975): 828–836.
Coetzee, Frans, and Marilyn Shevin Coetzee, 'Rethinking the Radical Right in Germany and Britain Before 1914', *Journal of Contemporary History* 21 (1986): 515–537.
Cornford, James, 'The Transformation of Conservatism in the Late Nineteenth Century', *Victorian Studies* 7 (1963–1964): 35–66.

Cronin, James E., 'Strikes and Power in Britain, 1870–1920', *International Review of Social History* 32 (1987): 144–167.

Cunningham, Hugh, 'The Language of Patriotism, 1750–1914', *History Workshop Journal* 12, autumn (1981): 8–33.

Daunton, Martin J., 'Inter-Union Relations on the Waterfront: Cardiff 1888–1914', *International Review of Social History* 22 (1977): 350–378.

Desmarais, Ralph, 'Lloyd George and the Development of the British Government's Strikebreaking Organization', *International Review of Social History* 20 (1975): 1–15.

Dutton, David, 'Unionist Politics and the Aftermath of the General Election of 1906: A Reassessment', *Historical Journal* 22 (1979): 861–876.

Dutton, David, 'The Unionist Party and Social Policy 1906–1914', *Historical Journal* 24 (1981): 871–884.

Fleming, Neil, 'The Imperial Maritime League: British Navalism, Conflict, and the Radical Right, c.1907–1920', *War in History* 23, no. 3 (2016): 296–322.

Fletcher, Barbara, 'The Government Were Determined to Make the Men as Strong as the Masters ... The Experience of the Shipping Federation, 1906 to 1910', *Maritime Policy and Management* 11, no. 4 (1984): 261–268.

France, John, 'Salisbury and the Unionist Alliance', in Robert Blake and Hugh Cecil (eds), *Salisbury: The Man and His Policies* (Basingstoke: Macmillan, 1987), 219–251.

Fraser, Peter, 'The Liberal Unionist Alliance: Chamberlain, Hartington, and the Conservatives 1886–1904', *English Historical Review* 77 (1962): 53–78.

Fraser, Peter, 'Unionism and Tariff Reform: The Crisis of 1906', *Historical Journal* 5 (1962): 149–166.

Fraser, Peter, 'The Unionist Debacle of 1911 and Balfour's Retirement', *Journal of Modern History* 35 (1963): 354–365.

French, David, 'Spy Fever in Britain 1900–1915', *Historical Journal* 21 (1978): 355–370.

French, David, 'The Edwardian Crisis and the Origins of the First World War', *International History Review* 4 (1982): 207–221.

Geyer, Michael, 'The Militarization of Europe, 1914–1945', in John R. Gillis (ed.), *The Militarization of the Western World* (New Brunswick, NJ: Rutgers University Press, 1989), 65–102.

Gilbert, Bentley B., 'Health and Politics: The British Physical Deterioration Report of 1904', *Bulletin of the History of Medicine* 39 (1965): 145–153.

Glickman, Harvey, 'The Toryness of English Conservatism', *Journal of British Studies* 1 (1961–1962): 111–143.

Godfrey, Emelyne, 'Urban Heroes Versus Folk Devils: Civilian Self-Defence in London (1880–1914)', *Crime, Histoire & Sociétés/Crime, History & Societies* 14, no. 2 (2010): 5–30.

Gordon, Michael, 'Domestic Conflict and the Origins of the First World War: The British and German Cases', *Journal of Modern History* 46 (1974): 191–226.

Green, E. H. H., 'Radical Conservatism: The Electoral Genesis of Tariff Reform', *Historical Journal* 28 (1985): 667–692.

Green, S. J. D., 'In Search of Bourgeois Civilisation: Institutions and Ideal in Nineteenth Century Britain', *Northern History* 28 (1992): 228–247.

Harrison, William, 'The British Press and the Russian Revolution of 1905–1907', *Oxford Slavonic Papers* (New Series), 7 (1974): 75–95.

Hendley, Matthew, '"Help Us to Secure a Strong, Healthy, Prosperous and Peaceful Britain": The Social Arguments of the Campaign for Compulsory Military Service in Britain, 1899–1914', *Canadian Journal of History* 30, no. 2 (1995): 261–288.

Hitchner, Thomas, 'Edwardian Spy Literature and the Ethos of Sportsmanship: The Sport of Spying', *English Literature in Transition, 1880–1920* 53, no. 4 (2010): 413–430.

Holmes, R. F. G., '"Ulster Will Fight and Ulster Will Be Right": The Protestant Churches and Ulster's Resistance to Home Rule, 1912–14', in W. J. Sheils (ed.), *The Church and War: Studies in Church History* (London: Basil Backwell, 1983), 321–335.

Holton, Bob, 'Syndicalism and Labour on Merseyside, 1906–14', in Harold R. Hikins (ed.), *Building the Union: Studies in the Growth of the Workers' Movement, Merseyside, 1756–1967* (Liverpool: Toulouse Press for Liverpool Trades Council, 1973), 121–150.

Hooper, Alan, 'From Liberal-Radicalism to Conservative Corporatism: The Pursuit of Radical Business', in Richard Bellamy (ed.), *Victorian Liberalism: Nineteenth-Century Political Thought and Practice* (London: Routledge, 1990), 193–212.

Humphries, Michael, 'The Eyes of an Empire: The Legion of Frontiersmen, 1904–14', *Historical Research* 85, no. 227 (2012): 133–158.

Jackson, Daniel M., 'Friends of the Union: Anti-Home Rule Demonstrations in Liverpool, 1912–1914', *Transactions of the Historic Society of Lancashire and Cheshire* 152 (2003): 101–132.

Johnson, Sam, '"Trouble Is Yet Coming!": The British Brothers League, Immigration and Anti-Jewish Sentiment in London's East End, 1901–1903', in Robert Nemes and Daniel Unowsky (eds), *Sites of European Antisemitism in the Age of Mass Politics, 1880–1918* (Waltham: Brandeis University Press, 2014), 137–156.

Jones, James R., 'England', in Hans Rogger and Eugen Weber (eds), *The European Right: A Historical Profile* (Berkeley, CA: University of California Press, 1966), 29–70.

Jones, Spencer, '"Shooting Power": A Study of the Effectiveness of Boer and British Rifle Fire, 1899–1914', *British Journal for Military History* 1, no. 1 (2014): 29–44.

Kennedy, Thomas C., '"The Gravest Situation of Our Lives": Conservatives, Ulster, and the Home Rule Crisis, 1911–1914', *Éire-Ireland: A Journal of Irish Studies* 36, no. 2 (2001): 67–82.

Kennedy, Thomas C., 'Tory Radicalism and the Home Rule Crisis, 1910–1914: The Case of Lord Willoughby de Broke', *Canadian Journal of History* 37, no. 1 (spring 2002): 23–40.

Maguire, Richard C., '"The Fascists ... Are ... to Be Depended Upon": The British Government, Fascists and Strike-Breaking during 1925 and 1926', in Nigel Copsey and Dave Renton (eds), *British Fascism, the Labour Movement and the State* (Basingstoke: Palgrave Macmillan, 2005), 6–26.

Mason, John W., 'Political Economy and the Response to Socialism in Britain 1870–1914', *Historical Journal* 23 (1980): 565–587.

McIvor, Arthur J., 'Employers' Organisations and Strikebreaking in Britain, 1880–1914', *International Review of Social History* 29, no. 1 (1984): 1–33.

Meachan, Standish, '"The Sense of an Impending Clash": English Working-Class Unrest before the First World War', *The American Historical Review* 77, no. 5 (December 1972): 1343–1364.

Melby, Christian K., 'Empire and Nation in British Future-War and Invasion-Scare, 1871–1914', *The Historical Journal* 63, no. 2 (03) (March 2020): 389–410.

Pellew, Jill, 'The Home Office and the Aliens Act, 1905', *The Historical Journal* 32, no. 2 (1989): 369–385.

Phillips, Gregory D., 'Lord Willoughby de Broke and the Politics of Radical Toryism, 1909–1914', *Journal of British Studies* 20 (1980): 205–224.

Ridley, Jane, 'The Unionist Social Reform Committee, 1911–1914: Wets Before the Deluge', *Historical Journal* 30 (1987): 391–413.

Rodner, William S., 'Leaguers, Covenanters, Moderates: British Support for Ulster, 1913–1914', *Éire-Ireland* 17, no. 3 (1982): 68–85.

Rubinstein, William D., 'Henry Page Croft and the National Party 1917–22', *Journal of Contemporary History* 9 (1974): 129–148.

Saluppo, Alessandro, 'Strikebreaking and Anti-Unionism on the Waterfront: The Shipping Federation, 1890–1914', *European History Quarterly* 49, no. 4 (2019): 570–596.

Saluppo, Alessandro, 'Vigilant Citizens: The Case of the Volunteer Police Force, 1911–14', in Matteo Millan and Alessandro Saluppo (eds), *Corporate Policing, Yellow Unionism, and Strikebreaking, 1890–1930* (Abingdon: Routledge, 2020), 222–241.

Searle, Geoffrey R., 'The Edwardian Liberal Party and Business', *English Historical Review* 98 (1983): 28–60.

Sires, R. V., 'Labour Unrest in England, 1910–1914', The *Journal of Economic History* 15, no. 3 (September 1955): 246–266.

Soloway, Richard, 'Counting the Degenerates: The Statistics of Race Deterioration in Edwardian England', *Journal of Contemporary History* 17 (1982): 137–164.

Stearn, Roger T., '"The Last Glorious Campaign": Lord Roberts, The National Service League and Compulsory Military Training, 1902–1914', *Journal of the Society for Army Historical Research* 87, no. 352 (2009): 312–330.

Stevens, Keith G., 'The Shensi Relief Column and the Legion of Frontiersmen, China Command, 1911–12', *Journal of the Royal Asiatic Society Hong Kong Branch* 51 (2011): 171–206.

Stocker, Paul, 'Importing Fascism: Reappraising the British Fascisti, 1923–1926', *Contemporary British History* 30, no. 3 (2016): 326–348.

Stokes, Eric, 'Milnerism', *Historical Journal* 5 (1962): 47–60.

Stubbs, John, 'The Impact of the Great War on the Conservative Party', in Chris Cook and Gillian Peele (eds), *The Politics of Reappraisal 1918–1939* (New York: St. Martin's Press, 1975), 14–38.

Summers, Anne, 'Militarism in Britain Before the Great War', *History Workshop* 1 (1976): 104–123.

Sykes, Alan, 'The Confederacy and the Purge of the Unionist Free Traders 1906–1910', *Historical Journal* 18 (1975): 349–366.

Sykes, Alan, 'The Radical Right and the Crisis of Conservatism Before the First World War', *Historical Journal* 26 (1983): 661–676.

Thackeray, David, 'Rethinking the Edwardian Crisis of Conservatism', *The Historical Journal* 54, no. 1 (March 2011): 191–213.

Voeltz, Richard A., '"A Good Jew and a Good Englishman": The Jewish Lads' Brigade, 1894–1922', *Journal of Contemporary History* 23, no. 1 (1988): 119–127.

Wald, Kenneth D., 'Class and the Vote Before the First World War', *British Journal of Political Science* 8 (1978): 441–457.

Warren, Allen, 'Sir Robert Baden-Powell, the Scout Movement and Citizen Training in Great Britain, 1900–1920', *English Historical Review* 101 (1986): 376–398.

Wilkinson, Paul, 'English Youth Movements, 1908–30', *Journal of Contemporary History* 4, no. 2 (1969): 3–23.

Williams, Rhodri, 'Arthur James Balfour, Sir John Fisher and the Politics of Naval Reform, 1904–10', *Historical Research* 60 (1987): 80–99.

Wrigley, Chris J., 'In the Excess of Their Patriotism: The National Party and Threats of Subversion', in C. J. Wrigley (ed.), *Warfare, Diplomacy and Politics: Essays in Honour of A. J. P. Taylor* (London: Hamish Hamilton, 1986), 93–119.

Zebel, Sydney H., 'Fair Trade: An English Reaction to the Breakdown of the Cobden Treaty System', *Journal of Modern History* 12 (1940): 161–185.

Zebel, Sydney H., 'Joseph Chamberlain and the Genesis of Tariff Reform', *Journal of British Studies* 1 (1967): 131–157.

Zweiniger-Bargielowska, Ina, 'Building a British Superman: Physical Culture in Interwar Britain', *Journal of Contemporary History* 41, no. 4 (2006): 595–610.

Theses

Allison, Michael J., *The National Service Issue 1899–1914*. PhD diss., University of London, 1975.

Foy, Michael T., *The Ulster Volunteer Force: Its Domestic Development and Political Importance in the Period 1913 to 1920*. PhD diss., The Queen's University of Belfast, 1986.

Hamilton, W. Mark, *The Nation and the Navy: Methods and Organisation of British Navalist Propaganda 1889–1914*. PhD diss., University of London, 1977.

Hebert, Raymond G., *Syndicalism and Industrial Strife 1910–1912: The Significance of the Cambrian Combine Strike, Liverpool General Transport Strike and London Dock Strikes as Barometers for a Better Understanding of the 'Labour Unrest 1910–1912' in the British Isles*. PhD diss., University of Maryland, 1975.

Holt, Charles E., *English Liberals and Russia 1895–1907*. PhD diss., University of Kentucky, 1976.

Leon, Claire Katherine, *Special Constables: An Historical and Contemporary Survey*. PhD diss., University of Bath, 1973.
Lunn, Kenneth, *The Marconi Scandal and Related Aspects of British Anti-Semitism, 1911–1914*. PhD diss., University of Sheffield, 1978.
Marsano, Viviana, *'Those Who Wish for Peace Must Prepare for War': The Ulster Volunteer Force and the Home Rule Crisis of 1912–1914*. PhD diss., University of California – Santa Barbara, 1996.
Pratten, John D., *The Reaction to Working Class Unrest 1911–1914*. PhD diss., Sheffield University, 1975.

Index

Action Française 5
Aerial League of the British Empire 15
air guns 42, 59–60, 102
Akers-Douglas, Aretas, first Viscount Chilston 139–140, 151
Aliens Act (1905) 22, 139–142
  impact on British Brothers' League (BBL) agitation 141–142
Aliens' Defence League 131
Amalgamated Society of Railway Servants (ASRS) 188, 190, 202
Amery, Leo 43, 52, 73, 255–256
Anglo-Irish Treaty (1921) 280
Anglo-Saxon race 7–8, 274
  contrasted with immigrant population 125, 128–129, 136, 277
  degeneration, risk of 21–24, 66, 118–119, 127, 133–134, 144, 149–152, 154–158, 162, 165–166, 277
  see also anti-alienism; British Brothers' League (BBL); eugenics; physical training; social degeneration
anti-alienism 119–129, 140–142
  England for the English (slogan) 22
  see also antisemitism; British Brothers' League (BBL); immigration
Anti-Socialist Union (ASU) 15, 19
anti-unionism 14, 17, 25, 131, 176–187 *passim*
  see also Collison, William; National Free Labour Association (NFLA); Shipping Federation; Volunteer Police Force (VPF)

antisemitism 2, 10–11, 119–122, 126, 129–131, 133–137
  Marconi Scandal 9, 142, 238
  Plunderbund and conspiracy theories 9–10, 130, 277
  Pogroms, threats of 277
  see also anti-alienism; British Brothers' League (BBL); immigration
army
  Army officers in the Ulster Volunteer Force (UVF) 230–231, 253–254
  use of troops in industrial disputes 190
  see also Boer War (1899–1902); Curragh incident; National Service League (NSL); Territorial Army
Army Annual Act (1911–1914) 257
Army Council (1904) 21, 60, 92, 101, 103, 110, 259
Army Motor Reserve (Volunteer Motor Corps) 100
Army Ordnance Department 40
Arnold-Forster, Hugh Oakeley 52–53
Asquith, Herbert Henry 8, 221, 237, 247, 252, 254–255, 257–259, 279–290
Association for Preventing the Immigration of Destitute Aliens 119
Astor, William Waldorf 49, 51–52
Australia 24, 55, 66, 73
  Defence Acts (1903–1914) 34n.71
  Immigration Restriction Act (1901) 126, 139
Automobile Association and Motor Union 194

Bachelor's Walk massacre 264
Baden-Powell, Robert, first Baron Baden-Powell 107, 161–164
Baillie-Grohman, William Adolphe 39
Balfour, Arthur James 56, 117, 136, 140, 142, 145, 155, 157, 165
Balfour, Gerald, second Earl of Balfour 123, 131–133
Ballymena 223
Ballyroney 223, 225
Balmoral (Belfast) 235–236
Bambatha rebellion (1906) 95
Banister, Joseph 133–134
Barrow, Gen. Edmund 56–57
Bartitsu 24, 167
Batty Tuke, Sir John 159
Beatty v. Gilbanks (1892) 188
bellicism 71
Belfast
  Belfast Dock and Carters Strike (1907) 189
  role in gun-running and arms logistics 229, 244
  shipyard workers and unionised labour 234–235
  see also Home Rule crisis (1912–1914); Ulster Volunteer Force (UVF)
Belloc, Hilaire 10, 11
Beresford, Lord Charles 56, 70, 157, 238, 243, 261, 270n.123
Birchenough, Sir John Henry, first Baronet 146
  see also Macclesfield Patriotic Association
Birmingham 42, 45, 47, 53, 59, 62, 96–98, 102, 109, 229, 242, 250, 252, 256, 263
Birmingham Small Arms Company 68, 84n.157
Birrell, Augustine 61, 258, 268n.82
Bisley ranges 38, 49, 61–62
  Miniature Bisley 48–50, 66
Black and Tans 27, 240
Blumenfeld, Ralph David 105
Boer War (1899–1902)
  Black Week 36, 38–39
  deficiencies in preparedness and physical fitness 107, 118, 143–144
  disparity in marksmanship between British and Boer forces 38–40

impact on military reform 15, 20, 52, 87
influence on the Right 3, 6, 20, 22, 51
see also army; civilian rifle movement; Legion of Frontiersmen; marksmanship training
Bonar Law, Andrew 2, 26, 221–222 227, 237, 247, 251–252, 255, 257, 259
Boulangerism 9
Bowman, Timothy 241
boxing 24, 102, 167, 205, 278
Boy Scouts 15, 21, 73, 75, 107–108, 161–163, 235, 276, 278
  see also Baden-Powell, Robert; Legion of Frontiersmen; militarism; youth organisations
Boyne, Battle of (1690) 223
Boys' Brigade 40–41, 64, 147–148, 226
Boys' Life Brigade 148–149
Brabazon, Reginald, twelfth Earl of Meath 40, 44, 46, 56–57, 90, 149, 155–157, 167
Brett, Reginald, second Viscount Esher 90, 111n.3
  Lord Esher's Committee [on the Reconstitution of the War Office] 52
Bright, John 7
Brighton 97, 99, 242
Britain
  analogies with the fall of the Roman empire 57, 117, 124, 162
  decline, relative 1
  modernity 1, 15, 274
  world position 3, 6, 9, 149
British Brothers' League (BBL) 5, 17, 22, 118
  antisemitism and racial demagoguery 121–122, 126, 129–131, 133–137
  comparison with British Union of Fascists (BUF) 143, 277
  mass rallies, propaganda and connection with Conservative politicians 120–142 *passim*
  paramilitary organisation 120–121
  violence and intimidation 122, 125, 131, 135
  see also Aliens Act (1905); anti-alienism; antisemitism; immigration
British Covenant 27, 256, 261–262

British Empire
  problems of defending 15, 87
  training for imperial defence 16, 20–22, 43, 55, 57–58, 69, 87–88, 90, 96–97, 143–145, 149, 163
  model of imperial citizenship 156–157
  Right, defence of imperial unity 5, 7, 10, 11, 18, 19, 110, 220–221, 251
  see also Anglo-Saxon race; Boer War; Home Rule crisis (1912–1914)
British Empire Union 211
British League for the Support of Ulster and the Union (BLSUU) 5, 8, 17, 27, 220–221
  firearms procurement 241–243
  military preparations 252, 256, 258, 260, 262–263
  recruitment 27, 239–242, 250–251, 253–254, 256, 263
  refusal of prominent Unionists to join 247–249
  relationship with British Covenant 255–256
  remobilisation for World War I 264
  threats of civil war 236–237, 243, 247, 249, 254–255, 257–258
  see also Home Rule crisis (1912–1914); Ulster Volunteer Force (UVF); Verney, Richard, nineteenth Baron Willoughby de Broke
British Medical Journal, The 155
British Rifle League 44–45, 48–49
British Rifle Union 45
British Union of Fascists (BUF) 277–278
Broadbent, William 159
Brodrick, St John, first Earl of Midleton 52
Brook-Ascough, Henry 45
Brown, Henry Phelps 14, 29n.7
Brudenell-Bruce, George, sixth Marquess of Ailesbury 90
Brunton, Thomas Lauder, first Baronet
  concern about physical deficiency 154
  military training in schools 40, 154
  promotion of physical preparedness 159–162
  see also National League for Physical Education and Improvement (NLPEI)

Bulkley Mackworth-Praed, Sir Herbert, first Baronet 37
Bull, William 109, 157, 200, 241
Bunyan, Tom 190

Cadet Corps 40, 54, 56, 60–61, 69, 154, 156, 278
Caine, Thomas H. H. 133
Camelots du Roi 5
Campbell-Bannerman, Sir Henry 59, 182
Canada 53, 55, 66, 144, 240
Cannadine, David 13
Cantlie, Sir James 150
Carlile, William Warrand 181
Carnegie, Andrew 179
Carpenter, William Boyd (Bishop of Ripon) 155, 159
Carson, Edward, Baron Carson
  chairmanship of the Ulster War Committee 142
  Ulster Unionism 8, 26, 221–236 *passim*, 255–256, 258, 260–261
  see also Home Rule crisis; Ulster Volunteer Force (UVF)
Cauvin, Antoinette (Madame Sorgue) 204
Cecil, Hugh, first Baron Quickswood 8, 9
Cecil, Robert, first Viscount Cecil of Chelwood 222, 247, 261
Chamberlain, Austen 249, 261
Chamberlain, Joseph 2
  campaign for imperial preference 7–8, 11
  immigration 119
Chamberlain, Neville 165
Chesterton brothers (Cecil and George) 10–11
Chicago 48, 180, 183–185
Childers, Erskine 105–106
Christian manliness 147–148
Church Lads' Brigade 47, 64, 147–148, 235, 278
Churchill, Winston 9, 140, 190, 194, 198–199, 223, 227
Citizen Army 24, 66
Citizen Guard 211
citizenship
  higher conception of 274
  ideals of patriotism 4, 149, 151, 156–157, 176–177, 180, 183,

citizenship: ideals of patriotism (cont.) 188, 192, 195–196, 198–199, 203, 205, 208
  military obligations 19, 20, 24, 36, 37, 51, 72, 75–76, 87, 93, 108, 274
  property defence 177, 190, 211
  see also civilian rifle movement; Legion of Frontiersmen; Volunteer Police Force (VPF)
Citizens' Industrial Alliance of Great Britain 177, 183, 186
Citizens' Industrial Association (CIA) 186
Citizens' Industrial Association of America (CIAA) 180, 181–184, 186
Citizens' League of Law and Order 209
Civic Service League (CSL) 177, 197
citizen-soldier ideal 19, 37, 41, 57, 90, 97, 273
  see also citizenship; militarism; nationalism
Civilian Force see Volunteer Police Force (VPF)
civilian rifle movement
  complement to conscription 20, 37, 51, 55, 57, 69, 76
  geographical spread 37
  schoolboys' rifle practice 40–41, 60–61
  wartime training contribution 20, 76
  women's participation 53, 60, 72–73, 75
  see also Roberts, Frederick, first Earl Roberts; Society of Miniature Rifle Clubs (SMRC)
Clarke, Charles Carlos 243, 251
Clements, Charles, fifth Earl of Leitrim 238
Cobdenism
  critique of 7, 9, 14
Coetzee, Frank 15–16
Coglan Horsfall, Thomas 146, 150–152
Coleraine 223
collectivism 7, 25, 193
Collison, William 177–187, 279
  see also Citizens' Industrial Alliance of Great Britain; National Free Labour Association (NFLA)
Comyn Platt, Thomas 237, 239, 256, 260, 267–8n.59
Committee of Imperial Defence 52, 54, 57, 70, 105

compulsory military service
  campaigns promoting 9, 11, 12, 16, 42–44, 57, 59, 66, 69–70, 166
  connection with eugenics 165
  controversy over 15, 16, 54, 72–73, 149, 150
  opposition to 40, 110, 149, 154, 160, 274
  physical regeneration, role in 23, 150–151
  relation to rifle club movement 20, 37, 51, 55, 69, 76
  social control, use for 151–152, 158
  wealthy classes, proposals for 278
  see also civilian rifle movement; National Service League (NSL)
Conan Doyle, Sir Arthur
  Bartitsu, popularisation of 167
  Legion of Frontiersmen, member of 95, 111n.3
  marksmanship, promotion 41, 51
  national defence, use of motorists for 93–94
  support for the British Brothers' League (BBL) 124, 135
Confederacy 18, 268n.59
conservatism
  core elements 18
  Edwardian crisis 1, 17
Conservative governments (1895–1905)
  civilian marksmanship, support for 36, 41–42, 45
  immigration policy 119–121, 131–135, 137–141
  military reform 20, 52
  physical training in school, promotion of 145
  see also conservatism; Conservative Party
Conservative Party
  factionalism 1, 7
  relationship with pressure groups 15–16
  rightward shift 2–6
  historiography 6–19
  Right, definition of 18–19
  see also Balfour, Arthur James; Bonar Law, Andrew; Conservative governments (1895–1905); Home Rule crisis (1912–1914)
Conspiracy and Protection of Property Act (1875) 179

Corelli, Marie 128
Cotes, Kenelm D. 274–275
Coventry 103
Crackanthorpe, Montague Hughes 165
Craig, James, first Viscount Craigavon 226, 243, 250–251
Craigavon 226, 244
Craik, Sir Henry, first Baronet 154, 159
Creagh, John 139
Cremer, William Randal 61
Croft, Henry Page 5, 8, 22, 24, 62, 66, 109, 142, 166, 264
　see also Citizen Army; Imperial Mission; militarism
Crosfield Rowlandson, George 152
Crozier, Frank Percy 27, 240–241
Crystal Palace 48–49, 107, 199
Curragh incident 259–260
Curzon, George Nathaniel, first Marquess Curzon of Kedleston 43–44, 152
Customs and Inland Revenue Act (1879) 230
Customs Laws Consolidation Act (1876) 226, 230
Cutcliffe Hyne, Charles John 95, 97

Daily Express 97, 105, 120
Daily Mail 70–71, 73, 89, 118, 120, 135, 181–182, 223–225
Daily Mirror 59, 74, 97, 164, 251, 253
Dangerfield, George 8
De Grey, John 200
De Hora, Manoel Herrera 94, 103
De Rutzen, Sir Albert 200
De Windt, Harry 94–95
democratisation 1, 2
　ascendancy of Labour 183
　opposition to 6, 13, 18, 118, 152, 163, 193, 279
Déroulède, Paul 10
Derry 223, 226, 232, 244
Dewar, Thomas 120, 122
Dicey, Albert Venn 281
diehards 2
　eugenics, views on 165–166
　militancy 12, 14, 18
　military ethic 12
　military preparedness, advocacy of 37, 46
　violence, openess to 12–13, 249–250
　see also Home Rule crisis (1912–1914); Verney, Richard, nineteenth Baron Willoughby de Broke
Digby, Kenelm 134
distributism 10
Douglas-Scott-Montagu, John, second Baron Montagu of Beaulieu 94, 194
drill instruction
　boys of school age 24, 40–41, 54, 60–62, 66, 145–148, 152, 154, 160–161, 163
　see also Cadet Corps; militarism; physical training
Driscoll, Lieut. Colonel Daniel Patrick 100, 105, 109–111
Dromore 223–225
Dublin 252
　Bachelor's Walk massacre 264
　miniature rifle clubs 73
　Ulster Volunteer Force (UVF) 232–233
Dublin Lockout 208–209, 236
Dunning, Leonard 197
Duty and Discipline Movement 157–158

East End 5
　overcrowding 22, 121–122, 125–127
　racial tensions 118–143 *passim*
　see also British Brothers' League (BBL)
Education Act (1902) 9
Edward VII 49, 241
Elgin Commission (1902) 52
Elias, Norbert 14
Emery, James A. 183, 186
Empire Day movement 156–157
employer associations in the United States of America 176, 179
　see also Citizens' Industrial Association (CIA); Citizens' Industrial Association of America (CIAA)
Ensor, R. C. K. 8
Enniskillen 223, 231, 235
Esher Committee 52
eugenics 11, 12, 15, 17, 23, 165, 166
Eugenics Education Society 117, 163–165
Evans-Gordon, William 120–122, 129, 130, 133–134, 138–139
Explosives Act (1875) 67

Extradiction Act (1870) 141
Eyre, Douglas 46

Farley, James 181–182
 see also strikebreaking; Volunteer Police Force (VPF)
fascism, British
 protofascism 10, 16–17, 167, 280
 relationship to Edwardian Right 28, 143, 211–212, 280
 see also British Union of Fascists (BUF)
Feilding, Rudolph, ninth Earl of Denbigh 37
First Aid Nursing Yeomanry (FANY) 15
First World War 210–211, 239–241, 264, 280
 Legion of Frontiersmen, service in 110
 physical trauma 167
 rifle clubs, mobilization for training recruits and home defence 75–76
Fitzalan-Howard, Henry, fifteenth Duke of Norfolk 45, 49, 53–54, 69
Fitzjohn, Lieut. Colonel Tudor 279–280
Flottenverein 15
Forde Ridley, Samuel 120, 127, 135
Foreign Enlistment Act (1870) 92
Francotte cadet rifles 53
Free Labour Press and Industrial Review 180–181, 186
Free Labour Protection Association (FLPA) 189, 213n.14
French, General John 89, 239, 259
French invasion scare (1858–1859) 37–38
Frivilliga Skyddskåren 187, 194
Frontiersman's Pocket Book, The 107–108

Gamage, Arthur Walter 49, 194–195
Gambetta, Léon 8
Gascoyne-Cecil, Robert, third Marquess of Salisbury 11, 20, 37, 42–44, 59, 118, 119–120, 131, 149
Gascoyne-Cecil, James, fourth Marquess of Salisbury 247–249
general strike, threat of 187, 195, 199, 279
General Strike (1926) 14, 211
Germany 4, 66–68, 71, 92, 94, 152, 210
 Anglo-German naval arms race 70, 106
 comparison with 11–12, 15, 39, 43, 64, 153
 fear of 4, 11, 21, 37, 44, 66, 70–71, 76, 105, 108, 276
 as model to imitate 7, 200
 see also invasion literature; spy-mania; Teutophobia
Gibson, Edward, first Baron Ashbourne 159
Giffard, Hardinge Stanley, first Earl of Halsbury 8, 159
Gilmour, Ian 2
Girl Guides 163
Girls' Life Brigade 148–149
Gladstone, Herbert, first Viscount Gladstone 141–142
Gladstone, William Ewart 221, 244
Glasgow 98, 147
 British League for the Support of Ulster and the Union (BLSUU) recruitment for 250, 258, 260–263
Gore, Arthur, sixth Earl of Arran 257
Gorst, Sir John Eldon 159
Great Labour Unrest (1911–1914) 25, 157, 189–212 *passim*
 see also Shipping Federation; special constabulary; Volunteer Police Force (VPF)
Green, E. H. H. 17
Grey, Albert, fourth Earl Grey 48, 53, 144
Grey, Sybil 48–49, 50
Grosvenor, Hugh, second Duke of Westminster 46
Gun Barrel Proof Act (1868) 241–242
Gun License Act (1870) 226
gun-running 8, 27, 103, 241–242, 243, 262, 264
gunmaking industry, British 57, 64, 68, 72, 84n.57
Gwynne, Howell Arthur Keir 59, 256
gymnastics 24, 34n.72, 101–102, 145–146, 148, 150

Haldane, Richard, first Viscount Haldane 60–62, 69, 73, 92–93, 96, 103, 159, 161, 164, 234, 278
 see also Territorial Force
Halsbury, Earl of 8, 19, 159

Index

Halsbury Club 8
Hamilton, Lord Claud 236, 256
Hamilton, Lord George Francis 200
Hamilton, General Ian 48, 57, 73, 80n.66, 115n.90
Hamilton, James, second Duke of Abercorn 5
  Civilian Force, presidency of 202–205
  Volunteer Police Force (VPF), presidency of 199–203
  see also Volunteer Police Force (VPF)
Hamilton-Gordon, John, first Marquess of Aberdeen and Temair 75
Harmsworth, Alfred Charles William, first Viscount Northcliffe 209
Harmsworth, Harold, first Viscount Rothermere 225
Harris, James, fifth Earl of Malmesbury 25
Harrison, Charles 204
Hay, Claude 136, 139
Health and Strength (magazine) 166–167
Healy, Tim 236
Help the Ulster Women Committee 252
Hely-Hutchinson, Richard, sixth Earl of Donoughmore 136
Hickman, Brigadier General Thomas Edgecumbe 239, 243–244, 252–254, 258, 263
hippology 102
Hobson, John Atkinson 26
Homeland Defence League 37
Home Office 68
  Aliens Act (1905) 140–141
  industrial disputes involvement 188, 192
  position on the British League for the Support of Ulster and the Union (BLSUU) 244
  stance on the Volunteer Police Force (VPF) 199, 200–203
Home Rule crisis (1912–1914) 8, 9, 12–13, 26–27, 73–75, 88, 109, 189, 221–222, 242–243, 255, 258–259, 264
  see also British League for the Support of Ulster and the Union (BLSUU); Carson, Edward, Baron Carson; Ireland; Ulster Volunteer Force (UVF)
horsemanship 21, 89, 97–98, 102, 104, 276
Houndsditch outrage 22, 142
humanitarianism
  right-wing opposition to 4, 11, 25, 97, 141, 193
hunting
  formative experience for imperial elites 21
  frontier skills 88
  training for war 4, 21

immigration
  criminality allegations 22, 119, 123, 137, 139, 142, 277
  Eastern European Jews 5, 22, 120, 125, 129, 130, 133, 137, 140
  low-wage labour 120, 130, 136
  racial dilution fears 127, 134, 136, 143, 277
Immigration Reform Association 136, 138
Imperial Maritime League (IML) 9, 71, 281n.1
Imperial Mission (organisation) 5, 22, 62
Imperial Pioneers (or Pioneers of the Empire) 109, 276
imperial preference 2, 7, 8, 22
  see also Croft, Henry Page; Imperial Mission; Tariff Reform League (TRL)
Imperial School of Colonial Training 107
Imperial Yeomanry 241, 254
invasion literature 4, 70–71, 105
Ireland 11, 13, 27, 73, 103, 189, 200, 220–264 *passim*, 280
  see also Dublin Lockout; Home Rule crisis (1912–1914); Irish Volunteers
Irish Citizens Army 208
Irish Volunteers 236, 262, 264, 280

Japan 98, 147, 167
Jevons, William Stanley 179
Jewish Lads' Brigade 47, 57, 148
Jones, John Joseph 192
Jones, J. R. 6, 9, 10
Joynson-Hicks, William, first Viscount Brentford 194, 211
ju-jitsu 24, 96, 167

Junior Constitutional Club 192, 255, 261

Kaiser Wilhelm II 25
Kennedy, Paul 10, 11
Kennedy, Admiral William Robert 89
Khaki election 4
King's Regulations and Orders for the Army (1908) 101
Kipling, Rudyard 36, 41, 72, 88–89, 222, 251
Kitchener, Herbert, first Earl Kitchener 76, 163, 264
Knowles, Sir Lees, first Baronet 96

Labour Party
  legislative programme in 1906 government 188
  right-wing accusations of revolutionary plotting 25, 199, 205
  rise of 178
  see also Taff Vale case; Trade Disputes Act (1906)
Lads' Drill Association 40, 52, 173n.137
Landa, Myer Jack 141
Lane, A. H. 17, 119
Larne gun-running 262
Laws, Cuthbert 182, 205
Leach, Lieut. Colonel Sir George Archibald 128
League of Covenanters 256
Lee-Enfield rifle .303 inch calibre 38, 57, 232
Lee-Metford rifle .303 inch calibre 38
Leeds 96–97, 110, 120, 142, 144
  Citizens' League 177
  Corporation strike (1913) 209–210
Lees, Elliot 56
Legge, William, seventh Earl of Dartmouth (Viscount Lewisham) 238
Legion of Frontiersmen
  Boy Scout connections 107–108
  organisation and activities 5, 21, 66, 87–111 *passim*, 276
  seeking official sanction 21, 92, 95, 101, 103–105, 111
  stewardship meetings of the Imperial Mission 22, 109
  wartime role (East Africa) 110

see also British Empire; Imperial Mission; manliness
Le Queux, William T. 70, 105
Leslie F. J. 197
Leslie-Melville, Ronald, eleventh Earl of Leven 41
Liberal governments (1906–1914)
  anti-patriotism allegations from conservative opposition 4, 6–9, 26, 92, 142, 211
  electoral strength and parliamentary position 6
  industrial relations policy 188
  Irish Home Rule legislation 221–222, 242–243, 255, 258–259, 264
  welfare reforms 188
liberalism
  right-wing critique of 1, 7, 9, 18, 19, 26
Liberty and Property Defence League 189
Ligue Maritime 15
Ligue pour le service de trois ans 15
Linehan, Thomas 16
Linz, Juan José 29
Lipset, Seymour 16
Liverpool 47, 128, 153, 184, 221, 236
  Civic Service League (CSL) 197–198
  general transport strike (1911) 189–192
  opposition to Irish Home Rule 226, 236, 246–247, 250, 255–256, 258, 263
Livesey, George 182
Lloyd George, David 9, 11, 12, 142, 157, 188
London
  British Covenant, 1914 Hyde Park rally 261–262
  coal porters and carmen strike (1914) 210
  transport workers' strike (1912) 205
  see also Crystal Palace; East End
London League 54
London Metropolitan Police 241
London Small Arms Company 68
Londoners' League 123, 129
Long, Walter, first Viscount Long 123, 256, 261
Lowther, Hugh, fifth Earl of Lonsdale 89, 90, 96, 98

Loyal British Waiters' Society 108
Luard, General Charles E. 42, 46–47, 49, 51–53, 62, 64
Ludovici, Anthony 17
Lyttelton, Alfred 134
Lyttelton, General Sir Neville Gerald 92

Macclesfield Patriotic Association 146–147
McHugh, Charles (Bishop of Derry) 244
McKenna, Reginald 202–204, 244
MacKenzie, John M. 21
McNeill, Ronald 243
Madden, Gerald 239
Manchester 44, 70, 96–97, 102–103, 128, 142–143, 154, 189, 210, 243, 250, 252, 262–263
Manchester School 7, 9
manliness 3, 11, 17, 19, 76–77, 88, 148, 167, 201
  decline concerns 19, 24, 149
  hyper-masculinity 167, 278
  imperial standing, effect on 153
  muscular and militarised ideals 3, 17, 19, 76–77, 201
  over-civilization as threat 15, 157, 162–163, 276
  reaction against bourgeois ideals 88
  training programmes 66, 107, 118, 150, 157, 160, 166–167
  see also citizenship; militarism; physical training
Mann, Tom 190
Mannlicher rifles 38
Marconi Affair 9, 142, 238
marksmanship training 20–21, 34n.71, 36–77 passim, 71, 102, 111, 154, 163, 227, 275–276, 280
  cult of the rifle 275
  vocation for killing 3–4, 61, 275
  see also civilian rifle movement; Society of Miniature Rifle Clubs (SMRC)
martial arts 89, 102, 167, 278
  see also Bartitsu; ju-jitsu; savate
Martini-Enfield rifle .303 inch calibre 229, 232
Martini-Henry rifle, original calibre (.577/450 inch) 257

Matheson, Sir Alexander, third Baronet 126–127
masculinity see manliness
Maurice, General John Frederick 144–146, 152–153
Maxse, Leopold 8, 11, 18, 43, 154, 276
Maxwell, Arthur, eleventh Baron Farnham 238, 268n.82
Mayer, Arno 13, 15
Mental Deficiency Act (1913) 165
Methuen, Paul, third Baron Methuen 89
middle classes 71, 158
  anti-strike mobilisation 26, 28, 176–177, 187–212 passim, 279
  perceived lack of military spirit 98
  physical training, interest in 166
militarism 2, 3, 6, 10, 12, 15–17, 23, 37, 52, 76, 87–88, 97, 102, 107, 110, 145, 156, 163, 234, 274–276
  definition 15
  in right-wing discourse 4, 9, 15, 47, 57, 274
  youth training 15, 21, 23, 40, 52, 54, 56–57, 59, 69, 73, 145–146, 149, 154, 276
  youth training, opposition to 41, 61
  see also civilian rifle movement; compulsory military service; drill instruction; National Service League (NSL); paramilitarism; physical training; youth organisations
Militia 39, 41–42, 46, 66, 69, 98, 150, 226, 278
Milner, Alfred, first Viscount Milner 1, 7, 8, 11, 44, 69, 167, 255–257, 261
Milnes-Gaskell, Evelyn 239–240
Model Course of Physical Training (1901) 145–147
Morgan, David John 139
Morgan, F. C. 200
Morning Post, The 59, 67, 111–112n.4, 203, 222, 256
Morrison-Bell, Clive 69
Mosley, Oswald 277
Mosso, Angelo 154, 159
Murray Guthrie, Walter 120

National Air Rifle Association 42
National Citizen's Union (NCU) 119

National Defence Association 59, 160
national efficiency 3, 11, 12, 15, 18, 150
National Free Labour Association (NFLA) 177–178, 180–181, 183–184, 186–187
National Front 277
National League for Clean Government 9
National League for Physical Education and Improvement (NLPEI) 159–161
National Party 281n.1
National Railway strike (1911) 26, 190
National Rifle Association (NRA) 37–38, 41, 45, 49, 51–53, 55, 57, 60–61, 67–68, 71, 73, 76, 95
National Service League (NSL) 15, 23–24, 42–44, 52, 55, 59, 69, 70–71, 76, 150–153, 272, 277
    relationship with Boy Scouts 161–162
    relationship with civilian rifle movement 37, 57
National Social Purity Crusade 158
nationalism 6, 17–19, 279
    cult of 9
    nationalist agitation through pressure groups 15
    resistant to irrationalism 7
    see also citizenship; militarism
Navy League (NL) 9, 15, 19, 71, 90
Newcastle upon Tyne 57, 96, 101–102, 182
Newman, Colonel John Robert Pretyman 254, 279
Nietzsche, Friedrich 17
Nightingale, W. H. 250
Norman, Henry 134
Norwich 102, 251

Ommundsen, Harcourt 76
Onslow, Richard, fifth Earl of Onslow 90, 111n.3
Organic society 6, 7, 9, 17, 18, 274
Organisation for the Maintenance of Supplies (OMS) 211
Owens, Charles John 62
Oxford 61, 71

pacifism
    depicted as unpatriotic or subversive 278

right-wing hostility to 19
Paget, Arthur 259
Palmer, William, second Earl of Selborne 237
Pan-German League 11
Parliament Act (1911) 8, 12, 189, 221, 238, 242
Patriotic Society, The 62–64
patriotism see citizenship
paramilitarism
    European comparisons 280
    see also British Brothers' League (BBL); Irish Volunteers; Ulster Volunteer Force (UVF)
Patterson, John Henry 231, 241
Peace Preservation Act 226
Pearson, Arthur 59, 182
Pearson, Karl 17
Peel, George 250
People's Budget (1909) 8, 9, 12, 157
Percy, Henry, seventh Duke of Northumberland 249
Peto, Sir Basil Edward, first Baronet 239
Physical Culture Society 102
physical efficiency see physical training
Physical Protection League 202
physical training 118
    to combat racial degeneration 8, 12, 15, 19, 22–23, 111, 146–152, 160–163, 166–167
    for military and national objectives 3, 22–24, 34n.71, 48, 60–61, 66, 69, 71, 118, 144–147, 150–153, 160–163, 276–277
    Swiss model as inspiration 24, 34n.72, 160
    see also Anglo-Saxon race; drill instruction; militarism; social degeneration
picketing 25, 183, 185–186, 195–196, 198–199
Pinkerton (detective agency) 177, 182, 196, 201–202, 205
    see also Volunteer Police Force (VPF)
Pink Ribbon League 128
Plutocracy 10, 22
Pocock, Roger 21, 87–108 passim, 276
Pole-Carew, General Reginald 89, 263
political violence 14, 22, 109

see also British Brothers' League (BBL); Khaki election; Legion of Frontiersmen; Imperial Mission; paramilitarism; vigilantism
populism 5, 11, 119, 123, 139
see also Conservative Party
Portadown 223–224
Portsmouth 102, 242, 252
Power, William Mailes
as founder and organiser of the Volunteer Civil Force 205, 208
as founder of the Volunteer Police Force (VPF) 109, 198–199, 202
Preparatory School Air Rifle Association (PSARA) 42, 61
Preparatory Schools Rifle Association (PSRA) 60–61
Pretyman, Capt. Ernest George 95, 106
Primrose, Archibald, fifth Earl of Rosebery 57, 153–154
Primrose League 20, 42, 59, 119, 251–252
Prince Louis of Battenberg 90
Pro-Boer Liberals 4, 59

radical Toryism 2
see also conservatism; Conservative Party
Radicaux Autoritaires 8
radical conservatism 19
Redmond, John Edward 221, 250, 254, 259, 264
Regis, Max 124
Repington, Charles à Court 234
Report of the Royal Commission on Volunteers and Militia (1904) 52, 150–151, 274
Report of the Inter-Departmental Committee on the Employment of School Children (1902) 155
Report of the Royal Commission on Physical Training in Scotland (1903) 155
Reveille group 8
Rex v. Bishop of Bangor 204
Rex v. Meade 230
Rex v. Pinney 274
Richardson, Lieut. General George 230–231, 243, 260
Rider-Haggard, Sir Henry 95

Ridgway, Hugh 239, 250–252, 255, 258
Rifleman, The 59, 72, 275
Rimington, General Michael 90
Roberts, Frederick, first Earl Roberts 5, 41, 54, 59, 110, 146, 152, 243, 263, 275, 278
belief in possibility of invasion 70–71, 72–73, 105
patron of the National Air Rifle Association 42
as President of the National Service League (NSL) 43, 57, 69–70, 157, 162
as President of the Society of Miniature Rifle Clubs (SMRC) 20, 36–37, 46, 52–56 *passim*, 59–60, 62, 64–66, 68–76 *passim*
see also civilian rifle movement; National Service League (NSL); marksmanship training; Society of Miniature Rifle Clubs (SMRC)
Roberts, Morley 95
Robertson, Thomas Herbert 127, 139
Rodgers, A. C. 138
Romania
Jewish immigration from 5, 22, 120, 125, 133
Ross, Charles 275–276
Rothschild, Walter, second Baron Rothschild 134
Royal Commission on Alien Immigration (1903) 134–135, 136–139, 140–141
Royal Commission on Physical Deterioration (1904) 155–156
Royal Irish Constabulary (RIC) 208, 229, 240, 258
Royal Naval Artillery Volunteers 106
Royal United Service Institution 43, 51, 60, 162, 164
Russell, Herbrand, eleventh Duke of Bedford 243–244, 257–258, 278
Russell, Oliver, second Baron Ampthill 257
Russia 90, 167, 211
conservative responses to the Russian Revolution (1905) 182
Jewish immigrants from 5, 22, 125, 129, 130, 133, 137, 140

Saleeby, Caleb 165–166
Salvidge, Archibald 247

Sanderson, William 17
Sandow Challenge Bowl 49
Sandow, Eugene 166
savate 167
Scally, R. J. 11
Scotland 27, 57, 138, 145, 155, 200, 238, 244, 246–247, 250–251, 256, 260–261, 264
  see also British League for the Support of Ulster and the Union (BLSUU); Glasgow
Scouts Defence Corps 163
Seebohm Rowntree, Benjamin 143–144
Serjeant, Col. William Charles Eldon 90, 103, 108–109
Seton-Karr, Henry 90, 108
Seymour, General Lord William 90
Shaw, William Stanley
  as founder and organiser of the British Brothers' League (BBL) 22, 118–143 *passim*
Shee, George Richard Francis 43, 150–151, 153
  see also National Service League (NSL)
Sheffield 40–41, 121, 138, 144, 192, 239
Sherard, Robert 129, 140
Shipping Federation 182, 204–205, 208
Silver, Gertrude 60
Silver, James L. 123, 126–127, 130, 135–136
Sinclair, Upton 184
Sinclair, William (archdeacon of London) 200
Smith, Frederick Edwin, first Earl of Birkenhead 221–224, 231, 252, 261
social degeneration 19, 24, 118
  association with urban life 5, 23, 143, 153, 155
  calls for social hygiene measures 156–160
  fears of physical decline in British population 143–145, 152–156
  immigration connections 4, 22, 118–143 *passim*
  military and physical training as remedy 15, 22–23, 111, 146–150, 151–152, 160–163, 166–167, 277
  see also compulsory military service; eugenics; physical training
socialism
  conservative opposition and critique 7, 15, 17–18, 19, 23, 25–26, 97, 136, 176, 182–183, 188, 193, 276, 278
  revisionism 10, 70, 151–152
  see also Great Labour Unrest (1911–1914); general strike, threat of
Society of Miniature Rifle Clubs (SMRC) 49–77 *passim*
  .22 calibre rifles 41, 47
  Martini-Henry rifles, converted to .22 calibre 44, 60, 68–69, 71–72
  Morris tube 45, 48–49, 51, 60
  see also civilian rifle movement; citizenship; militarism; patriotism; Roberts, Frederick, first Earl Roberts
Society of Working Men's Rifle Clubs (SWMR) 46–49, 64
Social Darwinism 11, 149, 162, 193, 274
social imperialism 8, 11, 17
Society for the Suppression of the Immigration of Destitute Aliens 119
Somerset, Henry, ninth Duke of Beaufort 44
South African veterans 90, 136, 239–241
South Wales coal strike (1910) 189
Special Constables Act (1831) 190, 197, 202
Special Constables Act (1923) 110, 211
special constabulary 109, 190–192, 194, 197–198, 201–202, 204, 211
Spencer, Victor, first Viscount Churchill 200
Spengler, Oswald 16
Spiess, Adolph 24
spy-mania 4, 5, 71, 105, 108, 276
  see also invasion literature; Legion of Frontiersmen; National Service League (NSL)
Stanhope, James, seventh Earl Stanhope 257
Stanley, Edward George Villiers, seventeenth Earl of Derby 197
Statham, Arnold 199–200, 203
Statute of Northampton (1328) 230

Stead, William Thomas 195–196
Stevens rifles 53
stick fighting 24, 102, 167
Stone, Dan 16–17
strikebreaking
  citizen-strikebreaker 210, 279
  pre- and post-war continuity 211, 279–280
  U.S. influence on British anti-labour practices 14, 179–180, 196
  see also Collison, William; National Free Labour Association (NFLA); Pinkerton; Volunteer Police Force (VPF)
strikes 138, 178
  expression of domestic disloyalty 179, 188, 199–200
  law and order concerns 189–190, 199, 211
  right-wing tendencies toward vigilantism 25, 26, 109, 192–193, 211–212, 279
  warfare analogies 195–196, 279
  see also general strike, threat of; Great Labour Unrest (1911–1914); strikebreaking
Suffragettes 2, 23–24
Sweden 68, 160
Switzerland 20, 24, 34n.72, 43–44, 150, 160
swordsmanship 102
Sykes, Alan 12, 17

Taff Vale case 182
Tannenbaum, Edward R. 17
Tariff Reform League (TRL) 15, 109, 115n.96
Taylor, William 153
Territorial Army 66, 69, 72–73, 254
Teutophobia 4
Times, The 36, 52–53, 55, 60, 94, 108, 139, 144–145, 154, 179, 181, 183, 187–189, 194, 201, 203, 205, 234, 237, 239, 242, 251, 261
Tippet, C. H. 239
Townshend, Charles 257
Trade Disputes Act (1906) 184, 187–188, 204
Trade Unionism
  allegations of subversion and disloyalty 17, 25–26, 177, 179

  perceived threat to economic freedom 183, 188–189
  post-war militancy 211
  see also Great Labour Unrest (1911–1914); Labour movement
Triple Alliance (trade unionism) 13, 211
Tristram, Major Francis 243
Trochu, Louis-Jules 274
Troup, Charles Edward 203
Twentieth Century League 147, 159

Ulster Covenant 225–226, 246
Ulster Union Council (UUC) 226, 238
Ulster Volunteer Force (UVF) 5, 27, 221
  composition 233–235
  gunrunning 227, 229–230
  as model for the British Right 9
  organisation 230–231
  propaganda 235
  training 229, 231–233
  see also Carson, Edward, Baron Carson; Home Rule crisis (1912–1914); Ireland
Union Defence League 256
Unionist Party see Conservative Party
United States of America 55, 66, 123–124, 128, 147, 177–180, 182–187, 196, 210, 262, 279
  see also employer associations in the United States of America; Farley, James; Pinkerton
Unlawful Drilling Act (1819) 227

Vane-Tempest-Stewart, Charles, seventh Marquess of Londonderry 5, 224, 261
Verney, Richard, nineteenth Baron Willoughby de Broke 5, 8, 11–12, 16, 19–27, 165–166, 223, 236–264 *passim*, 278, 280
  see also Conservative Party; British League for the Support of Ulster and the Union (BLSUU)
Vetterli-Vitali Rifles (Model 1870/87, 10.4mm / .41 calibre) 227, 241
vigilantism 19, 26, 139, 142, 179–180, 189, 196, 210–211, 279
  see also strikebreaking; Volunteer Police Force (VPF)
Vincent, Col. Sir Howard 43, 121, 125, 134–135, 140
Voluntary Aid Detachments (VADs) 15

Volunteer Police Force (Civilian Force) 5, 177
  government opposition to 199, 202–203
  organisational and operational structure 201, 203, 204–205
  support from conservative MPs and press 200
  uniforms, weapons and training 205–206
  use in London Dock Strike 205
  see also Great Labour Unrest (1911–1914); Shipping Federation; vigilantism
Volunteer Force 20, 36, 38, 41–42, 45, 52, 69, 98, 101, 146, 150, 198, 234, 274
  relation to rifle clubs 44, 47–49
  see also Report of the Royal Commission on Volunteers and Militia (1904)

Wales 42, 44–45, 100, 155, 188, 189, 192, 199, 244, 247, 264
Wallace, William 134
Wallop, Gerard Vernon, ninth Earl of Portsmouth (Viscount Lymington) 17
Walton, John Lawson 182
war
  as an index of national health 18, 273–274
  inevitability of war 3, 20
War Office 38, 41–42, 52, 57, 68, 71, 75, 90, 92–94, 101, 103, 110, 145, 259, 276
Ward, Arnold 200
Ward, William, second Earl of Dudley 46
Washburn, George Smalley 181
Webb, Capt. George 258, 260

Weber, Max 233
Webster, Richard, first Viscount Alverstone 147, 159
Wedgwood, Col. Josiah, first Baron Wedgwood 201–202
Wehrverein 15
Wellesley, Arthur, fourth Duke of Wellington 43
Welsh Church Disestablishment 9
Whetham, C. D. 17
White, Arnold 1, 11, 16, 119, 130, 135, 143, 165–166, 251
Wilkinson, Spenser 149
Williams, Job 137
Winchester rifles (various models) 47, 53–54, 57, 60
Wolverhampton 252
Wyatt, Harold Frazer 281n.1
wrestling 24, 104, 205, 278

xenophobia 2, 3, 11, 118–119, 277
  see also anti-alienism; British Brothers' League (BBL)

Yeomanry 20, 39, 52, 66, 69, 90, 101, 226, 239–240, 250, 260, 278
youth organisations
  military and physical training in 15, 20, 107–108, 146, 149, 161–163
  mitigate the growth of hooliganism 147
  moral disciplining 147–148
  see also Boy Scouts; Boys' Brigade; Christian manliness Empire Day movement; Lads' Drill Association; militarism; marksmanship training

Ziblatt, Daniel 2

EU authorised representative for GPSR:
Easy Access System Europe, Mustamäe tee 50,
10621 Tallinn, Estonia
gpsr.requests@easproject.com

www.ingramcontent.com/pod-product-compliance
Ingram Content Group UK Ltd.
Pitfield, Milton Keynes, MK11 3LW, UK
UKHW021826140426
5217IPUK00004B/114